diSh ———————————————

diSh

the inside story on
the world of gossip

JEANNETTE WALLS

SPIKE

AN AVON BOOK

AVON BOOKS, INC.
An Imprint of HarperCollins*Publishers,*
10 East 53rd Street
New York, New York 10022-5299

Copyright © 2000 by Jeannette Walls
Interior design by Kellan Peck
ISBN: 0-380-97821-0

Library of Congress Cataloging in Publication Data:

Walls, Jeannette.
Dish : the inside story on the world of gossip / Jeannette Walls.—1st ed.
p. cm.
"An Avon book."
Includes bibliographical references and index.
1. Gossip in mass media. I. Title.
P96.G65 W35 2000
302.23—dc21   99-059009

First Spike Printing: March 2000

Printed in the U.S.A.

FIRST EDITION

QPM 10 9 8 7 6 5 4 3 2 1

www.harpercollins.com

For John,
with love
and gratitude

CONTENTS

CONTENTS

viii

1

"citizen reporter"

"My reaction to having our speaker today at the National Press Club was the same as a lot of other members," Doug Harbrecht, the club's president and *Business Week*'s Washington bureau chief, told the two hundred journalists gathered before him on the afternoon of June 2, 1998. "Why do we want to give a forum to that guy?"

"That guy" was Matt Drudge, who, said Harbrecht, "mucks through the hoaxes, conspiracies, and half-truths posted on-line in pursuit of fodder for his website." Six months earlier, Drudge had posted the sordid story that had subsequently exploded into the biggest political scandal since Watergate. But while journalists had gloried in the heroic part they had played in Watergate, most reporters were repulsed by their role in the Lewinsky affair. Despite charges of Clinton's alleged perjury and obstruction of justice, this story was driven not by issues or by questions of national security and the abuse of power—but by sex. It was the stuff of *gossip* columns. Yet because the scandal dominated the news for months, Matt Drudge, who never studied journalism and had never worked for a news organization, became one of the best-known reporters in the country. Matt Drudge was the personification of how scandal had hijacked the news—and those in the establishment media hated him for it.

"So, Matt, know this," said Harbrecht. "There aren't many in this hallowed room who consider you a journalist. Real journalists pride themselves on getting it first *and* right; they get to the bottom of the story, they bend over backwards to get the other side. Journalism means being painstakingly thorough, evenhanded, and fair. Now, in the interest of good journalism, let's hear Matt Drudge's side of the story."

An awkward moment of silence followed, and then polite applause. Matt Drudge stepped up to the podium. He was only thirty-one years old, a young man dressed in old man's clothes: a cream-colored suit with unfashionably wide lapels, a blue shirt and striped tie, and tortoiseshell glasses. He was pale with a somewhat asymmetric face and small but intense dark eyes. He somehow appeared more vulnerable without his trademark fedora, which made him look more like a vaudeville character than a pasty-faced, self-described "computer geek" with a slightly receding hairline.

"Applause for Matt Drudge in Washington at the Press Club," Drudge joked. "Now there's a scandal." He was nervous at first, but just as his voice was about to falter, he reached over and grabbed his fedora and placed it on his head. With his talisman, this relic that evoked populist tabloid journalism of Walter Winchell's days, Drudge found his voice. For the next forty minutes, he spoke passionately—if not always eloquently—about his love of journalism, about the importance of the unfettered flow of information, about how scandals, while sometimes ugly, were important to democracy and to "individual liberty." Drudge spoke of being a loner, a little guy in a business dominated by conglomerates, about the importance of persevering to tell the truth, even when it embarrassed and infuriated powerful people.

" 'Freedom of the press belongs to anyone who owns one,' " he said, quoting the legendary journalist A. J. Liebling. The Internet, Drudge's medium, was a great equalizer, he insisted. Now, everyone who owned a laptop and a modem could be a publisher and a reporter, a "citizen reporter"—as Drudge called himself.

He looked forward to the day, he said, when everyone in America would have an equal voice and the country would be "vibrating with the din of small voices." The Internet was going to save the news, he declared: "It's freedom of participation absolutely realized."

Many journalists in the crowd were unimpressed. It was that elitism, those rules, they maintained, that had long kept lurid, irresponsible stories like Drudge's out of the press. The real reason that Matt Drudge had come to Washington that day, most of them knew, was that he was being forced to testify in his own defense in a $30 million libel lawsuit. Drudge had inaccurately reported that Sidney Blumenthal, a former journalist who had become an aide to President Clinton, had beaten his wife. Soon after he posted the erroneous item, Drudge posted an apology and correction. But he had made plenty of other bloopers, as well: He had posted items saying that Clinton had a bald eagle tattoo in his genital region, that Independent Counsel Kenneth Starr had seventy-five pictures of Bill Clinton and Monica Lewinsky together, and that Hillary Clinton was about to be indicted. He once estimated that he is accurate eighty percent of the time.

"Could you succeed as a journalist," someone in the crowd wanted to know, "if you worked for an organization which required an accuracy rate of one hundred percent?"

"I don't know what organization that would be," Drudge shot back.

There was some embarrassed laughter, and then applause. Despite Harbrecht's pronouncements about high standards of journalists, Matt Drudge and everyone else in the room knew that by the late 1990s, the media was in a state of absolute crisis. The always fuzzy line between news and gossip had become a complete blur. Tabloid topics and sensationalism repeatedly overshadowed serious news. It wasn't Drudge's mistakes that angered many in the crowd; it was the stories he got right: Clinton's trysts with Monica Lewinsky; the semen-stained dress; the infamous cigar. With the Internet, characters like Drudge could pursue—without the constraints and rules imposed by editors and institutions—scandals that were too juicy to ignore and too tawdry to explore. Matt Drudge was the future of journalism. And everyone else in the room was being forced to follow him.

The publication and dissemination of scandalous information about the rich and powerful has existed almost as long as the written word. Cuneiform tablets from the fifteenth century B.C. discuss allegations that a Mesopotamian mayor was committing adultery with a married woman. But the commercial publication of scandal and gossip as we understand it today began in the 1830s, with the Industrial Revolution and the birth of the penny press. Although these papers were filled with scandal, their information usually came from official sources, such as court proceedings and arrest records. The late nineteenth century saw the debut of the Society column, which contained information—descriptions of yacht trips, guests lists at debutante balls—that was usually sanctioned by the subjects.

Walter Winchell is often credited with inventing the modern gossip column by printing private and sometimes salacious information about famous people. Although some of the tidbits in Winchell's gossip column was the stuff of the old society columns, Winchell mixed in scandalous, unofficial information about pregnancies, divorces, and liaisons that riveted his readers. When Winchell's column first appeared in the 1920s in the struggling *New York Graphic*—a newspaper that would make modern-day tabloids look respectable—other editors saw what Winchell's column did for circulation and were quick to start up their own gossip columns. Soon, most newspapers in the country were carrying at least one gossip column and many had four or more. Throughout the 1930s and 1940s, gossip columns were an integral part of the news, and gossip columnists were loved and even respected by the public. At his peak in the 1940s, Winchell reached an estimated ninety percent of the American public through his columns and radio broadcasts, and was said to be, outside politics and religion, the most powerful man in the world.

So it is no wonder, perhaps, that Drudge would style himself after Winchell. Drudge was born in Takoma Park, Maryland, a middle-class suburb of Washington, D.C., not far from where he addressed the National Press Club that day. His mother was a lawyer and his father was a social worker; he would later describe his parents as "liberal hippies." He was a lonely only child, a stutterer and a latchkey kid who put on puppet shows under sheets and would sit in his bedroom narrating imaginary radio talk shows into a tape recorder. He constantly cut class, and was a D student. "I stopped learning at school at age twelve," he told the *Los Angeles Times*. "They were not able to stuff me like a sausage. Even then I didn't play by society's rules. I was a rebel all the way."

He was not so much rebel as outcast—so much so that he, rather prophetically, began throwing rocks at his classmates. Once, when someone threw stones back, he needed stitches. When Matt was in junior high school, his mother was hospitalized for schizophrenia; his parents got divorced not long afterward. The extent of his alienation and bitterness is evident from a mock "last will and testament" Drudge wrote when he graduated from high school in 1984: "To my only true friend Ms. thing VickyB I leave a night in Paris, a bottle of Chaps cologne and hope you find a school with original people—and to everyone else who has helped and hindred [sic] me whether it be Staff or students, I leave a penny for each days [sic] I've been here and cried here. A Penny rich in worthless memories. For worthless memories is what I have endured. It reminds me of a song, 'The Funeral Hyme.' "

Drudge didn't go to college. Instead, he bummed around Paris for a month, then moved to New York City for a year, where he worked in a grocery store. Still failing to find himself, he moved back to the Washington area and became the night manager at a 7-Eleven in Takoma Park. Matt Drudge hung out with a crowd of promiscuous, openly gay men and dated several of them. "He was a freak, but that's why we liked him," said Dan Mathews, a friend from that period who would later go on to be a highly visible activist for PETA (People for the Ethical Treatment of Animals). "He had a dark, brooding quality, but you never worried if he was going to snap, because it was like he already had."

"He loved to do wild, provocative things to draw attention to himself," according to David Cohen. Once, when Drudge and

Cohen were dating, they went to a nightclub, and by Cohen's account, Drudge got kicked out for throwing a pitcher of beer into the air that came raining down on everyone around them. "He loved to freak me out by telling me gossip that he found out about me," said Cohen. "It was very personal stuff and I have no idea how he found these things out about me." Cohen said that Drudge seemed very comfortable and open with his sexuality, though they never talked about it. "In all the time I knew him, I don't think we had a serious, in-depth conversation. It was always gossipy or shallow stuff. We were very young."

At twenty-two, desperate to start a new life for himself, Drudge moved across the country to Los Angeles. He moved into a grimy $600-a-month one-bedroom apartment on the ninth floor of a run-down apartment building near Hollywood and Vine. He lived there with a six-toed cat named Dexter. Drudge hoped to get a job in the entertainment business or writing for *Variety*. Instead, he got a $5-an-hour job as an errand runner for *The Price Is Right*. From there, he landed a job at the CBS gift shop in Studio City where he worked for five years.

Sensing that Matt was directionless, his father flew from Washington to Los Angeles to visit his son and dragged him into a Circuit City store on Sunset Boulevard to buy him a cheap 486 Packard Bell computer. "Oh yeah," Matt told his father. "What am I going to do with that?"

Drudge had long been an irrepressible gossip. He loved the way that knowing things made him more popular, made people want to talk to him, and, quickly figuring out what to do with his computer, he began to surf various web sites for gossip. Using the computer, it was easy to read foreign publications and wire news. Drudge got his information from places other than his computer, however. He eavesdropped on people's conversations, he volunteered in the CBS mailroom and intercepted memos, he fished around in the garbage and found discarded Nielsen ratings and confidential box office numbers.

Soon, he had so much gossip that he wanted a better way to spread it. Going to an established newspaper was out of the question. He had no experience and no college degree. "If I'd knocked on the door of the *Los Angeles Times* they'd have laughed at me," he recalled. So, in 1995 he set up a web site and began e-mailing his tidbits to friends, calling it "The Drudge Report." He began with only a few readers, then a couple of dozen, and within no time, one thousand. Drudge thought it had peaked there, but he kept adding more subscribers. In 1996, he was getting 10,000 hits a day and soon America Online offered him $36,000 a year to carry "The Drudge Report." Matt quit his job to work on his web site full time. By the summer of 1997, he was averaging 15,000 hits a day.

In many ways, Matt Drudge was still a loner, still working out of his crummy Hollywood apartment, which by now was furnished with a tattered rug, cheap couch, a satellite dish, and a police scanner that was on at all times. But his name was becoming well-known among his readers. He was getting hundreds of E-mails a day. His rogue status gave him a freedom and flexibility that more established journalists didn't have. "It takes ABC News twenty minutes to post a headline to their web site. It takes me ten seconds," Drudge once boasted. "I had Diana dead seven minutes before CNN did."

Some believed that one of the ways Drudge got his information was a high-tech version of the way he intercepted memos at CBS. Although Drudge insisted that he got the information from "sources" within the various news organizations, some editors began suspecting that Drudge had figured out how to hack into their computer systems. Editors at the *Washington Post* and the *New York Times* were alarmed that Drudge got stories that weren't available on its web site and then posted stories just as they would be sent to the news organizations that subscribed to their wire service—with certain key words and phrases intact. "Our presumption is that Drudge has someone who has access to the news service wire, and that's what he's put out," according to John Geddes, deputy managing editor of the *New York Times*. On other occasions, however, he posted stories well before they were released to the wires, and some media people suspected that he discovered a way to hack into the paper's computers. At one point, the *Times* considered legal action against Drudge, but decided that would be good publicity for him. Hacking into *Newsweek*'s computer system is how, some believed, Drudge in July

1997 scooped *Newsweek* on its own story by reporter Michael Isikoff that Clinton allegedly groped Kathleen Willey. A furious Isikoff blasted Drudge for "rifling through raw reporting, like raw FBI files, and disseminating it." Drudge maintained that he had "a source" at *Newsweek*—not Isikoff but one of his co-workers—who tipped him off about the story.

The Willey story, however, was nothing compared with the story that Drudge got on Saturday, January 16: Clinton was having an affair with an intern. Again, it was a story reported by Isikoff and again Drudge had the details from an unreleased story. Drudge hammered out the story in his typical hysterical fashion:

NEWSWEEK KILLS STORY ON WHITE HOUSE INTERN

BLOCKBUSTER REPORT: 23-YEAR-OLD FORMER WHITE HOUSE

INTERN, SEX RELATIONSHIP WITH PRESIDENT.

At 6 P.M. on Saturday evening, Newsweek *magazine killed a story that was destined to shake official Washington to its foundation: A White House intern carried on a sexual affair with the President of the United States!*

It was Sunday morning, January 17, when Drudge finished writing his story. The sun still hadn't come up. Drudge paused as he stared at his Packard Bell computer and his eyes began to fill with tears. "My life won't be the same after this," he thought, and he hit the Enter button.

For the next four days, no mainstream publication touched the story. A petrified Drudge hid out in his apartment, wearing boxer shorts, his chair jammed up against the door. Over 400,000 people tried to log on to "The Drudge Report," sending it crashing. To calm his nerves, he periodically did push-ups or scrubbed his bathtub. Finally, *Newsweek* published an on-line version of the story, confirming everything the cybercolumnist had written. Soon, it appeared on front pages of newspapers around the country.

Matt Drudge was being profiled in major newspapers and discussed on the television news. Then, on January 25, something astonishing occurred: NBC's Tim Russert invited Matt Drudge to appear on *Meet the Press*. The program was one of the oldest and most respected news shows on television. The other guests on the segment were some of the most revered journalists in the country: William Safire of the *New York Times*, Stuart Taylor of the *National Journal*, and *Newsweek*'s Mike Isikoff. Isikoff was still furious that this cybercolumnist had scooped him on his own story. "He not only poisoned the atmosphere for real reporting," Isikoff had said of Drudge, "he was reckless and irresponsible and he did a disservice to everybody involved." But, explained Russert, he's part of the story. The show had its highest rating since the Gulf War.

When Drudge exited the Washington offices where *Meet the Press* was shot, he was met by a cluster of reporters, television and print, who wanted to interview him. He launched into a lecture about the responsibilities of journalism. "What does this say about you—all you people here with all your resources—that a story like this can break out of a little apartment in Hollywood?" he said. "What are you guys doing here besides interviewing yourselves? There's a new paradigm here. That I can do this out of my stinky apartment and you've got your fancy newsrooms with your fancy rules!"

Suddenly, his outsider status was an asset, a subject of pride. It was the persona that Drudge would embrace, one that would lead his defenders to describe him as the "Thomas Paine of the Internet" and a "A town crier for the new age." Drudge also took pains to distinguish what he did from the work of conventional reporters. "I don't call it journalism," Drudge told students at New York University. "To me, that is a cuss word, simply because I think there was a period in the past twenty years when we got away from aggressive reporting."

Drudge was embraced by the far right, who claimed that ever since the Kennedy era, the left-leaning media had ignored stories that hurt the liberal cause. Drudge insisted that his only allegiance was to scandal. "I'm a partisan for news," he was fond of saying. "I go where the stink is."

The impulse to "go where the stink is" seemed to the dismay of many people—journalists, celebrities, the rich and powerful, and ordinary citizens—to have come to define the entire news industry. Gossip had coexisted vigorously—if not always easily— with more serious news during Walter Winchell's heyday. It had then disappeared almost completely from newspapers and television during the 1960s, only to reemerge during the 1970s, spread through the media like a virus in the 1980s, and completely consume it by the end of the 1990s. To understand how the modern media could have reached this bizarre state, how someone like Matt Drudge could come to play a pivotal role in American journalism at the end of the millennium, it is necessary to go back to 1957.

That year, there was an episode that has been all but forgotten by most media students today, but it was a pivotal event that shaped the direction of journalism for decades to come. It was the trial of *Confidential*.

the war against *confidential*

Spectators spilled into the corridor of Los Angeles's Hall of Justice those muggy days in the summer of 1957. Some wore their fanciest evening clothes, some wore short shorts or tight toreador pants, some even brought ballet or tap shoes and danced; they all hoped to catch the eye of the guard who had the power to grant them one of the few seats that had been set aside for the public. Court clerks had searched for hours trying to find a room big enough to accommodate the stars, defendants and witnesses, reporters and photographers, and hundreds of curious onlookers who crowded into the eighth floor of the Hall of Justice, craning their necks, hoping to catch a glimpse of the unfolding drama of America's favorite spectator sport: celebrity scandals. In its relatively short history, Hollywood had survived scores of sensational cases, but inside the packed green-and-gold filigreed courtroom that summer, scandal itself was on trial. *Confidential*—the magazine that had shocked and riveted America with tales of celebrity excesses and debauchery—had been indicted by the California Attorney General's office on charges of "conspiracy to publish criminally libelous, obscene and otherwise objectionable material."

"We will convict the filth peddlers that smear the names of Hollywood," vowed California Attorney General Edmund "Pat" Brown. The movie industry had been good to Brown and to California; it had endowed the state with millions of dollars in business and international fame. The film world is built on images and appearances, on fantasy and façades; *Confidential* made its money destroying those images, said Brown, "dragging people's names through the dirt and mire of gossip." Brown was a rising political star, a popular prosecutor who was planning to run for governor of California. He had already threatened to prosecute newsstand dealers who sold *Confidential*, effectively banning the magazine in California. Now Brown was going to finish the job, promising to "end *Confidential*'s reign of terror."

Celebrities had long endured—even embraced—gossip. The cleverly placed tidbit about a star's lavish lifestyle could actually help his career—or help keep a wayward actor in line. For years, celebrities and studio publicity departments worked with columnists like Hedda Hopper and Louella Parsons—planting items that were often concocted—about romances and marriages, and feuds and fights over film roles. The studios and stars controlled that sort of press; they used the gossip columnists as high-powered publicity machines. Despite their reputation for nastiness, the old-line gossip columnists were usually most vicious when it came to fighting with each other. Hollywood gossip columnist Sidney Skolsky was so certain that rival Louella Parsons got him fired from the *Los Angeles Examiner* because she didn't want the competition in her most valued outlet, that one day he retaliated by sinking his teeth into her arm. The gossip business had gotten very competitive.

The formula pioneered by Walter Winchell in the 1920s was so successful that by the 1940s gossip columnists were among the best read and most influential journalists in the country. Most newspapers carried several gossip columns; by the 1950s, there were more than four hundred full-time reporters covering Hollywood. Show business columns with announcements of romances and casting news like Hedda's and Louella's were becoming old hat. So were the New York columns like Walter Winchell's that chronicled Cafe Society and the Broadway scene. America was hungry for juicier scandals. In 1952 a flamboyant publisher named Robert Harrison gave it to them.

Harrison was intrigued by how America was spellbound in the early 1950s by the Kefauver hearings—the televised Senate investigation into mob corruption in the government. Housewives abandoned their chores, businessmen canceled meetings, people without television sets of their own crowded into TV-equipped bars. No one wanted to miss a minute of the unfolding scandal. Harrison, who at the time was churning out girlie magazines with names like *Wink, Titter,* and *Eyeful,* was so broke that he was posing as a cop or an irate husband for pictures in his own magazines to save the modeling fee. Harrison decided to try a different kind of titillation. "The daddy of *Confidential,* although he'd be shocked to know it, is Senator Estes Kefauver," said Harrison. "Behind-the-scenes stories. Inside, gossipy facts, it became clear that's what America wanted." The publisher was a fan of Walter Winchell's column; he took the gossip column format and combined it with the shocking exposé flavor of the Kefauver hearings, and in December 1952, began cranking out *Confidential* every other month. "People like to read about things they don't dare do themselves," Harrison said. "And if you can print these things about public figures, so much better." The scandal magazine was born.

Confidential's initial press run was only 150,000. Harrison didn't have the budget to publicize or get good distribution for his lurid tabloid. In 1953, he had a brainstorm. Walter Winchell—although still the most powerful gossip columnist ever—was starting to lose his grip on America. Winchell was desperately trying to break into the new medium of television, but the transition wasn't going smoothly. His look, his sensibilities, his causes, all seemed hopelessly mired in the past. In a desperate bid to preserve the old order that once had made him a success, Winchell made some dreadful misjudgments. His most notorious blunder was in 1951. When Josephine Baker accused Stork Club owner Sherman Billingsley of racism by giving her slow and sloppy service, Winchell sided with his old friend Billingsley. The controversy brought widespread attack from the liberal crowd that had always been Winchell's mainstay. As he became more isolated, Winchell lashed out against his enemies and embraced his allies. Harrison had worked as a copyboy at the ribald New York *Mirror* when Winchell was writing his "Broadway Hearsay" column for the tabloid; he knew the way Winchell operated and decided that even in his weakened state, Winchell could be a powerful friend. Harrison started running articles in *Confidential* to curry favor with the embattled columnist. "Winchell Was Right About Josephine Baker!" *Confidential* declared in its January 1953 issue. "Walter Winchell was virtually the only newspaperman in America who had the guts to stick out his chin and tell the world what a phony Josephine Baker was when she provoked the now-famous 'Stork Club Incident' last winter. For his pains, Winchell became an international target for charges of discrimination."

As soon as the article came off the presses, Harrison rushed over to Winchell's office with a copy. "He just loved it," Harrison recalled. Winchell flogged *Confidential* on his television show, holding up the magazine for the camera and urging his viewers to run out and buy an issue. "From then on, this thing flew," said Harrison. "We started running a Winchell piece every issue. We'd try to figure out who Winchell didn't like and run a piece on them." *Confidential* printed articles like "How Winchell Saved a Man from the Commie Kiss of Death" and "Broadway's Biggest Double Cross," which told about people whose career Winchell helped launch, only to have the person turn against him. "We kept plugging *Confidential*," Harrison said. "It got to the point where some days we would sit down and rack our brains trying to think of somebody else Winchell didn't like. We were running out of people, for Christ's sake!" Winchell brought *Confidential* to the attention of the public, but it was the magazine's celebrity scandals that kept them coming back. Readers went wild for the exposés: After only five years of publication, *Confidential* was selling nearly four million copies of each issue, making it the best-selling magazine on American newsstands.

While many older, more reputable publications were losing readers—often to television—*Confidential* became a publishing phenomenon. From 1952 to 1955, *Confidential*'s circulation went from 150,000 to 3.7 million an issue. In the same period, the *Saturday Evening Post* dropped from 1,742,311 to 1,547,341 an issue, and *Look* magazine fell from 1,153,525 to 1,001,068. *Confidential*, whose sales came entirely from the newsstands, resorted to increasingly sensational headlines to keep its sales up. Major advertisers shunned the tabloid: a typical issue carried only about $55,000 worth of ads, largely from places like correspondence schools and diet pills. By comparison, a single page in *Life* magazine, which in 1955 was fat with ads, cost $30,800. *Confidential*'s overhead, however, was low: While *Life* and other top magazines had huge staffs and bureaus around the world, Harrison had no advertising staff—what little the magazine had was handled by an outside agency—and a tiny editorial staff that rewrote articles that Harrison bought from freelancers for anywhere from $250 to $1,500. Harrison also kept costs down by printing on cheap paper. Most magazines used slick paper that in 1955 cost about $190 a ton; *Confidential* was printed on "super newsprint"—a stock that is just slightly higher grade than the newspaper—which in 1955 cost $134 a ton (newsprint was selling for $126 a ton that year). *Confidential* made Robert Harrison a very rich man.

More than a dozen *Confidential* imitators sprang up. Publications with names like *Suppressed, Top Secret, Hush-Hush, Inside Story, Exposed, Behind the Scenes,* and *On the QT* all competed for the most salacious dirt on movie stars. Harrison started publishing a second scandal magazine called *Whisper.* Scandal magazines became big business. Rather than being coddled and revered by columnists and fanzines, celebrities were suddenly being exposed and ridiculed in the press. Readers were riveted by stories like *Confidential*'s "Open Letter to General Mills: Here's Why Frank Sinatra Is Tarzan of the Boudoir." According to the article, the singer took breaks from his lovemaking to eat bowls of Wheaties. "He had the nation's front page playboys dizzy for years trying to discover the secret—Ava Gardner, Lana Turner, Gloria Vanderbilt, Anita Ekberg. How does that skinny little guy do it?" said the article. "Vitamins? Goat glands? Nope—Wheaties . . . After his *fourth* visit to the breakfast room, [an] unbelieving babe could plainly hear the crunch, crunch, crunch of a man—eating Wheaties." It was one of Harrison's all-time favorite articles, but when Sinatra read it, he went on a rampage.

"The Nude Who Came to Dinner," shocked fans of film noir star Robert Mitchum. "The menu said steak. There was no mention of a stew . . . and the party boiled over when one guest was not only fried—but peeled!" According to the June 1955 story, Mitchum stripped naked at a Hollywood dinner party and smeared himself with ketchup. "This a masquerade party, isn't it?" he reportedly said. "Well, I'm a hamburger, well done." *Confidential* continued: "The hamburger started dancing around the room, splattering the walls and all who came near." Mitchum was furious. "I never do such things because I have too much respect for the carpeting of my various hosts," he said. "If I were a catsup tosser, I wouldn't get invited to parties. And that would be tough. I just love parties."

The scandal magazines had a prurient yet Puritanical tone: They expressed outrage over Hollywood's hedonistic behavior— while describing each lurid act in detail. They exploited the peculiar paranoias of the 1950s. Articles about "Commies," the "Red Scare," and Cuba were common. So were stories about black stars mixing with whites. Typical was *Hush-Hush*'s September 1955 story, "His Passion for Blondes: Will It Destroy Sammy Davis, Jr.?" Homosexuality was also a big topic. While mainstream gossip columnists were reporting on Rock Hudson's various romances with Hollywood starlets, the scandal magazines were running the stories of the star's secret life that had been swirling around Hollywood for years. *TV Scandal*'s "How His Marriage Saved Rock Hudson from Double-Scandal!" reported that the star "was more comfortable with men than with women and had trouble keeping girlfriends." In its article, "Why Rock Hudson's Giving Hollywood the Willies!" *Uncensored* reported on various efforts by the studio to keep stories about Hudson quiet. Working for *Confidential* was a private investigator named Fred Otash—who played both sides of the fence. When Phyllis Gates wanted to divorce Rock Hudson, she hired Otash. The investigator taped a conversation of Rock and Phyllis discussing efforts to hide or "cure" his homosexuality.* Gates got everything she wanted in the divorce, and Otash got a little bonus in the arrangement: He went to Columbia Studios head Harry Cohn with the tape. "Rock is one of our biggest stars," Cohn pleaded with Otash. "If that stuff gets out, you'll ruin us." Cohn became a source and a client. "He handed me mug shots of one of his lesser stars, Rory Calhoun, who had been arrested and sent to prison earlier in life." *Confidential* did a story on Calhoun's early brush with the law and Cohn tossed more business Otash's way.

Hollywood tried to fight back. It made movies that slammed the exposé magazines, including the 1956 films *Scandal Inc.* with Robert Hutton and *Slander*, which was released with the tag line: "Who will be the next victim of this scandal magazine?" *Slander* starred Van Johnson, whose sex life was a regular topic for the scandal magazines. Some stars sued. Liberace filed a $20 million case against *Confidential* for a story that said the flamboyant pianist's theme song should be "Mad About the Boy." Maureen O'Hara, the star of *Miracle on 34th Street*, sued over an article, "It Was the Hottest Show in Town When Maureen O'Hara Cuddled in Row 35." The story reported that O'Hara and her "Latin Lothario" were kicked out of Grauman's Chinese Theatre for a "necking session [that was] so hot it threatened to short circuit the movie theater's air-conditioning system." Errol Flynn sued for $1 million, objecting to a story that he had taken several prostitutes as guests on his yachting honeymoon with Patricia Wymore.

Most celebrities, however, were worried that a court case would force out the rest of the story—the embarrassing details that *Confidential* held back. The story that did it—that made Hollywood decide it had to take action—was "The Real Reason for Marilyn Monroe's Divorce." The September 1955 article told how baseball hero Joe DiMaggio, hoping to catch the sex symbol he was divorcing in the arms of another man, conducted a raid on the apartment of a friend she was visiting. DiMaggio was still in love with Monroe; he was notoriously jealous and hot tem-

* It didn't bother Otash that Rock Hudson himself had also been a client. The actor had hired him to get some overly amorous ex-boyfriends out of his life.

pered, and he hired a private investigator, ex-cop Barney Ruditz-ky, and got his well-connected buddy Frank Sinatra to help with the ambush. DiMaggio, Sinatra, and their cronies followed America's hottest sex symbol to an apartment belonging to little-known starlet Sheila Stuart where, they suspected, Marilyn was having an affair with her vocal coach, Hal Schaefer.* There was some confusion and a couple of sidewalk conferences to discuss how to proceed, but at DiMaggio's insistence, the gang broke down the door and barged in. Once inside, the ambushers heard a woman's scream. The room was dark, but Ruditzky started taking pictures, using a flash on his camera, while the still-screaming woman tried to cover herself. Then someone turned on the lights. There, according to *Confidential*, the startled group of men saw a middle-aged woman "now sitting bolt upright in her bed, clutching her nightgown around her ribs and staring in utter terror at the invasion forces swarming around her boudoir." Then one of the invaders, realizing that they had broken into the wrong apartment, bellowed, "We're in the wrong place!"

During the debate over how to proceed, the hapless raiders lost sight of which door Marilyn had entered, and rather than catching the reigning film goddess in a compromising situation, they invaded the apartment of a bewildered middle-aged woman named Florence Kotz. Although several witnesses—including Kotz—recognized DiMaggio and Sinatra scurrying from the scene, the police department wrote off the incident as a bungled burglary until the blow-by-blow account appeared in *Confidential*. Hollywood's power elite was outraged—not with DiMaggio or Sinatra, but with *Confidential* for reporting the story.

Confidential had to be stopped. The heads of six major studios got together and discussed creating a $350,000 war chest to put *Confidential* out of business, according to a private detective named William Lewis, who met with *Wizard of Oz* producer Mervyn LeRoy to discuss the plan. That strategy was dropped, said

---

* There have been subsequent suggestions, including one from Hollywood private eye Don Crutchfield, that Monroe was actually having an affair with Sheila Stuart.

Lewis, because the studio heads were worried that the ploy would backfire. The movie community formed a committee "to consider proper ways and means to safeguard the welfare of the movie industry" that would "expose people connected with smear magazines and to alert the industry of their presence whenever they come around." Actor Ronald Reagan was on the executive committee and he turned to elected officials for help. Attorney General Edmund Brown was sympathetic. He was tight with Frank Sinatra, who would be a big contributor to his gubernatorial campaign. He was friendly with the Kennedy brothers, who knew that *Confidential* had the goods on their sexual escapades. In 1955, a California state senate subcommittee called the Kraft Commission investigated the scandal magazines to determine if private investigators were selling stories to them. The inquiry didn't produce any indictments, but it laid the groundwork for what was to follow. In May 1957, Brown and the State of California indicted *Confidential*, its owner, and its contributors, and charged them with "conspiracy to commit criminal libel."

"I love it," the *Confidential* publisher declared. "I've already told my lawyers to be prepared to subpoena every big-name star who ever appeared in the magazine." *Confidential* had turned its fifty-three-year-old publisher into a shameless publicity seeker. Harrison, nicknamed the King of Leer, was an effusive man who looked and spoke like a Broadway promoter. He had hooded eyes that darted back and forth, slicked-back black hair, a perpetual tan, and large, very white teeth. Harrison lived in a lavish Manhattan apartment off Fifth Avenue that he decorated to look like the nightclubs he frequented "with checkered tablecloths, a long bar and zebra stripes just like El Morocco," he boasted. He wore $250 tailor-made suits, a white fedora, and white polo coat, and drove around in a huge white custom-designed Cadillac Eldorado convertible. His flamboyance was his way, he insisted, of responding to suggestions that he go underground after getting death threats for articles his magazine had published. The *Confidential* trial would make him even richer and more famous, he insisted. "Can you picture that parade up to the witness stand?" Harrison loved a good scandal—even if it was about him. Like the time he was hunting for a male potency drug in the Dominican Republic and got shot by big-game hunter Richard Weldy. Earlier, *Confidential* had run an article that Weldy was a cuckolded husband. "No Wonder John Wayne Was the Topic of the Tropics," reported that while John Wayne was visiting his old friend Weldy in Lima, Wayne stole the hunter's wife, Pilar Palette. The jilted husband got into several public shouting matches with Harrison about the article. Eventually, Weldy took a rifle and shot at the publisher. The bullet hit Harrison in the shoulder, causing only a flesh wound. "Weldy is a nice fellow," John Wayne said after the incident, "but I deplore the fact that he is such a poor shot."

Weldy and Harrison both later claimed that the shooting was an accident, but it made headlines and the publisher happily posed for pictures from his hospital bed. Harrison even went on television where an aggressive reporter named Mike Wallace accused Harrison of faking the incident for publicity.

"[Mike Wallace] starts after me right away," said Harrison. "He's very sarcastic: 'Why don't you admit it, Harrison, that so-called shooting in the Dominican Republic was a fake, a publicity stunt, wasn't it? You weren't shot at all, were you?' "

"Would you know a bullet wound if you saw one?" Harrison asked.

Wallace insisted he would. The show was live and Harrison, a born showman, seized the moment; he took off his shirt in front of the stunned television crew. "Everybody is running around the studio like crazy!" Harrison recalled. "Those guys didn't know what to do, die or play organ music." The cameraman didn't notice the small puncture in Harrison's shoulder and instead zoomed in on a nickel-sized birthmark on his back. "On television, it must have looked like I'd been shot clean through with a cannon!" Harrison hooted. "That was funny! They never heard the end of it, about that show!" That was great publicity, Harrison said, but putting *Confidential* on trial—he declared—now *that* was going to be a headline bonanza.

Harrison hired private detective Fred Otash and his team of ten investigators to subpoena the biggest names in the movie industry: people like Clark Gable, Frank Sinatra, and Mike Todd, the high-profile producer of *Around the World in Eighty Days*, who was married to Hollywood's hottest star, Elizabeth Taylor. "Can you imagine those stars on the witness stand?" Harrison asked. "They'll have to testify that the stories about them are true!" He cackled.

"Hollywood's jitters have mounted toward hysteria," noted the New York *Daily News*. "Defense attorney Arthur J. Crowley says he is prepared to parade up to 200 movie colony greats including the 'king' himself Clark Gable before Judge Herbert V. Walker in an attempt to prove that *Confidential* magazine's exposés were true but not malicious." Crowley estimated that the trial would last at least six months. As the court date drew near, however, a funny thing happened in Hollywood: It emptied out. Frank Sinatra hid out in Las Vegas and put up other celebrities *Confidential* was trying to subpoena. Cary Grant stayed there and nervously kept tabs on the court proceedings. Clark Gable fled to Hawaii. Mike Todd and Elizabeth Taylor left the country for a yachting cruise. Errol Flynn, Dean Martin, Joan Crawford, and others were all hiding in various parts of the country. Stars were going to ridiculous lengths to avoid being subpoenaed. One day, Otash and his team cornered popular crooner Dan Daily at the Hollywood Bowl while the singer was giving a concert there. Otash posted detectives with subpoenas at all the stage door exits. "Daily walked boldly into a process server's ambush and escaped—without the dreaded summons—through an athletic display worthy of the elder Douglas Fairbanks," reported the New York *Daily News*. At the end of the concert, Daily took a deep bow and then shocked the fans as he "vaulted over the footlights when the curtain fell. Then as the surprised detectives gave chase, Daily snake-hipped through the aisles, jumped into a friend's car at a street entrance to the amphitheater, and rolled away."

Stranger things still happened to the witnesses. In the days before the trial, many of *them* disappeared, too. Some left the state. One, actress Francesca de Scaffa, who was also a defendant and a source for *Confidential*, fled to Mexico, where she hid in the trunk of her white Jaguar while deportation officials were in hot pursuit. Two other witnesses who were expected to testify died under suspicious circumstances. Polly Gould, a woman detective who gathered scandalous—but unpublished—details about Joan Crawford's sex life for *Confidential,* was found dead from an overdose of barbiturates. Police said it was an accident. A former featherweight boxer named Albert "Chalky" White, an ex-lover of Mae West who was the source of an article about the star's "Open Door Policy," was also found dead. He was drowned in his bathtub. Police said that that, too, was an accident. Insurance companies canceled *Confidential* staffers' policies, deeming them "poor risks." Otash and his detectives were able to subpoena only about one hundred stars. By this point, the once cocky Harrison had gotten nervous. He refused to go to California to be tried— fighting off several attempts by the prosecution to extradite him. The only defendants Brown's office was able to haul into court were Harrison's niece and her husband, Marjorie and Fred Meade, who ran the Los Angeles–based Hollywood Research, Inc., a small operation that gathered information for *Confidential.* The *Confidential* trial was held without Robert Harrison.

Even without the key defendants and witnesses, the *Confidential* trial was a great show for scandal fans; that became obvious from the moment Ronnie Quillan was called to testify. A collective gasp rose from the courtroom as Quillan, wearing a form-fitting white dress and gold sling-back heels, was sworn in. She ran her fingers through her shoulder-length red hair and gave her occupation as "prostitute." Ronnie Quillan was Hollywood's most notorious madam. What's more—she testified—she was also a paid informant for *Confidential.* "Mr. Harrison told me that he wanted stories concerning the activities of celebrities," Quillan testified in a bored, world-weary voice. "The more lewd and lascivious, the more colorful for the magazine." So Ronnie Quillan gave *Confidential* magazine the lowdown on television's most adorable husband—Desi Arnaz.

"Does Desi Really Love Lucy?" *Confidential* asked. "Arnaz is a Latin Lothario who loves Lucy *most* of the time but by no means *all* of the time," the magazine reported. "He has, in fact, sprinkled his affections all over Los Angeles for a number of years. And quite a bit of it has been bestowed on vice dollies who were paid handsomely for loving Desi briefly but, presumably, as effectively as Lucy." *Confidential* paid Quillan $1,200 for the information, she testified. She knew the story was true, she said, because she and two of her "girls" had serviced Arnaz. Arnaz angrily denied Quillan's story, calling it "baloney," adding, "I don't remember meeting the lady." Despite Arnaz's denial, America was shocked. Los Angeles, which had never read the Arnaz story because of Brown's ban of the magazine in California, was agog. The prosecutors had called Quillan as a witness against *Confidential** because they hoped her revelations would prove that Robert Harrison ran a sleazy operation. The prostitute's story turned out to be far more embarrassing to Arnaz and to Hollywood, however, than it was to *Confidential* magazine.

Quillan was just the opening act. Actress Maureen O'Hara angrily testified that the article about her alleged "necking session" at Grauman's Chinese Theatre was inaccurate and libelous; O'Hara had the passport stamps to prove she was out of the country at the time the incident was supposed to have occurred. But *Confidential* produced three witnesses to the disputed event, including James Craig, the former assistant manager of Grauman's, who testified that he asked O'Hara and her companion to leave the theater when things between them got too intimate. "The gentleman was facing the screen and Miss O'Hara was lying across the seats, across his lap," Craig told the jury in an impeccable British accent. "Her blouse was undone." Craig fixed his flashlight on the twosome, he said, and eventually O'Hara and her boyfriend "got back in their natural positions." Before long, however, Craig received a complaint that "they're at it again!" He returned, he testified, to find "Miss O'Hara sitting on his lap . . . I told myself 'This can't go on.' And I politely told them that I thought it best to leave." Craig drew charts and diagrams of the alleged incident and a female court employee was recruited to re-create the various positions that O'Hara had allegedly assumed atop her boyfriend. The jurors then requested a trip to Grauman's Chinese Theatre, where they got a first-hand look at the seats where O'Hara reportedly had her necking session.

---

* The defense claimed that the state threw out some prostitution charges against her in exchange for her testimony, which Brown's office denied.

Dorothy Dandridge, the elegantly beautiful star of *Carmen Jones* and the first black ever nominated for an Academy Award as best actress, also testified against *Confidential*. Dandridge had filed a $2 million lawsuit against the tabloid over the article, "What Dorothy Dandridge Did in the Woods." The case was settled out of court—Dandridge received an apology and $10,000. The actress told the jurors that the settlement proved that the story about her was a lie. *Confidential's* lawyer, however, insisted that Dandridge was given the relatively small sum of money because settling was much cheaper than a court fight would have been. What's more, the defense argued, by discussing the case, Dandridge had violated the terms of the agreement and *Confidential* wanted its money back. Even worse for Dandridge, the defense produced the source of the story, bandleader Dan Terry, and an affidavit from him declaring that he had the romp with Dandridge described in *Confidential*. Terry had been paid $200 for his story.

During the trial, a *Confidential* editor testified that the magazine got stories on Clark Gable because one of its regular sources was having an affair with the actor. The source, actress Francesca de Scaffa, was on the lam in Mexico, where she had attempted suicide. Reporters couldn't locate de Scaffa, but when they tracked down Gable in Hawaii for comment, he, like Arnaz, developed a memory problem. "I think I would remember her," Gable said, "but to my knowledge I never met the lady in my life." *Confidential* editors also claimed that Mike Todd was a big source for the magazine; Mr. Elizabeth Taylor at first denied the story, but then, when presented with detailed evidence of his participation in stories, he issued a "no comment." Scandals came out from stories that *Confidential* had decided not to publish, such as how one of Joan Crawford's adopted children ran away from home because the actress was "cruel to them."

The prosecution's star witness was former *Confidential* editor Howard Rushmore, a former Communist turned "anti-Red" crusader who had worked with Senator Joe McCarthy. Rushmore had resigned from *Confidential* in a huff over a number of disputes, including Harrison's decision to kill a lurid story Rushmore wrote about Eleanor Roosevelt's sex life. During the trial, it was revealed that several New York City and Los Angeles cops were on *Confidential's* payroll. A well-known Texas DJ had supplied the magazine with stories about Elvis Presley's outrageous sexual appetite.

The testimony in the trial was so ribald that newspapers around the country grappled with how to cover it. Some tabloids exploited the revelations with lurid banner headlines like: "Elvis Wriggled on Mag's Hook," "V-Girl Tells of Desi Smear" and "Clark Gable Linked to Vice Mag Party Girl." In Los Angeles— where many readers were getting the details of the stories for the first time—the conservative *Los Angeles Times* played down the story, but Hearst's bawdy *Examiner* put the story on the front pages and the paper sold out almost every day. Some editors, however, refused to publish details about the trial. Particularly in the South and in the Midwest, stories about the *Confidential* trial were heavily censored or banned altogether; the tales of nude parties and interracial romps were just too salacious for family newspapers. Even the tabloids that covered the trial in detail often expressed shock and outrage over the "sleaze mongers" and "dirt diggers." Some of the umbrage, however, was posturing. One reporter who was covering the trial for the New York *Daily News* was taken off the story after it was revealed that she contributed to *Confidential* under a pseudonym. Lee Mortimer, a gossip columnist for the New York *Daily Mirror* who wrote articles attacking *Confidential* and its publisher, was privately friendly with Harrison, according to the publisher. "Mortimer wanted to keep the controversy going," Harrison said. "We would meet at a phone booth in a little hotel on East Fifty-second Street and exchange information so that he could keep writing about *Confidential*. It was a big help to me."

The trial was turning out to be devastating to the Hollywood image that it was intended to protect. By the time Gloria Wellman, the adopted daughter of famed director William Wellman (*A Star is Born* and *Beau Geste*) and a self-described "naked model" and prostitute, testified that she was the source for a story on a "Naked Canapé" party attended by some of the movie industry's biggest names, stars were openly complaining that the strategy had backfired; stories that had been dismissed as tabloid trash were being confirmed on the witness stand by the sources. "Now that the whole world is reading what first appeared only in *Confidential*, it looks to me as if it were a mistake to bring this action into court," lamented singer John Carroll. "There is one thing for sure. Folks aren't going to be thinking from now on that we show people are like the boys and girls next door."

So, on August 19, when a sultry young singer and actress named Mylee Andreason took the stand and began to testify about a "star-studded naked rug party," she got only as far as identifying herself as a participant in the raunchy festivities before the prosecution interrupted her. The District Attorney's office appealed to Judge Walker, who was, himself, a former child actor and was sympathetic to the film community. Walker made a ruling that completely undermined the defense's strategy: he said that any new testimony had to relate to the few articles that the prosecution had already read into the record. Judge Walker's decision thwarted Harrison's plan for a parade of celebrity witnesses, or at the very least, an open discussion about their accuracy.

Then came another devastating blow to the magazine's credibility. Paul Gregory, producer of *The Naked and the Dead*, testified that Harrison's niece, Marjorie Meade, had tried to blackmail him. Gregory, the subject of a stinging *Confidential* exposé, produced a tape recording of a woman claiming to be Meade's secretary. In the recording, the woman demanded that Gregory meet Meade at a restaurant called Sherry to give her $10,000—or Gregory would be the subject of a scathing article in *Confidential*. The defense, however, proved that the restaurant Sherry wasn't even around at the time of the alleged blackmail attempt. What's more, they produced a witness who said Meade was out of town visiting a friend that day—and they had the tickets and receipts to prove it.

On September 16, after 6 weeks, 2,000 pages of testimony, and 164 exhibits—the case went to the jury. Attorney General Brown, however, wasn't finished with *Confidential*. While the jury was locked away in its deliberations, Brown announced that he was preparing new charges against the magazine. The prosecution vowed that *Confidential* and Robert Harrison would be "reindicted, regardless of the pending verdict." And this time, Brown vowed, Harrison would not be able to escape extradition to Los Angeles. Hollywood circled the wagons to make sure nothing like *Confidential* would ever publish again; the Motion Picture Industry Council formed a permanent committee to combat scandal magazines. "What we are trying to do," said a spokesman for the group, "is expose people connected with smear magazines and to alert the industry of their presence whenever they come around. Now that the wraps are off, we will act." Ronald Reagan headed up the board.

On October 1, the jury—exhausted by thirteen days of contentious deliberation, a rumor of jury fixing, screaming fights over where to have lunch, and smog that got so bad that one day several jurors collapsed—reported that it was "hopelessly deadlocked." Harrison, who had spent more than $400,000 defending *Confidential*—was emotionally and financially wiped out. Rather than go through another trial, he reached a plea bargain with Brown's office. The Attorney General would drop the charges if *Confidential* would change its editorial policy and publish only flattering stories about movie stars and politicians. Harrison was required to take out ads in New York, Chicago, and Los Angeles newspapers, announcing that *Confidential* was going to "eliminate exposé stories on the private lives of celebrities." Most of the stars dropped their suits against the magazine—although Liberace ended up getting a $40,000 settlement for the article suggesting he was gay. After several issues of celebrity-friendly articles, *Confidential's* circulation plummeted and Robert Harrison sold the magazine. *Confidential* limped along under various incarnations for over a decade.

Howard Rushmore, the former *Confidential* editor who was the key witness for the prosecution, briefly worked for other scandal magazines, but after *Confidential's* collapse, the exposé business wasn't the same, and Rushmore became depressed. One day, while riding up Madison Avenue in a taxi with his wife, Rushmore took a gun and blew out her brains, and then his own.

Robert Harrison disappeared from the headlines. When he ran into Walter Winchell on the street or at a nightclub, his old ally would practically run away from him. "How did I get mixed up with *Confidential?*" Winchell used to complain to friends. "I still don't understand it." Harrison tried to launch a few other magazines, including an "investigative journalism" newsletter called "Inside News," but none of his new ventures was very successful and he died virtually forgotten in 1978.

"This keyhole stuff is dead," Harrison glumly said several years after he lost *Confidential.*

He was wrong. *Confidential*'s legacy had just begun.

mike wallace—shaking the building

"The name of this program is *Night Beat*, and here's what it is all about," Mike Wallace said. It was 11 P.M. on October 9, 1956, the night of the debut of his new television talk show, and Wallace was sitting on a four-legged stool in the studio of WABC in New York. The room was dark except for an unforgiving spotlight; smoke from his cigarette curled up and encircled his face, which had been ravaged by acne when he was a teenager. The scars were now an asset, however; they made him seem tough as well as handsome, as if he'd been through a battle. "It's about *people*—people we think you will be curious about because they *are* news and because they *make* news," he went on. "Even if *Night Beat* must occasionally step on some toes, we will try to get you stories of success and sorrow, trial and error, hope, folly, and frustrations."

At the time, talk shows were tame, tepid chat fests. "They were pap, pabulum," said Wallace. "You'd put the microphone and the flowers on the table between the interviewer and the interviewee and the interviewee would say 'I wrote or sang or appeared in.' It was basically that. There was obviously a thirst for a different kind of interview." And Wallace delivered it. He set out to grill his subjects, and *Night Beat*, broadcast locally four nights a week from eleven to midnight, soon became a citywide sensation. Every morning, blurry-eyed New Yorkers were abuzz over what some stumbling, stuttering movie star or government official or society swell had confessed under Wallace's relentless interrogation. "Mike Wallace, a dark-haired 39-year-old with a prizefighter's face and the velvety voice of a musical-comedy performer has become one of TV's most talked about performers," noted *Newsweek*. "For his guests' pains, he has been called a muckraker and scandal monger; the Kukla, Fran, and Ollie of interviewers, as well as the bravest man on TV."

Wallace did do some important political interviews—but it was the scandals and salacious revelations he managed to produce that generated the most attention. His show became a forum for sex and scandal. It made headlines when social arbiter Elsa Maxwell blurted out: "Sex is the most tiring thing in the world. I was never interested for one minute, ever." Wallace asked society designer Mr. John why the fashion world attracted so many homosexuals. "That's not worth talking about," Mr. John snapped. When Jayne Mansfield was a guest, Wallace asked, "Are you irritated by the theory of evolution?" Of Zsa Zsa Gabor, he asked: "Tell me, Zsa Zsa, what are clothes *really* for?"

"As soon as Mike Wallace began his relentless prying and probing into the pasts, the actions, and the attitudes of the celebrities on his TV 'hot seat,' "Nightbeat" exploded into a television sensation that delighted and sometimes shocked New Yorkers," noted *Parade*. "The candor of Wallace's approach, the daring of his caustic questions, and the frankness of his victims' answers have started a revolution in television interviewing."

Most journalists sneered and scoffed. "Mike Wallace, the television inquisitor with a liking for blondes, became famous by cross-examining celebrities on embarrassing intimate matters," noted *Uncensored*, which, like *Confidential* and many other tamed scandal magazines, had taken to attacking sensationalism in journalism. "Sex has figured so largely in Wallace's questioning of men and women famous in Hollywood, and Broadway, on Park Avenue and in industry that loud-mouthed labor leader Mike

Quill once emerged from Wallace's verbal torture to call him 'the Peeping Tom of TV.' " Critics maintained that Wallace, whose previous credits included hosting game shows, serving as the announcer on *The Lone Ranger* and *The Green Hornet*, and starring in the Broadway musical *The Reclining Figure*, was more of a performer or entertainer than a reporter. "Wallace burst into the Tinker Toy world of timorous TV like a young bull storming into a china shop," noted *Hush-Hush*. "A moderately successful announcer even a few years ago, he became a national celebrity virtually overnight by getting answers to some rude questions no one else dared to ask on television. His wasn't the cliché interview program, plugging a star's upcoming epic or a delicatessen mogul's new king-sized franks. Mike's gimmick was to club his guests with queries on video's four taboo subjects—religion, politics, sex, and personal habits."

Wallace was accused of being a "muckracker and a scandal monger," and of having a prurient focus on sex. "Why be afraid of it," Wallace shot back. "As one of the basic drives in all human beings, it is a perfectly legitimate interest."

It was also a real ratings grabber: by 1957, the year of the *Confidential* trial, *Night Beat* had captured a then astonishing audience of more than 1.5 million New Yorkers a night and ABC asked him to take the show—the young medium's first real foray into the world of tabloid journalism and the true precursor to the "tabloid television" of the eighties—national.

Myron Leon Wallace was raised in what he would describe as a "Jewish/Irish section of Boston." Brookline, Massachusetts, was hardly a working-class neighborhood; Wallace's neighbors included John F. Kennedy and Leonard Bernstein. Both of Wallace's parents had immigrated from Russia as children; his father Frank, who changed his last name from Wallik, was a wholesale grocer and later an insurance broker. Wallace, the youngest of four children, was a B-minus student with a fairly happy childhood, marred primarily by his severe acne, which scarred his ego as well as his skin. "In some strange way [it] helped form my personality and character," he said. "You look into the mirror and you don't like what you see." Wallace's brother, Irving, recalled that Mike "was a moody kid, very self-centered, an egoist who was always searching for the purpose in life."

Wallace graduated from the University of Michigan in 1939, married his college sweetheart, Norma Kaplan, and had two children, Peter and Chris. He held a number of jobs as a radio announcer, including one at a 500-watt station in Grand Rapids, Michigan, with the unlikely call letters WOOD-WASH—it was owned jointly by a furniture store and a laundry service. In 1946, after serving in naval communications during World War II, he moved to Chicago, where he did regular newscasts for the *Chicago Sun-Times* and appeared on leading daytime radio dramas, including *Road of Life, Ma Perkins*, and *The Guiding Light*. In 1948, he and Norma were divorced. "I married too young," he said. His second wife was the beautiful and socially prominent actress Buff Cobb, whose grandfather was the humorist Irvin S. Cobb. In Chicago, he was the host of a number of television and radio shows, including *There's One in Every Family* and *I'll Buy That*, and, before their divorce in 1955, he and his wife co-hosted a breakfast-time television program called *The Mike and Buff Show*.

Still, *Night Beat* was merely a local show. When ABC head Leonard Goldenson came to Wallace and his producers and asked him to take *Night Beat* national, he was eager for the opportunity—and the exposure. It meant going from five days a week to once a week and a salary cut from around $150,000 to $100,000. "Leonard Goldenson was beginning to change the whole business," Wallace recalled. "ABC was third. He needed attention for his network. He made us an offer we couldn't refuse . . . it was the biggest mistake we could have made." Wallace's provocative questions worked well in New York, but Wallace wasn't sure if they would play with a national audience. Moreover, he was concerned that the often controversial content of the show would upset network officials. "Unless this building shakes every couple of weeks," Goldenson said, "you're not doing your job."

The Mike Wallace Interview went on the air in April 1957. It was broadcast Sundays at 9:30. Wallace took a cue from the legendary Edward R. Murrow and scheduled Joe McCarthy as his first guest. At the last minute, however, the ailing McCarthy—

who would die about a month later—canceled and the bookers scrambled to get Gloria Swanson. The actress was too savvy to be tricked into saying something indiscreet, and the show's debut was a disappointment. For his second national segment, Wallace was determined to create a stir. One of hottest subjects of the day was organized crime, and Wallace invited Mickey Cohen, the former mobster and confessed murderer, to appear on the show. Cohen, who had left the underworld and owned a flower shop and an ice cream parlor, did not disappoint. Once the cameras were rolling, he erupted into a tirade on live television, calling Los Angeles Police Chief Bill Parker a "sadistic degenerate," an alcoholic, and a "reformed thief."

Parker was watching the show. "I hope Mike Wallace has a lot of money," he said. Parker and the LAPD sued Wallace and every ABC station that carried the show for a total of $33 million. "Has Wallace's prying gone too far?" asked one reviewer. "There are those who believe that if Wallace continues sinking his scalpel too deep, it eventually will plant itself between his own shoulder blades." The network rushed onto air with a profuse apology and retraction, ABC made an out-of-court settlement with Parker, and Wallace was told to tone down the show. Things went downhill from there.

"Is he a sadist, as some contend?" *Newsweek* asked in September 1957. "Does he really think he is performing a public service by allowing ex-hoodlum Mickey Cohen and scandal sheet private eye Fred Otash to give their questionable views a public airing? What are his rebuttals to the charge that he is an untrained reporter and a sensation hound, and that his show, 'Mike Wallace Interviews,' is no better than the TV equivalent of *Confidential* magazine?"

Shortly after the Cohen fiasco, Wallace invited Drew Pearson to be a guest on his show. Pearson was at the time one of the most respected newspapermen in the country, an investigative reporter with a syndicated column who had dared take on the powerful Kennedy dynasty. In the late 1950s, Pearson had written a number of columns attacking the Kennedys, pointing out Joseph Kennedy's ties to organized crime and the disgraced anti-Communist Joe McCarthy. Pearson also wrote a column questioning the political ascendency of the young Senator John F. Kennedy. Wallace thought that the controversial but highly credible Pearson would make an ideal guest on his show.

"You wrote that Senator Kennedy's—and I quote—'millionaire McCarthyite father, crusty old Joseph P. Kennedy, is spending a fortune on a publicity machine to make Jack's name well-known.' " Wallace said to Pearson on air. "What significance do you see in this, aside from the fact that Joe Kennedy would like to see Jack Kennedy president of the United States?"

"I don't know what significance other than the fact that I don't think we should have a synthetic public relations buildup for any job of that kind," Pearson replied. "Jack Kennedy's a fine young man," the reporter continued, "but he isn't as good as that public relations campaign makes him out to be." Then Pearson let loose a bombshell: "[John F. Kennedy] is the only man in history that I know who won a Pulitzer Prize for a book that was ghostwritten for him."

Wallace's eyes grew wide with astonishment. "You know for a fact, Drew," he asked, "that the book *Profiles in Courage* was written for Senator Kennedy . . . by someone else?"

"I do," Pearson said, who maintained that Kennedy speechwriter Ted Sorensen actually wrote the book.

"And Kennedy accepted a Pulitzer Prize for it?" Wallace asked. "And he has never acknowledged the fact?"

"No, he has not," Pearson said. "You know, there's a little wisecrack around the Senate about Jack. . . . Some of his colleagues say, 'Jack, I wish you had a little less profile and more courage.' "

ABC executives didn't congratulate Wallace for his scoop. To the contrary. Joe Kennedy called his lawyer, Clark Clifford, yelling, "Sue the bastards for fifty million dollars!" And in no time, Clifford and Robert Kennedy had showed up at ABC and told executives there the Kennedys would sue unless the network issued a full retraction and apology. Mike Wallace and Drew Pearson insisted that the story was true and refused to back off. Nevertheless, ABC issued a full retraction and apology. Wallace was furious. It was one thing to apologize for the rantings of a former mobster like Mickey Cohen, but Pearson was a serious investigative journalist whose allegations about Kennedy's authorship of *Profiles in Courage* would later prove to be true. Nevertheless, Oliver Treyz, then head of the network, appeared on Wallace's show and offered a full retraction and apology. It was a terrible blow to Wallace and the credibility of his show. He became such a pariah around the network that John Daly, the vice president at ABC as well as the host of *What's My Line*, refused to moderate the show when Wallace was booked as the mystery guest. Wallace's appearance was canceled and Sammy Davis Jr. appeared instead.

"Along Madison Avenue it is no secret that veteran news commentator John Daly did not like the switch of headline-grabbing Mike Wallace to ABC. Daly is said to have stated that he did not believe there was any place for a show on TV that dealt with such controversial issues," noted one magazine.

Goldenson had assured Wallace that he wanted him to "shake the building," but the moment he did, the network executives were not willing to stand behind him. *The Mike Wallace Interview* went off the air in the summer of 1958. The networks were not yet ready for scandal.

4

the birth of a tabloid

At twilight on a warm day in early May 1957, just as the *Confidential* trial was getting underway in Los Angeles, a young publisher lumbered into the East Fifty-fifth Street restaurant L'Aiglon in New York City, took a seat at his usual table, and settled back to enjoy a taste of a world that was about to disappear. Generoso Pope Jr. had been having a rough time lately. Five years earlier, shortly after his twenty-fifth birthday, Pope had bought a floundering weekly tabloid called the *New York Enquirer*. In the first issue, Pope published his credo on the front page:

> In an age darkened by the menace of totalitarian tyranny and war, the *New York Enquirer* will fight for the rights of man—the rights of the individual, and will champion human decency, dignity, freedom and peace.

Decency, dignity, freedom, and peace didn't sell so well, so within a few months, Pope had turned the *New York Enquirer* into a scandal magazine. Recently, city and state officials had begun to take issue with the unseemly content of Pope's paper. Gene Pope didn't mind a battle; he was aggressive and cocky and came from a wealthy, influential family. He assumed he would always win. Besides, he had a powerful ally: the man he was meeting for dinner that night, his benefactor and godfather, gangster Frank Costello, who at that moment was perhaps the most powerful mobster in America.

Costello entered L'Aiglon shortly after Pope arrived. The two men embraced and ordered Scotches. The solicitous waiters arranged the carnations on their table and fussed over the men as they brought the food: risotto Milanese and piccata a la romana, served on plates so hot that you couldn't touch them—just the way Costello liked. Frank Costello was treated like a celebrity in New York. His incredible influence over city politics had been exposed several years earlier during the televised Kefauver hearings; Costello controlled Tammany Hall, appointed judges, and, the inquest concluded, controlled a "government within a government." Costello served some time for income tax evasion, but even from jail, his power was immense. The *New York Times* called him the Prime Minister of the Underworld, but to Gene Pope, he was still "Uncle Frank"—an old family friend who helped him out when he got into financial binds and political scrapes.

Several friends and business associates joined them that evening, but as usual during Pope's frequent dinners with Costello, Uncle Frank did most of the talking. The topic that night was Joe McCarthy. The news was yet to be released, but Costello had just learned that the controversial, communist-bashing Senator had died. "All that booze finally got to him," Costello said. McCarthy was such a heavy drinker that he sometimes ate a stick of butter before a night on the town just to coat his stomach against the alcohol. It wasn't simply his appetite for liquor that destroyed McCarthy, however; the senator did everything to extremes, and that, in Costello's opinion, is what created McCarthy's problems. "He was going after the Commies, and that was a good thing, right?" Costello said. "But then he started doing wrong things and accusin' everyone of being a Commie. Like I always say, you got to do things in moderation."

Gene Pope smiled and drank some champagne. He knew Joe

McCarthy. They were part of the same crowd, and they never did anything in moderation. Gene Pope was a big man, six foot four and bulky, with wavy, slicked-back hair, heavy eyebrows, a thick jaw, and cherubic lips. He spoke in a laconic baritone—a cross between Humphrey Bogart and Jimmy Stewart; his deliberate manner masked his stunning intellect. Pope had attended Horace Mann, the exclusive New York City boys school where he became best friends with Roy Cohn. He went on to attend MIT, graduating at nineteen with a degree in engineering, and briefly attended Columbia Law School. Gene's friend Cohn went on to become McCarthy's chief counsel and was brought down in disgrace when his tactics and nepotism were exposed by Democratic counsel Robert Kennedy during a televised Senate hearing.

Don't destroy yourself like McCarthy and Cohn did, Costello was telling Pope. "Like I always say," Costello said, "you got to do things in moderation. Too much of anything is no good." The mob boss may have been directing the comments toward himself as well, for that evening Costello had also learned that he was probably going back to jail—though he said nothing of the bad news to his friends. Costello picked up the $75 dinner tab, and the crowd went to Monsignore, further east on Fifty-fifth Street, for drinks. They ordered Scotches, except for Costello, who had coffee and two glasses of anisette. Pope wanted to go to the Copa to catch a show; Costello begged off. It was 11 P.M. and he needed to be clear-headed for an early morning meeting with his lawyer, Edward Bennett Williams. Costello bid his friends good night and took a taxi to his apartment building on Central Park West. There, a beefy thug walked up to Costello, put a gun up to his face, and said "This is for you, Frank" and shot the Prime Minister of the Underworld point blank.

The Costello hit was big news throughout the summer of 1957—occasionally knocking the *Confidential* trial off the front pages of the tabloids. Physically, Costello recovered, but he would never regain his old power.

Few were as shaken by the Costello shooting as Gene Pope. He was questioned by a grand jury about the shooting for fifty minutes, but repeatedly said he knew nothing. The interrogation wasn't what bothered Pope. The failed hit marked the end of an era—the young publisher's strongest remaining link to the world of political and financial power and corruption in which he had been raised. Pope had been jockeying for a solid position in that world, and had been counting on Frank Costello and the *New York Enquirer* to secure it for him. Now, after the shooting, he had only the *Enquirer*.

With the *New York Enquirer*, Pope was trying to achieve the same sort of political clout that his father had built up with his media empire. It was a tough act to follow. Generoso Pope Sr. had left his family in Pasquarielli, Italy, in 1906 to come to America when he was twelve years old and had $4 in his pocket. He quickly got a job hauling water at a sand and gravel outfit called Colonial; within five years he became a foreman. By 1918 he was half owner and a few years later, he took over the entire business. Colonial Sand and Gravel became one of the country's largest construction companies, helping to build some of New York City's most important landmarks, including Rockefeller Center and Radio City Music Hall.

Pope Sr.'s business clout led to political connections—and vice versa. In 1925, he organized Italian Americans to back Tammany Hall politician Jimmy Walker for mayor; in gratitude, Walker appointed Pope Sr. to several high-level positions, including chairman of the newly formed Aviation and Airports Program, which planned the construction of airports. Such appointments gave Pope both social prestige and political power. The cozy relationship between Walker and municipal contractors like Pope prompted an investigation by the Seabury Commission in 1931, but no charges were filed against Colonial.

It wasn't Pope's construction company or his political appointments that gave him real status, however. That came from his media holdings. In 1928 Pope bought *Il Progresso Italo-Americano*, the country's largest and oldest Italian-language daily newspaper. Pope paid $2 million for *Il Progresso*, which had a circulation of 90,000. Some thought the cost was too high, but the clout that came with it was priceless. Pope went on to buy most of the Italian newspapers in New York, including *Il Bollettino della Sera* and *Il Corriere d'America*, and by 1930, he essentially controlled the Italian press in New York. He added to his holdings by buying radio station WHOM in 1946. Pope used his papers to encourage his readers to learn English, become American citizens, and vote. He was honored by Francis Cardinal Spellman and began organizing the Columbus Day Parade, an important celebration of ethnic pride for Italian-Americans in New York. Pope became an important ally and friend of Franklin Roosevelt.

Some of Pope's causes, however, got him in trouble. *Il Progresso* supported Fascist dictator Benito Mussolini, who invited Pope to Italy. Pope was accused of hiring thugs to intimidate anti-Fascist editors and in 1931, someone tried to kill the publisher with a mail bomb, which blew up prematurely, taking the lives of two postal workers. When Mussolini invaded Ethiopia, Pope used his considerable clout with Roosevelt, urging him to maintain neutrality in the war. He came under increasing fire as Mussolini drew closer to Hitler, but redeemed himself by blasting Fascism in 1941 and working for the American War effort—organizing an Italian-American war bond drive. When the feds came after Frank Costello, *Il Progresso* ran a series of articles and editorials defending the mob leader. Suspicions arose that Pope was connected to the Mafia, and he came under FBI surveillance, but no link was ever proved. Frank Costello, however, did become a loyal friend and ally.

Generoso Pope Sr. personified the immigrant dream. Through hard work and ruthless ambition—as well as some dubious political connections—he acquired incredible wealth and power. Like an Italian Joe Kennedy, he hoped to pave a path of respectability for the next generation. Pope had married the beautiful and aristocratic-looking Catherine Richcichi in 1916, and together they had three sons, Fortune, Anthony, and on January 13, 1927, Generoso Jr., the youngest. His sons were handsome and well educated; he had dreams that one them would become president.

Gene was chauffeured to school at Horace Mann from the family's lavish sixteen-room apartment at 1040 Park Avenue. His best friend, Roy Cohn, who lived several blocks north at 1165 Park Avenue, would sometimes ride in the limousine with him. Roy's two other best friends at Horace Mann would also go on to become important people in the world of media: publishing scion Si Newhouse, and the future *New York Times* columnist Anthony Lewis, whose father Kassel Lewis—originally Kassell Oshinsky—and his brothers owned Crown Fabrics, one of the leading firms in the garment center. The four young men formed a clique of boys who were fascinated by power, the media, and politics.*

Roy and Gene would visit Roy's father, the influential liberal Bronx Judge Al Cohn, at his courthouse. They liked to drop by City Hall, where they met politicians and became friendly with fixers like Tammany Hall boss Carmine DeSapio and Sammy De-Falco, who got appointed a judge through Costello. Gene's father arranged for the boys to visit the White House, where they met President Harry S. Truman. By the mid-1940s, they were hanging out at the Stork Club with people like J. Edgar Hoover and Damon Runyon and other members of Cafe Society. It was an exclusive world, an informal club in which the members shared their power and traded secrets.

Gossip columnists in that era were among the most powerful journalists in the country; they were valued by their papers and followed religiously by their readers. "It was a different time, a golden age for gossip columnists," recalled Igor Cassini, who wrote Hearst's widely read Cholly Knickerbocker column. "We were treated like royalty. We were always coining words and fighting over scoops." In addition to Cassini, there was Dorothy Kilgallen, Earl Wilson, Doris Lilly, Leonard Lyons, George Sokolsky, Nancy Randolph, Louis Sobol, Ed Sullivan, Danton Walker, and, of course, Walter Winchell, who took credit for having introduced Roy Cohn to his friend J. Edgar Hoover.

Gene Pope Jr. and Roy Cohn were big men in this world. Cohn edged out the promising young Robert Kennedy for the highly coveted job of McCarthy's chief counsel and would leak stories praising McCarthy and digging at Kennedy to his buddies like Winchell and Hearst columnist George Sokolsky. Gene Jr. was being groomed to take over his father's media empire. The sand and gravel business, young Pope said, "didn't intrigue me," but he loved working at WHOM and at *Il Progresso*, which he

---

* Lewis later had an ideological break from his friend Cohn over Robert Kennedy.

started running in 1947 when he was twenty years old. He basked in the power that the media gave him. Then, on April 28, 1950, at the age of fifty-nine, Generoso Pope Sr. died of a heart attack.

When Pope Sr. died, Frank Costello got Mayor Bill O'Dwyer to give Pope Jr. several high-profile appointments. The elder Pope had been the treasurer of O'Dwyer's election campaign; after Pope Sr. died, O'Dwyer made Pope Jr. an honorary deputy police commissioner and gave him a seat on the prestigious Board of Higher Education. Pope Jr. started running the city's Columbus Day Parade like his father had. That summer, however, O'Dwyer was forced to resign amid charges that he was connected to the mob. Then, in October, Pope Jr. ruffled feathers during a radio broadcast of the Columbus Day celebration by praising his political friends and being dismissive of his political enemies. "Whatever his merits or failings, Gene Pope Jr., ex–Mayor O'Dwyer's 23-year-old appointee to the Board of Higher Education, isn't going to win any popularity contests," noted the New York *Herald Tribune*. "His political elders, who have been smarting under Gene's arrogance since he took over the enterprises of his late father, are doing a brand new slow burn over his antics at the Columbus Day Parade."

Another controversy erupted later that month when Pope was accused of being a front for Frank Costello. Pope was stripped of his position as honorary deputy police commissioner. "I highly value my commissionership," Pope said, "but I gladly give it up rather than compromise my freedom of expression."

Then Gene's world collapsed even further. His brothers, resentful, he said, that he was running the family empire that had been left in a trust for all three of them, voted Gene out of the business. "I was supposed to run the company," Pope later said. "My brothers decided I was going to work for them. I told them to take a walk."

By the end of 1950, Gene Pope had lost his father, his career, and his position in New York politics. His next move was a peculiar one: he went to Washington to work for the CIA. There, Pope worked in a department specializing in psychological warfare. He quit after about eighteen months. "I got fed up with the bureaucracy and the red tape," he once said. "You'd spend weeks trying to get something done, and then they wouldn't let you do it." Some who knew Pope, however, believe he never completely severed his ties with the agency.

Gene Pope cast about a bit, trying to decide what to do with the rest of his life. In 1952, while hanging out at a Greenwich Village nightclub, he heard that the *New York Enquirer* was going on the block. The newspaper had a peculiar history. William Griffin, a newspaper advertising man, founded the tabloid as a New York Sunday afternoon paper in 1926 on a loan from his mentor, William Randolph Hearst. In return, Hearst used the paper as a testing ground for new ideas. Hearst used the good ideas for his own papers; the *Enquirer* was free to keep the bad ones. It was New York's only Sunday afternoon newspaper—and thus had a brief moment of glory when it scooped the other publications in town with New York's first published account of the bombing of Pearl Harbor. The paper's credibility was badly undermined, however, by Griffin's tirades against U.S. involvement in World War II. These attacks were so vitriolic that Griffin was accused of being a Nazi and was indicted on charges that he used the *New York Enquirer* to undermine the morale of U.S. troops.

By 1952, the *New York Enquirer* was a mishmash, carrying sports scores, theater profiles and news, and racing statistics. Its circulation had dwindled to a mere 17,000, and it had only one full-time employee. Griffin by then had died and his son was hoping to sell the tabloid for $75,000. Most people thought the asking price was exorbitant. Pope was nearly broke, but he was so eager to get back into the publishing business that he borrowed $10,000 from Frank Costello and another $10,000 from Roy Cohn. After taking a taxi to close the deal, he realized he didn't have the cash to pay the cab fare, so he paid it with a lucky silver dollar he had carried around for years.

Before long, Pope turned the *New York Enquirer* into a scandal magazine. He hired an aggressive seventeen-year-old police reporter named John J. Miller* and used a network of stringers,

---

* Father of WNBC reporter John Miller Jr. Miller was also with Costello the night he got shot, as was Miller's wife, who was nine months pregnant with the future TV reporter.

often ones who worked at other papers and wrote for the *New York Enquirer* under pseudonyms. Using his government and mob contacts, Pope began exploiting the seamy underworld of New York. Three topics, however, were taboo: staffers were forbidden to write anything negative about the mob or the CIA. And they were not allowed to write anything remotely negative about actress Sophia Loren, with whom Pope was infatuated.

Pope got the circulation up to 250,000, but still had trouble making ends meet. "I couldn't pay the rent," he later recalled. "I spent ninety percent of my time in the first six years borrowing from one guy to pay off the other guy. I was thrown out of banks because all the checks used to bounce." He turned to his Uncle Frank for help. Each week, Costello would lend Pope $10,000 to meet operating expenses, and Pope would repay the loan the next week as money from newsstand sales came in. "Although Mr. Pope spent most of the day at the paper, he rarely left his office," according to former writer Reginald Potterton. "He was accessible only to key executives, to his barber who called once a week, and to an intermittent procession of pinkie-ringed male visitors who arrived in twos and threes wearing white-on-white and expensive shot-silk suits."

By 1957, government officials were cracking down on scandal magazines, and Pope was considering taking the *New York Enquirer* in a new direction. One day, while passing the scene of a grisly car crash, Pope watched a crowd gather. Although the onlookers recoiled in dismay and disgust, they also strained their necks for a better view. People were drawn to gore, Pope realized, so he gave it to them, hiring an editor named Carl Grothman, who boasted, "If a story is good, no matter how vile, we'll run it."

Pope and Grothman packed the *New York Enquirer* with grisly stories and bloody photographs about horrific crimes, deformed children, and tragic accidents. Mothers who went berserk and killed their babies, spurned lovers who tortured the women who rejected them, hapless horses that were decapitated when they stuck their heads out of moving trailers, and random violence and senseless tragedy were the *New York Enquirer*'s fare. "Mom Uses Son's Face as Ashtray!" blared one headline. "I'm Sorry I Killed

My Mother, but I'm Glad I Killed My Father!" declared another. "Teenager Twists Off Corpse's Head to Get Gold Teeth." Sometimes, exploitative articles were disguised as altruism, such as the time the tabloid tracked down the "World's Ugliest Little Girl— she's so ugly that she's not allowed to go to school!" The *Enquirer* paid for her plastic surgery and plastered her haunting face across its pages for weeks.* More often, however, the tabloid's subjects had died horribly. If they had already been hauled off to the morgue, a *New York Enquirer* photographer would have to "raid a morgue," according to a former reporter. "When you 'raid a morgue' you pull the corpse out of a special drawer, photograph the deceased, then return the body to where you found it," explained ex-*Enquirer* staffer George Bernard. "Imagine the anguish, the despair and the hatred generated towards the *Enquirer* by the family and friends of the deceased when they saw their loved ones plastered through the pages of what was then the most terrifying tabloid in the country. Not a very pleasant business."

Nonetheless, the formula was a success. The circulation skyrocketed to about 1 million. Pope decided to take his grisly publication national and in 1957, he changed the name of the *New York Enquirer* to the *National Enquirer*. Pope became the pioneer of gore exploitation magazines, much as Robert Harrison discovered the scandal market several years earlier. Soon, imitators sprang up. In the late 1950s and early 1960s, more than forty titles catered to a macabre taste for gore; tabloids with names like *National Exposure*, *National Mirror*, and *National Limelight* saturated the newsstands. Their combined circulation was estimated at 7 million. "In view of this popularity, it is surprising that tabloids have been so widely ignored by serious commentators on the press," noted Reginald Potterton, a mainstream reporter who went to work for the *Enquirer* in 1963 during the newspaper strike. "They represent a significant condition in our culture, yet few people talk about them."

Indeed, gore magazines were the demented cousins of the

* The child, unfortunately, looked the same in the "before" and "after" photographs.

publishing industry. Pope's outrageous formula for the *National Enquirer* worked wonders for circulation, though it didn't help him much in the prestige department. The *National Enquirer*, Gene Pope quickly learned, wasn't going to open doors for him the way *Il Progresso* did for his father. Quite the opposite. Pope's children were once asked to leave the Catholic school they attended when the mother superior discovered what their father did for a living.* New York City administrators were worried that the *National Enquirer* and magazines like it were taking over the newsstands and tainting the minds of the young. The tabloid was banned in some areas and Pope was forced to resign his position on the Board of Higher Education because of the *Enquirer*. Police Commissioner Stephen Kennedy refused to give Pope's staff the police press cards they needed. Pope sued Kennedy in New York Supreme Court, charging him with "restricting freedom of the press." He didn't win the case.

To stay ahead of the competition, Pope, who actually grew faint at the sight of blood, kept upping the gore quotient on the cover of his paper because the gorier it was, the better the sales. But he also continued to tinker with the mixture, and by the late 1950s, included other ingredients in his formula. One was heartwarming stories about common folks that made readers feel good about themselves. Pope also rediscovered celebrities. After *Confidential* folded, there was a void for stories about celebrities. Scantily clad women had long been featured in the *Enquirer*, but by the late 1950s, they were mostly starlets like Angie Dickinson and Gina Lollobrigida. "Wolf Whistles Are Music to Any Girl's Ear," Angie Dickinson supposedly told the tabloid for a July 5, 1959, cover story. "The ultimate purpose of a girl is to make a man feel like a man—all over," Dickinson, said, adding that she "can't understand why girls get angry when they're referred to as a 'broad.' . . . Long as they talk about girls, what's the difference?"

---

* Pope had a total of six children by three wives. His first wife, socialite Patricia McManus, was institutionalized. His second marriage was brief and ended badly. In 1963, Pope wed a beautiful former actress and show girl named Lois Berrodin, the young widow of MCA agent George Wood, who was allegedly connected to the mob. Lois and Gene stayed married until his death.

That issue's hodgepodge content revealed the paper's transition from a hard-boiled men's tabloid to a celebrity gossip sheet targeted at middle America: It included a 'Who's Sexier' competition, based on an alleged feud between Jayne Mansfield and future *Gilligan* star Tina Louise; a series of photographs of a toddler getting his first hair cut; a racing column; a photograph of a blood-soaked woman crumbled on the floor of her mobile home after a game of dominoes turned ugly; a political column updating readers on Richard Nixon and Jimmy Hoffa; gossip columns telling about Cary Grant and Gina Lollobrigida holding hands and Fernando Lamas showing up nude at a party; a boxing column; and news of Liz Taylor's outrage over a bootlegged film of her wedding to Eddie Fisher.

The mixture, however odd, was working. In 1958, the *National Enquirer* was in the black and by 1959, it was turning a solid profit. Generoso Pope Jr. was well on his way to creating a publishing empire that would rival his father's—but would turn him into a pariah in New York's social and political circles.

By then, Gene Pope's eldest brother, Fortune, had emerged as a respectable and powerful figure in New York. He had inherited his father's position—the one Gene had expected to—and was running the family business and overseeing the Columbus Day Parade. Fortune had brought Colonial public and was, according to press accounts of the time, both "fabulously wealthy" and "incredibly powerful." "Fortune Pope is regarded by many in this country—and by nearly everyone in Italy—as the spokesman for the Italian-American community," the *New York Times* wrote in 1960. "If you want to import Italian lace, or sell machinery to Italy, or just would like to have an appointment with the President of Italy while you're there on a visit, Fortune Pope is the first person you go to see."

Meanwhile, the authorities were closing in on Gene Pope. Censors were trying to shut down the *Enquirer*. He was being investigated by the FBI. Pope's mother blamed it on his continued association with members of the mob, especially Pope Sr.'s old friend, Frank Costello. "Some company you keep," Catherine Pope told Gene when she heard that he had dined with Costello the night the mobster was shot. "The sins of the father will be visited upon the children," she warned her youngest son, "and your father has sinned so, therefore, you keep this up, and you'll ruin your life as well as he did."

Catherine Pope's prediction was directed to the wrong son. In July 1960, Fortune and Anthony Pope were indicted by a special grand jury. The twelve-count charge against them included allegations of corporate theft and fraud. The two brothers were accused of taking more than $375,000 from the publicly held Colonial Sand and Stone and diverting the money to their privately held companies. They were also charged with billing the city for $176,599 worth of rock salt that they never delivered. The two brothers initially denied the charges, but eventually pleaded guilty to five of the counts against them, and no contest to five more counts. They were fined $500,000 and began a slow fade from their prestigious public life.

Generoso Pope Sr.'s dream of a political dynasty ruled by his sons foundered, just as Gene Pope Jr.'s publishing empire was taking off. The timing was not coincidental. The charges against Fortune and Anthony were gathered by Costello's ally, Judge Sammy DeFalco. The source of much of the information used in the indictment, according to several members of the family, was Gene Pope. "He was bitter about being edged out of the family business," said his son Paul.

By 1966, Pope started phasing the gore out of the *Enquirer*. "I didn't want to be with that crowd," he said. "I wanted to put out a paper a woman, say, at the supermarket, would pick up and take home, expecting to find something in it that would mean something—that would be of some practical or educational value to her in this life of decency most of us are trying to live." The real reason Pope cleaned up his act was that the market for gore was leveling off. Circulation hit 1 million and would go no further. "There are only so many libertines and neurotics," Pope observed.

Another reason for the *Enquirer*'s flat sales was that there was, at the time, a radical drop in the number of newsstands, which had been run out of business by newspaper strikes that had shut down publications across the country. With so many newsstands closing down, Pope looked for a new sales rack and found it in the nation's 50,000 supermarkets. Pope had to find a new place to peddle his ware; he was impressed with *Reader's Digest*'s circulation of 17.9 million. One of its primary outlets was grocery stores, but there was no way that supermarkets would carry the *National Enquirer*'s mix of cheesecake and gore. Pope began to think about repositioning the paper yet again, this time focusing on celebrity gossip, real-life heroics, and self-help and medical stories. "I decided to clean up the *Enquirer* and turn it into a condensed version of *Reader's Digest*," Pope said in 1969.

Around this time, Pope ran into his good friend Frank Costello. "Stay away from me," the once powerful mobster cautioned him. "You must stay away now. Don't be seen with me. You'll get hurt. Stay away. Don't come near me anymore. It won't be good for you, my son." The incident spooked Pope. Shortly afterward, he moved from New York City to Englewood, Cliffs, New Jersey. But he didn't feel safe there either.

In 1969, Pope was badly shaken by another event. The young publisher identified with Rupert Murdoch who, like him, was the son of a media magnate and was drawing the contempt of the media elite. That year, Murdoch and his wife went home to Australia for Christmas and left their Rolls Royce back in London for their executives to use. One day, the wife of one of Murdoch's executives was kidnapped while she was driving the car. The kidnappers thought that she was Murdoch's wife, Anna, and when they realized their mistake, killed the woman and fed her body to some pigs.

The following year, another incident occurred that would forever close the door for Pope on New York and the world in which he had grown up. The delivery trucks that distributed the *Enquirer* were distributing fewer papers than he was sending out. Pope suspected that someone—possibly the Teamsters—was trying to cheat him. He called on an old contact named Angie La Pastornia, who had recently been released from prison. Angie agreed to ride on one of the trucks that Pope suspected was stealing from him. The next day, when the truck came back, Angie was inside, dead.

A note attached to the knife that was stuck in his chest read simply, "Don't fuck with us."

Pope packed up his house and his office and told his family and staff to meet him at the train station, where he handed out tickets and boarded a train for Florida. Pope had a printing press in Pompano Beach, and he was moving his entire operation to nearby Lantana. Shortly after he arrived, he got his friend Roy Cohn to set up a meeting with Richard Nixon. On the promise of favorable press from the *Enquirer*, Nixon invited the heads of fourteen supermarket chains to the White House and talked them into selling the now cleaned up *National Enquirer* at their check-out stands. Pope would no longer be dependent on newsstand sales, which meant he would not be beholden to the Teamsters.

"It's politics," Pope later said of his deal with Nixon. "One hand washes the other." Pope would rule over the area around Lantana, Florida, population 8,000, and it would become known as Tabloid Valley, a place where a certain type of journalism was allowed to take root, to grow and flourish.

"they've got everything on you . . ."

"How can I take this kid seriously?" Walter Winchell said when John F. Kennedy was running for President. "He spends half his time screwing every girl that comes around. I've seen lots of nothings like him around the Stork Club and other places where the sons of rich men go and waste their time and money." By then, Winchell's power was declining, but he was still the most powerful gossip columnist in the country, and he thought that if John F. Kennedy really wanted power, he would eventually have to bow to him. Winchell had reason to believe that he had some power over Kennedy. Although Winchell was past his peak, he had the dirt on the young politician. Joseph Kennedy had once hired Winchell to get the goods on a woman John Kennedy was dating. One of Winchell's all-time best sources, J. Edgar Hoover, regularly gave Winchell files on Kennedy. So did Bobby Kennedy's nemesis, Roy Cohn, who was another big source for Winchell.

But during the election, Winchell was quite evenhanded and invited Kennedy to appear on his foundering television talk show. When Kennedy, who could nurse a grudge and who was also aware of Winchell's ratings, turned him down and instead went on Jack Paar's *Tonight Show*, Winchell was furious. He saw it as a snub, which it was—a very portentous snub. It foretold the decline of gossip columnists and the rise of celebrity-friendly TV talk shows. After Kennedy was elected, *Confidential*, which since the 1957 libel trial had ironically taken to attacking gossip writers, chortled about the slight. "President Kennedy has no time to waste on gossip columnists," the former scandal magazine declared. "As soon as he took office, the White House welcome mat was withdrawn as far as WW was concerned. And Walter, longing to share the confidences of the great and powerful, was out in the cold."

Winchell began to attack the President in his column. Some attacks were legitimate, such as the stories he reported linking Kennedy to organized crime, but most were hysterical, personalized attacks, accusing Kennedy of being soft on Communism and calling the White House the "Pink House" or the "oddministration." Irritated, Attorney General Robert Kennedy met with Hearst executive Richard Berlin and put pressure on him to delete anti-Kennedy comments from Winchell's column. When the gossip columnist found out about the meeting, he went on a tear. "I say the Administration's attempt to transform the American press into a propaganda weapon is as iniquitous as it is perilous," Winchell wrote.

The aging gossip columnist didn't stand a chance against the charismatic young president. Winchell lost his television show, and by the early 1960s, his column, which was once syndicated in 2,000 papers, was now printed by only 150. Within a few years, the man who had been the most powerful gossip columnist in history was taking out ads, begging some publication to print his column. "Never claimed being a newspaperman, Mr. Editor. Always called myself a newsboy," he said in a 1967 ad in *Variety*. "Peddling papers. Why not audition the column for one month?" There were no takers.

The gossip industry has always involved a struggle between journalists and the wealthy and powerful—be they politicians or movie stars—for control of information about their private lives. During the sixties, the Kennedy family, through a variety of tactics, prevailed in that struggle. While it's true that politicians have always tried to control what is said and written about them, the Kennedys' success in doing so was unparalleled before or since. In fact, their willingness to retaliate against reporters who tried to probe behind the mediagenic family myth goes a great distance in explaining why the gossip industry—which had thrived in the 1930s and 1940s with several gossip columns in most major newspapers and during the 1950s with the aggressive tabloid magazines like *Confidential*, *Hush-Hush*, and *On The QT*—withered in the sixties. During the Kennedy administration, gossip largely disappeared from the establishment press.

The mood of the times played an important role in this development. The national optimism of the early 1960s made the public reluctant to read unflattering details of the lives of political leaders. The decline of the print media and the rise of television during the late 1950s and early 1960s—particularly in its scandal-shy early years as experienced by Mike Wallace—were also factors in the suppression of gossip published about the family. But the power of the Kennedy family and the Kennedy charisma cannot be underestimated.

It wasn't that John Kennedy disliked gossip; to the contrary, he was obsessed with it, a connoisseur of gossip. He understood its power to make or to destroy people. He pumped his Hollywood contacts for the lowdown on celebrities; he quizzed his society friends for the latest scandals; and he regularly debriefed his friends in the press for inside information on the news business. He knew individual reporters' strengths and weaknesses, their jealousies, even their salaries. "It is unbelievable to an outsider how interested Kennedy was in journalists and how clued in he was to their characters, their office politics, their petty rivalries," Kennedy's friend, *Washington Post* executive editor Ben Bradlee once wrote. "He soaked up newspaper gossip like a blotter."

Kennedy used his knowledge of journalists to court, seduce, and co-opt them. He granted access in exchange for what amounted to partisan loyalty, and no journalist had more access or was more loyal than Bradlee. Bradlee had lived in Europe from 1951 until 1957; when he moved back to the United States and became the Washington bureau chief of *Newsweek*, he felt like an outsider in a city in which contacts meant everything. "I had fewer politicians as friends than most of my colleagues and all of my competitors," Bradlee admitted, "and I worried about it."

So when Jack Kennedy and his glamorous wife Jacqueline befriended Bradlee, who with his wife Toni Meyer Bradlee lived near the young Senator in Georgetown, the journalist latched on to the politicians and clung to the relationship at the expense of his own integrity. He wrote only flattering things about Kennedy and ignored anything potentially damaging or embarrassing. Bradlee, for example, was the only journalist allowed to spend the evening of the West Virginia primary with Kennedy, which they spent watching a pornographic movie called *Private Property* about a housewife who is seduced and then raped by hoodlums. Bradlee didn't mention the film in the otherwise highly detailed account of Kennedy's West Virginia campaign that he wrote for *Newsweek*. He wouldn't have written anything, he has admitted, that would have hurt Kennedy's chances of getting into the White House. "I wanted Kennedy to win," Bradlee once wrote. "I wanted my friend and neighbor to be President."

After Kennedy was elected, Bradlee became the envy of the Washington media world because of his access to the President. The President had weekly dinners with Bradlee, telling him what subjects *Newsweek* should cover and which reporters it should hire. They went sailing together, and Kennedy had highly personal conversations with the journalist, confessing, for example, that he had always been embarrassed by his rather pronounced mammaries, which he called the "Fitzgerald breasts." Bradlee told Kennedy what was in upcoming issues of *Newsweek*, and Kennedy would let Bradlee know what was going to be in future issues of *Time* magazine, where he also had contacts. Kennedy was often an off-the-record source for Bradlee—and the President even gave Bradlee items for the magazine's gossipy "Periscope" section and would advise him on tactics for his political coverage. When Bradlee told Kennedy that *Newsweek* was working on a profile of New York Governor Nelson Rockefeller, whom the president expected to be his opponent in the next election, Kennedy said, "You ought to cut Rocky's ass open a little."

In addition to rewarding Bradlee when he was obedient, Kennedy would punish him when he was disobedient. The journalist temporarily lost his treasured position in Kennedy's inner circle, for example, when he was quoted in *Look* magazine discussing Kennedy's manipulation of the press. Bradlee insisted that his comments to *Look* were supposed to have been off the record, but Kennedy banned him from the White House and refused to speak to him for months.

In the fall of 1962, however, Kennedy needed Bradlee's services again. At the time, a story was making the rounds—and had appeared in print in some disreputable publications—that before John Kennedy married Jackie, he had been wed to a socialite named Durie Malcolm. The "other wife" story wouldn't go away—largely because the White House refused to directly deny it. Kennedy's spokesman, Pierre Salinger, made Bradlee a proposition: The administration would give Bradlee access to classified government documents if he would write an article for *Newsweek* discrediting the "other wife" story. But Bradlee was presented with a remarkably restrictive set of conditions: He could not copy the government papers, he could not say he saw them, and if he or *Newsweek* was sued, they would not have access to the documents again. What's more, Salinger insisted that Kennedy would have the right to edit or kill Bradlee's story before it ran. Bradlee—eager to get back into Kennedy's graces—agreed. After the article appeared, when any reporters pursued the story, the White House referred them to *Newsweek*. Bradlee's article, Kennedy later told him, essentially killed the "other wife" story.*

Bradlee later insisted that he—unlike just about every other reporter in Washington—was unaware of Kennedy's infidelities. He even claimed that he didn't know that Kennedy was having an affair with his sister-in-law, Mary Pinchot Meyer. "Extracurricular screwing was one of the few subjects that never came up" in his conversations with Kennedy, Bradlee later wrote, "and in those days reporters did not feel compelled to conduct full FBI field investigations about a politician friend."

In addition to Bradlee, Kennedy also befriended *New York Times*

---

* Twenty-five years later, Seymour Hersch resurrected the Durie Malcolm story in his book *The Dark Side of Camelot* and declared it true.

publisher Orvil Dryfoos and the *Times*'s Washington bureau chief, James "Scotty" Reston. As a result, neither the *Times* nor the *Washington Post* would print Kennedy's dirty little secrets—and in the early 1960s, those two newspapers set the tone for the rest of the establishment media. In early 1963, when a *New York Times* reporter told his editor that he had observed Angie Dickinson repeatedly visiting President Kennedy's New York hotel suite, the editor said, "No story there." Once, when a reporter suggested looking into the Durie Malcolm story, Reston declared, "I won't have the *New York Times* muckraking the President of the United States!"

"Even if we had written about the girlfriends, our editors would never have published the information," observed Maxine Cheshire, the society writer for the *Washington Post*, who was as close as the paper had to a gossip columnist. "That simply was not the way one covered the presidency at that time."*

The Kennedys' sex life was not the only topic off limits. On occasion, the journalists whom Kennedy had befriended refrained from printing information they'd learned about questions of national security. The *New York Times*'s Reston would tell a story about how once, while covering the summit conference in Vienna in 1961, Kennedy came into his hotel room after a meeting with Soviet leader Nikita Khrushchev. The President sat down on his couch. "Khrushchev raped me," the President told Reston. Kennedy felt that the Soviet leader didn't respect him because of the Bay of Pigs fiasco. "I have to show him we're not gutless," Kennedy said to the journalist. "The only way to do it is to send troops into Vietnam. . . . I've got to do it, Scotty, it's the only way."

"Reston told me this story at a dinner party hosted by [*Times* writer] Steve Roberts," says former *Times* reporter Sidney Zion. "I

---

* Apologists would later dismiss the self-censorship, arguing that until the tabloidization of the press in the late 1970s and 1980s politicians' private lives were off limits. That is simply not the case. Throughout American history, politicians' sex lives have been the subject of newspaper articles. The very first newspaper in America, *Publik Occurrences Foreign and Abroad*, reported in 1790 a rumor that the King of France was sleeping with his daughter-in-law. Thomas Jefferson's affair with his slave, Sally Hemings, was first reported in the *Richmond Record* in 1802. When Andrew Jackson got married before his wife's divorce was legal, the papers tormented him with stories about bigamy, and Grover Cleveland's illegitimate child was so widely reported that it became the stuff of nursery rhymes.

couldn't believe my ears. I said, 'You've got to write that story, dammit.' There were all sorts of wild conspiracies going on as to why we were in Vietnam—that it was Johnson's fault, that it was all started by the arms manufacturers—and here was the simple, pure truth as told by the President himself. I was shocked. I said, 'You've got to write that story. You owe it to the readers.' There were other reporters from the *Times* at the dinner, and they were kicking me under the table trying to make me shut up. Kennedy was so popular among the press that betraying him by printing the truth was absolutely unthinkable."

The same held true for the President's wife. When Cheshire was working on a series of articles about how Jacqueline Kennedy was putting pressure on people to donate money toward redecorating the White House, the president called *Post* publisher Phil Graham. "Maxine Cheshire is making my wife cry," he complained. "Listen, just listen. Jackie is on the extension!" The President's wife got on the phone and, sure enough, she was sobbing so loudly that Graham could plainly hear her. Several subsequent pieces in the series were killed, including a well-documented story on illegal kickbacks that the Kennedys had given one of their suppliers.

Jackie Kennedy was openly disdainful of reporters like Cheshire. "My relationship with Jackie Kennedy was never one of even strained civility," Cheshire later wrote. "In my opinion, she seemed to be acting as if she lived in a monarchy rather than a democracy." Nonetheless, her editors refused to allow her to portray the first lady's darker side. Once, when a reporter for another paper was interviewing the First Lady, who was hugely pregnant at the time, Mrs. Kennedy nonchalantly stripped down to nothing but her maternity panties in the reporter's presence. "The woman's own paper had cut the item from her story and stashed the deleted material in a vault," according to Cheshire. She confirmed the incident and wrote it up, but *Washington Post* editors killed her story. The only stories they would publish were so relentlessly flattering that some of her competitors scolded her for doting on the First Lady.

When the Kennedys couldn't count on the loyalty of journalists, they regularly resorted to the tactics they had used against Mike Wallace.

At times, however, they did more than merely apply pressure to reporters' publishers. In June 1963, for example, the New York *Journal-American* ran a story by Don Frasca and James Horan saying that one of the "biggest names in American politics" had an affair with Suzy Chang, the British model and actress. People in political and media circles knew that the unnamed politician was John Kennedy; writers Frasca and Horan also told colleagues that they had proof he had had group sex with a nineteen-year-old London call girl named Marie Novotny and two other prostitutes. After the article appeared, Robert Kennedy told executives at the *Journal* that they could expect to be hit with an antitrust suit—which, as Attorney General, was under his jurisdiction—if the paper printed any more stories that could embarrass the President. The editors told their reporters to back off.

Anyone who tried to expose such heavy-handed tactics was also punished. While *Look* was preparing a story on Kennedy's manipulation of the press, Robert Kennedy and two burly associates showed up unannounced at editor William Arthur's office. "They sought to suppress the article by making a series of threats," according to journalist Herman Klurfield who for years worked as Walter Winchell's ghostwriter. The editor went ahead with the article, but after it appeared, anyone who cooperated with the story was denied access to the White House.

Then there was the peculiar fate of Igor Cassini. When Kennedy took office, Igor Cassini was one of the nation's best-read gossip columnists, with an estimated audience of 20 million. He wrote for the Hearst newspapers under the pseudonym Cholly Knickerbocker, which he took from the famed Maury Paul after Paul died in 1942. Cassini had long been close to the Kennedys. His wife, Charlene, had grown up near the Kennedy's Palm Beach house. He was Jackie Kennedy's favorite gossip columnist, his brother, Oleg Cassini, was Jackie's dress designer, and both brothers were friends with patriarch Joe Kennedy.* When Kennedy was

---

* Oleg set up dates for patriarch Joe Kennedy; they met every Tuesday night at eight at the swank midtown Manhattan restaurant La Caravelle. "I would usually bring some lady friends—top models or society girls," according to Oleg, "although, on several occasions, Joe did the honors and, believe me, he knew some real beauties." Jack Kennedy had an affair with Oleg's wife, Gene Tierney.

elected, Cassini was at the top of his profession and, he thought, invincible. "The world was my oyster," he said. He had hired a diligent young assistant from Texas named Liz Smith, who often wrote much of his column. He opened an exclusive night spot, Le Club, the Jet Setters version of the Stork Club.* He had his own TV show on NBC, and hired as an assistant, a woman who was dating his friend, Roy Cohn. Her name was Barbara Walters.

Oleg was trusted by the Kennedys for his discretion and devotion. Igor, however, wasn't discreet. "My dilemma was that private lives were my stock in trade," Igor said. The President constantly complained to Oleg about what his "damned brother" had written. "He's basically a newspaperman," Kennedy fumed. "He can't keep a secret."

"It was my problem," Cassini later wrote. "I wrote about my friends and crowd. I always wrote everything I knew. It got me into trouble." His trouble with the First Family began in September 1962, when he wrote a revealing article for *Good Housekeeping*, "How the Kennedy Marriage Has Fared." Although the article ostensibly praised Jack and Jackie's devotion to each other, it also included some details that at the time were quite shocking, including tidbits about how lonely Jackie was during John's frequent absences, how Jackie didn't mix well with the Kennedy clan, and how her sisters-in-law teased and called her "The Queen"—mimicking her breathy, little-girl voice. It also reported a rumor—which Igor later said had been told to him as fact by Joe Kennedy—that a fed-up Jackie was ready to leave her philandering husband but that Joe Kennedy offered her $1 million to stay married. The Kennedys were so infuriated by the article and by Igor's other lapses that the columnist was temporarily banned from the White House. But the punishment didn't end there. Robert Kennedy began investigating him.

Cassini had a sideline business—he ran a public relations firm, Martial, and would regularly plug its clients in his column. Cassini insisted that his bosses knew about his double dealing and that it was even sanctioned by tradition. "My predecessor Maury Paul—

---

* Igor Cassini actually coined the phrase "Jet Set." His predecessor, Maury Paul, had coined the phrase "Cafe Society."

and he is not the only one to have done so—used to take checks from socialites," according to Cassini, "aspiring or real, in payment either for what he wrote or for what he knew but graciously did not say."

Cassini's blatantly biased plugs may have represented unethical journalism, but they weren't illegal. The incident for which Robert Kennedy indicted him—acting as an unregistered agent of the Dominican Republic—was illegal. It was also arranged by the Kennedys themselves.

It began one day when Cassini mentioned to Joseph Kennedy that a friend—playboy Porfirio Rubirosa, who had been the ambassador to the Dominican Republic—was worried that the country was on the brink of a Cubalike coup. Joe Kennedy passed the information along to his son John Kennedy, and the President asked Cassini to make a diplomatic trip to the Dominican Republic. "With all the billions this country spends on its State Department and Central Intelligence Agency," noted the *New York Times*, "it will be interesting to learn why the White House turned to a society columnist as the initiator of a special mission to the Dominican Republic."

The incident was also seized on by reporter Peter Maas, who wrote an exposé of Cassini in the *Saturday Evening Post*. A month later, Attorney General Robert Kennedy indicted Igor Cassini as an unregistered agent of the Dominican Republic.* "I was prepared to fight the charges, but the legal bills were very high and I was running out of money," Igor later explained. "Robert Kennedy sent word through my brother that I should plead no contest. He said, 'Don't worry, everything will be fine.' I had done nothing illegal. He promised everything would go back to being the way it was."

Igor was forced to resign the Cholly Knickerbocker column—it was taken over by Aileen "Suzy Knickerbocker" Mehle. As a result, he lost most of his public relations clients. He also lost his status in society. Igor's brother Oleg was still invited to the White

---

* If Cassini was paid for his services, he would have been required to register with the Justice Department under the Foreign Agents Registration Act of 1938, which was enacted to identify spies. Cassini has always maintained that he was never paid and, indeed, a check was never found.

House, where he was teased by the Kennedy sisters who would say, "Bobby's going to put your brother in jail."

"They've got everything on you," Oleg once told his brother in a frantic phone call. "They don't care whether you're innocent or not. Bobby Kennedy has told me he'll put you in jail for ten years!"

"That self-righteous bastard!" Igor replied. "I know the redhead he's sleeping with!" Igor claimed that he later discovered that Bobby Kennedy was taping the call.

Igor's wife, Charlene Wrightsman, had been a longtime friend of the Kennedys, but she had become increasingly depressed over her husband's indictment. The couple became such pariahs that her socially prominent father, Charles, and his wife Jayne Wrightsman, wouldn't let Charlene or Igor visit when they were entertaining the Kennedys. On March 31, 1963, Charlene wrote a desperate letter to her former friend and neighbor John Kennedy:

Dear Mr. President:

I have hesitated writing you before, but now I feel I must appeal to you. . . . We always considered ourselves good friends of the Kennedys and [Igor] still cannot understand why the son of a man whom he considered one of his closest friends for 17 years, and who so often advised him in all matters, should now be determined to bringing him down to total ruin. . . . I hope, Jack, that you will not resent my writing you this letter. We've been friends for so many years, and now in this terrible moment in which our family needs help, I appeal to you.

Charlene waited for a reply, but it never came. Several months later, at age thirty-eight, she killed herself with an overdose of sleeping pills.* "I was ruined," Cassini said. "I lost my job. I lost my wife. Nothing was ever the same again. The Kenne-

---

* *Confidential* again took the opportunity to bash a gossip columnist. "The Truth About that Jet Set Suicide" claimed that Charlene Wrightsman killed herself over her husband's infidelities.

dys, who were supposed to be my friends, ruined me because I became an embarrassment to them."

Such tactics help explain why Jack Kennedy's affair with Marilyn Monroe was left untouched by the press. The relationship was common knowledge among gossip columnists. In early 1962, Monroe confided to her good friend and confidante, gossip columnist Sidney Skolsky, that she was having an affair with "The Prez."

"Are you surprised?" Marilyn giggled.

"No, nothing you do surprises me," Skolsky sighed. Skolsky, who wrote a Hollywood column for Hearst, had been friends with Monroe for more than fifteen years. The actress complained to him how difficult it was to have private time with Kennedy—when they got together at Peter Lawford's beach house, she said, they had to leave the light on or the Secret Service men took it as a signal to burst in and "rescue" the President. Monroe told the gossip columnist that she expected to be able to spend more time with him in the White House sometime soon. Skolsky, however, never mentioned the affair in his column. "In a society that boasts of freedom of the press, no reporter, including myself, dared to write about Marilyn Monroe's affair with John F. Kennedy," Skolsky once admitted. "I accept my share of the blame. I also confess that I still find it grim to speculate on what might have happened to me if I had tried to write about this romance in my column."

Skolsky wasn't the only reporter afraid to print what he knew. "If I dared print but one-half of one percent of all I know about these people, I'd be run out of Hollywood on a rail in five minutes flat!" said Hollywood columnist Ruth Waterbuy. Peter Lawford's mother gave Hedda Hopper an interview in which she complained about Kennedy and his extramarital affairs. Hopper never published it.

Gossip columnist Dorothy Kilgallen, who was among the most fearless writers in the country, was getting increasingly obsessed about Kennedy's relationship with Monroe. She used to regale her friends with tales of Kennedy's indiscretions.

"Why don't you write that?" one asked.

"I couldn't possibly," Dorothy said. "Nobody would." But as

Kennedy's philandering started getting more brazen, Kilgallen took to hinting at it in her column. When Monroe sang "Happy Birthday" to the President in May 1962, the two danced together five times. "Marilyn Monroe is cooking in the sex appeal department," Kilgallen wrote not long afterward. "She has appeared vastly alluring to a handsome gentleman. A handsome gentleman with a bigger name than Joe DiMaggio in his heyday—so don't write her off."

After the item appeared, Kennedy, deciding that on this occasion flattery would work better than intimidation, invited Kilgallen and her eight-year-old son Kerry, for a private tour of the White House. The President personally greeted Dorothy and her son, and fussed shamelessly over young Kerry: gave him a ballpoint pen with the Presidential seal on it, and pinned a gold PT-109 pin on the school tie of the beaming boy. Kilgallen stopped writing blind items about Kennedy.

But the Kennedys did persecute and discredit one news source whom they were afraid might disclose Jack's affair with Monroe and Bobby's unofficial, and secret, trip to her apartment in the wake of her suicide: Fred Otash, the private investigator and former *Confidential* informer.

Early in the morning on August 4, 1962, Fred Otash was jolted by a call from Peter Lawford. The actor was upset, Otash remembered, he seemed nervous or drunk, maybe. "I have a big problem," Lawford said. "I need to come over and see you." Otash invited the Kennedy in-law to drop by his Laurel Avenue office.

Otash had once been the most powerful, feared private detective in Hollywood, but business had never been quite the same for him since *Confidential* had folded. Otash had known Kennedy's brother-in-law, Peter Lawford, when he was a vice cop for the L.A.P.D. (Lawford's name, according to Otash, was in the black book of almost every high-class prostitute in Los Angeles.) When Otash became a private detective and started working as a source for *Confidential*, he would get new clients—his list included Howard Hughes, Judy Garland, Edward G. Robinson, Lana Turner, and Bette Davis—by promising to keep them out of the scandal magazine. One day, Lawford called him. "Fred, I know *Confiden-*

tial has something coming out on me," Lawford told him. "Now that I'm married to Pat Kennedy, I really can't afford this horse-shit." If Otash would get the story killed, Lawford would become a source for him. The story was duly killed and Lawford duly began passing Otash information on other Hollywood celebrities.

Coincidentally, another Otash client was Marilyn Monroe. According to Otash, the actress thought she could protect herself from any possible retaliation from the Kennedy family over her affair with Jack if she had her own evidence of her conversations with him and his associates. So, according to Otash, at the recommendation of their mutual friend gossip columnist Sidney Skolsky, Monroe hired him to bug *her*. Otash not only tapped Marilyn's phone for her, he gave her a recording device for her purse, as well as one that could be hidden in her wristwatch.

Then in 1961, according to Otash, he was approached by the Teamsters Union leader Jimmy Hoffa, an old client, who said he was being investigated by Attorney General Robert Kennedy, and according to Otash, the union boss wanted a little something to use to fight back. Otash knew that Jack Kennedy had seen Monroe at Peter Lawford's Santa Monica beach house. With Lawford's approval, according to Otash, he arranged for the actor's sound man, Bernie Spindel, to wire the house where Kennedy and Monroe would meet. According to Otash, he actually acquired several tapes of these sessions. He passed them on to Hoffa but they disappeared.

Lawford arrived about 2 A.M., "half crocked and half nervous," Otash recalled. "[Lawford] said he had just left Monroe and she was dead and that Bobby had been there earlier," Otash later told the *Los Angeles Times*. "He said they got Bobby out of the city and back to Northern California and would I go on out there and arrange to do anything to remove anything incriminating from the house."*

According to Otash, Lawford said Bobby Kennedy, who was also reportedly sleeping with Monroe, had been to her house the

---

* Lawford denied this account to the *Los Angeles Times* and offered to take a lie detector test. When the *Times* took him up on it, he declined. He died shortly thereafter.

previous evening and the two fought over their relationship. "According to Lawford, he had called [Monroe] and she had said to him that she was passed around like a piece of meat," Otash said. "She'd had it. She didn't want Bobby to use her anymore."

Lawford told Otash that he had been to the actress's house to try to clean out any evidence of the affairs with the Kennedys, according to the detective, but he wanted Otash to double-check. "He said, 'I took what I could find and destroyed it—period,' " said Otash. "But he said, 'I'm so out of it, I would feel better if you went there.' " Otash was worried he'd be recognized, he said, so he sent someone else who found and destroyed incriminating material such as letters that Lawford may have missed.

Otash became convinced, after that night, that he was in trouble. He felt he knew too much. In 1959 he had been convicted of conspiracy in a racehorse-doping incident, and though he claimed he had been set up and though the conviction was later reduced to a misdemeanor, the California Bureau of Private Investigators and Adjusters revoked his license in 1965 citing evidence of "moral turpitude." Edmund Brown, who had prosecuted Otash in the *Confidential* trial, was by then the Governor of California. He was also a close political ally of the Kennedys, having helped Jack win the California primary in 1960, and Otash was convinced that his license had been revoked on Brown's orders and that the Governor was acting at the behest of Robert Kennedy. "That son-of-a-bitch Bobby Kennedy," Otash claimed, "had been trying to get me for years."

It was the end of Otash's career as the world's premiere gatherer of sleaze—he went on to become the head of security for the Hazel Bishop beauty salons and during the 1970s and 1980s was manager of the Hollywood Palladium. Otash died in 1992 at the age of seventy. His infamous tape of Marilyn Monroe, however, would surface nearly three decades after it was made and would help change the direction of tabloid television.

6

the divas

In September 1964, Louella Parsons, the greatest Hollywood gossip columnist who ever lived, broke her hip. Louella had been feeble for a while both physically and mentally; but after she broke her hip, she never fully recovered. For a while she gallantly tried to continue writing her column, making the slow, painful trip from her bedroom down the hall to her office, but she never really wrote again, and the next year, at age eighty-three, the grand dame of gossip went into a Hollywood nursing home.

The dowager ruler of Hollywood had finally left her throne. "She was Queen of Hollywood," *Life* magazine proclaimed, "the very embodiment of its hopes, its dreams, its fears and its responses . . . her home on Beverly Hill's Maple Drive was the closest thing to Buckingham Palace the movie industry ever boasted."

When word of Louella's retirement reached her nemesis Hedda Hopper, the slightly younger, always less powerful Hopper spent the night celebrating. It was Lucille Ball Day at the New York World's Fair, and the seventy-nine-year-old former showgirl literally kicked off her shoes and danced until dawn. Her rivalry with Louella was so all-consuming that Hedda didn't notice that the kingdom she had inherited had all but vanished. Two years later, on January 30, 1966, Hedda caught double pneumonia and died within two days. News of Hedda's death reached Louella at her Hollywood nursing home, where the former queen of gossip had become virtually mute, silently watching old movies on TV all day. When she was told that Hedda had died, however, a smile crossed Louella's face and she spoke for the first time anyone there could remember. "GOOD!" she said.

If the gossip industry had a golden age, it coincided with the "golden age" of the Hollywood studio system in the 1930s and 1940s. And, like Hollywood during those years, the gossip industry had its constellation of fixed stars. Chief among them was Walter Winchell, who is often credited with inventing the gossip column. Just below Winchell in the firmament were "the ladies," as the syndicated columnists, and legendary rivals, Louella Parsons and Hedda Hopper were referred to jointly. Like Winchell, "the ladies" were more famous and more powerful than many of the movie stars they covered. Louella, the more influential of the two, was, by most accounts, Hollywood's first gossip columnist (Winchell started out as a Broadway columnist). "Hollywood loved her," noted writer Paul O'Neil. "She was Queen—the one it deserved—and she reigned for forty years."

Indeed, the accolades and honors bestowed upon Louella during the years when her power was at its peak routinely invoked royalty. When Louella's boss, William Randolph Hearst, threw a party for her in 1948, eight hundred of Hollywood's most famous movie stars and most powerful moguls jammed Cocoanut Grove in Los Angeles's Ambassador Hotel to pay homage.

"No queen," Louis B. Mayer toasted her, "could wish for richer jewels than the bright crown of friendship you possess."

"You have a heart," Darryl Zanuck declared, "as big as the church itself."

It wasn't, of course, Louella's heart that Hollywood loved, but the one thousand or so newspapers that carried her daily column. During the 1930s through the 1950s, she and Hedda were an unofficial but essential part of the Hollywood studio system. Studio executives, well aware that the public curiosity the columnists fed with their items about the stars heightened the box office appeal of those stars and thus increased studio profits, parceled out items to Hedda and Louella every day. They also forced stars to cooperate in giving exclusives to the two women. In return, Hedda and Louella were careful never to antagonize the studio moguls themselves. And in fact, they were ardent defenders of the studio system.

Louella often referred to Hollywood as "this marvelous town" and sang the praises of "our magnificent industry." Although she is remembered as a shrewish harridan, she was, in fact, a protector of the stars. She knew much more about them than she ever revealed. In fact, since her husband, Docky, was a urologist for Twentieth Century Fox and frequently administered tranquilizers or testosterone shots to stars, she often found out about their medical conditions before the stars themselves did—and she usually kept quiet about them. While she did, from time to time, chide or even attack stars, the scoldings usually took place when actors and actresses violated moral codes—as when Ingrid Bergman scandalized American moviegoers by becoming pregnant out of wedlock—or when they disobeyed the orders of studio executives. "This is the first time I have publicly spanked Judy," Louella wrote in 1949 after Garland failed to lose fifteen pounds as directed by MGM. "But I can't understand her attitude after all that has been done for her."

Hedda Hopper was more caustic than Louella, but even she saw herself as a champion of Hollywood, as a promoter of its stars and its values. She liked to think she played the role of a stern—but loving—aunt. Hedda, for example, felt that she had practically discovered Elizabeth Taylor, and would privately advise the star on her wardrobe and her love life. When Taylor confided to Hedda that she was having an affair with Eddie Fisher, Hedda broke the story as though she had a moral obligation, not only to her readers but to Hollywood at large and the actress herself, to do so. "I had no regret," she said. "Without a sense of integrity, you can't sleep at nights."

The two columnists' truly vicious behavior usually involved their rivalry, their fights over scoops. For example, when Clark

Gable and Carole Lombard got married in 1939, Louella banned them from her column for several months because they didn't give her the story exclusively. Joan Crawford was careful not to make the same mistake; when she got married to Philip Terry in 1948, she notified Louella immediately. That, of course, infuriated Hedda. Upon reading Louella's scoop, Hedda telephoned Crawford and declared: "I will ruin you!" When Crawford ran into Hedda at a Hollywood party, she stretched her arms toward the columnist and begged for forgiveness. Hedda abruptly walked away. So when Rock Hudson married Phyllis Gates in 1955, they played it smart. As soon as vows were exchanged, Rock got on the phone and called the story in to Louella Parsons while Phyllis was on the other line, giving it in to Hedda Hopper.

In the 1950s, when stars like Jimmy Stewart and Bette Davis began defecting from the studios and hiring independent agents, the studio system that had produced so many classic movies began to fall apart. New stars like Marlon Brando and James Dean held the system, and Hedda and Louella, in contempt and refused to cooperate with them. The columnists, for their part, continued writing about aging studio stars like Clark Gable—Louella invariably referred to him as "the king"—and ridiculed the new generation.

At the same time, many of the newspapers that carried their columns began to fold. In late 1962, a printers' strike that lasted 114 days killed or seriously crippled a number of New York papers, including the New York *Mirror*, Winchell's home base. Louella's hometown outlet, the *Los Angeles Examiner*, folded in 1962. In 1966, the great *Herald Tribune* folded. In 1967, the *World Journal Telegram*, a conglomerate of papers hoping to join forces in an effort to stay alive, collapsed. Most towns were left with only one newspaper—usually the more established, upscale paper—and the tabloid wars that had characterized the pretelevision era disappeared. Editors in one-paper towns began to reevaluate the role of their publications. Without the need to use blaring headlines, scandal, and gossip in the old daily competition for circulation with other papers, they could afford to refine the definition of news, to distinguish it more sharply from entertainment, to make it more serious and more sober. Socially conscious editors and reporters also became openly disdainful of Hollywood and celebrities. The once feared and revered Louella, in particular, became a source of ridicule, an aging and somewhat daffy relic. In one oft-repeated, perhaps apocryphal incident, some friends dropped by Parsons's home to take her to a movie screening and the gossip diva answered the door buck naked except for red shoes and a matching hat and handbag. She then excused herself, went into the rest room and ten minutes later came out declaring, "Well that was the worst damn picture I ever saw!" John Barrymore called her "that old udder" and Marlon Brando referred to her as "The fat One." "[Louella's] column limited itself almost completely to trivia—production news from the studios and items concerning the love affairs, marriages, quarrels, divorces, peccadilloes and pregnancies of featured players," a snide *Life* piece noted at the time of her retirement. "But if she was narrow, semi-illiterate and often moved by blubbering sentimentality, so were many of her peers in the movie colony."

With Hedda and Louella gone, many assumed that the era of gossip was dead. "Who shall replace the Mmes Parsons and Hopper?" Bob Thomas, the veteran Hollywood correspondent for the Associated Press, wondered in an article in 1968. "Probably no one. Their successors are pretenders to thrones that no longer exist. Gone are the days when Hollywood was a tight little town that ruled the entertainment world and hence could be ruled by feminine columnists."

There was, however, a small but determined group of gossip columnists who were ferociously vying for the position. They were a peculiarly determined lot, trying against the odds to persuade reluctant editors around the country that gossip still mattered. One of them was Cindy Adams.

The former Cindy Heller was an almond-eyed former beauty queen and stand-up comic from Queens who had a string of fifty-seven dubious beauty titles, including Miss Coaxial Cable 1949, Miss Torso of 1949, Miss Upswept Hairdo of 1948, Miss Brooklyn Dodgers of 1947, Queen of the Night Club Division of the March of Dimes, Miss Bagel, Miss Manischewitz Wine of 1948, and Miss Bazooka Bubble Gum of 1948. Cindy had tried to use her string of unlikely titles to break into show business—performing stunts like blowing Bazooka bubbles at Bergen Junior College in Teaneck, New Jersey, to demonstrate inflation. Then, in 1951, Cindy Heller met comedian Joey Adams, who was on the periphery of Sinatra's Rat Pack and was married to Walter Winchell's sister, Mary. She became Cindy Adams on Valentine's Day, 1952. Although she would later claim that she was seventeen when she got married, according to an announcement at the time, she was twenty-one. A friend insists that even then, she was shaving off a few years.*

Joey introduced Cindy to his friend Frank Sinatra and various political leaders he had entertained, and, after failing to make it as a singing and dancing sidekick in Joey's standup comedy act, the young Mrs. Adams decided to cash in on these contacts by becoming a gossip columnist. By 1960, her column "Cindy Says" was syndicated in ten newspapers, including the Miami Beach *Sun* and the Bridgeport *Herald* in Connecticut. Although her success was modest, the beautiful young wife of the older Borscht Belt comedian cut quite a figure, and she played it to the hilt. She wore stunning jewels, rode in a limousine, decorated her apartment in red, dressed only in red clothes and wrote only with a red pen. "I even think in red," she told *Editor and Publisher* in 1960. "I go out seven nights a week, go to all the plays on opening night. I know everybody, go to parties all the time and report it all in a brassy and breezy way."

In 1961, Joey and a group of performers were chosen to make a "Good Will Tour" of Southeast Asia on behalf of Kennedy's Cultural Exchange program. Cindy Adams came along and addressed the crowds in their native tongues, just like Jacqueline Kennedy had done, Joey said. "The payoff was to be a better understanding of the democracy that is America," he noted. "It was my thought that maybe we could bring a little joy to a troubled world."

Not everyone agreed. A House appropriations subcommittee questioned the wisdom of spending more than $250,000 on a vaudeville act. It also expressed outrage that the "goodwill" mission was characterized by feuding among its members, that Cindy

---

* A newspaper article from January 1949 gives her age as nineteen.

Adams addressed the Prime Minister of Afghanistan as "honey," and that she wrote a column calling three members of the Laotian royal family "those three cranky princes." Rival gossip columnist Dorothy Kilgallen ridiculed Adams and company in her column, calling it a waste of taxpayers' money. "Mrs. Adams is bombing around the globe," she wrote. Kilgallen wrote:

> *Joey Adams, a comedian whose talent I will not attempt to evaluate, is touring around the globe with a bunch of performers under the auspices of the State Department to the tune of $10,000 a week to prove that the United States has tap dancers and a fellow who can blow up balloons in the shapes of giraffes and elephants. I am not making this up.*
>
> *What's more, Mr. Adams's wife, Cindy, is along on the junket for the sole purpose of introducing the various acts in the language of the country being entertained. . . . If our diplomats abroad need Joey and Cindy Adams to convert the shepherds of Afghanistan to democracy, then we are in real trouble.*

A gossip feud erupted, and Cindy accused Dorothy of being jealous of her, as a younger, sexier gossip columnist. Cindy called Dorothy "a vulgar old crone" and wrote a vitriolic attack in which she accused Kilgallen of being an alcoholic. Kilgallen filed a $1 million suit against Adams, and Cindy and Joey countersued.*

Despite the publicity from the feud, Cindy was having trouble breaking into any major newspapers, and in 1965 she parlayed her newfound friendship with foreign despots into a book-writing career. Amid rumors, denied by Cindy, that she had an affair with mass murdering Indonesian dictator Sukarno, Cindy Adams wrote *Sukarno: An Autobiography*.† Sukarno's "autobiography"

---

* Both sides eventually dropped the suits.

† The opening line of Cindy's follow-up book, *My Friend the Dictator*, did little to dispel the rumors: "The simplest way to describe Sukarno is that he is a great lover." She then, however, went on to write, "He loves his country, he loves his people, he loves women, he loves art, and best of all, he loves himself." She also wrote about fending off his ham-handed advances. "Listen, honey, face the facts," Cindy claims she told Sukarno while wiping her lipstick off his mouth after he planted an uninvited kiss. "With all the legal and illegal love affairs you've got going for you, you're getting more than enough exercise for a fella your age."

was met with mixed reviews, to put it kindly. Dan Kurzman wrote in the *Herald Tribune* that "The book often reads as if it were the handiwork of a high school freshman struggling to pass an English course."* Then, Sukarno was overthrown in 1968, a new government took power in Indonesia, and Cindy's lifetime visa was canceled. She cozied up to her pals Imelda and Ferdinand Marcos and the Shah of Iran and continued to write for small, local newspapers. She would resurface later when the climate was kinder to gossip.

Another gossip columnist trying to make a name for herself during this period was Doris Lilly. Doris was a holdover from Cafe Society, a vivacious, socially connected, tall blond beauty who dated, among others, John Huston, Joe DiMaggio, Evelyn Waugh, Walter Winchell, and Cary Grant. Lilly was raised near Santa Monica, and moved to New York in 1946. She got her entree into the world of celebrity through John Huston, whom she met in a drugstore. The director was eager to get the beautiful young woman in bed, according to Lilly, and he agreed to marry her when she was still in her teens. They flew to Juarez, Mexico, where they had a quick ceremony witnessed by Humphrey Bogart. Within a matter of months, Lilly caught Huston in bed with another woman and filed for divorce—and learned that her marriage was never legal in the first place. Huston, Lilly said, had got a bit actor from his movie *Treasure of the Sierra Madre* to pose as the priest and had convinced Bogart to go along with the ruse. Lilly was furious and consulted lawyers, but, she said, Huston talked her out of suing, persuading her he could help her career more if they remained friends and allies. And it was true. The director introduced her to Hollywood's elite. Mike Todd soon signed her up to be in a show, and in the years to come she had steamy affairs with some of the best-known actors of her time,

---

* Cindy's grande dame shtick wasn't going over well, either. "Because Sukarno ordered every Indonesian embassy and consulate to buy copies of Mrs. Adams's biography of him, 425,000 hardcover copies are sold," Leonard Lyons wrote in the *New York Post*. "As a result, she has a chauffeur-driven white Rolls Royce." Lyons chided Adams for leaving the Rolls parked outside WABC-TV's offices when she went in to cover a poverty program.

including Gene Kelly, who was then married. She was less impressed with lovers Ronald Reagan, who wrote rather vapid love letters to her,* and Joe DiMaggio, who, she said, was "about as exciting in bed as a bowl of cornflakes."

Lilly also flirted shamelessly with Walter Winchell, who regularly put her in his column. She became quite friendly with Truman Capote, who used her as an inspiration for Holly Golightly in *Breakfast at Tiffany's*.† Capote urged Lilly to write a book based on her adventures. It was good advice. *How to Meet a Millionaire* was such a smash that it was made into the movie *How to Marry a Millionaire*, inspired a line of clothing, and made Lilly a household name. In 1952, she was hired to write a society column for the New York *Mirror*, and in 1958, she was hired by Dorothy Schiff, the politically liberal owner of the *New York Post*, to write a three-times-a-week column. The column was a success but it struck many journalists as dated and oddly apolitical in a paper with a strong progressive agenda. "Miss Lilly puts together, often at 4 A.M., a bubbly gossip column which gets high readership in a town where society page writers have little real social news and concentrate on the foolish irrelevancies of that curious breed: Cafe Society," *Newsweek* noted in 1960. "While many of the militantly liberal *New York Post*'s writers are fretting about civil rights and civic wrongs, columnist Doris Lilly concerns herself with the civilities and incivilities of the Colony, at charity balls, and on the zebra-striped banquettes at El Morocco."

Even so, by the mid-1960s, Doris Lilly had emerged as one of the most likely successors to Hedda and Louella. She had become a regular on Merv Griffin's talk show. She was feuding with rival Aileen "Suzy" Mehle, whose column also appeared in the *Post* and who was actually dating media-hater Frank Sinatra. She had also become friendly with Roy Cohn, who was a good source

---

* Doris Lilly caused a flap when she sold some love letters in 1988. The letters were bought by Malcolm Forbes, who is said to have given them to his friend Nancy Reagan. She, word has it, promptly destroyed them.

† After the release of *Breakfast at Tiffany's*, a woman named Holly Golightly sued, saying that the book invaded her privacy. Lilly testified on behalf of Capote, who said the book was based on her. Capote privately said that Holly Golightly was also inspired by Carol Marcus and Oona Chaplin.

of items for her—especially regarding the Kennedys. On one occasion, Cohn invited her to the Bahamas with him.* On her return she wrote an item about the trip. "I got a memo from Mrs. Schiff saying that she'd rather not see Roy Cohn's name mentioned in the newspaper," Doris said. "When I saw Dorothy, whom I knew quite well—we used to go to the theater together, have lunch together, things like that—I said 'Dorothy, I thought that being liberal meant that you were liberal with everybody. What is wrong with Roy Cohn? Why can't I mention Roy Cohn's name?' "

"He's controversial," Schiff said obliquely.

"We had our first big disagreement over that," Lilly said, "because I didn't think it was fair. Mrs. Schiff's bottom line was 'It's my newspaper and I can put whatever I want in it.' " Doris, however, continued to rely on sources like Cohn while attacking icons like the Kennedys—much to the anger of Schiff, a big Kennedy supporter. Doris also became somewhat obsessed with Jackie Kennedy. But she was not a fan of the former First Lady, considering her a hypocrite who was in truth a darker, more complicated person than the saintly widow the public saw. For example, Doris tried to report that in August 1962 while Jackie was visiting Fiat mogul Gianni Agnelli she sent a Secret Service plane back to Washington to pick up her diaphragm. Schiff, however, killed the story. Doris knew a lot of tidbits about Jacqueline Kennedy—that the former First Lady, who so assiduously protected her own privacy, was herself an incorrigible snoop and gossip. When she moved into her Fifth Avenue apartment, she put a telescope in her living room and used it to spy on her neighbors. But every time Lilly tried to put something like that into an article, it got killed. Truman Capote had told her that Jackie read everything that was written about her. "If she sees a photograph of herself in a book or an article she will write a note to the author and request the original 'for her scrapbook,' " according

---

* During the trip, she met Barbara Walters for the first time. "I have to tell you the truth about Barbara, she didn't make an impression on me," said Lilly. "As I understood it at the time, she was his secretary. . . . Later I understood they had some kind of romance."

to Lilly. "During her White House days, the walls of her bedroom were lined with pictures of herself."

In 1968, Doris Lilly heard from her friend Truman Capote that Jackie was going to marry Aristotle Onassis.* She was ecstatic about getting the story. The world's most glamorous woman marrying the world's richest man was the gossip item of the decade. Tabloids had been speculating about the former First Lady's love life, and getting the scoop on it was, Doris figured, the best thing that could happen to her career. Doris wrote about Jackie's engagement to Onassis in her *New York Post* column and—just to be sure that she got credit for breaking the story—she also went on Merv Griffin's show with the news.

The Griffin show had a live studio audience, and Lilly wasn't prepared for the crowd's reaction. "There were loud boos and catcalls," she recalled. "People couldn't believe that Jackie—Caesar's wife, their saint, their Virgin Mary—was marrying a short, fat old Greek." Lilly was quickly ushered off the stage. But as she tried to leave Griffin's studio, she was met by a throng of angry Jackie lovers who had already gathered outside. As Doris tried to pass through the crowd, they attacked her. She was hit, her hair was pulled. One woman dug her nails into her arm, drawing blood. "Jackie would never marry anyone like that!" Doris heard a particularly distraught woman cry out. Doris went back into the studio and got a police escort to help her to the car.

Despite landing the "scoop of the decade," Lilly was fired from the *New York Post* a few months later. Dorothy Schiff had decided that in 1968—a year that saw the assassinations of Martin Luther King and Robert Kennedy, the upheaval at the Democratic convention in Chicago, the intensified bombing campaign against North Vietnam—Doris's kind of journalism didn't belong in a paper like the *Post*, even though it was a tabloid. Gossip, many editors and publishers had come to believe, disgraced the serious

---

* The *Washington Post*'s Maxine Cheshire actually had the story before Doris Lilly, but her editor, Ben Bradlee, killed the story. "I really don't believe it," Cheshire recalled Bradlee saying. "I don't believe she's going to do it." When it became obvious that he was wrong, Bradlee was outraged. "That goddamn greasy Greek gangster," he bellowed as he punched his fist against an office wall.

news it was supposed to offset. Nothing illustrated this more clearly than the outraged reaction of journalists and critics that same year to the television appearances of Rona Barrett in Los Angeles.

People who had tuned into KABC-TV in Los Angeles one evening in December 1966 couldn't believe what they were seeing. There, on the nightly local news, was the station's newest hire. Standing at just over five feet tall, with elaborately coifed hair resembling a platinum-frosted artichoke, heavily-lined eyes conjuring images of Elizabeth Taylor in *Cleopatra*, and an obviously sculpted nose shaped into a pert little stump, Rona Barrett looked, one critic later noted, like a "human Kewpie doll." That, like so many of the comments about Rona, was unkind in the extreme. One thing she certainly *didn't* look like was a newscaster, however. But then she wasn't being billed as one. She was a gossip reporter. And there she was interviewing her good friend Tina Sinatra.

"What movie star is it," Barrett asked in a slightly Betty Boopish voice that still honked with traces of Queens, New York, "that you would model yourself after in your aspiring career?"

"Oh, no one," Tina replied. "I'm told my beauty is so unique and my acting ability so fantastic, I won't remind anyone of anyone!"

The Sinatra family was outraged. After the show, Tina's mother Nancy called up Rona, practically hysterical. "Tina has never said any of those things!" Rona recalled Mrs. Sinatra screaming. "You've dubbed her voice! It's someone else's voice on the track! All you're looking to do is use the Sinatra name to further your own career. You're like everyone else!" Although Rona considered herself to be close to the Sinatras—"a third daughter" as Frank had once put it—the family refused to speak with her after the disastrous interview.

Undeterred, Barrett produced one scoop after another in the weeks and months that followed. She was the first to tell the world that Elizabeth Taylor and Richard Burton were breaking up. She broke the news that Cary Grant was divorcing his wife, actress Dyan Cannon—a case that went on to become the sensation of Hollywood when Grant, the epitome of cinematic charm and sophistication, was accused by Cannon of beating her and was also revealed to be a devoted user of LSD.* When Mia Farrow and Frank Sinatra were having marital problems, Rona reported that Mia danced with Robert Kennedy until the early-morning hours. Rona's biggest scoop, she always maintained, was the news, in 1967, that Elvis Presley was going to marry Priscilla Beaulieu. "That was the story," Rona boasted, "that really 'made' me."

The city of Los Angeles was riveted. There on the television news—amid the grim dispatches about body counts in Vietnam, race riots in the big cities, unrest on college campuses, and poverty in Appalachia—was something that the viewers enjoyed hearing. Almost instantly, Rona became one of the best-known personalities in Los Angeles. Her face was plastered on billboards and full-page newspaper ads. "Rona Barrett—First to put Hollywood's private secrets on public record." Watching Rona became an event, not only for movie fans, but for Hollywood executives and even the celebrities she covered. "All over Los Angeles, people sit back to play the campiest after dinner game since charades: watching Rona Barrett, or 'Miss Rona' as she is called, deliver the Hollywood news," one reviewer noted. "Elegant hostesses stop their dinner parties dead; weary studio executives make themselves stay up for The Event; and even the stars who curse her existence most furtively tune in."

When KABC-TV hired Rona Barrett, it was the third-rated station in Los Angeles. Within months, its ratings nearly doubled and it had become number one. Competitors sneered that it had climbed to the top by the cheapest, easiest way possible: pandering to viewers' basest instincts with gossip. It was a charge the station's executives didn't bother to deny. "I don't care *how* we did it," KABC-TV's station manager said. "We did it."

With Walter Winchell jobless and begging for work, Hedda Hopper dead, Louella Parsons in a nursing home, and Doris Lilly fired from the *New York Post*, the consensus was that gossip was

---

* The effect of LSD on Grant was peculiar. Whereas he once assiduously avoided the press, after taking the drug he actively pursued gossip columnists and would pour out his heart to them, which may explain his brief romance with Doris Lilly.

dead. "Newspapers were dying around the country. Editors were cutting back," Barrett said of those days. "No one believed the era of Hollywood would continue." But within little more than a year after arriving at KABC, Barrett had reconfigured the calling for television, and by 1968 no less a voice than the *New York Times* had anointed her the official successor to Hedda and Louella. "A lot of locals have been fighting for the empty throne," the *Times* wrote. "As of right now, Rona Barrett has it. She is the queen of the gossips, and she sits, if a little uneasily, on that tarnished throne, clutching her silver screen orb and waving her Oscar-gold scepter at all those wicked subjects."

Like so many gossip columnists, Rona Barrett was first and foremost a fan—a fan with dreams of becoming a star herself. She was born Rona Burstein in the working class neighborhood of Astoria, Queens, where her father owned a grocery store and her mother was a housewife. Young Rona was not a beautiful child: She had a huge nose and was overweight. She was terribly self-conscious—a problem compounded by a form of muscular dystrophy that gave her problems walking. Hoping to correct the problem, Rona's mother had her fitted with a heavy leg brace, but when Rona showed up to school the next day, her classmates taunted her mercilessly. "Someday, so help me," she recalled thinking, "I'll be so important, so famous, not one of you will ever be able to touch me again."

Rona retreated into the fantasy world of celebrity. In high school she began signing her name "Rona Starr Barrett." She idolized Elizabeth Taylor and had a big crush on Eddie Fisher. While she read Louella Parsons religiously, she thought the column covered too many has-beens like Clark Gable and Joan Crawford; Rona and her friends hungered for news about the new breed of stars that were emerging, actors like Paul Newman and Tony Perkins, and singers like Frank Sinatra, Elvis Presley, and particularly, Eddie Fisher. When Rona was thirteen, she became chief coordinator of the Eddie Fisher Fan Club, taking the subway into Manhattan and working at the Blackstone publicity office answering the young singer's fan mail. By then, Rona had her leg brace removed and was more confident about her looks, and one day she coyly flirted with her idol, asking him why he didn't date Jewish women. "Jewish girls are no good for fucking" he said, as she recalled in her autobiography *Miss Rona*. Rona, stunned and disillusioned, asked the singer what he meant. "They think they're doing you a big favor when it comes to the sex department," he said. "Before you know it, you've got a depleted bank account because this Jewish broad has bribed you into buying every goddamned newfangled goody in the world just to get a piece of ass."

The next day, Rona Barrett resigned as chief coordinator of the Eddie Fisher Fan Club, and went to work instead for the Steve Lawrence Fan Club. She attended New York University but dropped out when she was eighteen to work for a fanzine. She gravitated toward a group of aspiring actors, including Michael Landon, and in 1958, she got a call from Landon—who had not yet achieved fame from the TV series *Bonanza*—and went to Los Angeles to live with him and his wife, Dodie.

Once there, she became friendly with producer Bob Evans, Warren Beatty, and Frankie Avalon.* By 1960, she had a column in a fanzine called *Motion Picture*, and a year later, the North American Newspaper Alliance began distributing her column, seven days a week, to more than one hundred newspapers. Although they were small, local papers, and paid her only $75 a week apiece, not many reporters were writing about celebrities, and Rona, aggressive and eager to please the stars, acquired remarkable access. As writer Jacqueline Susann noted, "In this business, you've got to have the guts of a burglar. Rona has them."

She also set out to transform herself physically. She dyed her brunette hair platinum blond and had her nose bobbed. Her low forehead gave her a dull-witted appearance, and she corrected this by having her hairline raised through electrolysis, just as Rita Hayworth had done. She hired Kim Novak's masseuse to help her lose weight, and she visited a speech therapist who helped turn down her nasal Queens accent. By the time of her debut on

---

* She wrote an item about two groupies who lived in a car outside Avalon's house. In July 1961, when one of the women hit Avalon with a paternity suit, Rona helped him keep the scandal under wraps. When the story of Avalon's paternity suit got out, Avalon cut Rona out of his life, she said, because "I knew too much."

KABC, dark, roly-poly Rona Burstein had become svelte blonde Rona Barrett.

Her appearances proved so popular with the public that within a year Rona's reports were being picked up by all eight of ABC's owned and operated stations, including KGO in San Francisco, WBKB in Chicago, WXYZ in Detroit, and WABC in New York, where she appeared nightly on *The 11 O'clock News with Roger Grimsby*. "Which gives me forty percent of the American public," Rona boasted. "Like New Jersey and Connecticut watch me from my New York outlet. I've got the centers, baby."

Rona's segment usually appeared toward the end of the news show; some said it was because it wasn't real news, but others whispered it was really because producers knew that people would stay tuned for it. When Barrett's reports were on, ratings went up. "Greetings everyone!" Rona would open her segment, occasionally delivering her scoops in a dramatic stage whisper. "Her shrill little yentalike voice is swept along on gushes of scandalous innuendo," observed one critic. "Like Hedda and Louella before her, Rona is genuinely fascinated, titillated, and alarmed by who was seen where with whom, why so-and-so was signed, and which star isn't speaking to which director."

From the beginning, she faced resistance from the regular anchors and reporters at those stations, and as her success grew, their disapproval turned to contempt. Although Rona raised ratings at WABC in New York, anchorman Roger Grimsby introduced the gossip columnist with comments such as "Here's Rona Barrett, Hollywood's tripe caster" or "Here's Rona Barrett, keyhole ferret." One night, Grimsby introduced Barrett after a segment on the sanitation strike by saying, "and speaking of garbage . . ."

"They don't like the fact that I'm a ratings-getter, the news guys," Barrett said. "Tough! Now they have to acknowledge me— reluctantly." She tried to be a trouper about it all and one night even poked fun at herself by saying: "This is Rona Rumor." For the next four nights she was blacked out on the WABC-TV screen.

Serious news people weren't the only ones who hated Rona. Celebrities made a sport of ridiculing her. "Rona doesn't need a

knife," Johnny Carson said. "She cuts her steak with her tongue."
Rona impersonations became a fixture on comedy shows. Ruth
Buzzi mimicked her as "Mona Blarit" on *Laugh In*. Frank Sinatra
took to calling her a "bow wow." Comedienne Carol Burnett did
a wickedly funny takeoff called "Rona Rumor," though when she
had a movie to promote, she happily sat for an interview with
the woman she regularly impersonated.*

Some celebrities were not content merely to make fun of
Barrett. At one Hollywood party, Mia Farrow dumped champagne
over her head. Ryan O'Neal sent her a live tarantula in the mail.
Rona didn't mind—or at least she said she didn't. She understood
the publicity game. "Carol Burnett's show helped me more than
any one thing," she said. "People remembered it." The public
knew her name—that's what mattered. "Any publicity helps. And
you know what? People remember the bad."

By the early 1970s, Rona Barrett had, as she vowed to do
when her classmates mocked her leg brace, became a genuine
star. In 1973 she married William Trowbridge, a former radio
disc jockey turned Hollywood producer. Her 1974 dishy autobiography, *Miss Rona*, was a best-seller, and she wrote a follow-up,
How You Can Look Rich and Achieve Sexual Fantasy, in which
she advised her female readers to "mold chocolate fudge around
his toes and dine on it before the rest of him." She recorded an
album of Hollywood's greatest hits, including "Over the Rain-
bow" and "As Time Goes By." She bought Hoagy Carmichael's
former house for the then-exorbitant price of $1.5 million and
spent another $400,000 fixing it up. She bought a Rolls Royce
with the license plate MS RONA. She launched several fanzines.
"Most any star will return my call in a matter of seconds," she
said in 1974. "When you are on television, being seen by a mini-
mum of thirty or forty million people a day, well that's a lot of
influence." Once, when asked to name her favorite stars, Barrett
replied, "Paul Newman, Barbra Streisand, Burt Lancaster—and
me!"

---

* "I don't read movie magazines because I don't care about all that," Burnett
was quick to explain. "I watch Rona from a comedic standpoint, not to learn
who's doing what to whom."

In 1975, Rona Barrett was hired by ABC, becoming the first gossip columnist to appear in a national newscast. Again, she raised the ratings, but the serious news people resented her presence. "I hear Elmer Lower, the head of ABC News, sends memos daily to get me fired," Rona said shortly after she was hired by the network. "But I don't care. I mean, it annoys me, but I don't *care*. . . . I am a very big moneymaker that gives the station a very enormous rating. Elmer Lower's ratings *stink*."

The truth is, Rona did care. After joining the national network, she decided she wanted to be taken seriously. "It grieves me that they categorize me as a gossip," she said in 1977. "I have brought the business of entertainment to the American public." She also informed people that they should no longer call her "Miss Rona." And she began making demands. She considered celebrity news, which the network was increasingly emphasizing, to be her exclusive territory. She liked to maintain that she had pioneered the format of the long celebrity interviews, and she became resentful at the growing number of such assignments being given to a woman who was politically shrewder than she was, Igor Cassini's former assistant and Roy Cohn's former "girl-friend," Barbara Walters, whom ABC had lured away from NBC with a salary of $1 million.

Rona was a regular on *Good Morning America*, but she complained that Barbara Walters was upstaging her and that all of her good ideas were being given to Walters. "I'm smarter than Barbara and I do a better job than she does on the specials," Rona complained. "She has invaded my turf." The ever diplomatic Walters knew better than to get into a catfight with Rona. "Rona is entitled to her opinion," Walters said. "I have great respect for her."

Rona wasn't calmed. In April 1980, she poured her heart out to Tom Snyder on the *Tomorrow* show. "I feel raped!" she told him. "I can't watch my ideas be given to somebody else. There's an old expression, you can steal my wife, but don't steal my ideas. . . . There is nothing worse than feeling raped. You feel sick. And you feel violated." Rona quit ABC in 1980 and was hired by NBC, where she was paid $1 million a year and teamed up with Tom Snyder. "This is not a ploy to get more money," Rona declared. "It's an artistic decision."

With Snyder broadcasting from New York and Barrett from Los Angeles, NBC had great hopes for the show, but it was a disaster from the beginning. For Rona's debut episode, she had taped an interview with Mary Tyler Moore. Shortly before the segment was to air, however, Moore's son killed himself. Moore's estranged husband, Grant Tinker, the former head of NBC, advised Moore that it would be unseemly for her to appear gossiping and giggling with Rona Barrett on national TV shortly after her son committed suicide. Barrett begged Moore to help her update the segment, but the actress refused. Barrett then threatened to run the interview without Moore's approval, introducing it by noting that the actress was devastated by the tragedy. "Mary said that if Rona did that, she would issue a public statement blasting Rona," according to a source. "Snyder sided with Moore against Barrett." So, on her heralded *Tomorrow* debut, Rona Barrett discussed politics.

The second show went even worse. Rona was scheduled to interview Victor Navasky, author of the McCarthy era chronicle *Naming Names*, but Snyder, according to sources, was unhappy because he felt Barrett was invading his territory by tackling such a serious subject. When the broadcast began, Snyder told viewers that Rona would not be part of that evening's show because of "communications difficulties." In truth, he simply refused to turn any part of the show over to his West Coast co-host. Barrett was left stranded in her Hollywood studio with Navasky, humiliated and furious.

"He told me I was trying to steal his program," Barrett later said. "I was stunned." It was her understanding, Barrett said, that she and Tom were supposed to be equals on the show. That was not Snyder's understanding. "It's Tom Snyder's show, not hers," Snyder's agent, Ed Hookstratten said. "She can be an integral part of it, but she can't be co-host. It's not her show."

Snyder wasn't Rona's only enemy. The critics were also vicious. "Poor little Miss Ro-Ro," wrote the *Washington Post's* Tom Shales, referring to the "one blessed night" when Snyder refused to throw the show over to her. "Yesterday only a few people knew about The Rona Syndrome. It used to be known as biting off more than you can chew, even if you have a very big mouth. Miss Rona reached—for the stars! And not just Burt Reynolds, either. She wanted more than glamour, more than fame, more than daily morning exposure on television with her tattered Tinseltown tidbits. She wanted RESPECT. But Rona and Tom together was one shrieking peacock too many even for the peacock network."

Although NBC's executives valued the viewers that Barrett brought to the show, they balked at giving her celebrity reports equal billing with the "hard news" that was Snyder's beat. The feud continued to escalate until one day in June 1981, Rona simply refused to show up for work. "I don't want to be on any show with Tom Snyder anymore," she said. "No matter who I got as a guest, no matter how important, they never put me first up. If NBC doesn't like what I have to say I'm really sorry." She insisted on hosting her own show, declaring, "I won't play second fiddle to [Snyder] or anybody else any longer." She had hoped to stay with NBC, but left the network entirely not long afterward. "It's really mind-boggling the way NBC has treated me," she said, "and I'm tired of being the good little girl."

In 1985, Rona was hired by *Entertainment Tonight*, the all-celebrity nightly newscast started by Paramount in 1981. She was reportedly making $700,000 a year and her contract stipulated that if her segments ran longer than eighteen minutes, she was to be paid an extra $1,200 per minute. But the show's producers soon realized that Barrett's reports contained no greater revelations, and drew no more of an audience, than the pieces by the junior reporters, who were paid much less and who were less difficult to work with. The audience was tuning in for information about celebrities and didn't particularly care who reported it. Rona and *Entertainment Tonight* parted company after nine months. She tried doing an industry newsletter, "The Barrett Report" but at $1,200 a year, it was considered overpriced for information that could be found in other places, and it soon folded. Rona tried a number of TV and radio shows, including a short-lived return to NBC, but nothing worked. Her personal life wasn't going much better. She had split from her husband. The form of celebrity news that Rona had given birth to had outgrown her. "Hedda and Louella had it easier," Rona complained in 1986. "Today, if Ingrid Bergman got pregnant, it would be lucky to make the inside pages."

That same year Macmillan announced that it was canceling the sequel to Barrett's best-selling *Miss Rona* and asked for the return of the $300,000 advance. By the end of the eighties, Rona finally acknowledged that her brief reign as America's premiere gossip columnist was over. "As Walter Cronkite once said, now and then there's a fabulous story and I go for my fireman's hat and I say, 'Where's the fire?' " Rona said in 1989. "And that's when I remember that I don't have the forum."

Rona Barrett's legacy, however, was lasting. During the late 1960s and early 1970s, she had proved—against all odds and despite the contrary feelings of so many newspaper editors—that the public was still interested in celebrity news, and that for fledgling television stations, gossip was the surest, quickest route to profitability. Once that had been established, it wasn't long before the "legitimate" print press would rediscover the formula was well.

tabloid glory days

Late at night on July 29, 1975, Secret Service agents spotted a slim young man with a mustache and aviator glasses behind the Georgetown home of Secretary of State Henry Kissinger. The man was in the process of heaving five green plastic garbage bags into the trunk of his 1968 Buick. The agents confronted the man and ordered him to return the trash. He refused. They argued with the man and tried to reason with him, but he held fast. He was, he said, keeping the garbage. The Secret Service agents were puzzled—they had been trained to deal with terrorists, but not with garbage thieves—and they called their supervisor, who ordered them to bring the man in for questioning.

At Secret Service headquarters, the agents interrogated the man, a twenty-seven-year-old named Jay Gourley. The theft of the trash seemed so bizarre that the agents were at pains to establish the man's mental stability. But Gourley was quite sane, even lucid and articulate. He argued that garbage, by definition, had been abandoned by its owner, and therefore he couldn't be accused of stealing anything. After two-and-a-half hours, the Secret Service concluded that, indeed, Gourley had not broken the law.

Since they couldn't charge him with any crime, they took his photograph and reluctantly released him. Gourley had neglected to tell the Secret Service that he was a reporter on assignment for the *National Enquirer*, but as soon as he was free he telephoned his editors in Lantana, Florida. "Operation Trash," he reported, was accomplished.

Most of Kissinger's garbage, as the tabloid reported the following week, was simply garbage: an empty vichyssoise can, used packages of antacids, empty yogurt containers, two unread copies of the *New York Times*, a lot of empty cigarette packs (his wife, Nancy, was a smoker), and a prescription for a bottle of Seconal. The *Enquirer* also found what it boasted were "hundreds of Secret Service documents." Among the booty were copies of Kissinger's daily agenda, including appointments with corporate leaders that weren't on the official agendas distributed to the media. One classified document explained a coded light signal system that was being tested by the Secret Service for use in all of its limousines. Another detailed the amount and kind of ammunition carried by each Secret Service limousine.

When the *National Enquirer* published its findings, the story made headlines around the world. Kissinger was outraged, "Really revolted," he said. His wife Nancy was in "anguish." The article so alarmed the Hollywood community, that in Beverly Hills an ordinance was passed forbidding garbage theft. And when furious officials at the Secret Service complained that sensitive information like that should never have been made public, the *Enquirer* turned the admonishment into vindication. Generoso Pope, the *Enquirer*'s editor-owner, insisted that the tabloid wasn't violating the Secretary of State's privacy; it was performing a service to the American public—indeed to Henry Kissinger himself—by showing how easy it would be for an assassin or a Communist spy to get his hands on the classified documents that were in Kissinger's trash. Then, using the classic tabloid tactic of moralizing about prurient detail in order to justify serving it up, the *Enquirer* followed up its initial story with the headline: "Secret Service Admits: Confidential Documents That *Enquirer* Found in Kissinger's Trash Was a 'Breach of Security.' "

*　　*　　*

For most of its twenty-year history under Gene Pope Jr., the *Enquirer* had been beneath notice, as far as the establishment press in America was concerned. But after the headlines generated by "Operation Trash," its audacity—or shamelessness, depending on one's point of view—as well as its success began to receive attention.

Since Pope had moved the tabloid to Florida in 1971, housing it in a nondescript low-level office building in an area near the coastal town of Lantana that became known as Tabloid Valley, circulation had climbed from 2 million to over 3 million in 1975, giving it the largest circulation of any newspaper in the country. Its gross earnings for 1974 were reportedly $41 million, versus $17 million a year earlier. It received nearly 2 million pieces of mail a year and had its own zip code. And according to one study, the 20 million people who read the *Enquirer* every week were not, as was commonly believed, "trailer park trash" at the very bottom of the demographic chart, but women aged twenty-five to forty-nine with high school or college educations.

The man who had created this wildly successful handbook of the middle class, middle American housewife was unrecognizable as the New York power broker who had fled the Northeast in terror in 1971. The man who had dined with mobsters, hob-nobbed with political fixers, whose arrogance infuriated the city reformers had come to distrust and loathe the powerful crowd he once personified. The MIT grad had become an anti-intellectual. He was worth an estimated $150 million, but he drove a beat-up white Chevy and ate brown bag lunches of lettuce, tomato, and American cheese on rye. His clothes—short-sleeved shirts and baggy work pants in either blue or gray—came from Sears. New hires at the *Enquirer* often mistook him for the janitor because he spent so much time checking the thermostat in the company's offices (it had to be at *exactly* seventy-five degrees) and tending to the grounds (the grass, which he would measure with a ruler, had to be *exactly* three inches high). Generoso Pope Jr. was a man intent on controlling his environment.

The only indication of his tremendous fortune was the fourteen-room mansion he had built on a bluff overlooking the ocean in Manalapan, a five-minute drive away from the *National Enquirer's* offices. It was largely a concession to his wife, Lois, a former Broadway showgirl and cabaret singer who had not taken to life in the swamplands of Florida quite as easily as her husband. Within a few years, however, Lois came around and eventually she and several of Gene Pope's six children were working for the *National Enquirer.*

Despite, or perhaps because of, his publication's relentless investigations into the private lives of the famous, Pope himself liked to remain anonymous. In fact, his name didn't appear on the tabloid's masthead. But there was no question that Gene Pope *was* the *National Enquirer.* He worked incessantly. He chain-smoked Kents and came into the office six days a week, usually bringing piles of work home with him each evening. Pope approved or killed every story idea—about six to nine hundred were submitted every week—and read each page proof, signing off with a rubber stamp: "Passed. G.P." He never took vacations, and since moving to Lantana, which was just outside of Palm Beach, the farthest he had traveled was to one of his printing facilities in the next county to the south.

As a manager his behavior alternated between astonishing generosity and tyranny. He quietly paid for an expensive operation for the local barber; when one editor needed an expensive bone marrow transplant, Pope assigned a researcher to find the best specialist in the country and footed the bill. Then he turned around and fired half a dozen staffers a few days before Christmas.

Pope's peculiar mixture of kindness and self-aggrandizement was epitomized by his annual "Christmas present" to Lantana: the world's tallest Christmas tree. It started out as a 21-foot spruce outside the *National Enquirer*'s offices in 1971. Some motorists stopped by to admire it. The next year he erected a 40-foot tree, and crowds gathered. Within a few years, it became a massive operation: teams were dispatched to the Pacific Northwest, sometimes bribing officials or local Indian tribes to circumvent regulations and let them cut down the largest tree they could find in existence. Over the years, the tree's usual height was over 125 feet. It had to be chopped into pieces, put on a train, and reassembled with cranes and teams of workers in Lantana. It was decorated lavishly, with hundreds of feet of lights, garland, moving teddy bears, and Santa's helpers. Busloads of families made pilgrimages each year to gawk at the tree. It was rumored to cost close to $1 million; Pope would never comment on the price, saying merely, "It's a Christmas present." Much to Pope's anger and dismay, he could never get it listed in the *Guinness Book of World Records* as the world's tallest Christmas tree. It was just another example, Pope would grumble, of the establishment's refusal to recognize his achievements.

The newsroom of the *Enquirer* had an incredibly competitive atmosphere. Many of its reporters came from England, Scotland, or Australia and imported the aggressive Fleet Street brand of reporting. "They're the masters of the *Enquirer*'s kind of 'hit-and-run,' make-a-story-out-of-one-fact journalism," former articles editor P. J. Corkery once observed. "The English support a half dozen national newspapers like the *Enquirer*. In fact, that's how I got interested in this stuff. For a long while when I was in England, I was fascinated by the fact that every Sunday morning, sober, respectable people would leave their churches and homes to pick up papers much more lurid than even the *Enquirer*. The reason for this is that while the stories are often outlandish, the reporting is exceptionally well organized and researched. They come up with all sorts of small details that are very revealing. In fact, the better papers of this kind in England are fun to read."

To motivate staffers, Pope paid them $100 for any idea that resulted in a published story and "The Far Out Story Idea of the Week" was worth $1,000. Pope also liked to pit editorial teams— two editors and six reporters—against each other to see which could come up with the most provocative, shocking stories. Editors who got the most stories in the tabloid received the highest pay; the number of stories each reporter produced was posted in the newsroom. Those in the bottom third were put on thirty days' notice; if their ranking didn't improve in a month, they were fired. One Friday, thirteen reporters were fired for not producing more.

Turnover was so high at the *Enquirer* that its rival, the *Globe*, moved to nearby Boca Raton in the early 1980s so it could more easily hire fired *Enquirer* employees. But Pope never had trouble finding replacements; starting salaries at the *Enquirer* were among the highest in the industry, and the perks were unparalleled.

"Money was no object to him," noted former freelancer Colin Dangaard. "Planes, yachts, traveling to wherever. Whatever it took, he [Pope] didn't care. I used to freelance stories to him during my lunch hour when I was a reporter at the *Miami Herald.* For what took me thirty minutes of work on the telephone for the *Enquirer* once a week, I was paid almost as much as I made for the entire week from the *Herald.* And these were little human interest things, not even celebrity stories."

The reporters and editors themselves, in addition to being compensated handsomely, funneled money to their sources. The publication had an editorial budget of $15 million. It made some 5,000 payments a year to sources for tips and spent $850,000 on stories that went unpublished. Reporters were given thick wads of $20, $50, and $100 bills to use as bribes in getting stories. "You go into a bar and you leave twenty dollars. You have one drink, you leave twenty dollars. You have no drinks, you leave twenty dollars. You use the phone, you leave twenty dollars," said Mike Walker. "This was back in the 1970s, when twenty dollars really meant something. We can easily spend $20,000 for something that's going to end up in the trashcan." "I would walk into that newsroom and I could do anything I wanted," said Tom Kuncl. "To be able to do that, to have those sorts of resources, was truly exciting."

Contrary to charges made by its critics, the *National Enquirer* didn't have an official policy of making up stories. It merely sensationalized them. Its reporters knew just how to manipulate people into giving them the quotes the magazine needed. Pope himself spelled out the techniques in a confidential memorandum in 1975. "Prod, push and probe the main characters in the story," Pope wrote. "Help them frame their answers," he advised. The memo gave this imaginary interview between an *Enquirer* reporter and an inarticulate source:

"How did it feel?"
"I don't know, it just hurt."
"Was it a sharp pain?"
"No."
"Was it more like a toothache?"
"No."

"Have you ever felt anything like it before?"

"Not really, but it was something like an electrical shock."

"Where did you feel it?"

"It hit me in the back of the neck and it went down my spine."

"Did you scream?"

"I couldn't."

"Let's see if I've got this straight. You said, 'The pain hit me. It was like an electrical shot that started in my neck and shot down my spine. I wanted to scream, but I couldn't. I've never felt anything like it."

"Yes, that's it."

The "quotes," Pope cautioned, had to be believable: "A Japanese carpenter should not sound like Ernest Hemingway, or vice versa," he noted, but "We need quotes that tug at the heart." For example, Pope wrote, "Take the story about the mother who had the flag that covered her son's coffin stolen. The writer wrote, 'I wish they'd bring it back.' But it was changed to 'If they don't bring it back, God help them.' " "We should touch our readers' souls," Pope wrote. "Cause them to smile, to get lumps in their throats, to break down and cry."

Pope was looking for what he called "Gee whiz stories"—a phrase coined by Joseph Pulitzer. And indeed, Pope was in many ways following in the footsteps of Pulitzer and that other master of yellow journalism, William Randolph Hearst, both of whom he viewed as role models. Pope, like Hearst and Pulitzer, understood that to capture the masses, journalism had to be entertaining. Feel-good articles run by the *Enquirer* included "Amazing Candy and Chewing Gum Diet," "TV Can Prolong Life," "After 56 Men Refuse to Coach Little League Baseball Club, Housewife Takes Job and Wins Championship," and, perhaps most ironic, "How to Stop Vicious Gossip." On one occasion, former articles editor P. J. Corkery submitted a list of story ideas to Pope, including a suggestion for an article on how to throw parties.

"Parties?" Pope asked incredulously. "You mean like with hats?"

"We can leave the hats out of it," Corkery said.

Pope was dismissive. "People don't go to parties," he said as he killed the story.

Pope was well aware that people do go to parties, Corkery knew, but he also realized that many people who bought the *Enquirer* weren't invited to parties or didn't have the time or money to give them. "The boss never wants the reader to feel bad about his or her life," Corkery noted. "The job of the paper, aside from getting people to buy it each week, the boss says, is to entertain. Ameliorate . . . Never make our readers feel as if they're missing something. Like parties. With or without hats."

Another staple of the *Enquirer* was the harmlessly zany, believe-it-or-not story. On one occasion, a group of *National Enquirer* reporters decided the biggest scoop in the history of mankind would be if aliens landed on earth. "So we decided to do it," said one of the editors involved in the charade. "We thought it would tell our readers a lot about human nature." The *Enquirer* orchestrated a light show and a "landing" in a small town in Texas known for its UFO sightings. They hired a Hollywood makeup artist and a special effects team to disguise an *Enquirer* reporter as an alien. "I swear to god, he looked like a Martian," said the editor. "So we drop him off in a small town. He walks up to people and says, 'Take me to your leader.' They fucking nearly killed him. He's running away, screaming, 'Stop, I'm with the *National Enquirer*.' They said, 'The hell you are. You're a damned alien.' " The article never ran. "It sure as hell did tell us something about human nature," the editor said, "but it's not something that our readers would have liked hearing about themselves."

While the *Enquirer* tended to avoid writing about politicians, it made an exception with the Kennedy family. "Business will be fine as long as Ted Kennedy stays in the news," Pope once said. The *Enquirer* pursued the Senator so tenaciously that eventually he struck a deal with the tabloid: His office would supply them with stories if they would hold back on some of the more salacious stuff they had uncovered—a deal that a number of Hollywood stars were to strike with the publication in the 1980s. The deal was negotiated by Kennedy's brother-in-law, lawyer Steven Smith, according to Rick Burke, the Kennedy staffer who was assigned as the *Enquirer* contact. "I was the contact man," Burke once admitted. "Once a week, I received a call from an 'inquiring' reporter to see if there was any family news to report."

Because the mainstream papers were ignoring the Kennedy scandals, the tabloids were having a field day with them. For years before the story was legitimized by "credible" journalists like Seymour Hersch, the tabloids were filled with Kennedy scandals.*

During this time, some of the most respected investigative reporters in the country were turning to publications like the *National Enquirer* to get stories on the Kennedys printed; no upscale publications would touch them. Articles by reporters like Jack Anderson and Drew Pearson began appearing in the *National Enquirer*. Peter Lawford, who had been banned from the Kennedy circle after the Marilyn Monroe embarrassment, and after *Confidential* disappeared, became a source for the *Enquirer* and regularly sold stories about the clan to the tabloid.† There, tucked between stories of freaks of nature and violent crimes, stories started appearing in the tabloid—complete with photos—about Kennedy's infidelities and mob links that no other publication would run.‡

---

* As early as 1964, an article appeared in *Photoplay* magazine reporting that Robert Kennedy was at Monroe's house the day of her death.

† When Lawford died in 1988, the Kennedys allegedly refused to pay the cost of his burial and the tab for a ceremony to have his ashes scattered at sea was picked up by the *National Enquirer*.

‡ Because the *National Enquirer* was one of the few newspapers in the 1960s and early 1970s that *would* print scandals about the beloved slain President, in February 1976 it broke an astonishing story that was all but ignored by the mainstream press: that Ben Bradlee's former sister-in-law, Mary Pinchot Meyer, had an affair with the President shortly before she was killed, shot once in the head and once in the chest, while walking along Washington, D.C.'s Chesapeake and Ohio Canal, where she used to go with her friend Jacqueline Kennedy. A drifter was charged but never convicted of the murder. The *Enquirer* described Meyer and Kennedy smoking pot together and revealed that, after Meyer's death, her diary detailing the affair was located, with the help of Ben Bradlee, and given to the CIA to destroy. When the story broke, a *Washington Post* reporter called Bradlee, who was vacationing in the Virgin Islands. Bradlee wouldn't comment on the record, but off the record he excoriated his former friend Jim Truitt, a former vice president with the *Washington Post*, who was the source of the story.

Perhaps even more shocking than what appeared in the *Enquirer* was the method by which material was obtained. Reporters went to extraordinary, and frequently appalling, lengths to investigate the private lives of public figures. "Probably the sleaziest thing I had to do while at the *Enquirer* was when Art Carney was in some kind of accident and alcohol was rumored to be involved," a former reporter recalls. "My assignment was to go to Carney's hometown and hit all the liquor stores to see if he was a drunk, then check into his hospital to see if he was in detox. But I couldn't find any dirt, and I thought I was going to get axed for it." Indeed, eventually, like so many of the *Enquirer*'s reporters, he was.

Despite the search for and publication of such material, Gene Pope frequently insisted, and genuinely seemed to believe, that in contrast to the cynical, pessimistic tone of much of the journalism of the early 1970s, his magazine offered an upbeat, optimistic view of the world. "We refuse to run anything that is depressing," Pope once said. "We try to make sure that when you read the *Enquirer*, you're never depressed. You feel good about it and yourself."

To make this point, Pope had a time capsule buried in front of his headquarters and above it installed a plaque with this inscription:

The National Enquirer newspaper on February 28, 1974, buried here a sealed capsule containing good news items of 1973. When opened on February 28, 2074, these items will prove that despite the many crises of the year 1973, Americans still showed the courage, kindness and strength that made this country great.

8

---

60 minutes

March 4, 1975, was a smoggy, somewhat soggy Tuesday in the swank Hancock Park section of Los Angeles when Mike Wallace sat down in H. R. Haldeman's elegant living room and pumped the convicted Watergate conspirator about the scoops and scandals which CBS News had paid him $100,000 to reveal. Nixon's former chief of staff was one of the most notorious men in the country. He was the former President's closest confidante, his hatchet man. "Every President needs a son of a bitch, and I'm Nixon's," Haldeman once famously said. "I get what he wants done and I take the heat instead of him." He had recently been convicted of perjury, conspiracy, and obstruction of justice for his role in covering up Watergate. That's what made him such a ripe subject for 60 Minutes, the highly respected "news magazine" of crusading investigative journalism.

Haldeman had refused to speak to any reporters for the previous three years, but in October 1974, shortly before his case went to trial, his agent Ron Konecky had approached CBS and said that Haldeman might be willing to talk. Bill Leonard, the network's senior vice president for news, and Gordon Manning, CBS vice president for hard news, met with Haldeman in Washington to negotiate the interview. Over dinner, Haldeman handed Leonard and Manning an outline for a tell-all book he was planning to write; it promised to deliver sizzling anecdotes about Nixon, Henry Kissinger, John Mitchell, and John Ehrlichman. Those stories, he told them, could be presented on CBS first. What's more, Haldeman had a potential gold mine: he had privately used a Super 8 mm camera to film dozens of hours of behind-the-scenes activities of Nixon and his top aides. It was, in essence, actual film footage of the events leading up to Watergate.

Haldeman wasn't motivated by the public's right to know. For the interview and the film—which he wouldn't show to CBS before the deal was struck—Haldeman was asking $200,000. CBS had a written policy against paying news sources, but there were ways to hide or disguise such payments. Besides, earlier that year, when *60 Minutes* paid convicted White House burglar G. Gordon Liddy $15,000 for an interview, the results were explosive, and the fee didn't become much of an issue. An exclusive with Haldeman would add some muscle to a show reviewers said was "an intelligent weakling," "having brains but lacking brawn." CBS negotiated Haldeman's payment down to $100,000 and quietly signed a contract.

When Leonard got back to New York, he called Mike Wallace into his office. Leonard asked Wallace if he'd like to interview H. R. Haldeman. A contract had been signed, Leonard said. Wallace would have six hours to question Haldeman off the record; there were no ground rules and no topic was off limits. Wallace leaped at the chance.

In the days leading up to the actual interview, Wallace and the *60 Minutes* team had spent nearly forty-four hours with Haldeman, pumping him for details, prepping him on what he was going to say. The conversations went well. Haldeman had a reputation for being rigid and elusive. Yet, Wallace found him more likable, more "amiable" than he had expected. Haldeman, who for years had worn his hair in a militaristic buzz cut, had let it grow "modishly long," Wallace noticed. He smiled and joked a lot. Wallace had high hopes for the interview.

The interview took place over two days, March 4 and 5, 1975.

Haldeman and Wallace were miked, the lights were on, and the cameras started rolling. The Grand Inquisitor bore in, and he found out why some journalists called Haldeman "The Berlin Wall." He was impenetrable.

"Mr. Haldeman," Wallace asked the convicted perjurer, "has it never occurred to you to confess?"

"If I felt I were guilty of any crime for which I have been charged or any other crime, I'd confess to the guilt of that," Haldeman replied. "But on the basis of living with yourself, I've got to be able to know that I'm in a truthful and honest position. And a plea of guilty would not be truthful or honest on my part and so I can't do it."

Was Watergate the result, Wallace wanted to know, of a White House that was paranoid about "enemies"?

Haldeman looked slightly taken aback. "I don't think there was any mind-set that led to Watergate," he said.

Haldeman backpedaled from things he had said before the interview. During the off-camera conversations, Haldeman had called Nixon "the weirdest man ever to sit in the White House." Once the cameras were rolling, however, Haldeman insisted that he simply meant that the disgraced President was "a very paradoxical man." When pressed, he offered this insight: "Richard Nixon's complexities are not surface complexities that by study and exposure one can see through and then deal with."

When presented with a truly tough question, he would say, "You know, Mike, that's a good question. I wish I knew the answer." or "Hmm. Let's get to that question on the next reel." Somehow, that next reel never came. Haldeman's much-touted film footage of Nixon and his staff behind-the-scenes was an even bigger bust. CBS had bought exclusive rights to twenty-five hours of grainy images like a smiling Nixon waving at the camera, Nixon taking Kissinger for a ride in a golf cart, and White House staffers sitting beside a hotel swimming pool. CBS found only four minutes worthy of putting on air, including one shot of Kissinger eating a hamburger.

Still, some network officials argued that anything coming from the elusive convicted Watergate conspirator was potentially newsworthy, and CBS announced that "H. R. Haldeman has granted

Mike Wallace an extensive, exclusive interview." Executives at the other networks were shocked by the news of CBS's exclusive. Haldeman's lawyer had also approached them, and they knew that he was only willing to talk for a fee. CBS News's much-touted policy, laid forth in its carefully drafted News Standards Outline, strictly forbade the network from paying news sources. The so-called Tiffany network had violated its own standards, and other news organizations were quick to attack the network that so often sneered at them.

"Paying is the second issue," said Frank Reuven, the former president of NBC news. "The first is whether a man like Haldeman should be given a platform, knowing full well that he will try to manipulate the medium."

The episode sparked a debate on checkbook journalism. "The competition for exclusive news between networks or between newspapers has always been keen and often savage, but usually the prize has gone to the side with the best legs, brains and imagination," James Reston wrote in the *New York Times.* "If CBS will pay this kind of money for Mr. Haldeman, won't other big shots or notorious characters demand their price?" Paid sources, one of the arguments went, were little more than performers. The whole issue of "checkbook journalism" blurred the all-important distinction between news and entertainment.

Embarrassed CBS officials insisted they had stayed within the boundaries of network guidelines. The network's policy permitted the payment of fees to newsworthy people for their "memoirs." CBS had paid "honorariums" to both Lyndon Johnson and Dwight D. Eisenhower for their televised memoirs. That's what this was, CBS News president Richard Salant insisted, Haldeman's *memoirs* of his years at the White House. To further prove that point, CBS announced that the Haldeman interview would not run on *60 Minutes*—because it was a news show. It would run as a two-part special: "Haldeman: The Nixon Years—Conversations with Mike Wallace."

No one bought it. The Haldeman segments had been produced by *60 Minutes* staffers, using their equipment and their offices, and the interview was running in the *60 Minutes* time slot. "CBS was flat out wrong on this," said ABC News president William Sheehan. It was, he said, "an outright buy of a news exclusive."

Indeed, the whole issue of checkbook journalism might have been forgiven outside the small circle of journalists who debate this sort of thing—if CBS had delivered the goods. But when the show was broadcast March 23 and 30, both the critics and the public were outraged.

"Mr. Haldeman was paid for the privilege of staunchly arguing his innocence on an invaluable national forum," one reviewer wrote.

"Liddy's fanaticism was fascinating," noted another critic. "Haldeman's impersonation of a Boy Scout was not."

"Bob Haldeman is no more innocent than I am," John Dean wrote in the *New York Times*. The former White House Counsel, who had pled guilty for his role in the Watergate cover-up, piously noted that the *Times* did not pay him for writing the review.

Wallace was especially stung by Dean's criticism. He claimed that Dean was upset because *60 Minutes* had turned down an offer to pay *him* for an interview six weeks earlier. "I didn't think he had anything to say that was worth the money," said Wallace. He scrambled to distance himself from the mess. "Let me make it clear that I had nothing to do with the negotiations," Wallace protested. "I was presented with a fait accompli. I'm paid to do this kind of work. I was presented with a chore."

CBS admitted that it may have made a mistake. "I'm going to reexamine the whole question," Salant said. "I may have slipped here." The real crisis over the Haldeman interview, however, was that it was a snooze. Although *60 Minutes* promised it would never again pay for an interview, it did on several occasions. It was just careful never again to pay for such a *boring* interview.

Although neither its producers nor its reporters would ever admit it, the legendary *60 Minutes*, which achieved its great success at the same time that the *National Enquirer* became the most widely read magazine in the country, employed many of the same disingenuous and arguably unethical tactics as the *Enquirer*. In fact, the story of the rise of *60 Minutes* illustrates how television adopted the techniques pioneered by the *Enquirer*, with much the same commercial results, a development that paved the way for the "tabloidization" of television in the eighties and nineties. Geraldo Rivera's true godfather is Don Hewitt.

Hewitt had long been the bad boy of TV news. He was a wunderkind and an enfant terrible who joined CBS in 1948—the year that the number of television sets in the country jumped from 15,000 to 190,000. Except for the time that he predicted that Barbara Walters would never make it as a newscaster, Hewitt had an almost uncanny knowledge of what would work in television. He produced the televised debate between Nixon and Kennedy, he worked for famed newsman Edward R. Murrow, and he soon became executive producer of the *CBS Evening News with Walter Cronkite*.

Hewitt, however, was given to gimmicks and stunts. Once, for example, while trying to report a story in Texas, Hewitt disguised himself as a sheriff to find out a competitor's coverage plans. On another occasion, he beat NBC's story on Winston Churchill's funeral by calling the airline carrying NBC's tape and pretending to be with NBC. "Don't take off," Hewitt told the Royal Canadian Air Force. "There's more videotape on the way." On another occasion, he encouraged prisoners in a New Jersey jail to resume a riot so he could get good footage of the uprising. The escapade that really got Hewitt in trouble, however, occurred during the 1964 convention, when he stole an NBC producer's confidential handbook detailing the network's plans for coverage. Hewitt was fired from Cronkite's show and was put in charge of CBS's documentaries.

Hewitt loathed the assignment. Though he could become so giddy over a good story that he would literally jump up and down in glee, he openly admitted that he was bored by most news and liked to boast that he had the shortest attention span in the television industry. The earnestly ponderous news documentaries CBS produced at the time hopelessly bored him. "I hate the word *documentary*," he declared. "No one wants to read a document, for God's sake. Who wants to watch a documentary?"

Hewitt found very few ideas that he thought deserved an hour-long show, the standard length for CBS documentaries at the time. He also thought that news documentaries could be more entertaining if they were packaged differently. "Bill Moyers did a thing called 'CBS Reports: Illegal Aliens.' It was great," he said, "but it should have been called 'The Gonzales Brothers,' and the ads should have shown the immigration service chasing two wetbacks through the back alleys of Los Angeles."

In 1968, Hewitt came up with the idea of using the magazine format in television—mixing in three or four "articles" on a variety of topics: politics, show business, crime. These pieces would, like the magazine articles after which they were fashioned, employ texture, conflict, a strong point of view, and the struggle between good and evil. They would not only have drama, they would *be* dramas. And furthermore, Hewitt thought, it would be important to position the newscasters as characters in a drama. "It's very much a question of marketing in this business," Hewitt said. "I told [CBS news head Richard] Salant that if we packaged this show like Hollywood and centered it around personalities, I'd bet we could double the documentary audience."

Not everyone welcomed his idea. "Entertainment under the guise of news," Salant objected. "I thought the idea was terrible." Nevertheless, Hewitt persuaded CBS executives to give his show a shot.

For his star reporter, Hewitt brought on Mike Wallace. The man who had pioneered tabloid television before leaving ABC in 1958 had floundered professionally for several years. He hosted game shows, conducted fluffy celebrity interviews for a show called *PM*, filmed toilet bowl cleaner commercials, and became a pitchman for Parliament cigarettes. Then, in 1962, Wallace went looking for his son Peter, who had disappeared while on a camping trip in Greece. He discovered his son's body off the side of a cliff, where he had fallen. Devastated, Wallace reevaluated his own life. He decided he wanted to get back into journalism, but almost no news organization would have him. Wallace was tainted by show business and commercialism. Finally, in March 1963, he accepted a huge cut in pay to become an anchor at a local TV station in Los Angeles. Word had spread that a redemptive Wallace—so eager to cleanse his commercialized past—had offered to buy up all the Parliament ads he had appeared in. The rumor wasn't true, but it so impressed CBS news head Dick Salant that he reconsidered his decision about Wallace. Salant hired Wallace to try to rescue the ever-stumbling *CBS Morning News*, which was getting beaten badly by *NBC's Today Show with Barbara Walters*.

At age forty-five, Wallace was being given another chance, but not everyone welcomed him. Harry Reasoner looked at the former game show host "like I was a hair in his soup" Wallace later recalled. "We were all quite contemptuous," CBS writer Joan Snyder said. "Why on earth, we wondered, had this sleazy Madison Avenue pitchman been chosen to anchor a CBS News broadcast? I would have preferred Johnny, the Philip Morris bell-hop." Wallace worked hard to prove himself, clocking in long hours, yelling at writers and producers when their work was below par—frequently dismissing bad copy or uninspired ideas as "baby shit."

Wallace left the *CBS Morning News*—it was not a good fit, especially after the time was moved up to 7 A.M. and the perennial night owl found the hours difficult. He became a field correspondent, and CBS was trying to figure out what to do with Wallace when Hewitt decided he was an ideal character for the new show *60 Minutes*.

When *60 Minutes* debuted on September 24, 1968, it was a bomb, ranking dead last of the seventy-two shows in prime time. Hewitt tinkered with the formula. He tried devoting the program to a single topic, with Harry Reasoner being positive and upbeat about the subject while Mike Wallace took a negative point of view, but that only confused viewers. Hewitt even briefly tried adding cartoons. Nothing worked. At the same time, CBS's programmers kept moving the show to various time slots—in its first three years, the show was broadcast on Mondays at ten P.M., Tuesdays at ten, Thursdays at eight, and Fridays at eight, but it was clobbered by entertainment shows like the popular *Marcus Welby*. To make matters worse, in the midst of all this shuffling Reasoner was hired away by ABC.

In 1971, *60 Minutes* was moved to Sunday at 6 P.M. It was considered a deadly time slot, but up against local news on other networks, its ratings improved slightly. What's more important,

Hewitt had further honed his formula for the program. Just as the magazines sold at newsstands had to be saucier and more sensational than the ones delivered through subscription, Hewitt's TV news magazine had to be more aggressive than the evening news, which had a built-in audience. Like the *Enquirer*, it needed to shock, to scandalize, to titillate. One segment showed well-known liberal supporters of busing sending their children to private schools. An interview with fugitive Black Panther leader Eldridge Cleaver elicited a government subpoena for the program's film and notes. Hewitt by then was mixing celebrity profiles in with the serious news segments. In one broadcast, Liz Taylor and Richard Burton bantered about his "pockmarks" and her "slightly fat belly." In another, Barbra Streisand, under questioning by Mike Wallace, broke down in tears.

Hewitt also started employing some of the more controversial tactics that are associated with tabloid journalism: ambush interviews and, especially, checkbook journalism. CBS news has repeatedly denied that it practices checkbook journalism, but *60 Minutes* has frequently paid for hot stories. A year after CBS paid Haldeman $100,000 to sit down for an interview, an ex-con claiming to know the whereabouts of Jimmy Hoffa's body demanded $10,000 in cash for the information. Amazingly, CBS News drew out ten $1,000 bills in order to buy the far-fetched Hoffa tale. The story didn't materialize and the informant absconded with the cash without leading the CBS news crew to Hoffa. The informant, Chuck Medlin, was later apprehended in a New Orleans hotel where he was playing poker with what was left of CBS's money. Medlin had tried to sell the Hoffa story to several local papers, but they had all taken a pass. "He was obviously a nut," said Charlotte Hays, a former reporter with *Figaro*, a small New Orleans weekly who spoke with him. "We got rid of him as soon as possible. He called us cowards and all sorts of other names and told us he'd be at the local Holiday Inn in case we changed our minds." The editor of *Figaro* contacted officials and told them where Medlin was staying. When the FBI burst in on Medlin, he was sitting on the floor of his hotel room, playing cards with an Arab seaman and a black hooker. Medlin handed over what was left of CBS's money: $3,100 that he had stashed under the rug. Hewitt and CBS declined to press charges against the fraudulent informant. The debacle was hugely embarrassing to the network; still, it didn't dissuade the *60 Minutes* team from whipping out the checkbook for stories. The program simply became more discreet about how the money made its way to the subject.

One way it would do this was to pay an "intermediary" who was then free to pass along a percent of the fee to the source. In 1981, for example, *60 Minutes* paid $10,000 to two fugitive gun runners, Frank E. Terpil and George Gregory Korkala. CBS insisted that it would never pay criminals for news, but admitted paying $12,000 to an "intermediary" whom network officials refused to identify. And in 1984, *60 Minutes* paid $500,000 for an interview with Richard Nixon. That money didn't go directly to Nixon; rather, it went to a former aide, Frank Gannon, who coincidentally had dated CBS correspondent Diane Sawyer. Gannon did the actual interviewing and then paid Nixon. And CBS News has repeatedly offered newspaper reporters nationwide "finders' fees" of $500 to $1,000 for tips leading to stories that make it onto *60 Minutes*. The show sometimes pays a source a "consultant" fee as it did "consultant" Jeffrey Wigland in its 1995 Brown & Williamson tobacco story.

Payments to its sources was only one of the troubling ways that *60 Minutes* gathered news. To heighten the drama in his pieces, Hewitt encouraged his correspondents to adopt a confrontational style. Balanced news, he felt, seldom made for entertaining, compelling, theatrical stories. "Tell me a story!" Hewitt used to insist. "Each segment has to be its own little morality play." While the tactics produced money-making episodes, the critics who felt that they violated journalistic standards of fairness and objectivity included CBS's own Walter Cronkite, who told the *New York Times*, "The confrontational form that sometimes produces more heat than light, I quarrel with. It is not my style. Some of the camera techniques bother me. The extreme close-up would make almost anybody look guilty. Under the hot lights perspiring, the slightest eye movement appears to be furtive."

Hewitt and his correspondents ignored such complaints. Instead of reforming their tactics, they devised elaborate new methods of staging interviews and manipulating their "news magazine" stories for dramatic effect. In one favorite ploy, *60 Minutes* crews would bring only one camera to interviews, which meant that instead of shooting the correspondent and the subject simultaneously they had to film the interview in two "takes." In the first take the camera remained on the subject, and then when the interview was over the camera would be turned to the correspondent who would then be filmed reasking the questions. Often, the correspondent would first ask the questions in a very friendly manner, lulling the subject into thinking the interview was sympathetic, only to use a very different tone, one frequently expressing shock, dismay, or surprise, when asking the questions the second time around. "I was very surprised to note that they seemed to care as much about the question as the answers," said the writer Jerzy Kosinksi, who was once interviewed by Mike Wallace for a segment on the director Roman Polanski. "I noticed it after the interview was over, when they turned the cameras around to film Mike reasking the questions. The process is very studied and very precise: He assumed an expression that was at once that of a man who knows and a boy who wants to find out, a fascinating mixture of the inquisitive and the inquisitional."

Wallace, whose background was in acting, was the preeminent practitioner of this technique. In 1976 he interviewed Gene Pope and the *National Enquirer*'s editor Iain Calder for a segment on the tabloid. During the interview, Wallace first posed his questions in a friendly manner and then in the second taping adopted an accusatory tone. When Pope later complained about the unfairness, Wallace unapologetically replied, "Gene Pope was present, right?" Wallace asked. "Then he should have interrupted." The story adopted a tone of moral indignation over what it claimed was the tabloid's practice of printing falsehoods, and to prove its point, it disputed an *Enquirer* report that Walter Cronkite earned $750,000 a year by airing a tape of the anchorman saying, "That's *not* the way it is. Not even close! Not half that!" In fact, Cronkite had a base salary of $650,000 and also received perks and three months of paid vacation that valued his total compensation at $750,000. Then to discredit a story the tabloid had run about a hot romance between Raquel Welch and Freddie

Prinze, *60 Minutes* had footage of Rona Barrett disputing the story. "Everything they wrote is totally false," said Barrett. "They are totally made up quotes. So said Raquel Welch to me!"

Before taping interviews, Wallace would sometimes cozy up to subjects off camera, making them think they were friends, joking or sympathizing with their plight, luring them into a false sense of security, hoping to get them to say something off guard on camera. Once in a while, however, the ploy backfired. In 1981 Wallace was preparing a segment on whether the San Diego Federal Savings and Loan was making loans to low-income families, especially poorly educated minorities, who couldn't afford to repay the loans. Wallace was interviewing a bank officer named Richard Carlson, and during a break in filming, Wallace started kidding around with Carlson about how complicated the loan forms were. "You bet your ass they are hard to read," Wallace said to Carlson, "if you're reading them over watermelon or over tacos." Although *60 Minutes* cameras weren't rolling, the bank had set up its own cameras. Wallace, who thought the bank's cameras were off, was furious.

Several months later, Wallace received a call from a *Wall Street Journal* reporter asking about the incident. Wallace was able to persuade the reporter that there was no story. The *60 Minutes* correspondent then called the bank, complaining that the *Journal* was trying to "destroy" him and asking the bank to erase the tapes. "Look," Wallace reportedly said, "I know this is not a very good thing to ask in this era of erased tapes [but] I would be exceedingly grateful if you would excise them for me." Wallace had almost forgotten about the incident—and, some say, the segment—when the *New York Times* called. Again, Wallace talked the paper out of writing about the incident. Then, a reporter from the *Los Angeles Times* called. Under the same sort of aggressive questioning he himself employed, Wallace admitted that he has a "penchant for obscenity and for jokes," and he tried to justify his comments about "tacos" and "watermelons" by arguing that the remark had been partly tactical, intended to elicit "some hint of [Carlson's] feeling toward the minority community."

On other occasions, Wallace was accused of conflicts of interest, such as when he accepted a speaking fee from Amway, a company he had recently investigated, or when he put pressure on his colleague, Ed Bradley, to go soft on an investigation of Haiti, where his then wife had family and business concerns.

Hewitt and Wallace also had reputations as incorrigible womanizers. When Hewitt was called in to rescue Sally Quinn during her disastrous stint as co-host of CBS *Morning News*, he informed her they were going to have an affair. Quinn declined, explaining that she was dating Ben Bradlee. "Don't give me that shit," Hewitt told Quinn, according to her account in *We're Going to Make You a Star*. When she continued to rebuff him, he stopped helping her show, but told her: "Well, if you won't sleep with me, I'll sleep with Barbara Walters." According to one report—which Hewitt vehemently denied—he once pinned a subordinate against a wall and stuck his tongue down her throat. She freed herself by kneeing him in the groin. Hewitt's star reporter, Mike Wallace, also had a reputation for unwelcome sexual friskiness with co-workers: slapping their bottoms, undoing or snapping their bra straps, or putting his hands on their thighs. "One producer said that basically, Mike Wallace and Don Hewitt thought this was their right," according to Mark Hertsgaard, who wrote about *60 Minutes* for *Rolling Stone*. Hertsgaard later claimed that after Hewitt called and complained to editor Jann Wenner, the most shocking details of the piece were cut. "Sexual harassment was not the point of the investigation," according to Hertsgaard, "it was just so pervasive at the time that you couldn't miss it."

"I'm just an old fashioned guy," Wallace said in his defense. "I come from a time when joking about that sort of thing was commonplace. And that's what I was doing. Joking." Hewitt chose not to comment on the allegations.

Despite Hewitt's reputation as a womanizer, he apparently had few qualms about broadcasting a segment in which Kathleen Willey accused President Clinton of groping her in a manner much less offensive than Hewitt's own alleged advances. "It was odd to me, seeing Don quoted in the *New York Times*," Hertsgaard later noted. "He's talking about what [Clinton allegedly did to Willey], and I just thought of that old Dylan song [lyric], 'You've got a lot of nerve.' "

Critics charged that Hewitt's team had coached Willey and

edited the tape to make her look good. Some said it was to make the story stronger. Some said Hewitt was motivated by revenge. Several years earlier, when Bill Clinton's candidacy was nearly derailed by Gennifer Flowers's charges that they had been sexually involved, it was a *60 Minutes* segment that put his campaign back on track. "They came to us because they were in big trouble in New Hampshire," Don Hewitt reportedly said later. "They were about to lose right there and they needed some first aid. They needed some bandaging. What they needed was a paramedic. So they came to us and we did it and that's what they wanted to do." According to columnists Jack Germond and Jules Witcover, Don Hewitt told Bill Clinton just before the interview: "The last time I did something like this, Bill, it was the Kennedy-Nixon debates, and it produced a President. This will produce a President, too." Hewitt heard afterward that Hillary Clinton was upset because she didn't like the way the segment had been edited. Clinton adviser Mandy Grunwald complained to Hewitt that the candidate and his wife had wanted to discuss politics. "I said to Mandy, 'You know, if I'd edited it your way, you know where you'd be today? You'd be sitting up in New Hampshire looking for the nomination.' He became the candidate that night." To Hillary, he says, he wrote a letter. "Sore losers I understand. Sore winners are beyond me. What are you sore about?" Although he says he never doubted Gennifer Flowers's story, it had already been out. Good television had to be a revelation—even if you didn't believe what was behind the revelation.

Despite the personal and professional behavior of Hewitt and his star reporter Wallace, *60 Minutes* became both one of the most profitable programs in the history of network television and was celebrated as a model of journalistic integrity. It climbed from seventy-second in the ratings in its 1968 debut to fifty-second in 1975, to eighteenth in 1977 and to number four in 1978. By the late 1970s, *60 Minutes* was the envy of the other networks. "As the most honored show on television, with dozens of Emmys, Peabodys and Polks to its credit, '60 Minutes' has added immeasurably to its network's prestige," the *New York Times* noted in 1979. " '60 Minutes' is CBS's only regular entry in the top 10 and as such is able to charge as much as $215,000 per commercial minute. Since the show is, by television standards, comparatively inexpensive to produce, coming in at around $200,000 a week, and since each show offers six commercial minutes, the profit margin is significant."

"There's nothing tabloidy about ambush journalism," Mike Wallace insisted. "Unless you're doing it for drama, in which case it's to be deplored. . . . After a while, we realized that we had become, to a degree, caricatures of ourselves because we were paying more attention to the drama than to the illumination of an issue."

Through shrewd packaging and an uncanny understanding of which targets to aim for, Don Hewitt had created a news magazine that escaped the label of tabloid, but it was, in fact, exactly that: entertainment disguised as news. By the late 1970s all of Don Hewitt's past transgressions had been forgiven or forgotten and the man who staged interviews and paid sources for stories was lecturing at colleges and journalism centers about the evils of tabloid television and the relentless quest for ratings.

"I think that sensationalism is a wonderful word," said Wallace, "if by sensationalism you mean, 'Hey! Holy shit! I didn't know that!' That's really what we do."

From time to time, Hewitt also acknowledged his role in the tabloidization of television news. " '60 Minutes' has single-handedly ruined television," he once admitted. "No one can report news today without making money."

9

---

gossip goes mainstream

Cher was the sort of celebrity, Dick Stolley knew, who sometimes needed to be protected from herself. It was 1976, two years after Time Inc. had launched the much-maligned but wildly popular *People* magazine with Stolley at the helm, and Cher was one of the magazine's favorite cover subjects. During the 1970s, Cher and *People* would work to serve each other well—both riding that decade's rediscovery of celebrity voyeurism. It was a symbiotic relationship, one that depended on reciprocal cooperation. Cher would appear on the cover of *People* magazine more than any other star in the 1970s—and nearly every issue became that year's best-seller. Over the years, *People* frequently came across—and ignored—embarrassing information about the flamboyant singer, including the time she and Sonny had his-and-her nose jobs and how Cher had her breasts lifted and they had become infected from the surgery. Although Cher had a neurotically shy side, she also was an exhibitionist who loved publicity; back before she was famous she would stand in front of a mirror and practice telling paparazzi and autograph hounds to leave her alone. "There are too many of you," she would tell the imaginary crowds. "I just don't have time for all of you." Cher had the conflicting feelings toward fame that is so common among celebrities—she would complain about invasions into her privacy while telling reporters details about her latest est session. She loved saying outrageous things to the press. "Feel my ass," she once told boyfriend David Geffen while a journalist was just trying to interview him. "Hard as a rock." Then, still in full view of the reporter, she ran her tongue all over Geffen and stuck it in his mouth.

By September 1976, Cher had dumped Geffen, had a Vegas wedding to Gregg Allman, whom *People* called a "coked-out cracker of a rock star," had an on-air reunion with Sonny while she was pregnant with Allman's baby, and encouraged Allman to testify against his friends in a very messy drug trial. "Our whole world as we knew it was shot to ratshit," Cher complained. "I ought to write a soap opera." Instead, she decided to tell all to *People.* "The Hollywood community was a little appalled that someone would talk so openly about her husband's drug problems," said a *People* editor, who decided that the drama would make a good cover story. A reporter visited Cher at the Beverly Hills house she had shared with Allman, who had swelled from reed-thin to two hundred pounds and bopped around the house during the interview wearing sandals. "Why do you feel so strongly about this drug issue?" the reporter asked Cher.

"Because," Cher matter-of-factly told the reporter, "my father was a heroin addict."

Back at the Time-Life building, top *People* editors had a meeting to discuss what to do with this explosive bit of information. They decided, first, to make sure it was accurate. They located Cher's father, John Sarkisian, who was living in a retirement community. "The story was true and would have been very big news at the time," said Stolley. "Everybody in this man's retirement community knew that he was Cher's dad, but nobody knew about his history with addiction. He most definitely did not want it made public."

Stolley consulted with *People*'s lawyer. "He said we could go with it," said Stolley. "We had it nailed. It wasn't libel. The privacy issue was a close call, but we could probably get away with it." Stolley had the information edited out of the story. "I was not going to ruin that old man's life," he said, "just for the sake of gossip."*

Stolley said he has no regrets. "I think gossip can be the enemy of civilization," Stolley declared. He actually banned the word *gossip* from the pages of *People* when he was the editor there. "I think the dissemination of cruel, mean-spirited information which is fundamentally disturbing to a human being, to his family, to his friends, is a blow to civilized society." Such sentiments may sound surprisingly high-minded coming from the founding editor of *People* magazine—the publication that brought tabloid topics out of Tabloid Valley and into the mainstream—but Stolley wasn't motivated solely by the moral issue at hand; there was also a strong element of pragmatism in his philosophy. At the time Cher told *People* about her father's addiction, she was happy for the magazine to use it. But, Stolley knew, such spontaneous revelations often came back to haunt celebrities. In its early days, *People* protected its subjects from such self-destructive disclosures.

The Cher episode was not an isolated incident. There was the time that a then wildly popular country and western singer told *People* that the only reason he married his wife was because he got her pregnant. Or the time Truman Capote, fresh out of an alcohol rehab center, invited *People* to accompany him to a gym to do an article on his new healthy lifestyle. During the interview, Capote downed two glasses of vodka and kept falling over, but the *People* reporter helped prop the writer up on a Nautilus machine long enough to get pictures.

"Celebrities were very naïve back then," said Stolley. "We had to be very, very careful about what we would let them say. They would talk about their problems or their ex-husbands or ex-wives in the most scurrilous ways. They were venting. It was like they were talking to their psychiatrist. We constantly had to censor them to protect them from themselves."

Stolley knew that if *People* magazine started to burn its subjects—even if it was with the star's own words—celebrities would stop coming to the magazine with their stories. It would mean

* John Sarkisian died in 1985.

the end of a cozy relationship that had made *People* magazine the publishing phenomenon of the decade. "*People* will never stoop to the cheap thrill," Stolley vowed when the magazine was launched in 1974. "We will not pander to baser instincts." Of course, he wasn't about to fill *People* with articles about Vietnam or Watergate, either. He had already worked for a magazine that did that, and it all ended in one of the most traumatic experiences of his life.

That December morning in 1972 was still vivid in Stolley's mind. He was an assistant managing editor of *Life* magazine, and had been summoned with three hundred other journalists to the eighth floor auditorium of the Time-Life Building that cold, overcast Friday to listen as a succession of men in gray suits struggled to justify the inevitable. The crowd was filled with some of the most world-weary photographers and editors in the country, but sometimes even they succumbed. Faces were streaked with tears, and occasionally a body here or there would heave with stifled sobs. Even the men at the podium, the bean counters and the top corporate editors who made the decision, were so distraught that their voices cracked in midsentence:

". . . I deeply regret to tell you that after this issue, *Life* magazine will be no more. . . ."
". . . the emotional agony behind this move . . ."
". . . we did everything possible . . ."
". . . this painful decision . . ."
It was a wake for what many believed to be the absolute best that the world of journalism had to offer. *Life* was only thirty-six years old, but it had the aura of an immortal. One by one, the other great picture magazines had died: the esteemed *Saturday Evening Post* succumbed in 1969, and *Look* fell in 1971. For months rumors had swirled that *Life* magazine was next, but no one believed them. Then, on that Friday, December 8, 1972, came the official word that those terrible rumors were true.

Life was still a great magazine. It ran intelligent articles and important photographs on the issues of the times: shocking picture essays of Vietnam and the My Lai massacre, revealing photos of Woodstock, horrifying shots of race riots in Birmingham. *Life* was an expensive operation, with a huge staff and bureaus around the world. Circulation was still very high: 5.5 million, but the figure was misleading; Time Inc. was so eager to keep the number up that it was charging readers less than it cost to publish *Life*. Almost all the magazine's sales came from subscriptions, and Time Inc. offered deals so that many people were getting *Life* for about ten cents an issue; it cost twenty-six cents an issue to produce and mail. The difference was supposed to be made up in ad revenue, but by 1971, a one-page color ad in *Life* cost $50,000— more than a one-minute commercial on prime time television. Advertisers had been deserting the magazine for television, and if *Life* tried to increase revenue by hiking its ad rates, it would lose even more advertisers. *Life* magazine had lost more than $47 million over the previous three years.

Not everyone mourned the death. "It's no great loss," said an ad executive from Ted Bates & Co. "*Life* didn't die of a sudden heart attack, but rather of hardening of the arteries." Wall Street applauded the move: The day of the announcement, Time-Life's stock went up $6.50. The next day it was up again, a total of ten points for the two days, to $59.

The hardest thing, some thought, would be breaking the news to Clare Booth Luce, the feisty widow of Time-Life founder Henry Luce. She was a big champion of *Life* in its early years and continued to be a brilliant cultural arbiter. Reached at her home in Honolulu, Luce said, "I was wondering when you fellows would get around to it."

The still-shaken *Life* staff headed back to their offices to put together a farewell issue. "We have this last issue to cling to," said Stolley, "and suspend belief that it's all over." Then, a reporter from a local television station came in and started nosing around with his camera crew, trying to interview people. Most turned their backs or left the area to avoid the intruder, but famed photojournalist Co Rentmeester feared no one. When the TV reporter approached the photographer, and asked a question or two, Rentmeester hauled off and belted the television man squarely in the jaw. Some *Life* staffers cheered him on, others tried to hold him back. Everyone, however, knew that no matter who won the fight, *Life* had lost the battle. "I have that same terrible feeling you have when you hear a declaration of war," said Jozefa Stuart, editor of *Life*'s entertainment department. "It's that feeling you get when you know that there's going to be a terrible change in your life."

By 1973, the world was changing, and Time Inc wasn't. The company had faltered in several attempts to break into the television industry, and efforts to come up with new print titles weren't faring much better. Time Inc. hadn't successfully launched a weekly magazine in twenty years. Executives there put together a team of experts—dubbed the Magazine Development Group—whose sole purpose was to come up with a magazine that the public wanted to read. They analyzed spending patterns, devised flow charts, contemplated social trends, and quizzed demographic groups without success. They proposed a magazine for liberated women, a fitness and health magazine, an upscale photography magazine, but none of their ideas tested well in the marketplace. At the time, the two best-selling weeklies in the country were the *National Enquirer* and *TV Guide*, but Time Inc. was considered a reputable publisher that didn't traffic in that sort of fare.

Then, Andrew Heiskell, the chairman of the board at Time Inc., came up with a proposal for a magazine devoted exclusively to covering people. No events, no issues, just people. The idea was not warmly received. The MBAs who were consulting to the Magazine Development Board called it "one of the stupidest publishing ideas we'd ever heard of." Members of the group ridiculed the idea and dragged their feet, but because the idea came from Heiskell, it was pushed through. The Time chairman would periodically pop by, asking "How you doing with my *People* idea?" When a test issue was put together, it was widely held in contempt at Time Inc. "The consensus [on *People*] was powerfully negative," recalled one member of the Committee. "The words most often used were 'sleazy' and 'cheap.'"

A copy was sent to Henry Luce's unsentimental widow. She liked it. More important, she showed the magazine to her manicurist, secretary, maids, cook, and hairdresser. They loved *People*—and they were the potential readers. "Please let me know how you make out with the advertisers," Clare Booth Luce wrote. "If you make out well, nothing can stop *People*."

In 1973, Dick Stolley was considering getting out of the journalism business. "The death of *Life* was a terrible experience," he said. "When one magazine has broken your heart," he said, "why give another one the same chance?" Stolley had fallen in love with journalism at a very early age; he became the sports editor of his hometown paper in Pekin, Illinois, when he was fifteen years old; he would rise at 5 A.M. and head to the newspaper office before going to high school. After attending Northwestern's journalism school, he had a few newspaper jobs before he ended up at *Life*, where he spent nineteen years. Stolley was one of *Life*'s brightest stars. He ran the magazine's biggest bureaus, including those in Los Angeles, Washington, and Paris. It was Dick Stolley who negotiated the famous, if somewhat controversial, deal to pay $150,000 for the exclusive rights to the Zapruder film of Kennedy's assassination. When *Life* folded, Time executives were eager to keep Stolley and parked him on the Magazine Development Committee. Stolley wasn't sure he'd stay. He was considering quitting the business altogether, going back to Illinois and running for political office, or possibly becoming a professor or getting a degree in law. Anything but journalism, which seemed to be a dying industry.

Then Stolley saw the test issue for *People* magazine. The cover featured a grinning Liz Taylor, decked out in a denim cap and an embroidered denim jacket. Inside were grainy photographs of Taylor and Burton, who had just been through one of their many very public battles, attempting a reconciliation at Sophia Loren's villa. The pictures looked as if they'd been shot with a paparazzo's telephoto lens; the short, jagged text seemed to have been hammered out on an ancient typewriter in somebody's basement. Other articles in the issue peeked at Ali McGraw's romance with Steve McQueen and at Faye Dunaway's various escapades. There was even a shot of Barbara Carrera, then the Chiquita Banana Girl, topless. The entire package was appallingly cheap and obvious. "It looked," Stolley recalled, "like a whore house magazine."

As Stolley thumbed through the tawdry, vulgar magazine that

was so unlike his beloved *Life* or anything that the distinguished Time Inc. had ever published, his spirits lifted and the bounce returned to his step, because he realized that maybe there was a future for print journalism after all.

In August 1973, Time Inc. tested its Liz Taylor issue in eleven cities; the results were startling. In some areas, it sold 38.4 percent of issues on newsstands, which is quite respectable, but in cities where *People* was promoted on television, it sold an almost unheard of 85.2 percent. The message was clear: *People* was aiming for the television audience.

"I said, 'I want to run this magazine,' " Stolley said. "I liked it, but I really wanted to redesign it, because it looked like a piece of shit . . . In that form it seemed sleazy, shocking. To make it work, you had to encase it in a comfortable, conventional format." The first thing to go was the topless motif; several distributors refused to carry the test issue of *People* because of the risqué Chiquita Banana photo. "Boy, I learned my lesson on that one," Stolley said. "You could print hair-raising information about people's relationships, sex lives, and finances . . . but no breasts."

Stolley had to figure out what the magazine would be. "It's hard to understand, today, in this celebrity-saturated world, how revolutionary *People* was. Newspapers and news magazines were totally ignoring personalities," said Stolley. Women's magazines still had cakes and crochet on their covers. "There wasn't a niche. There was a wide open crevice."

Although newspapers and magazines across the country were closing or cutting back, investigative reporting was going through an almost unprecedented vogue. Watergate dominated the papers. Carl Bernstein and Bob Woodward were stars, role models that just about every other journalist in the country followed. There were more students enrolled in journalism schools than there were journalism jobs. In the mid-1970s, journalism was serious business. "It was a time when individuals got submerged, buried," Stolley recalled. "For the most part, the news was depressing." *People* would not be. *People* made no pretensions to being an indepth magazine. Many items were very short, a few paragraphs, and the upper limit for most stories was 1,500 words. The entire issue would be limited to 13,000 words. Stolley would actually sit there counting them. "This was going to be a quick, easy read," said Stolley, "which most of the magazines were not."

People was done on the cheap; Time Inc. wasn't completely committed to the project, and didn't want to get caught up in the expensive news-gathering operation that *Life* had become. The entire editorial staff numbered only thirty-four, a minuscule number for a weekly magazine. *Life*, at its peak, had more than ten times as many. Most of the reporting was done by a staff of sixty-six stringers, often newspaper reporters who were paid $7.50 an hour. The articles were usually rewritten by editors in a snappy, chatty style. Stolley—determined not to make the magazine a reincarnation of *Life*—didn't want to hire too many of his colleagues from the recently folded magazine. It wasn't a problem. Not many wanted to join. In fact, very few people from inside the Time-Life corporation wanted to be part of the new enterprise.

The first year was rough. Ad pages were cheap, $4,550 for black and white, $5,800 for color—slightly more than one-tenth what *Life* had charged. Nevertheless, the first several issues of *People* were quite thin. The first issue carried twenty pages of ads, and there were only 601 advertising pages that year. "The advertisers remembered *Confidential*," said Stolley, "and it scared the hell out of them."

The cover of the first regular issue, dated March 4, 1974, featured Mia Farrow, who was starring in *The Great Gatsby*, nibbling on a strand of pearls. Inside was a little something for everyone: profiles of authors Alexander Solzhenitsyn and Clifford Irving, as well as pieces on porn star Linda Lovelace, *Exorcist* author and producer William Blatty, kidnapped socialite Patricia Hearst, gymnast Cathy Rigby, actresses Debbie Reynolds and Joanne Woodward, and Lee Harvey Oswald's widow, Marina. The magazine was still clearly trying to find its market, but wanted to make it clear that it was not *Confidential* revisited. "We think of *People* as a very contemporary magazine," Stolley noted, "one attuned to the free-wheeling seventies and its mood of burning curiosity, wry detachment, and tolerance for other people's manners and morals. We want *People* to reflect the times."

People was greeted with hoots of derision and howls of protest. It was referred to as "Peephole." It was parodied in *Esquire* and in *National Lampoon*. It was called "celebrity pap" and "fluff and puff." *Newsweek* predicted that it would run out of people to profile. "We were universally scorned and put down by our journalistic colleagues," former executive producer Jim Seymore recalled. His friends at serious publications would mock *People* at cocktail parties, but as soon as they were alone, they would corner him and ask him what various celebrities were *really* like.

William Safire, the esteemed columnist for the *New York Times*, was perhaps the harshest critic. "By the choice of topics, the *Time* editors . . . give us their frank assessment of [*People*'s] audience: A collection of frantic, tasteless fadcats, deeply concerned with social climbing and intellectual pretensions, panting for a look at celebrities in poses that press agents staged back in the thirties," he wrote. "Maybe there is money in this sort of thing; if so, publishing empires whose executives harrumph about social responsibility should leave the field to upstart publishers more adept at grubbiness." Stolley tacked Safire's essay to his bulletin board. Whenever he got tired or discouraged, he'd read Safire's sneering putdown, start seething, and he'd find the energy to go on.

The reaction inside the Time-Life building was even more hostile. "It was very tough in those first few years," said one former reporter. "We were putting in these eighty- and ninety-hour weeks, working until four or five three nights a week, and you'd hear people joking in the elevator about how we weren't really journalists. If they knew you were with *People*, they'd just sort of be quiet and move away, as if they were afraid they might catch something. I dreaded taking the elevators."

"Do you know the word *pariah*?" Stolley said. "Well, that pretty well describes how we were regarded. . . . There was great concern—especially with the distinguished *Life* having recently died and the body hardly cold—that we were cheapening the precarious coin of the Time Inc. realm." Then one day, Stolley rode down in the elevator with a *Time* writer, who turned to him and said, "I know you're taking a lot of crap about this magazine, but I'm telling you, it's getting better. I like it." He paused then added, "More important, it's going to pay my pension some day."

* * *

In the early issues, *People* editors were still trying to figure out exactly what sort of celebrity stories America was interested in reading. The common wisdom was that contemporary stars were all unglamorous and boring and that the public was more fascinated by the Golden Age of Hollywood. As an experiment to gauge the public's interest in that period, *People* located one of the great old gossip columnists to contribute to the first issue. Walter Winchell, Dorothy Kilgallen, Hedda Hopper, and Louella Parsons were all dead, but the great Sheila Graham was still alive. Graham, who sometimes was lumped together with Louella and Hedda as "The Unholy Trio," was the least famous of the three, but toward the end of their careers, Graham was actually syndicated in more newspapers than either of her rivals. She also had the most fascinating life. Born Lily Sheil, Graham grew up in an orphanage in London's East End. She wanted to become a writer, but was terribly insecure about her lack of a proper education and took jobs as a domestic, a toothbrush demonstrator, and a showgirl in London before she came to Los Angeles, with hopes of launching her writing career. "No one there could embarrass me with erudite conversation," she later explained. "Hollywood was notorious even in London for the ignorance of the people who made the films." Within three years, she had a syndicated column that, she claimed, earned $5,000 a week. She had an affair with F. Scott Fitzgerald, whose career was on the skids and who tutored Graham, giving her lists of books to read and quizzing her on them afterward. They had a tortured relationship, however; he refused to leave his institutionalized wife Zelda, and he frequently went on drunken rages during which he would mock Graham relentlessly about her ignorance and her Jewish background. Fitzgerald used Graham as the inspiration for Kathleen from *The Last Tycoon*, and he died in her arms. She wrote about their relationship in *Beloved Infidel*, which in 1959 was made into a movie.

People asked Graham, who had recently retired and moved from Hollywood to Palm Beach, to write an article for its first issue, comparing the film community she had left with the old money society she had recently entered. When Graham handed in her manuscript, the editors were shocked. "It turned out that the poor woman couldn't put two words back to back," according to Hal Wingo, the editor who oversaw the piece. "She was almost illiterate. It was almost comical. Here she was F. Scott Fitzgerald's mistress and this fabled writer of columns all these years and she could hardly construct a sentence."

Buried deep inside the piece was a startling bit of information: In discussing how someone with an unsavory past could make it in Hollywood, Graham wrote "you can be a illegitimate, as Marilyn Monroe was" you could "have a juvenile delinquency record, as Steve McQueen did," or you could be a call girl, "as I was." "I remember very clearly when I read this my jaw dropped," said Wingo. "I said, 'Well this is an interesting admission on her part anyway.' " Wingo rewrote much of Graham's story, but, he said, he carefully read back the entire text to her—including the explosive "call girl" sentence.

When the issue hit the newsstands, Graham went ballistic. She had never, she insisted, written that she was a former call girl. It was a typo, she maintained, and should have read "J" was a former call girl—"J" was the anonymous author of the best-selling book, *The Sensuous Woman*. The article was libelous, Graham said, and she hired lawyer Edward Bennett Williams to sue *People*. Getting sued for such a howler of an error in its first issue—by the person who ostensibly wrote the article—would have given *People*'s many critics additional ammunition. "The whole joke about *People* from the beginning was that we would have a staff of three writers and ten lawyers, so this was not good for our first issue," said Wingo. *People* paid for Graham to come to New York, during which time she was treated like a star, and ran a "clarification" in the "Chatter" section of the magazine. "From Sheila Graham comes word that the eyebrow-raising phrase in her by-lined story . . . should have read "former 'chorus' girl," the item explained. It went on to quote Graham, "As I have written in several of my books, I have always believed in love. I was so busy in this area that I didn't have time to consider the financial aspects."*

---

* Graham's disclaimer was slightly disingenuous. Graham was obsessed with money and once confessed that she often used sex to get what she wanted. Her first marriage was to a man twenty-five years her senior, who would arrange dates with wealthy men, and he and Graham sometimes lived off the proceeds of the "gifts" the dates gave her.

One of the truly startling things about the Sheila Graham debacle is that hardly anyone noticed. *People* had accidentally called one of the most famous gossip columnists of her time a call girl, and no one seemed to care. It was a clear sign that *People* shouldn't cater to a nostalgia for Hollywood. What many other editors had long interpreted as a lack of interest in gossip was in fact, merely boredom with the old stars they continued to write about.

The public's apparent aversion to gossip was also, at least partially, the result of a more than decade-long vilification of gossip columnists. It was a crusade that went into full throttle at the *Confidential* trial and was continued through the 1960s by some of the nation's most popular stars, such as Frank Sinatra, and beloved politicians, like the Kennedys. By the mid-1970s, the *idea* of gossip was repugnant to most Americans, but they had never lost their appetite for juicy tidbits about celebrities. Readers liked gossip best, *People* realized, if it wasn't served up by gossip columnists.

Readers weren't the only ones hungry for celebrity news. The celebrities themselves were starved. "Stars clamored to be profiled," remembered one reporter. "We could really call the shots. We'd set these conditions back then that we had to be allowed into the celebrity's home, they had to tell us personal and private things. There were so many stars wanting to be interviewed, that once, in a single day, I had breakfast with Nelson Rockefeller, lunch with Gloria Swanson, and dinner with Sophia Loren."

Dick Stolley worked hard to ensure the notion that *People's* brand of gossip was harmless fun. "I think it was important that the magazine established a reputation for not only fairness and decency but also kindness," he said. "*People* is a good cheer magazine and always has been. It is also a magazine that has tended to be kind to people—not to say it hasn't embarrassed people and hurt people." Nevertheless, *People* staffers were continually shocked by the confessions celebrities would make.

Celebrities, and even politicians, were so unfamiliar with dealing with the press that they used to blurt out things that they never would have a decade later. "Sex and money were two of the things no one had asked celebrities about before," said Stolley, "and damned if they didn't answer." Rosalynn Carter told *People* about her plastic surgery. Gloria Steinem caused an uproar when she posed for photographers in a bubble bath.

"The awfulest things about them would come out of their own mouths and they often had no idea what they were saying," said Stolley. "There was a kind of wonderful innocence then. Particularly when it came to people talking about themselves or their spouses, children and all the rest—we were very, very careful about what we let people say."

People was rewarded for its kindness. Stars lined up to appear in the magazine. One of them was Elizabeth Taylor. *People*'s original cover girl, Stolley discovered, sold every time she appeared on the cover. One of the things that the *People* editors realized was that a celebrity didn't sell well just because he or she was famous; the star had to be *doing* something to be newsworthy. "Elizabeth Taylor was always doing *something*—getting married, getting divorced or having medical emergencies," said Stolley. "She had a great sense of drama about herself . . . and she regularly made herself available" to *People* in the early days. "Readers loved her," says Stolley. "She represented tough American glamour at its best."

Early on, *People* wasn't always reverential to old stars. In its second issue, the magazine ran an interview with Lucille Ball. "She looked, but did not act, her age," noted the writer, who reported the sixty-three-year-old actress's diatribes against contemporary films (she blasted them as "a marathon of sex and perversion"), Marlon Brando, who was starring in the sexually provocative *Last Tango In Paris* ("I'll hit him when I see him," Ball said. "I'll punch him right in the nose, and I hope I have these rings on."), and her loose false eyelashes. ("Goddamn this thing won't stay on!") Angry letters to the editor followed.

When Joan Crawford died, *People* commissioned gossip columnist Doris Lilly to write an article about her. Lilly, who lived in the same building as Crawford and was quite friendly with the actress, believed that the Hollywood legend had committed suicide and had compelling evidence to support the theory.* Lilly

---

* Such as the way that Crawford sent away her beloved dog, from whom she was never separated, the weekend that she died. The theory has since been put forward by recent biographers.

also had delicious anecdotes about Crawford's eccentricities.* "The last time I saw her was two weeks before she died," Lilly wrote. "She had hurt her back scrubbing floors. We gossiped. Joan Crawford *loved* to gossip. She said, 'The so-called actresses of today look like they don't bathe and they don't memorize their lines. I think most of them took acting lessons from the A&P.' " Lilly also wrote that Joan Crawford had a love affair with Clark Gable—which would have been a big scoop for *People*. It, and much of the rest of the article for which Lilly was paid $500, was cut. *People* wasn't interested in the Golden Age of Hollywood and it wasn't interested in exposing love affairs or other scandals.

Even during this honeymoon period, however, *People* clashed with a few celebrities. Warren Beatty was one. Beatty had a peculiar relationship with the press. During the filming of his breakthrough 1961 movie, *Splendor in the Grass*, Beatty was living with Joan Collins, whom he had recently convinced to get an abortion, and co-star Natalie Wood was married to Robert Wagner, in what was widely believed to be one of the film world's happiest marriages. Then columnist Dorothy Kilgallen reported that Beatty and Wood were "staying up nights rehearsing their next day's love scenes." Hollywood was shocked.[†] Around that time Beatty had another unpleasant media experience when he was interviewed by Joe Hyams for *Show Business Illustrated*. Beatty rambled almost incoherently during much of the conversation, pausing only to scratch his head or pick his nose. Hyams was shocked by the number of times "fuck" erupted from Beatty's mouth at a time when movie stars didn't talk like that. Hyams was not impressed and said so in the article.

After that, Beatty, for the most part, refused to give inter-

---

* During a sanitation strike, for example, Crawford had her trash put in Bergdorf Goodman boxes complete with big purple bows before she had them taken out. Despite rumors that her house was all carpeted in white, Crawford had all her carpets thrown out because she could never get them entirely dirt free. She also had all her furniture and even her walls coated in plastic so she could clean them better.

† Louella Parsons declared it the greatest tragedy since Mary Pickford and Douglas Fairbanks split. Elizabeth Taylor, who had recently busted up Debbie Reynolds and Eddie Fisher, claimed that the scandal had traumatized her so badly that she had to sedate herself with tranquilizers and take to bed.

views. "Most of what I say is unprintable, anyway," Beatty told Rex Reed. "Most movie stars are not interesting, so to sell papers and magazines in the fading publications field, a writer has to end up writing his ass off to make somebody more interesting than he is, right? What do I need with publicity?"

But in 1975, Beatty was releasing *Shampoo* and very much wanted publicity. *People* was the perfect outlet. "I wanted to challenge the assumption that a hypersexual character with women, a Don Juan, is a misogynist or a latent homosexual," said Beatty, who had been linked with Michelle Phillips, Julie Christie, Jean Seberg, Susannah York, Leslie Caron, and others. "Even the promiscuous feel pain." The profile was mostly flattering, but reporter Barbara Wilkins reported an alleged encounter in which Beatty tried to seduce a photographer on one of his movies, unzipping her pants on the set of the film and getting her fired when she rebuffed his advances. After the story appeared, Beatty called Stolley, furiously denying that any such incident occurred and demanding a retraction.

"We had several screaming conversations," says Stolley. "I tried to calm him down, tried to do damage control." Stolley refused to run a retraction, and got ready to be blackballed by the power elite of Hollywood. It didn't happen. "I think Warren was more isolated than we thought at this point," Stolley said. "No one in Hollywood would believe his story, and I think we worried unnecessarily." Eventually, Beatty dropped the issue, and the two men ran into each other at a Hollywood party, shook hands, and chatted about politics. "Being on the cover of *People* was a pretty big deal then," said Stolley. "No one was going to alienate himself from the magazine entirely."

People was on its way to becoming one of the most successful magazines in the history of publishing. Stolley quickly realized that he had to cater to public tastes, not dictate them as *Life* had done. The strategy was a radical departure for upscale magazines. It was also a survival tactic.

In a further effort to avoid the same fate as *Life*, *People* avoided the high price of postage and in its early years, was available only on newsstands. It lived or died, therefore, on the appeal of its cover. A dud meant a $1 million drop in ad and newsstand revenue. Choosing a cover was the most important decision for each issue, and Stolley carefully studied patterns of what worked and what didn't. "We were very pragmatic," said Stolley. "If someone didn't work well on the cover, that person didn't make the cover again." Some would call it a movement toward populism, but many in the industry blasted it as shameless pandering. Stolley remained unapologetic. "A cover is not a benediction," he bristled. "It's a marketing tool."

Early on, Stolley found that imaginative or artistically compelling covers weren't necessarily good sellers. *People*'s second cover depicted eccentric billionaire John Paul Getty. It was a stunning photo, taken by famed *Life* photographer Alfred Eisenstadt, in which Getty was backlit, his craggy, deeply lined face in stark contrast to a perfect, delicate daffodil he was holding. It bombed on the newsstands.

Celebrities were just about the only subjects that could be counted on to sell well. Politicians almost always sold poorly. Much to everyone's surprise, Teddy Kennedy was one of the first year's worst sellers. He was beaten by Joan Kennedy. Even Watergate, the hottest political story in the country, didn't interest readers. *People* ran three Watergate covers during its early years. "They didn't sell worth a damn," said Stolley. Ideally, the cover subject had to be recognized by eighty-five percent of Americans—which ruled out most politicians and many actors. "Liv Ullman is an example," said Stolley. "She had acted in mostly art house films. She may have *deserved* a *People* cover, but she didn't belong there." Once, when *People* was doing an issue on celebrity gardening, Stolley realized that none of the actors in the story was a big enough star for the cover. He called his good friend, actress Ann-Margret. "I'm in a jam," he told the actress. "Do you ever garden?"

The actress was somewhat perplexed. "I have a gardener," she said.

Stolley was desperate. "Didn't you ever plant a seed when you were a kid?"

"Yes," Ann-Margret said.

"That's good enough for me," Stolley declared. "I'm going to have you photographed in the next twenty-four hours."

Common wisdom held that singers and musicians didn't sell well on covers, but when an Olivia Newton John cover nearly sold out, the editors reconsidered the rules. Television actors, surprisingly, usually sold better than movie stars. Themes emerged and Stolley developed what is known as "Stolley's Formula." It went:

> *Young is better than old*
> *Pretty is better than ugly*
> *Rich is better than poor*
> *TV is better than music.*
> *Music is better than movies*
> *Movies are better than Sports*
> *And anything is better than politics.*

The findings, which critics considered the ultimate triumph of marketing over journalism, turned on its head the conventional hierarchy of news, where nothing was more sacred than politics, and television was perhaps the lowest order. Beyond Stolley's Formula, he devised what he called the X Factor. Some people just fascinated the readers. Mary Tyler Moore, much to his surprise, didn't. "Under my formula, she should have sold through the roof," said Stolley. "The public loved her, but they had no curiosity about her. There was no X factor."

Then, in 1977, *People* discovered a Pandora's Box. Tony Orlando was having troubles and he didn't want *People* to censor them; he wanted the world to know what he was going through. A few years earlier, Orlando had been very hot, with his own television series and several number one hit songs, but he had suffered a nervous breakdown and dropped out of television for a while. The singer's publicist called *People* to say Orlando wanted to talk, so the magazine sent reporter Judy Kessler to interview him. Once Orlando started talking, he didn't seem able to stop. He told about being unfaithful to his wife, about his cocaine abuse, and about the suicide of his dear friend, Freddie Prinze. The story ran with the headline: "Tony Orlando's Breakdown."

It became one of the magazine's all-time best-sellers. As a result, *People* began exploiting what Stolley called O.P.P.—Other People's Problems. "We realized that for a number of reasons, a lot of prominent people would talk to us about these problems if we sent a sympathetic reporter and photographer," said Stolley. "They felt this was helpful to them to tell America who they were and what was happening in their lives." And they discovered that America loved reading about it. *People* started out as a feel-good magazine, but by the late 1970s, melodramatic stories about the traumas suffered by stars became its staple. Karen Carpenter's anorexia, Drew Barrymore's drug problems, the breakdown in Farrah Fawcett's marriage appeared regularly. The stories all came from the stars themselves, and *People* treated O.P.P.s with extraordinary sympathy.

People's greatest innovation was packaging tabloid content in an upscale package with the imprimatur of a reputable publisher. Circulation hit 1 million in less than a year and 2 million within three years. In the first several issues, advertisers stayed away, but as the magazine caught on with readers, advertisers flocked to buy pages. Within eighteen months, *People* was in the black, a record; *Sports Illustrated*, by comparison, had taken ten years to turn a profit. *People*'s advertising pages shot up from 601 pages in 1974 to more than 3,000 pages in less than four years. It went on to become the most successful magazine in the history of publishing. The rest of the publishing world didn't know whether to throw stones or follow suit.

Other celebrity publications sprang up. Australian publisher Rupert Murdoch, who had been having huge success with tabloids in England, was trying to enter the American market. Murdoch had tried to buy the *National Enquirer* from Pope, and got Pope's buddy Roy Cohn to try to broker the deal. Talks fell through. Around this time, Pope told associates that he turned down an offer to buy the paper for $50 million—and Murdoch was used to buying on the cheap. So in 1974, the same year that Time-Life launched *People*, Australian publisher Rupert Murdoch started publishing the *National Star*.* It was somewhat slicker

---

* Later shortened to simply the *Star*.

than the *Enquirer*, though less slick than *People*, and Murdoch promoted it with a million-dollar ad campaign.

In 1976, the tabloidization of the mainstream press went into high gear when Murdoch bought the intellectually elite but financially beleaguered *New York Post*. Murdoch transformed the tabloid with screaming headlines and a full page of gossip, and went after the *Daily News*'s blue collar readers, ridiculing its competitor for trying to be like the *New York Times*.

The *Daily News* hired Igor Cassini's former assistant, Liz Smith, to write a daily gossip column. "I said, 'Well, I just don't think people want to read gossip anymore,' " she said. "I guess I just thought the Winchell thing had ended." She was wrong; New York's tabloid wars had begun.

Within three years after *People* was founded, virtually every publisher in the country had entered into the field. While Dick Stolley was getting credit—or blame—for being a pioneer of celebrity journalism, he was, in fact, just traveling over territory that Gene Pope had blazed long ago. Stolley didn't invent—or even rediscover—personality journalism. He just made it respectable.

"They stole our idea," said *National Enquirer* columnist Mike Walker. "They ripped us off." Stolley maintained that *People* was in no way inspired by the *National Enquirer*, but it's hard to believe that Time Inc. didn't at least notice the *National Enquirer*, which in 1974 had a circulation that was nudging 4 million—and climbing. "If not the mother or father" of *People* magazine, said *National Enquirer* editor Iain Calder, "we're certainly the midwife."

In the three years since *People* was founded, gossip had gone from virtual extinction to a renaissance, and the trend was lamented by journalists everywhere. Outraged cover stories appeared in magazines like *Esquire*, *Newsweek*, and *New York* magazine. "Gossip columns, which had all but vanished with the deaths of Winchell, Kilgallen, Hopper and Parsons—not to mention their papers—are back in bolder typeface than ever," noted a *Newsweek* cover story in May 1976. "Not since the giddy old days of American journalism has so much space been devoted to so little."

"The doleful fact is that the celebrity industry has reached the point at which the demand is outstripping the supply," according to another article. "There is hardly a major newspaper in the nation that hasn't launched its own gossip or names-in-the-news column."

"To everything there is a season, and if this seems to be the season for anything at all, then that thing is gossip," *Esquire* noted. "You can bet that Time Inc. isn't publishing *People* as a public service." The magazine went on to report the gossip on gossip columnists. (Louella Parsons used to wet herself in restaurants, Rona Barrett's real name is Rona Burstein.) "So what is it with you? Why, all of a sudden, are you so interested in this stuff?" *Esquire* asked. "Are you ashamed of yourself? Should you be? . . . Does anybody care? DOES ANYBODY CARE!"

Readers not only cared, they cared a great deal. They cared more than they did about Watergate or Vietnam or race riots, and any publisher who ignored what people really cared about— and tried to tell them what they should care about—was headed toward extinction. *Life* magazine had found that out, but if *Esquire* or anyone else needed further proof, it came one hot August day in 1977. It was the ultimate tabloid event.

the death of a king

Shortly after midnight, on August 16, 1977, Elvis Presley drove his Stutz-Bearcat through the music-sheet-inspired iron gates in front of 3764 Elvis Presley Boulevard. Fans were waiting at the gates as usual, and one of them snapped the singer's picture with a $20.95 instamatic camera. When Elvis got home, he sang "Blue Eyes Crying in the Rain" and "Unchained Melody," ate some cookies and a bowl of ice cream, and then played racquetball until 6 A.M. He changed into gold-colored pajama bottoms, and, clutching some reading material—friends maintain it was a book on the Shroud of Turin, others say it was actually pornography—Elvis went to a second floor bathroom. There, the forty-two-year-old, two-hundred-sixty-pound performer took a handful of pills. Moments later, he collapsed.

Elvis's fiancée, Ginger Alden, was asleep in the next room and heard nothing, but at 2:15 that afternoon, she said, she went into the bathroom and discovered Elvis's body sprawled on the red shag carpet. She called for help. Al Strada, a bodyguard, was next on the scene, then came Elvis's road manager, Joe Esposito. Soon, the bathroom was filled with members of the "Memphis

Mafia,'' some of them sobbing hysterically, others desperately trying to revive him.

"Don't die!" Presley's guitarist cried as he knelt over the singer's body. "Please don't leave us!" Elvis's elderly father Vernon
was having heart troubles and collapsed on the floor beside his
son. Nine-year-old Lisa Marie stood at the doorway. "What's
wrong with my daddy?" she asked, but no one answered.

At 2:33 P.M. the dispatcher for the Memphis Fire Department
notified paramedics. "Unit Six, respond to 3764 Elvis Presley
Boulevard. Party having difficulty breathing. Go to the front gate
and go to the front of the mansion." Paramedic Ulysses S. Jones
Jr. tried to resuscitate Presley while Charlie Crosby drove the
ambulance the seven miles to the Baptist Memorial Hospital;
there a "white male, approximately forty, under CPR, no response" was admitted to the emergency room at 2:56 P.M. On
the admittance form, he was listed as Mr. John Doe and across
the top were the words: NO PUBLICITY.

At 3:30 P.M. Elvis's personal physician, Dr. George Nichopoulos, came out of the emergency room with a grim expression
on his face. "He's gone," Dr. Nichopoulos told the sobbing entourage. "He's no longer here."

August 16 was a sweltering hot, otherwise slow news day
when *National Enquirer* Executive Editor Iain Calder called his
closest aides into an office and closed the door. It was about 3
P.M. "Elvis Presley is dead," Calder said. The news hadn't been
announced—even the family hadn't been given the official word—
but the *Enquirer* had a source inside Graceland. A reporter was
on his way to the mansion before the ambulance got there. The
announcement would be delayed for at least half an hour so that
Elvis's father Vernon could be notified.

This was no time for mourning. This wasn't just a big story,
it was the biggest. Elvis Presley's death—more than any other
story in the *National Enquirer*'s history—was monumental to tabloid readers. To the masses who read the *National Enquirer*, it
was what John Kennedy's assassination was to the *New York
Times*'s readers.

The staff of the *Enquirer* began to mobilize. Calder had al-

ready chartered a Cessna Citation jet to take a team of four reporters and a photographer to Memphis. Sixteen more would be
flown in from around the country to join them. Operation Elvis
would have an unlimited budget and a simple mission: get the
story, get it first, and get it exclusively. Calder needed a commander to oversee the effort. He turned to Tom Kuncl, an aggressive 6-foot 2-inch, 215-pound former war correspondent with a
caustic sense of humor and a booming voice. "Tom, what have
you got going right now that's important?" Calder asked. The
editor had just killed a story that Kuncl had worked on for
months, and the reporter was in a sulk. "Nothing," Kuncl mumbled. "You," Calder ordered Kuncl, "go to Memphis."

By 6 P.M. the *Enquirer* crew was in flight on its chartered
Cessna and headed to Graceland.

In midtown Manhattan, up on the twenty-ninth floor of
Time-Life's sleek skyscraper on Avenue of the Americas, Dick
Stolley was in the final stages of closing that week's issue of *People*
magazine when he heard that Elvis Presley had died. Stolley
sighed. He was not an Elvis fan, but he knew he should somehow
acknowledge the death of the once-revolutionary singer. Stolley
didn't even consider putting the story on the cover of *People*;
Time Inc. had a policy of not picturing the deceased on its magazine covers. To do so would have been considered unseemly, exploitative. "You didn't spend a lot of time covering dead people
back then," Stolley later said, "unless they were world figures,
presidents and the rest, and even then probably not on the cover."
When John F. Kennedy was assassinated, *Time* didn't put him on
the cover, and he was a beloved president. Elvis was a flabby,
over-the-hill crooner who gave concerts in Vegas. Besides, the
cover of that week's *People* was already finished: it featured Marty
Feldman and Dick Stolley's good friend Ann-Margret on the release of their movie, *The Last Remake of Beau Geste*. Stolley decided to put the news of Elvis's death in "Star Tracks"—a two-
page section of photographs with paragraph-long captions that ran
toward the back of the magazine. He had a picture editor round
up shots of Elvis and chose a recent one of the singer in concert,
looking jowly and ludicrous, his paunchy belly pushing up against

his rhinestone-studded belt. *People* gave Elvis's death a 169-word write-up. The "late Elvis Presley" shared the page with a couple of other people in the news, including Dorothy Hamill, who made it into the "Star Tracks" section because a toy company was marketing a Dorothy Hamill doll. "It was the biggest mistake of my career," Stolley later admitted. "I probably should have been fired for not putting Elvis on the cover."

A few blocks away, at 745 Fifth Avenue, the young hipsters who worked for *Rolling Stone* were also about to put their latest issue to bed. It was a special New York edition, celebrating the magazine's move from San Francisco to Manhattan. Editors and production people were congratulating one another on a job well done when word spread through the moving-crate-littered offices that Elvis Presley had died. Music editor Peter Herbst went to Jann Wenner's office to share the news with his boss. "His face sort of scrunched up and he started crying," said Herbst. "These tears were rolling down his face, and he was trying to say something, but I couldn't understand." Then finally, the grief-stricken editor gathered his composure enough to speak. "It's . . ." Wenner sobbed. "It's a cover." The music editor protested. The New York issue had been put together in the midst of the transcontinental move and involved tremendous effort from everyone. The staff was particularly proud of the results. An Andy Warhol portrait of Bella Abzug was on the cover and everything inside was very New York and very hip. Wasn't Elvis sort of . . . hokey? "It's a cover!" Wenner practically screamed. "It's a cover!"

But Wenner didn't want just a new cover—he wanted an Elvis Presley issue. The magazine was ripped up and redone in four days. *Rolling Stone*'s deadline was pushed back and writers were dispatched to Graceland, and to Elvis's birthplace, Tupelo, Mississippi. His movies were reevaluated; his records re-reviewed. Jann told staffers that he wanted them to evoke the slim, hip swinging rock-n-roll rebel of the fifties—not the bloated recluse that Elvis had become. Some of the young editors and photo researchers rolled their eyes; as usual, Wenner was acting less like a dispassionate, unbiased journalist and more like a fan. That, however, was the secret of his success.

*   *   *

It was a late-breaking story for the networks to cover. The story wasn't formally announced until 4 P.M. The networks usually started feeding footage to local stations at 5 P.M. for the 6 P.M. news. At NBC, there was no question what the lead story would be. Anchor David Brinkley was a North Carolina native. "The truth is that I never liked Elvis Presley's music," Brinkley later said. "But I knew millions of others did." Brinkley opened the news with the death of Elvis, and spent nearly three minutes eulogizing him—an extraordinary time in network news. At Brinkley's urging, NBC immediately began putting together a late-night special tribute to Elvis, which they broadcast that evening.

ABC also led with the Elvis story—devoting two minutes to the segment. Upon hearing the announcement of the NBC special, ABC scrambled to put together its own special, which was hosted by a long-haired reporter and Elvis fan who had recently joined the network to give the news a little pizzazz: Geraldo Rivera.

News executives at CBS, however, didn't think Elvis's death was a significant story. The Tiffany network led instead with the news that former President Gerald Ford had endorsed the Panama Canal treaties. The minute-long report on Elvis's death was buried six minutes inside the broadcast. "We thought the [Panama] story was terribly important," said Burton Benjamin Jr., the program's executive producer. Several staffers, including anchor Roger Mudd who was filling in for the vacationing Walter Cronkite, protested the decision—people *care* about Elvis, they said. The staffers were overruled—rather vehemently. The Panama story was *significant*; the Elvis story merely *interesting*. CBS Evening News with Walter Cronkite, which regularly led in the ratings, was badly beaten by both NBC and ABC.

CBS executives said they had no plans to broadcast an Elvis tribute like the other two networks, but on Wednesday, when they saw the high ratings that NBC's and ABC's Elvis specials had pulled in, CBS did an about-face. On Wednesday the network announced that it would broadcast a special on Thursday evening. It was put in a tough time slot—opposite NBC's *Tonight Show*, but the CBS tribute had the network's highest ratings of any late-night show that year—with forty-one percent of viewers—twice those who were tuned in to NBC.

Newspapers that played the Elvis story big were finding an almost insatiable appetite for details of his death. Some papers reported selling more copies than they had when they carried the news of John Kennedy's death. The *St. Louis Post-Dispatch*, for example, printed 370,000 copies of the paper, 100,000 more than usual, and it still sold out. One person bought 500 copies. A driver delivering copies of the *Post Dispatch* was forced off the road and a man carrying a baseball bat stole fifty copies of the paper. Around the country, papers with Elvis's death on the front page were being resold within hours of hitting the newsstand for five dollars or more.

Tom Kuncl didn't really get this whole Elvis thing. He thought the story was just another celebrity death. He had been a war correspondent, a police reporter, and a political writer. He sometimes covered celebrities for the *National Enquirer*, but his favorite articles were ones about government waste, dumb crooks, and astonishing human feats. "I didn't know sic 'em about Elvis," he said. But Generoso Pope had this idea that America was obsessed with Elvis, that all this "King" stuff wasn't said in jest, that for some of his followers, Elvis held a monumental, almost religious, significance. As soon as the *Enquirer*'s plane landed in Memphis, Kuncl knew Pope was right. The city had erupted into mayhem. Its streets were clogged with thousands of mourners who—upon hearing the news of Elvis's death—had left their jobs and their houses to make pilgrimages to Graceland. They clutched record albums or photographs or paintings of the singer. Some clung to teddy bears. Many of them were in a state of shock. Others wept openly and inconsolably. Dozens of mourners collapsed from grief and from ninety-degree heat.

Throngs of grief-stricken fans had "simply gathered up their children, got in cars and headed for Memphis when they heard the news that Elvis had died," according to one account. "They had packed no bags; most had made no plans beyond telling friends or neighbors to notify their employers that they had gone." The three Tripper brothers who lived in Buffalo, New

York, heard about Elvis's death when they were playing softball. "There was no question," said Charlie Tripper. "We just stopped to get money for gas and took off. He was the man. He was it." He was still wearing his softball outfit. A woman from Pennsylvania told a reporter, "Thirty of us decided to come down here because there'll never be another one like him. He was the king. He was the king of everyone and especially of our people. He was *ours*."

A hundred vans delivered 3,116 floral arrangements. Every flower in the Memphis area was sold by noon Wednesday, and more were shipped in from other states. The Floral Telegraph Delivery (FTD) recorded its biggest volume of shipments ever. Arrangements arrived shaped like hound dogs, broken hearts, and blue shoes. Liberace sent one resembling a guitar. Elton John sent a huge bouquet with a note, "For All the Inspiration." Tributes poured in from stars and heads of state. "If there hadn't been a Presley, there would have never been any Beatles," John Lennon said. "Nothing really affected me until Elvis." President Jimmy Carter issued a statement that noted, "Elvis Presley's death deprives our country of part of itself." Even the government of the Soviet Union sent flowers.

For the funeral, Elvis's coffin was carried by a silver Cadillac, followed by a caravan of seventeen white Cadillacs, that snaked its way through two-and-a-half miles of mourners on the way to Forest Hill Cemetery. "The crowd was unbelievable," said Memphis Police Director Buddy Chapman, who was put in charge of the mourners outside the ornate iron gates around Graceland on Elvis Presley Boulevard. "They had crushed people up against the fence to the point where we had to rescue some people." But unlike most crowds of this size, they weren't angry or moblike. "They were—I don't want to say like zombies, but they were almost like in a daze."

Before long, the docile, exceedingly polite crowd became somewhat crazed. Fans descended on the floral arrangements and plucked them bare for souvenirs. They ripped out chunks of grass from Graceland and from the mausoleum where Elvis was buried. A distraught, drunken driver plowed his 1963 Ford Fairlane into a crowd of mourners at 55 miles an hour, killing and critically injuring several of them. Three men were arrested and charged with a plot to steal Elvis's body and hold it for ransom. They later said they were just trying to prove that Elvis had never really died.

The hundreds of reporters who came to Memphis fought for rental cars and hotel rooms. Adding to the bedlam, 16,000 Shriners had already come to town for a convention, taking up most of the city's 9,000 hotel rooms, so many of the reporters had to set up campsites outside Graceland with the mourning fans. The competition to interview anyone who knew Elvis was insanely intense. "I was a war correspondent and had covered the war in Bangladesh and two wars in the Middle East and a revolution in Ethiopia," said one *National Enquirer* reporter. "Well, covering Elvis was a war too. A journalistic war." "The Elvis death coverage—that was the Normandy landing," said another writer for the tabloid. "Other reporters were the enemy."

One of Pope's Fleet Street imports was Iain Calder, a native of Scotland who was so cold and direct that his staff called him the Ice Pick. Calder became Pope's right-hand man, was named editor in 1975, and once fired his best friend for not delivering the goods on stories. The mandate for the Elvis story was to get exclusives, pay whatever it cost to get exclusives, and throw caution—and ethics—to the wind.

The *National Enquirer* took over the top floor of a seedy boarding house. The main area—a place that the owner of the boarding house called the Card Room—was set up as command central. Within hours, a bank of twenty-two private phone lines was installed. "It was a trick that Pope learned from his CIA days," said an *Enquirer* reporter. "Whenever possible, we wouldn't go through switchboards or hotel operators. That way, we could make calls posing as friends or relatives or people from other papers and people calling back wouldn't get suspicious or be able to check us out."

It was the *National Enquirer* at its best—and at its worst. The tabloid had seemingly unlimited resources, and *Enquirer* reporters infiltrated Memphis, handing out $100 bills like they were business cards. Their aggressive tactics appalled the mainstream reporters. Some *Enquirer* reporters were assigned to get their competitors too drunk to work. They befriended and bribed telephone operators at other hotels who would keep them posted on what the other journalists were doing. Kuncl had his people track down the two paramedics who drove Elvis from Graceland to the hospital. They were paid off and put under exclusive contract with the *Enquirer*. Likewise dozens of groupies, band members, and Elvis hangers-on. The *Enquirer* located Robert Call, the fan who had been waiting in front of Graceland when Elvis returned home on the day of his death and who snapped the singer's picture with the $20.95 instamatic camera; the *Enquirer* bought the photograph for $10,000 and ran it under the headline: "Last Photo of Elvis Alive." One *Enquirer* reporter faked a toothache to get an emergency appointment with Elvis's dentist. Dee Presley, who had been married to Vernon for seventeen years, was put under exclusive contract with the *Enquirer*. Although she had divorced Vernon, she was a valuable source for the *Enquirer*. She gave them the story—disputed by Elvis's inner circle—that the singer left a suicide note.*

The *National Enquirer* locked up an exclusive interview with Elvis's fiancée Ginger Alden. She gave the tabloid a graphic account of how Elvis looked when she discovered his body: "His eyes were closed and his face was a purplish color and swollen looking. His tongue was sticking out of his mouth and he'd bitten down on it." There were some inside Graceland who were convinced that it was Ginger Alden who initially leaked the news of Elvis's death to the *National Enquirer*. Dick Grob—a member of Elvis's entourage—claimed that Alden placed a call to *Enquirer* reporter James Kirk shortly after she discovered the body—as early as 11:30—well before she alerted Elvis's entourage. Alden admitted she did sell an interview to the *Enquirer*, but insisted that she didn't call the tabloid before she called for help. Still, many in the Memphis Mafia were suspicious of Elvis's last girlfriend and banned her from their inner circle.†

---

* Years later, Dee Presley would also sell the *Enquirer* a story that Elvis was gay and had been involved in a love affair with his mother, Gladys.

† Alden didn't even get her full fee from the *Enquirer*. The payment was cut from $105,000 to $35,000 because she also spoke to the Memphis *Commercial Appeal*, voiding the interview's exclusivity.

Then there was the controversy over the cause of the death itself. The official word was that Elvis had died from "cardiac arrhythmia brought on by an irregular heartbeat caused by undetermined causes." Elvis's physician, Dr. George Nichopoulos, initially denied that Elvis had any drug problems, although he would later be charged with overprescribing drugs to Elvis—some 10,000 pills in the last twenty months of the star's life. Because Elvis's death had been ruled the result of natural causes, under Tennessee law, the findings of the autopsy did not have to be released. That didn't stop the *Enquirer;* within hours they had the names of all twelve people present at the autopsy. "We knew virtually every substance that was in Elvis's body," said Kuncl. Among those substances were codeine, Quaaludes, Valium, pentobarbital, butabarbital, and phenobarbital. They were all "downers," and the codeine itself was enough to kill most people.

The *Enquirer* knew that Elvis used psychics, so Kuncl called all the physics listed in the Memphis Yellow Pages, and asked them if they had ever treated Elvis. Sure enough, one of them had seen him shortly before his death, and Elvis had expressed morbid fears of death. That yielded the epic scoop: "ELVIS KNEW HE WAS GOING TO DIE."

In those weeks after Elvis's death, the *Enquirer* was riding high, scooping the mainstream press and beating the television news. It was, however, getting fierce competition from its new nemesis, the *National Star.* Rupert Murdoch's four-year-old tabloid was proving to be more competition than Pope had expected, and had scored a scoop in the Elvis story that was hard to match. Shortly before the singer died, Murdoch's star reporter Steve Dunleavy learned that three of Elvis's bodyguards had been fired. Dunleavy interviewed the men, Red West, Sonny West, and Dave Hebler, hoping to turn their stories into a three-part series for the *Star.* After the initial conversations, however, Dunleavy realized he had struck gold. Until then, Elvis's private life was a very closely guarded secret. These three bodyguards told Dunleavy jaw-dropping tales of debauchery and decadence: drug abuse, kinky sex, and violence. "I realized we were dealing with an incredible story about the biggest star since Valentino," said Dunleavy. He consulted with Murdoch, who agreed to pay the bodyguards a flat fee of $50,000 for their story. Dunleavy spent a month in a Los Angeles hotel taping the bodyguards' stories. More than thirty publishers had asked to read the manuscript, but only Ballantine bid. The imprint is a division of Random House, which at the time was owned by RCA, Elvis's label. They knew that anything with Elvis's name on it sold. *Elvis: What Happened?* was published on August 1, 1977, a few weeks before Elvis's death, with an initial print run of 400,000 copies. Within six hours of Elvis's death, Ballantine ordered an additional 250,000 copies. Eventually, K-Mart alone ordered 2 million copies, the biggest single shipment ever for a book. Some of the details contained in *Elvis: What Happened?* were so lurid that the head of Ballantine later confessed that he didn't know "whether the book was legally publishable." And Rupert Murdoch's *Star* had exclusive excerpt rights to the book.

"Read the book the world is talking about!" The *Star* headlines blared for weeks. The book gave shocking details about the extent of Elvis's pill habit, calling the singer "a walking pharmaceutical shop." It revealed that Elvis "firmly believes he has the powers of psychic healing by the laying of hands. He believes he will be reincarnated. He believes he has the strength of will to move clouds in the air. He firmly believes he is a prophet who was destined to lead, designated by God for a special role in life." The excerpts reported Elvis's obsession with firearms, and revealed that he usually carried two or three guns on him; he even carried a gun on stage in concert, tucked into his boot. Elvis would shoot holes in television sets when he didn't like a particular show.* According to the book, he ordered one of the bodyguards to kill the karate instructor who was dating his ex-wife Priscilla. The book also revealed Elvis's then top-secret visit to the White House to meet with Richard Nixon in hopes of becoming a federal drug enforcement officer.

Although the book became a huge best-seller, at the time it was dismissed by the mainstream press. One of the bodyguards, Red West, remembered tuning in to *Good Morning America* the

---

* Or when his nemesis Robert Goulet appeared.

morning after Elvis's death. Geraldo Rivera, who was then a "serious" journalist for the show, was blasting *Elvis: What Happened?* as a bunch of tabloid trash. "I met Elvis, and he seemed pretty straight to me," Geraldo said, and while Elvis's death was tragic, "at least 'The King' had not followed in the melancholy rock 'n' roll tradition of Janis Joplin, Jim Morrison, Jimi Hendrix, and all the others" who died of drug abuse. "It was like we were defectors," said West. "Nobody wanted to believe what we had to say."

"The main attitude at the time was one of awe," said a reporter who covered Elvis's death for the *Pensacola News Journal.* "Nobody wanted to delve into the seedier side. Now, I keep wondering why we didn't ask more questions."

The Memphis Mafia was doing its best to hold off the press. No reporters were allowed into Graceland to view Elvis. Much to the dismay of Elvis's inner circle, however, one reporter did get in. Her name was Caroline Kennedy. The daughter of the late President had been working as an intern at the New York *Daily News.* Columnist Pete Hamill, who was dating Jackie Onassis, got Caroline a summer job at the newspaper. When the news of Elvis's death broke, Hamill was staying at Hyannis Port with the Kennedys. He immediately left for Memphis, taking the cub reporter with him.

When Caroline went to Graceland, people didn't know that she was there as a journalist. Other reporters who noted her presence in Memphis assumed she was there as a celebrity visiting Elvis's family, like actor George Hamilton, soul singer James Brown, and actress Ann-Margret. Elvis's family and friends were honored that John Kennedy's daughter was there to pay her respects. "Well, we were all impressed," said Elvis's friend, Memphis disc jockey George Klein. "We'd always been such Kennedy supporters, you know." Elvis's father, Vernon Presley, was especially touched by the gesture. "The bell rang, and I opened the door and said, 'Caroline, come on in,' " Klein said. "That was a mistake. A big mistake." Until he saw what Caroline wrote, Klein had no idea that she was there as a reporter. "That was a cheap shot way to get a story," Klein said.

The *Daily News* decided not to run Caroline's article. Some say she missed her deadline, others say the writing was simply terrible. *Rolling Stone* publisher Jann Wenner snatched up the rejected story. Jann was friendly with Jackie and had escorted Caroline to the theater. He also knew the impact of a Kennedy byline. He gave the manuscript to an editor who, staffers say, had to almost entirely rewrite the piece. "Graceland: A Family Mourns" didn't contain any scoops or stunning insights; rather, it was a somewhat flat, cold-eyed description of Elvis in his coffin, surrounded by his mourning family and cronies. "The director of police, who looked like the advance man from *Nashville*, invited me into the house where a scarlet carpeted hall led into a large room filled with gold and white folding chairs," Kennedy wrote. Priscilla Beaulieu Presley offered Kennedy a Coke or Seven-Up and introduced her to Elvis's father, Vernon, some of his aunts and uncles, and his eighty-two-year-old grandmother. "At the far end of the room was the gleaming copper coffin that contained the body of Elvis Presley," the article continued. "His face seemed swollen and his sideburns reached his chin . . . Potted plastic palms surrounded the coffin and on the wall was a painting of a skyline on black velveteen. . . . 'He doesn't look anything like himself,' the woman beside me said softly."

The article struck some as an astonishing breach of taste—coming, as it did, from someone whose mother not long ago had waged a bitter war with William Manchester over his account of John F. Kennedy's assassination in his book, *The Death of a President*. Caroline—who would later write a book on peoples' rights to privacy—made no apologies for the article. But when Vernon Presley read Caroline's revelations, he was devastated. "She not only insulted the memory of Elvis," Vernon said, "she insulted her own family name."

Even without any Kennedys on staff, the *National Enquirer* was coming up with a fair number of Elvis exclusives. But no matter what they got, Pope seemed underwhelmed. "He kept screaming at us and giving us incredible grief," recalled Kuncl. "He said that we didn't have any blockbusters." Members of Operation Elvis feared for their jobs. Then one reporter, the son of a funeral director in Brooklyn, had an idea. At his father's mortuary, he said, it was the custom to photograph the departed at rest in their coffins. The pictures made unique souvenirs of the funeral. Why not do the same for Elvis?

The *Enquirer* staff bought every camera they could find for miles around. They handed out the cameras—along with cash and promises of a lot more—to anyone who could snap a decent photo of Elvis in his coffin. "We thought it was a long shot," said P. J. Corkery, then a features editor for the tabloid, "but we overlooked the fact that relatives and retainers and others would prove to be extraordinarily greedy. That night, people kept sneaking into the viewing room, snapping photographs and holding others with the same idea at gunpoint. Next morning, our cheeseburger-littered nerve center was also littered with photos of Elvis lying in state."

The picture of Elvis in his white suit and copper coffin was plastered across the front page of the September 1, 1977, issue of the *National Enquirer* with the headline "ELVIS AT PEACE." It became the best-seller in the history of the tabloid: 6,668,563 issues were sold—more than a million over the previous record holder, "How Freddie Prinze Rehearsed His Own Suicide."

According to *National Enquirer* lore, the infamous picture was taken by a cousin of Elvis who used a $300 Minox supplied to him by the *Enquirer*. He was paid anywhere from $35,000 to $75,000. The Presley family hired a private detective to track down the traitor; he allegedly has been ostracized.

In another peculiar postmortem to the episode, after the picture ran, a group of *Enquirer* reporters stole it. The photograph was worth a lot of money to Elvis collectors, and the office burglars were tracked down, charged with corporate theft, and led away from the *Enquirer* offices in handcuffs.

The "Elvis at Peace" issue spawned an *Enquirer* tradition, indelicately referred to as the "celebrity in a box" picture. *Enquirer* reporters became notorious for trying to photograph stars in their coffins. *Enquirer* reporters used a ham operator to break into the walkie-talkie conversations of the security guards standing watch at Liberace's funeral. A paparazzi working for the *Enquirer* parachuted onto Rock Hudson's hearse. When Bing Crosby died, the tabloid's religion reporter disguised himself as a priest to get pictures of the singer. On the way out of the church, the reporter, still dressed in cleric's robes, was stopped by ABC's Geraldo Rivera, who asked him for an interview. The "priest" obliged and then chastised Rivera for invading the privacy of the mourning family. Not every "celebrity in a box" ended up on the cover of the *National Enquirer*, however. When Kurt Cobain committed suicide in 1994, the *Enquirer* editors had what one described as a "raging newsroom debate" about whether they should run a photo of the grunge star in his coffin. They ultimately decided not to, said one, because they thought it was "in bad taste"—although another source says the real reason was that they knew their readers weren't Kurt Cobain fans.

The editors at the *National Enquirer* realized that their readers loved Elvis, dead or alive. The tabloid came up with plenty of excuses to put Elvis on its cover even after his death, reporting JFK-like conspiracies about the singer's death: That Elvis was rubbed out by the Mafia to keep a lid on a $2 billion bond scam he knew about; that Elvis's death was staged by the FBI so that the singer could become an undercover agent for the government; and, most popularly, that Elvis had faked his own death to escape the prying media.

Dick Stolley also learned a lesson from Elvis's death. Because he—and the high-minded Time Inc. corporation—didn't want to exploit the dead, *People* missed the biggest story of the decade. The magazine wouldn't make that mistake again. On the first anniversary of the singer's death—and on at least four occasions after that—*People* concocted a cover story about Elvis. Dead celebrities would become one of *People*'s sure-fire formulas for a best-selling issue: When John Lennon was shot in 1980, *People* put him on the cover without hesitation. That issue sold 2,664,000 on the newsstands—about a million more than usual, making the John Lennon memorial issue *People*'s best-seller to date. Thus, an amendment was added to Stolley's "Pretty is better than ugly" formula of cover stories that sell. The new axiom: "Nothing is better than a dead celebrity."

Many in the mainstream press were appalled by the coverage

of Elvis's death. "Elvis was not an icon," wrote syndicated Chicago *Sun-Times* columnist Mike Royko, "he was a con." Royko was outraged that so many people seemed more distraught by Elvis's death than they were when Kennedy was shot. "I think what Presley's success really proves, is that the majority of Americans—while fine, decent people—have lousy taste in music."

While editors and producers around the country may have agreed with Royko's sneering assessment of Elvis's music, the verdict on Elvis as a news subject was undeniable: he sold like crazy. That was a significant discovery in 1977, when newspapers were struggling to stay alive and network news producers were first grappling with the choice between profitability and respect. CBS News President Salant maintained that editors should base their news decisions on "what is important, rather than what is merely interesting," but if they did, the viewers simply changed the channel. Elvis Presley's death was a turning point in news coverage; it, more than any other single news event in recent history, proved to newspaper editors and television producers around the country that if you don't cater to your audience, you lose it.

Two years after Elvis's death, the episode was still fresh in the minds of producers at ABC who were looking for a way to rescue their nascent news magazine, *20/20*. The program was still in the trial stages, it was broadcast irregularly, and like *60 Minutes* in its early years, it was having trouble finding an audience.

Geraldo Rivera had been tapped as one of the show's regular correspondents, and the biggest ratings grabber he had done for *20/20* was a segment on the bizarre life and death of Howard Hughes. "If it worked with Howard Hughes, it would work again," Geraldo recalled. "I remember brainstorming it with [producer] Charlie Thompson, casting about for another larger-than-life celebrity who had lived and died under mysterious or at least unexplained circumstances." The first person who came to mind was John F. Kennedy, but Geraldo had recently done a segment on Kennedy for another show, *Good Night America*. Rivera was a fan of actor James Dean, but he worried that Dean didn't have the mass appeal he was looking for. Then he remembered Elvis, and what a ratings blockbuster his death had been. Now all he needed was controversy. Geraldo had publicly and repeatedly disputed reports that Elvis had died of drugs, but now he was prepared to reverse his opinion. His producer Thompson had worked for the Memphis *Commercial Appeal* and was able to get into the "shit files" of the newspaper—where one of the paper's reporters had dug up some unreleased results of the autopsy. The *Appeal* hadn't published the information, which it allegedly considered too controversial at the time. By using the *Appeal*'s banned autopsy finding and Thompson's contacts in Memphis, Geraldo came up with some explosive footage about the facts behind Elvis's death. He and Thompson showed the executive producer for *20/20* what they had, and he decided to make it *20/20*'s season opener and to dedicate the entire program to it. The show, "The Elvis Cover-up," was slotted for Thursday, September 13, 1979. If the ratings were low, it would probably signal the end for *20/20*.

"The official investigation of the death of Elvis Presley, at least insofar as we have been able to determine, must rank among the worst, most unprofessional investigations of this type ever made," Geraldo said. "Reporting this story has been a melancholy experience for me, because I wanted it not to be true. . . . But it was true. By the end of his life, Elvis had become a medical addict."

Geraldo's anguish was alleviated somewhat by the ratings for the "The Elvis Cover-up." Forty-three percent of all people watching television that evening tuned in to watch the Elvis conspiracy. It ranked a stunning fourth that week, beating all other news show; only entertainment shows—*Charlie's Angels*, *The Love Boat*, and *Three's Company*—did better. Most important, it beat the highly rated, highly respected *60 Minutes*. "It established me as top gun among *20/20* correspondents," said Rivera, "and it established my team as the ass-kicking class of the industry." Geraldo's exposé would remain the most-watched segment in *20/20* history until Barbara Walters's interview with Monica Lewinsky some twenty years later. Because of Elvis, *20/20* was awarded a regular time slot. Network news would never be the same.

11

the networks go tabloid

On August 11, 1977, when an unemployed postal worker was arrested and charged with a series of shootings that had terrorized New York City for 379 days, Roone Arledge, the new head of ABC News, saw the opportunity he had been waiting for: a big news event with entertainment value. It was 3 A.M., but Arledge, dressed in his trademark flashy but casual attire, hurried down to the police headquarters in lower Manhattan. Walking around with a glass of Scotch and a walkie-talkie, he personally directed the coverage for what he had decided would be a massive package on the story for the next *Evening News*. He summoned Barbara Walters, who a year earlier had been hired by the network amid a firestorm of controversy, to ABC headquarters to introduce the story from the site. And he assigned Geraldo Rivera, whom he had recently hired for the *Evening News* after the combustible young reporter had been fired from *Good Morning America*, to provide a high-impact "investigative" piece.

The so-called Son of Sam murders had gripped the New York City area since the evening of July 29, 1976, when an unidentified man walked up to two women sitting in a car in the Pelham Bay section of the Bronx and shot them with a .44 pistol. By the following spring, the murderer had attacked four more times, always at night, killing three more people and wounding three others, all of them young men and women who had been talking on the front steps of their homes or kissing in cars or walking home along quiet streets in Brooklyn or Queens or the Bronx.

The murderer sometimes left notes behind referring to someone named Sam, so the New York police began calling the unknown killer "Son of Sam." In April, the killer left a note signed "Son of Sam" beside the bodies of two more people he'd murdered. He was clearly reading—and enjoying—the hysterical tabloid coverage of his crimes. The murders occurred during a pivotal time for the news industry. In New York City, where the newspaper business was struggling for survival, the tabloids went wild over the serial murders, fanning and exploiting the hysteria with increasingly outrageous headlines that followed each development in the case. (For a more detailed discussion of how the tabloids reacted to the killings, see Chapter 15, "The Rise of Tabloid Television.")

The sensational coverage was, until Arledge came on the scene, by and large confined to the tabloids. The reporting in the *New York Times* was restrained, and the producers of the network news shows, considering it a local story, had given it scant attention. But in May of that year, Leonard Goldenson, the head of ABC, had put Arledge, who'd been running the network's spectacularly successful sports division, in charge of the ABC News division and Arledge, who had been told to raise the viewership and profile of the ABC *Evening News*, was eager to milk a story that seemed like a cop thriller come to life.

After he arrived at the news division, jokes were made about the "Wide World of News." *Time* compared Arledge's hiring to the satirical film *Network*, in which cynical television executives engage in shameless theatrics to boost ratings. Peter Jennings and Ted Koppel, afraid that Arledge would undermine the integrity of their broadcast with sensational reporting and vulgar gimmicks, actually asked for a meeting with ABC head Fred Pierce and tried to block Arledge's appointment.

Arledge did indeed believe news could be snappier and more

entertaining. Shortly after his promotion, he urged his staff to study commercials, where powerful messages could be delivered in thirty seconds. The fears of Jennings and Koppel seemed confirmed. Then, at a corporate retreat for all senior producers and correspondents that was held in Montauk, Long Island shortly after taking up his new post, Arledge further alarmed many of those present by expressing his admiration for Geraldo Rivera. Even more distressing to the news veterans was Arledge's suggestion that the *Evening News* create some sort of Washington "gossip column." At this, a few of the senior people rose from their chairs and made passionate speeches about what correspondent Sam Donaldson would call "the integrity of the news."

When ABC old-liners tuned in to the evening news the day after the Son of Sam arrest, their worst fears were confirmed. The usually staid half hour had been turned into a Son of Sam extravaganza. The package that night had five different Son of Sam segments and consumed nineteen-and-a-half minutes out of the twenty-two minutes broadcast. Rivera joined Walters, who was back at the anchor desk, to introduce his own piece. Much to the horror of ABC News's old-liners, the mustachioed Geraldo, dressed in jeans and a tee-shirt and speaking off the top of his head, described Berkowitz as a "fiend," a "beast," a "monster," and a "murderer," and when he did remember to use the word *alleged*, which he didn't always, he spoke it in a voice dripping with scorn and sarcasm. "I tripped over the world *alleged*, which we were required by our legal department to use in all criminal matters pending trial," Geraldo later explained. "I said it with sarcasm because I wanted to remind our viewers that this butcher had essentially confessed to his crime."

After the package, with some two minutes left on the broadcast, Walters turned to Howard Smith in Washington, who noted dryly, "There *were* some other things that happened today."

The traditionalists at ABC News were appalled. They were particularly galled by Geraldo's performance. "Roone later admitted to me that he had placed too much emphasis on the Son of Sam story after [David] Berkowitz's arrest, that he had run two or three stories too many before cutting away to other news,"

Geraldo recalled. "But these were not my decisions. These were not my stories. My story was a valid sidebar looking at the circumstances of the arrest, delivered perhaps with a shade more enthusiasm than what was comfortably allowed by journalistic convention. Still, I got the blame for the entire broadcast, and I carried the Son of Sam rap for years."

In fact, so appalled were the traditionalists that a group of them in the Washington bureau, including Brit Hume, Frank Reynolds, and Sam Donaldson, wrote a letter to Arledge in protest. The letter, while not mentioning Geraldo by name, raised concerns about the journalistic obligation to protect the rights of the accused by using words like *alleged*. It also questioned the tone of the coverage. The letter's signers considered their declaration so sensitive that they did not even make a copy of it. They wrote it, signed it, sealed it in an envelope, and sent it to Arledge. Nonetheless, Frank Swertlow, a columnist for the *Chicago Daily News*, found out about the letter and summarized its contents in a column, which reportedly annoyed Arledge as much as actually receiving the letter did. A clear battle line seemed to have been drawn at ABC between those who believed in pure, unadorned news and those who were eager to employ flash and drama to enliven the news. Under Roone Arledge, ABC News became an aggressive pioneer in the tabloidization of network news. It was a harrowing journey, with several casualties.

Putting Arledge in charge of the news was, indeed, a drastic move, but by 1977, ABC needed something drastic. Its news division had long been the also-ran of the networks, a laughingstock among elite news gatherers.

The network was begun as an offshoot of NBC, when RCA owned what it called the Red and the Blue radio networks, but in 1943, government regulators forced RCA to sell one of them. Life Savers magnate Edward J. Noble bought the Blue network and renamed it ABC—the one RCA kept was NBC. By 1952, it was clear that television—not radio—was the wave of the future. But Noble didn't have the money to expand into television, so he sold ABC to theater chain magnate Leonard Goldenson.

For a long time, it was a distant third in the industry. "It was third only because there were three," Goldenson once said. "If there were ten, it would have been tenth." It was nicknamed the Almost Broadcasting Company, but during the 1960s and early 1970s, ABC made a name for itself in entertainment with shows like *The Untouchables*—then the most violent show on television—and *Peyton Place*, the first prime-time soap opera. The entertainment division's success continued into the 1970s under Fred Silverman, with such hits as *Happy Days* and *Starsky and Hutch*. The sports division under Roone Arledge was also hugely profitable. The news division, however, always languished. It had gained some respect by hiring Harry Reasoner away from CBS in 1970 at the then handsome salary of $200,000, but the ratings were still anemic. Then in 1976, ABC stunned the industry by hiring Barbara Walters, for the then astronomical salary of $1 million, to co-anchor the *Evening News* along with its existing anchor, Harry Reasoner.

Walters had come a long way since working on Igor Cassini's short-lived NBC show. The woman who had "dated" Roy Cohn had become—through default—the co-host of NBC's immensely successful *Today Show* and, as a result of the success of her fifteen-year run there, a major force in television.* But Walters was seen as a product of the entertainment division, which produced the *Today Show*, and not the news division, and the decision to elevate her over all the network's seasoned correspondents was greeted with outrage. The *Washington Post* called Walters "A Million Dollar Baby Handling 5-and-10-Cent News." CBS's Richard Salant asked, "Is Barbara Walters a Journalist, or Is She Cher?"

Reasoner particularly felt slighted. He complained to people that while ABC's news department desperately needed new equipment and new staff, the network had gone out and squandered $1 million—five times Reasoner's salary—on a woman with no hard news background. Reasoner had been lured away from CBS's elite group of *60 Minutes* correspondents, and he had ex-

---

* In her contract was a clause forgotten by NBC that stipulated that if Frank McGee ever left the show she could co-host. "Nobody expected Frank to leave the show, I guess," Walters said. "Then he died and I remember they put out all kinds of statements saying they were looking for a new host." Her agent pointed out the clause, and Walters became co-host of the *Today Show*.

pected to be sole anchor. It was a humiliating setback. Furthermore, his marriage, which would end in divorce a few years later, was deteriorating. He felt thwarted and unhappy at work and at home. He barely spoke to Walters off the air; on the air, the chill between them was perceptible. Reasoner looked for opportunities to slight. Once, for example, Walters commented on air, "Henry Kissinger didn't make too bad a sex symbol." "You would know more about that than I would," Reasoner shot back. The quarreling between the two was so constant they became known as "the Bickersons."

"He felt I was hired for the wrong reason. He was terribly unhappy about it," Walters later said. "I'd walk into the studio and Harry would talk to everybody there except me. He cracked jokes with all the guys about the latest baseball scores, and he would go across the street every day to Café des Artistes [a restaurant that was a favorite of the ABC crowd] and spend an hour before the show and an hour after complaining about me. Had I known how violently opposed he was, I wouldn't have come. It was the toughest period of my life."*

Resolving the anchor situation was Roone Arledge's first big challenge. He realized quickly that it would be impossible for the two anchors ever to work together harmoniously. He also felt Walters was misused in the static role of anchor. "Barbara was great at so many things that reading the news opposite a grumpy guy who didn't want her there was not in her best interest," Arledge's boss, Leonard Goldenson, said. "But there was no way

---

* During this period, Liz Smith called Walters and suggested the two get together. Walters eagerly accepted Liz's offer. Walters not only enjoyed gossiping—she long counted irrepressible gossips Roy Cohn and columnists Sidney Skolsky and Jack O'Brien among her confidantes—but she also recognized the importance of having a columnist like Liz Smith on her side. The two went to Café des Artistes, where they started an old girls club that helped counterbalance the old boys club headed by Reasoner. "Instead of it being a professional lunch, we were very friendly and dishy and had a lot of fun," Smith said, according to Walters's biographer Jerry Oppenheimer. "Afterwards, she invited me to her parties and introduced me to people like the Kissingers. . . . There's a difference between writing a column and having any kind of social acceptance. While I wasn't really looking for social acceptance, because of Barbara, I got a lot of it." Liz became a loyal friend and supporter of Walters, but Aileen "Suzy" Mehle, a bitter rival of Liz, refused to write about Walters—much to the detriment of her own career.

I could take Barbara off that program and keep Harry on it without leaving her tremendously damaged. So poor Harry had to go."

Walters, however, had a clause in her contract giving her virtual veto power over a new anchor. To circumvent this, Arledge decided to dispense with the anchor system altogether and instead create a series of "desks"—headed up by Peter Jennings in London, Frank Reynolds in Washington, and Max Robinson in Chicago—who would divvy the broadcast's introductory newsreading assignment more or less evenly. The format, which debuted on July 10, 1978, left Walters without a formal role in the nightly broadcast. Reasoner called it, "the Arledge shell game," and went on to say, "He more or less successfully concealed from the public the fact that Barbara was no longer any kind of anchor."

By then, however, Arledge had already launched *The Barbara Walters Specials* that would prove such a distinctive, and commercially successful, blend of entertainment and news. The first, which aired on December 14, 1976, featured Walters interviewing Barbra Streisand and her then boyfriend Jon Peters, and Jimmy Carter and his wife Rosalynn. The critics panned it. "If this is a preview of future Walters specials," *Variety* noted, "she may be doing irremediable damage to the reputation she's trying to cultivate as a journalist." The public, however, loved it. It pulled in thirty-six percent of the TV audience—a record for a show of its type. The celebrities were more popular than the politicians. "As time went on, we found that the audience didn't want the political [guests], no matter who we did," Walters recalled. "We had King Hussein and his wife, Queen Noor. We had Vice President [Walter] Mondale. That's not what they wanted. They wanted television stars, movie stars."

Arledge's second major task was to create a news magazine. By the late 1970s, *60 Minutes* was the envy of the other networks. It received more awards than any other television show—including Emmys, Peabodys, and Polk awards. It was a source of great pride for CBS and, more important, it made money.

Taking the news-as-entertainment—very profitable entertainment—further, Arledge decided ABC needed its own *60 Minutes*. Unlike the CBS show, however, Arledge wanted ABC's news magazine to be younger and hipper, infused with Arledge's signature flash and dazzle. Bob Shanks, who had worked on late-night and early-morning programming, was named executive producer of what would be *20/20*. For potential hosts, he turned to some of the biggest names in print, auditioning Ben Bradlee of the *Washington Post*, writer Pete Hamill, television critic Marvin Kitman, and Watergate reporter Carl Bernstein. Ultimately, he decided on a co-host format and chose Harold Hayes, the legendary former editor of *Esquire* magazine, and Robert Hughes, the Australian art critic for *Time* magazine. The similarity in their names—Hughes and Hayes—was confusing enough. On top of that, Hayes had no television experience. Hughes had some, but not a great deal, and his Australian accent was so thick as to be almost unintelligible to the viewers.

As the show's star correspondent, Arledge chose Geraldo Rivera. In the late 1970s, *60 Minutes*'s cast of graying Cold War–era journalists in their tailored suits and trenchcoats was decidedly unhip. Geraldo, with his relative youth and his unapologetically open liberal politics, would be a hip, ethnic version of Mike Wallace.

When Geraldo first burst on the scene, he was seen by many as a welcome alternative to the largely Anglo-Saxon cast of television reporters who saw themselves as the direct descendants, if not the contemporaries, of Edward R. Murrow. Half Jewish, half Puerto Rican, a former lawyer for the street gang Young Bloods, a former advocate for the legalization of marijuana, in 1970, at age twenty-seven, Rivera had been tapped by WABC-TV news, which was trying to increase its ethnic representation.* There, Geraldo almost instantly became a hit. His award-winning 1972 exposé on the grim conditions at Willowbrook, a mental institute on Staten Island, brought him national accolades. Geraldo seemed to be an updated version of the turn-of-the-century crusading journalist. *Newsweek* called him an "outspoken young mod with a passionate commitment to social reform." A fawning profile in

---

* Rivera had, from time to time, tried to Anglicize his name, including Jerry Rivers, but the news director at WABC advised him to use the ethnic Geraldo Rivera. He has long been hounded by rumors that his real name is Jerry Rivers but, in fact, his father's name was Cruz Rivera.

Life that year explained how to pronounce his name ("Hair-ALL-dough"). "He is the golden Puerto Rican," panted *New York* magazine. "His shoulders taper to hips so minor he has to hold up his jeans with a strip of video."

He became a celebrity in his own right. Geraldo had joined *Good Morning America* in 1975 and started a late night show called *Good Night America*, in which he explored sensational tabloid topics like UFOs, the Kennedy assassination, the Bermuda Triangle, and prostitution. When *Good Night America* was taken off the air in June 1977, Geraldo was so angry that he threatened to leave ABC. Much to his surprise, ABC accepted his resignation before Roone Arledge tapped him, first for the News Department (the week after his Son of Sam reporting, Arledge sent him off to Memphis to cover the death of Elvis), then for *20/20*.

The news magazine debuted on June 6, 1978. The show included political cartoons, a Claymation Jimmy Carter singing "Georgia on My Mind," and, as segues into and out of commercials, the definitions of supposedly obscure words like *exegesis*. There was even a gossip segment called "Cries and Whispers" that featured a couple exchanging secrets in bed. The lead story was a virtual parody of investigative reporting by Geraldo on how rabbits—cuddly, pink-eyed, helpless rabbits—are killed in the training of greyhounds. Wearing a red bandana around his neck and an open-collar Western shirt, the reporter looked into the camera and with grim indignation intoned, "The rabbits don't stand a chance." The debut show also included an alarmist segment on terrorism, an irreverent review of the week's news called "The Wayward Week," and dazzling graphics. *Washington Post* critic Tom Shales called it "probably the trashiest stab at candy-cane journalism yet made by a TV network. 20/20 managed to take a gross leap backward and a garish leap forward at the same time, and if at first it gave us the giggles, it may on second thought justifiably give us the creeps."

Roone Arledge had viewed an early version of the premiere and had ordered some changes. The evening the show was broadcast, however, he was out on a date with Ethel Kennedy, and the next day he was so embarrassed by the reaction to the debut of his news magazine that he claimed he hadn't seen it before it was broadcast. "Frankly, I was appalled," he told the *Washington Post.* "I hated the program," he said to the *New York Times.*

Arledge fired Hayes and Hughes, demoted Bob Shanks, and hired the staid but reliable Hugh Downs as anchor. He also eliminated the bizarre graphics and lead-ins, and the show's second episode—restrained and conventional, with a piece by Geraldo on the homeless—bore virtually no resemblance to the first. "Roone Arledge didn't become the Toscanini of TV sports technology without learning when to hit the stop-action button," wrote Harry Waters in *Newsweek.* "In went Hugh Downs and a journalistic sobriety that, while not as slick as CBS's '60 Minutes,' at least tapped the program's potential."

Nonetheless, Arledge continued to think he could revitalize ABC News by importing people from outside television. He hired Carl Bernstein—whom he had earlier interviewed to be the host— to be ABC News's Washington bureau chief. Bernstein, for all his genuine investigative accomplishments during Watergate, not only had never worked in television but also had never held a management position and indeed, while at the *Post*, had tended to be contemptuous of managers and bureaucrats. Furthermore, since the success of *All the President's Men*, which became the best-selling nonfiction book to date, and the release of the movie version starring Dustin Hoffman as Bernstein, the reporter had come to think of himself not as a journalist but as a celebrity.

The disaster that followed seemed inevitable. "He'd have his clothes on all backward like he just got up, and he'd have come back from New York where he stayed some place dancing with Bianca Jagger and he was full of show biz stories and name dropping," said Washington producer John Armstrong. "Bernstein became a joke," said Charles Gibson. "He tried to bluff his way through the job and people would ignore him. He spent more and more time in that office, with nobody going in there and nobody talking to him." Once, while working on a story in England, he borrowed £500 from a producer and lost it all gambling. After fourteen months, Arledge removed him as bureau chief and made him a correspondent, where he fared somewhat better, but parted company with the network in 1984, and devoted much of his time to writing and lecturing about the evils of gossip.

ABC also hired Ron Reagan Jr., the son of the President. He was widely liked by colleagues, but some remember with amusement that during the height of Nancy Reagan's "Just Say No" campaign against drug use, he was growing his own pot. "He told me that when the Secret Service agents came to tell him that his father had been shot," recalls one co-worker, "he was absolutely terrified because he thought they were coming in to bust him." When called for comment, young Reagan denied that he grew pot, but admitted that he smoked it.

But Geraldo remained Arledge's most memorable—and controversial—hire. He was, to begin with, notoriously promiscuous, even in the sexually uninhibited world of television journalism. "I was like a pig," he once admitted, "a grunting, voracious pig in heat." He once did a report on hookers and then, by his own account, took the services of two of them for free. He once had sex in the boiler room with two college interns. In his autobiography, *Exposing Myself,* he boasted of bedding Bette Midler, the former Canadian Premier Pierre Trudeau's wife Margaret, and Marian Javits, the wife of the well-known senator Jacob Javits. He had Mick Jagger and Rudolf Nureyev dancing provocatively in his Lower East Side apartment, where his walls were painted all black. He even seemed attractive to the remote Barbara Walters, on one occasion declaring that he thought she had "great tits." He later added, "I'm a big fan of hers. . . . She's a sexy woman. She's a real good lookin' old broad."

It wasn't just his unchecked libido that annoyed his critics, it was the way he injected his testosterone-fueled personal style into his reporting. As a roving correspondent for *20/20*, Geraldo pioneered a form of participatory, point-of-view television journalism that had its print counterpart in the Gonzo school of New Journalism originated by Hunter Thompson and Tom Wolfe. The stories Geraldo did tended to fall into two categories: one was what could be called Geraldo Goes on an Adventure; the other could be called Geraldo Investigates. In the former category, the correspondent ran with the bulls at Pamplona, swam with whales in the Caribbean, descended in a shark cage off San Francisco, boxed with Mohammed Ali, and shot hoops with Johnny Matthis. In the investigative category, Geraldo explored traditional news magazine topics like Agent Orange and fetal alcohol syndrome. But he also ventured into what had previously been considered tabloid territory, including his hugely successful "Elvis Cover-up."

While Geraldo's investigative stories received considerable attention, they were also often attacked as irresponsible and unfair and lacking journalistic credibility. He and ABC were sued by a group of Chicago businessmen he had secretly taped with a hidden camera, which is illegal in Illinois, in a story accusing them of buying slum tenements, insuring them, and then burning them down without regard for the tenants. He was sued by an Ohio judge he accused of accepting sexual favors from prostitutes in exchange for lenient sentences and then sued by one of the women he had interviewed for describing her as a "hooker." And all of those compromised broadcasts took place in just one year. Rivera won the case in the hooker story. The arson case was settled out of court.

By the early eighties, *20/20* had hit its stride. It was using broadcast news for the sorts of stories hitherto confined to the tabloid press. In the process it became adept at what some considered staging real news. In 1980, for example, in an exercise that recalled *New York Post* editor Steve Dunleavy's appeal to the Son of Sam to surrender to him, Barbara Walters persuaded radical fugitive Abbie Hoffman to "surrender" to her on camera. They met on two boats in one of the lakes in upstate New York. While the story generated incredible publicity for Walters, Hoffman had already made a decision to turn himself in, and, critics observed, his real motive in granting the interview was to promote his new book, *Soon to be a Major Motion Picture*. In other words, the purported "surrender" was simply another Abbie Hoffman publicity stunt in which Walters had willingly participated.

Walters, however, always seemed to get away with such behavior. It wasn't just her regal bearing and poised, dry, at times intimidating, style. Nor was it her vast array of friends and contacts. Barbara Walters was a team player in a way that Geraldo never was. Despite her often tabloidy topics, she was clearly a member of the establishment, and she would back off a topic when she was told to. Geraldo basked in his bad-boy reputation, but by the mid-eighties Roone Arledge, the former sports producer who, having established the success of ABC News, now began to yearn for establishment approval, began to see his former protégé as a liability. "Geraldo had become a symbol in many people's minds of how the line had been blurred between news and entertainment," Arledge said to his biographer, Marc Gunther. He complained that people would say, "Yeah, they're good, but they're not really serious or they wouldn't have Geraldo on."

Arledge began distancing himself from his former star reporter. He stopped returning Geraldo's calls. He began looking for an excuse to dump him. Then, in late 1985, he got one. In October, *20/20* put together a segment that promised to be a blockbuster. Correspondent Sylvia Chase and producer Stanhope Gould had a twenty-six-minute piece that linked Marilyn Monroe to the Kennedys and the mob. Based largely on Anthony Summers's well-documented book, *Goddess: The Secret Lives of Marilyn Monroe*, the segment also included an on-camera interview with Fred Otash, the detective who worked for *Confidential* and who claimed to be involved in tapping Marilyn Monroe's house for Jimmy Hoffa. Sylvia Chase was one of the show's most respected reporters; *TV Guide* once called her "the most trusted woman on TV." She was responsible for a segment on flaming gas tanks on Ford's subcompact Pinto that revealed that Ford had tested a safer gas tank but never used it. Producer Gould was also respected in the industry, and had won an Emmy for his work. "I've never seen anything comparable in shock value," Milo Speriglio, a private detective who worked on the program as a consultant, said of the program. "I believed it would not just change our way of looking at a notorious real-life Hollywood drama, but our thinking about the Camelot years."

There was some concern that Arledge, who had dated Ethel Kennedy, would kill the piece because of his ties to the Kennedy family. His links to the Kennedys went beyond Ethel. His top aide, David Burke, was a former high-level aide to Teddy Kennedy.* Ethel's

---

* Burke officially recused himself from the piece, but privately is said to have called it "sleazy."

daughter Courtney Kennedy had married Arledge's longtime assistant Jeff Ruhel. Ethel's son Michael Kennedy was married to Vicki Gifford, the daughter of Frank Gifford, one of Arledge's closest friends. And Arledge was quite close to Stephen Smith, a Kennedy brother-in-law. Roone had earlier killed a piece on Chappaquidick, but he insisted that his numerous ties to the Kennedy clan didn't influence his coverage of the family. "Ethel Kennedy is a friend of mine like hundreds of people we do stories on," Arledge said. "That has never affected our judgment."

The Marilyn Monroe story was originally scheduled to air on the season premiere, September 26, 1985. At the last minute, however, Arledge declared that the segment "needed work" and bumped it to the next week. The segment was also cut from twenty-six minutes to seventeen. On October 3, while Sylvia Chase was getting her makeup done to go on the air with the Kennedy story, she learned that it would be delayed again. It was replaced by a piece on sniffer dogs and was cut down again, from seventeen minutes to thirteen. The next week, it was bumped again, and finally, ABC announced that the piece would not run at all. "It was gossip-column stuff," said Arledge, and "did not live up to its billing."

Inside ABC, there was outrage. *20/20* co-anchor Hugh Downs said that he thought the story had "air-tight" documentation. "All of us felt jolted by this preemptive strike against what we considered a balanced and revealing piece of television journalism," Downs said. "I honestly believe that this is more carefully documented than anything any network did during Watergate."

No one was more infuriated than Geraldo. "This is a fucking outrage," he declared to his colleagues. "Arledge should resign." He went to Barbara Walters and Hugh Downs and argued passionately that they should join forces and publicly protest the decision. Walters and Downs low-keyed their complaints, but Geraldo took his protest where he knew it would be most read: to *People* magazine and to Liz Smith's gossip column. "The decision smacks of cronyism," Rivera told *People*. "We were appalled that the head of this network would suddenly show such an interest in a particular story when he hasn't shown interest in so many others we've done," he told Liz Smith.

"My objection to the piece as it stands is that it's a piece of sleazy journalism,"* Arledge told Smith. "It's just not good enough for us."

The piece was killed and so were any chances Geraldo had for staying at ABC. Soon after the Monroe flap, Geraldo's girlfriend, C. C. Dyer, who was also his associate producer and would later become his wife, was accused of using an ABC messenger to pick up an ounce of marijuana from a friend at CNN. Dyer claimed that the marijuana, which had been hidden in a package containing news videotapes, was not for her but for another friend. Dyer resigned and Roone Arledge, seeing the incident as an opportunity to get rid of her boyfriend as well, called Geraldo at home to tell him it was time for him too to part company with the network.

"I want you to quit," Arledge told his former star reporter.

"Bullshit," Rivera said. "I'm not quitting."

"Show me the contract, Geraldo," Arledge said. He knew that Rivera hadn't been given a new contract and had been working for ABC—at $1 million a year—based on a verbal agreement and a handshake. He was now being told that the agreement wasn't binding. "Where's the contract?" Arledge kept saying to him. "We have no contract."

"Are you saying I'm fired?" Rivera asked.

"You can use whatever words you want," Arledge said. "But I don't think you're going to work here anymore."

Like Mike Wallace nearly twenty years before him, Geraldo had been hired by ABC to create controversy and was then fired for creating controversy. The Marilyn Monroe story in particular and ABC's overall experience with Geraldo epitomized the dilemma the networks faced when dealing with tabloid news. They craved the ratings and the publicity, but flinched at the disapproval. Once Geraldo succeeded in helping establish *20/20*, he became an embarrassment.

---

* Arledge later denied using the world *sleazy*, but Smith, who considered Arledge a friend, stood by her report. "I'm sorry, but that's exactly what he said to me," Smith said. "I even asked him, 'is that really what you want to say?' . . . He probably didn't mean it as a reproach to his people, [but] he did use the word *sleazy* and even I was sort of taken aback."

"Geraldo did two interesting things for ABC News," Roone Arledge told Marc Gunther. "He helped us tremendously up to a point, in our early growth. And he helped ABC News immensely by leaving."

celebrities fight back

"I feel like Rocky," Carol Burnett declared. The comedienne stood on the steps of the Los Angeles County Superior Court on March 11, 1981, surrounded by photographers, camera crews, and fans. Her usually elastic face was fixed in an expression of steely determination; her bright red hair had faded into its natural gray-streaked brown. Burnett was about to slug it out in court with the *National Enquirer*, the tabloid bully that no one else in Hollywood would dare fight. "I have gone the distance," she told the throng of admirers. The crowd cheered.

"We love you!"

"We're behind you!"

"We hope you win!"

Carol had endured sleepless nights, years of depositions and subpoenas and disastrous negotiations, and had spent more than $200,000 in legal fees in her $10 million lawsuit against the *Enquirer* over an item that appeared on March 2, 1976. The 66-word story said that a "boisterous" Burnett had an argument with Henry Kissinger at a Washington restaurant and then later "traipsed around the place" offering diners a taste of her food. Then, according to the item, Burnett "accidentally knocked a glass of wine over one diner—and started giggling instead of apologizing."

Burnett was furious. "I was lied about and I don't think anyone has the right to do that," Burnett said. "It portrays me as being drunk. It portrays me as being rude. It portrays me as being uncaring. It portrays me as being physically abusive. It is disgusting and it is a pack of lies."

The *Enquirer* had tried to keep the case from going to trial. It had run a retraction and apology, but the apology had done nothing to mollify Burnett. "It's like you're hit by a hit-and-run driver," she said, "and you're in the hospital and they send you a bouquet of crabgrass."

Lawyers for the *National Enquirer* also tried to offer the actress an out-of-court settlement. Burnett had settled a similar case before. In 1971, *Inside TV* and *Movie World* published stories that quoted sources saying the star would condone the use of marijuana by her children. After suing the magazines for $2 million each, the actress eventually settled out of court. This time, however, Burnett wasn't interested in a deal. "Every time they tried to settle, I said, 'No. I want to go to trial. You are the bad guys,'" Carol said. "If this sucker goes on fifty years, I'm going to be there in a rocking chair facing the jury."

Then the *Enquirer* apparently considered playing dirty. Talk reached Burnett that some tabloid reporters were snooping around her daughter, Carrie, who was having drug problems. Burnett's friends were worried that the *Enquirer* was going to blackmail her by threatening to run the dirt on her daughter. Carol made a preemptive strike and, like Tony Orlando had done two years earlier, gave the entire story to *People* magazine, which put it on the cover. "Carol Burnett's Nightmare," read the October 1, 1979 headline. "For the first time, she reveals her daughter's battle to conquer drugs."

"It was a wrenching story, and Carol told us everything," said *People* editor Dick Stolley. "It only enhanced Carol's standing in the film community. It was a big seller for us and it helped establish *People* as a place to go if you had a terrible secret to tell. We would handle it gracefully and sympathetically."*

By the late seventies, the *National Enquirer* had lost the virtual monopoly on gossip it had enjoyed only a few years earlier due to Time Inc.'s launch of *People* in 1974, followed that same year by the birth of Rupert Murdoch's *Star*, a tabloid like the *Enquirer* except with four-color photography. The upscale papers were also venturing into gossip. In 1977—over the objections of Bob Woodward—the *Washington Post* added a gossip column, written by Nancy Collins. "You can write about anyone but Mrs. Graham's friends," her editor once instructed her. Soon after violating that rule, "The Gossip Column" was axed.†

Even the New York Times Company entered the fray. In 1977—much to the dismay of many *Times* editors and writers—the company spent $3 million to launch *Us* magazine, a blatant rip-off of *People*. The publisher himself seemed embarrassed by the venture. "It's not going to be my favorite dish of tea," publisher Arthur Ochs Sulzberger said. "But it's the kind of thing people want to read." The magazine was doomed to failure by the antigossip culture of the company that produced it. An editor's letter in the premiere issue noted, somewhat condescendingly, that the magazine was "created for a generation that has grown up in an era of visual communication." *Us* magazine went through $10 million and five editors in ten years, but didn't turn a profit. The New York Times Company was so desperate to unload it that at one point, executives at the company offered to *give* the magazine to Generoso Pope if he would assume the debt

---

* For years afterward, celebrities took their cue from Carol Burnett. When they found out that the tabloids were sniffing around about a potentially damaging story, they would often turn to *People*, which they knew would be sympathetic. That was Drew Barrymore's strategy when she found out that the tabloids had checked one of its reporters into rehab to get a story on the thirteen-year-old. That was also Michael J. Fox's strategy in revealing his struggle with Parkinson's in late 1998. The *Enquirer* had the story and Fox went to *People* to break it.

† Collins was somewhat redeemed at the *Post* after she got hold of an advanced copy of H. R. Haldeman's book, *Ends of Power*, which, despite what he had told Mike Wallace, was explosive.

and subscription list, according to someone familiar with the negotiations. After investigating, Pope passed.*

The competition among all these publications became fierce. Since they were targeted for women, and since they depended on newsstand sales rather than subscriptions, they tended to be bought and displayed at supermarket checkout counters. By the late seventies there were more publications than there was space at many checkout counters. If a new arrival was to succeed, it would literally have to displace one of its competitors on the racks. "A magazine really has to move briskly to hold its own at the checkout," the *New York Times* noted in 1979. "The competition is so fierce that some checkouts are magazine saturated. If a new publication gets on display, a slow mover must be booted out to make room for it."

Space at the checkout counter wasn't the only thing the tabloids were competing for; they were fighting one another for stories, too. Since a magazine earned its place on the checkout counter racks by delivering more celebrity gossip than its competitors, and since all these publications were writing about the same narrow world of movie and television personalities, the scramble for the scandalous scoop intensified tremendously. At the *National Enquirer* the dozen or so articles editors were each required to submit thirty story ideas every day. The story ideas were reviewed at a weekly editorial meeting called The Hour of the Jackals, according to former articles editor P. J. Corkery: "It was usually not held in the offices, but in a Holiday Inn on the beach where dozens of martini pitchers, beer mugs, brandy glasses, and Bloody Mary mugs with the celery untouched littered the table. A couple of editors would follow their cheese smothered steaks with hot fudge sundaes. 'I want to be buried in a piano case,' said one as he plunged into his second sundae. . . . Why hold the meetings on Fridays? 'Because,' I as told, 'that gives the janitor time to wash the blood from the walls.' "

After the embarrassing and expensive Carol Burnett suit, however, the *Enquirer* also established more rigorous procedures

---

* The magazine was sold to Macfadden Company in 1980 and Jann Wenner. Wenner later bought it outright.

for verifying what it published. Pope hired a former Time Inc. employee named Ruth Annan to head up a twenty-six-person fact-checking team. Annan instituted a fact-checking system which—although it would do little to raise the credibility of the tabloid in the eyes of its critics—would make the *National Enquirer* one of the most strictly verified publications in America. Annan required three sources for most stories, including one who was on tape. "They're so concerned about scrubbing up their image," complained one reporter, "that I was actually asked to get somebody on tape for a story about how to spruce up leftovers." *Enquirer* reporter R. Couri Hay complained: "Gossip is so documented now it's not even gossip anymore. I know people in hospitals dying of complications from face-lifts, but I can't print it unless I know the name of the doctor, the time of the operation, the room number in the hospital, and have two eyewitnesses."

The rigorous fact-checking led to huge clashes between the freewheeling reporters and Annan's staff, which was sometimes referred to internally as the Secret Police or the IRS. In fact, some would allege, the fact-checking process was so strict that it encouraged reporters to fudge not facts but sources. To get the requisite three sources, according to some *Enquirer* foes, reporters would often give tip fees to people who hadn't actually given them stories. The canceled checks would be "proof" that they had sources. Sometimes reporters used even more elaborate tricks to get around the rigorous fact-checkers. Once, according to P. J. Corkery, a reporter had a story about a cow who glowed in the dark because a UFO had contaminated it with some alien substance that gave it a neon effect. Pope wanted a credible scientist on the record discussing the glowing cow. The reporter produced a taped interview with a Nobel Prize winner, clearly declaring he was "baffled" by the story. Ruth Annan was suspicious. She was right to be. The reporter did, in fact, interview the Nobel Prize winner, but when he identified himself as being with the *National Enquirer*, the scientist said he was "baffled and confounded that you would have the effrontery to call me up and waste my time." The reporter took what he wanted from the professor's taped comments, and, with a little editing, inserted his own questions. When the truth came out, the reporter was fired.

By 1978, when its circulation peaked at an astonishing 5.7 million, the *National Enquirer* was no longer the amusing if somewhat annoying fringe publication it had been when it first moved to Tabloid Valley seven years earlier. It had become a major force in the media industry. And, since nothing sold as well as celebrity scandals, it had also come to epitomize media invasiveness into the private lives of the rich and famous. "We cover Hollywood the same way the *New York Times* or the *Washington Post* would cover the Pentagon," said the *Enquirer* editor-in-chief Iain Calder. "We don't wait for a story to break. If you have a new hit show, chances are we have a cameraman there who works for the *Enquirer.* Or the top star, we'll probably have her hairdresser who works for us, her P.R. guy, or someone in her lawyer's office, maybe her boyfriend, maybe her husband. Basically, you've got to look at it like a military exercise."

It's not surprising that celebrities increasingly felt the need to fight back. Johnny Carson's sidekick, Ed McMahon, filed a $2.5 million suit over a story that he had had a face-lift. Dolly Parton sued over a story that called her the "Ghengis Khan of Country Music." Former sex siren Hedy Lamarr sued for $10 million for a story that said she was a virtual recluse. Liz Taylor's ex-lover, former used-car salesman Henry Wynberg, sued over a story suggesting he was a gigolo living off her money. Comedian Paul Lynde sued for $10 million after an article claimed he was forced off "Hollywood Squares" because he drank too much. "It's worth a lawsuit to find out the source of the story," said Lynde, who insisted he left the show "to pursue other options." Even Elvis Presley's former dentist filed a lawsuit against the tabloid.

By the time the Carol Burnett case went to court, everyone who was anyone in Hollywood had a *National Enquirer* horror story. "They went to my grade school in Forest Hills, and tried to get into my school records to prove I used to be a stinky, rotten, little racist kid," complained Carroll O'Connor, who played *All in the Family*'s bigot Archie Bunker. Photographers from the tabloid flew over O'Connor's Malibu estate in a helicopter. The star went to the balcony of the house to moon them, but O'Connor's wife pulled him away from the cameras. "Can you imagine a shot of your behind in the *National Enquirer?*" she pleaded with him. "That's just what they want."

Various stars proposed different plans for a concerted counterattack against the *Enquirer. Dallas* star Larry Hagman, furious over a story reporting that as a child he shot birds and tore up his brother's photo album, suggested forming a "war chest" to force the tabloid into bankruptcy. "Isn't it about time we banded together to get rid of that piece of garbage?" Hagman asked. But many in Hollywood were reluctant; they remembered how the *Confidential* trial embarrassed so many stars. Some were afraid that they would be revealed as sources for the tabloid. Others were reluctant to be cross-examined about the truth of the details of their private lives that the tabloid had reported, fearing quite rightly that such a process would reveal even greater details. Celebrities needed someone who was unafraid of doing battle with the *Enquirer.* That was when Carol Burnett stepped forward.

Dozens of lawsuits had been filed against the tabloid over the years, but they had all been settled, dropped, or thrown out. When the Carol Burnett case went to trial in the spring of 1981, it was the first time that any star had ever actually gotten the tabloid into court, and all of Hollywood was watching. Other stars showered her with support and letters of encouragement. Dinah Shore sent an expensive box of candy. Henry "The Fonze" Winkler sent flowers and a note that said, "All our love." Leonard Nimoy attended the trial. Governor Edmund "Jerry" Brown, whose father had brought the libel case against *Confidential,* telephoned Carol to express his support. Henry Kissinger, who didn't appear in court but who did give a sworn deposition, told the media that Carol "acted in a perfect ladylike fashion." "This is an important day for all of us," declared producer Marty Ingels as the trial began. "If Carol wins her suit, it will open the floodgates for the entire field of libel." Ingels and his wife, singer and actress Shirley Jones, who played David Cassidy's mother in *The Partridge Family,* had filed a $10 million suit against the *Enquirer* for an article that called Jones "a crying drunk."*

---

* Ingels wasn't eager to testify, according to some reports, because he had in the past been a source for the tabloid.

The trial provided a rare peek inside the workings of the nation's most notorious tabloid. The Burnett story, which appeared under the byline of Steve Tinney, had actually come from *Enquirer* contributor R. Couri Hay. Hay told executive editor Mike Walker that he had it from two different sources that Burnett had been drinking at the Washington restaurant Rive Gauche. "He went on to say that she had bumped a table somehow and that wine was spilled," Walker testified, "and she started giggling and the guy at the table did not take it very well and that he somehow nudged over a glass of water and some was spilled on her dress." An hour before deadline, Walker, who actually wrote the item, asked another reporter, Gregory Lyon, to double-check Hay's information. Lyon called a spokeswoman for Rive Gauche who, in two phone conversations, told him that Burnett was indeed at the restaurant and that she and her party "were having fun in a loud way." She denied, however, that anyone spilled wine or water or that anyone was "obnoxious" or "tipsy." The spokeswoman told Lyon that Burnett "was just very happy and was going around giving everyone samples of her dessert." The spokeswoman also told Lyon that Burnett's party of five stopped by Kissinger's table as they left the restaurant and had a "spirited conversation." *National Enquirer* reporters followed up that call with two conversations with the headwaiter, who insisted that the story wasn't true but, according to *Enquirer* reporters, contradicted himself. The *Enquirer* people thought they'd play it safe by not actually saying Carol was drunk—they didn't even say she was drinking. Rather, they called her "boisterous" and "giggling"—"much like the television character for which Carol Burnett is known and loved," the tabloid's lawyer tried to argue.

The *Enquirer*'s editors believed they could persuade the jury that, although the story contained some inaccuracies, they had sources for the information and had acted responsibly when they were informed of the item's problems. What they didn't count on was Burnett's passion about the subject of alcohol and how the public would respond to that passion: Burnett had become an active crusader against alcoholism because both her parents had drunk themselves to death at age forty-six. She told a spellbound jury about her parents, how her mother was a violent, "hostile, drunk" and how her father was the opposite, a gentle, loving man. "I remember asking him if he loved me would he stop [drinking]," Burnett testified. "When he did start again, I thought he didn't love me." Burnett's testimony, which included the admission that despite her concerns with alcoholism she had in fact drunk "two or three" glasses of wine during the lunch, moved several jurors to tears.

In the midst of the trial, Johnny Carson rallied the entire country against the *National Enquirer*. The talk show host's rocky marital life, his high salary, and fights among members of his staff had long been fodder for the tabloids. They had reported that he had had a face-lift. They called him "The Laziest Man in TV" and printed details of his cushy work schedule. They had snooped around the drinking problem Carson once had had. In fact, during the Carol Burnett trial, the *National Enquirer* ran a cover story with the headline "Johnny Carson Marriage in Serious Trouble."

Carson was furious and used the occasion of the trial to blast the tabloid on his talk show. "I think [people are] becoming very aware in this country, especially during the past few weeks because of the national publicity via certain lawsuits that have been filed against this publication, how the *National Enquirer* works," Carson said on the *Tonight* show one evening while the trial was in progress. "It's based on innuendo, it's based on gossip, it's based on half-truths, it's based on speculation." The audience cheered and clapped enthusiastically. Carson called the story about his marital difficulties "a pack of lies"* and blasted the "creep" who wrote it. "I'm going to call the *National Enquirer* and the people who wrote this 'liars,'" he proclaimed. "Now that's slander, so they can sue me for slander." Then he looked directly into the camera and declared: "You know where I am, *gentlemen*." The crowd went wild. They gave Carson an extended ovation.

Carson's *Enquirer* diatribe was the talk of Los Angeles. It almost derailed the trial because at least two jurors saw or heard

---

* Carson's wife later admitted that their marriage was, indeed, by this time on the rocks, exacerbated by a drinking problem. "When I did drink," Carson admitted, "rather than a lot of people who become fun loving and gregarious and love everybody, I would go the opposite."

about the talk show host's commentary, and the tabloid's lawyer asked for a mistrial. Carol Burnett, however, was thrilled. "I thought he was wonderful," she beamed. "Johnny was defending himself. He wasn't talking about me."

The *Enquirer*, by comparison, was friendless. Other publications, usually quick to defend any newspaper or magazine being sued, distanced themselves from the tabloid and its dubious First Amendment right to snoop on celebrities. The *San Francisco Examiner* called the *Enquirer* "a disgrace to journalism" and media reporter Jonathan Friendly wrote in the *New York Times* that journalists "cannot be comfortable riding in the same First Amendment boat with the *Enquirer*."

On March 26, after two weeks of testimony and four days of deliberation the jury reached its verdict: $1.6 million—$300,000 in actual damages and $1.3 million in punitive. The courtroom erupted in cheers. Burnett gasped, clasped her hands to her face, and sobbed with joy. "There is a God," she declared and ran over to the jurors and shook their hands. She hugged them and gave several her autograph. Flashbulbs erupted as Burnett left the courtroom and announced that she was giving the money to charity—to journalism schools. Vowing to appeal the case, the *Enquirer*'s lawyer, William Masterson, declared, "This is the equivalent of capital punishment for a publication."

After the Burnett verdict, an array of other stars decided to take similar action against the *Enquirer*. Cary Grant filed a $10 million suit over a story that suggested that his fifth wife pressured him into marriage. Raquel Welch sued over a story that declared: "Fading sex bomb Raquel Welch was fired from her latest movie [*Cannery Row*] because she threw temper tantrums, made outrageous demands for changes in her script and acted like an indispensable superstar rather than a hopeful has been." Elizabeth Taylor and her latest husband, Virginia Senator John Warner, announced that they were going to sue if they didn't get a full retraction on an article that announced: "Seventh Marriage Crumbling: Liz Taylor and Hubby in Raging Public Fights." By the end of 1981, the *Enquirer* was facing more than ten cases totaling over $62 million in libel charges. There was talk that the *National*

Enquirer was headed for the same fate as *Confidential*—crushed under the weight of lawsuits from a Hollywood united in anger against it.

But the *Enquirer* didn't retract its Liz Taylor story, and by the end of the year, she and John Warner did indeed split up. A court also determined that the tabloid's comments about Warner and Taylor were essentially true. Johnny Carson and his wife separated the next year. All the other $100 million in suits pending against the *Enquirer* at end of the trial were either dropped, dismissed, or settled. Even Carol Burnett's award was cut in half by the judge and was eventually settled out of court, reportedly for a mere $200,000.

The ultimate lesson that celebrities learned from the Carol Burnett case was that lawsuits were an expensive, arduous, and not entirely effective way of protecting themselves. Their real power, they discovered in the 1980s, was to be found not in the courts but in their star power; in the *access* they could grant to or withhold from the increasing number of journalists who wanted to write about them. A pioneer in the rediscovery of this reawakened power of celebrity was Elizabeth Taylor—or more accurately, her publicist, Chen Sam.

When she first started representing Elizabeth Taylor, Chen Sam was known as Hurricane Chen or the Dragon Lady. Petite at five feet, four inches, she always wore heels and had waist-length dark hair. She chain-smoked Marlboros and was sometimes curt or rude to the journalists who were accustomed to being courted by her predecessor, veteran P.R. man John Springer. "Chen and I had some rocky times, particularly at the beginning of her tenure," says Liz Smith. "I had known Elizabeth for years and enjoyed a good relationship with John Springer. Chen was different, dicier, and to my mind, sometimes overly protective."

Chenina Samin was born in Cairo to an Egyptian father and an Italian mother. She was raised in a strict Muslim tradition, with a veil covering her face. She fled from an arranged marriage at age fifteen and went on to study physiotherapy. She married a man forty years her senior, whom she later divorced. Chen was practicing pharmacology in South Africa in 1975 when she was called to treat Richard Burton, who had been stricken with malaria while on his second honeymoon with Elizabeth Taylor. "She had to have a Zulu native sit on Richard's chest while she treated him," says a friend of Sam. "He was delirious with fever. She saved his life. Richard adored Chen from the beginning, but Elizabeth took longer to warm to her."

While Chen was staying with the Burtons, she learned that her eleven-year-old son had died. She was grief stricken and stayed with the Burtons while she was mourning. When the Burtons split up a year later, Richard decided that Taylor should get "custody" of Chen. "He was still quite fond of Elizabeth and felt she needed Chen," says the friend. "He was tired of the sycophants and the hangers-on—he called them 'all those fags'—who surrounded Elizabeth. He saw in Chen someone who was smart and pragmatic. Richard gave Chen a six-month crash course on the care and feeding of Elizabeth Taylor, including how to light her for the cameras."

Chen took on the secretarial and scheduling duties for the star, eventually edging out her long-time publicist Springer. Taylor's career was in crisis at that point. At forty-nine she could no longer play romantic leads; she became the butt of fat jokes. She was overweight, overaged, and given to tantrums. No producer wanted to hire her. After her marriage to Virginia Senator John Warner ended in 1981, she was at a loss over what to do with herself. Despite her world fame, she was essentially another unemployed actress. Chen Sam set out not to revitalize Taylor's acting career but to give her a new career—one in which being famous was itself her full-time occupation.

"Perhaps because Chen didn't have a background in P.R., she didn't follow all the old rules," says a former employee. "She invented new ones." One of the things that Chen had to address was that Taylor had become too *accessible*. "We were told that whenever someone wanted her to appear at a function we were to say Miss Taylor is *so* busy these days," says the source. "It's all about saying no, until you create an appetite in people," Chen used to say, "and knowing the exact right moment to say yes."

Another way that she upped Taylor's celebrity image was by making outrageous and sometimes capricious demands. Taylor had a seven-page list of requirements on how her hotel room should be prepared for her stays. When she appeared in *Little Foxes* at the Victoria Theatre in 1982, she not only insisted that the walls of her dressing room be painted violet to match her eyes, but she also had a violet carpet installed, violet flowers delivered daily, and demanded a huge tank of exotic tropical violet-colored fish.

Chen also started to charge for Taylor's appearances and interviews. "If she was looking to promote something, fine, the interview was free," says the source. "But if someone just wanted time with Elizabeth, Chen always demanded money. "Why should we give it away?" she would ask. Sometimes, there were misunderstandings over fees. In 1985, Chen accepted an offer of $1 million from Bob Guccione to pose for *Penthouse* magazine. "Chen and Elizabeth were both very excited by it," says a source. "They had several meetings with Guccione to discuss the details. Then Bob asked what Elizabeth wanted to wear in the pictures where she'd be dressed. There was some confusion, and then Bob realized that Chen and Elizabeth thought they were going to get $1 million for her posing *with* clothes. Bob couldn't believe it! Chen and Elizabeth were furious and stormed out. But that was the way that Chen was marketing Elizabeth."

Chen Sam, according to those who knew her, believed she was also the mastermind behind Taylor's "relationships" with men like Michael Jackson and Malcolm Forbes. It was she, says a source, who arranged the "romance" between the actress and publisher Malcolm Forbes, who was gay. "Chen came to me and asked me if I knew of any rich men who'd be willing to donate money to Elizabeth's charity," says a former editor for *Forbes* magazine. "I knew that Malcolm was looking for a beard. Chen hooked them up."

Similarly, when Saudi arms dealer Adnan Khashoggi was looking for entree into respectable society, he started escorting Taylor around. He donated $1 million to her charitable organization. "She gave people credibility and Hollywood cachet," says a source. "They gave her money."

By that time, Taylor had successfully repositioned herself not just as a scandalous tabloid fixture but as a genuine celebrity icon.

Nothing demonstrated this more clearly than the success of her line of fragrances: Passion, White Diamonds, and Black Pearls, which grossed some tens of millions of dollars. "We did tours of department stores and sometimes the managers of the stores were unprepared for the onslaught of fans when Elizabeth appeared," says a former employee of Sam. "They were like rock concerts. We would give store managers a list of things they had to do for crowd control, like turn down the thermostats so that people wouldn't get overheated. One store manager refused to comply. He said, 'Oh, we've had celebrities here before. We had Cindy Crawford here once.' But they had no idea about the incredible drawing power of someone like Elizabeth Taylor. We said, 'You haven't seen true stardom in effect until you've seen Elizabeth Taylor.' But they didn't believe us. It got overcrowded, and people fainted. It was mayhem."

Other celebrities tried to imitate this marketing strategy, but without similar success. When Karl Lagerfeld created a fragrance called Sun, Moon, Stars, Chen Sam was hired to do the publicity. "Karl Lagerfeld chose Daryl Hannah to be the face behind the fragrance because at the time she was dating John Kennedy Jr. and the Europeans are obsessed with anything Kennedy," says a source who worked on the campaign. "Chen made up a list of the publications Daryl should talk to and the cities she should visit. Daryl refused to do any of the interviews or make any appearances. She told us, and I quote, 'I am the next Jacqueline Kennedy. I have to be careful who I give myself to.' Our jaws all dropped. We all called her the mute spokesperson." Eventually, she did start talking, and some wished she had stayed mute. When asked if she wore Sun, Moon, Stars all the time, Hannah replied, "I don't wear perfume." The fragrance bombed.

By the late eighties, celebrities had rediscovered the tremendous power of celebrity. Stars have long had a reputation for being spoiled and demanding, but by the late 1980s, they were making increasingly capricious demands for special treatment. Demi Moore asked that the studios foot the bill for her entourage of bodyguards, nannies, trainers, and makeup artists. Demi's personal staff cost the producers of the clunker *Scarlet Letter* more than $877,000.

As the years progressed, some of these demands became obscene. When John Travolta was negotiating to appear in *The Double*, *Variety* reported that producers agreed not only to his $17 million salary, but also agreed to foot the bill for more than a dozen assistants, trainers, makeup artists, stand-ins, security guards, and massage therapists. He wanted his personal cook as well as approval over the catering staff for the rest of the cast and crew. What's more, he insisted that the studio had to rent his private plane from him for the Paris-based shoot and that the trailer he normally uses in Los Angeles be shipped to Europe. (By the time it arrived, Travolta had dropped out of the film.) During the shooting of *Ace Ventura 2*, Jim Carrey asked for a chef not only for himself but for his pet iguana as well. When producers balked at that expense, Carrey compromised: they shared the cost of the iguana chef.

In the most notorious and capricious of all celebrity demands, the rock group Van Halen had it written into their contract that a large bowl of M&M's had to await them in the dressing room of any place they played and that all brown M&M's had to be removed before they arrived. If a brown M&M was found, the group would receive full pay and didn't have to play. "Word got around that we really meant it," lead singer David Lee Roth once said. If Roth found a brown M&M in his dressing room, he would throw a fit. He would hold the offending M&M in his hand and bellow "What is this?" The promoter would be called. "How could you do that to Dave?" his manager would bellow. The Rolling Stones mocked Van Halen's demand by putting in their contracts that they wanted only brown M&M's. (Once Mick Jagger bought a used Volkswagen, had it painted like a brown M&M and parked it in front of Van Halen.) But the Rolling Stones made their own outrageous demands as well, insisting on pool tables, a golf driving range, and imported caviar.

"Celebrities love to play power games—to see how high people will jump for them," says one Hollywood producer. When on the set of *Star Trek Generations*, William Shatner insisted that Volvic mineral water be delivered to his trailer, Patrick Stewart insisted on the same perk. "It's the principle of the thing," he reportedly explained. "I remember once Bruce Willis called all these [film] heavyweights to his ranch to discuss film projects," said the producer. "There was about four feet of snow outside and Bruce suggested they go out for a stroll. They had shown up in these paper-thin, custom-made Gucci loafers and these light-weight Southern California coats, but they all swallowed hard and went out and traipsed in waist-high snow. Then Willis stops at a snowbank and says, 'You know, last week I lost the rearview mirror in this very spot.' Then he looks all wistful. 'Sure do wish I could find it.' Then he looks at the moguls expectantly. They all dived into the snow and Willis stood there with this big shit-eating grin watching them."

As celebrities became more coddled and more powerful, they expected gentler treatment from the publications that covered them—at a time when those publications were getting increas-ingly aggressive. Even *People*, that onetime celebrity-fawning mag-azine, was finding itself at loggerheads with the stars it covered. Jim Gaines, a former editor from *Saturday Review* and writer for the national affairs section of *Newsweek*, became managing editor of the magazine in 1987. Unlike Dick Stolley, who left *People* to head up a revived *Life*, or Pat Ryan, who succeeded Stolley, Gaines didn't feel the need or desire to protect celebrities from themselves. He was an ex-reporter, with a taste for news, and felt that *People* was there to tell its readers the truth about the rich and famous. The different philosophy led to some nasty conflicts between *People* and its celebrity subjects. "They surrounded themselves with fire walls of P.R. people who began trying to manipulate the press," Gaines said. "They became obnoxious, difficult barriers to the truth. It became very confrontational." The most serious of those clashes, and the one that would for years affect the relationship between *People* and celebrities, was over a profile of Robin Williams.

In early 1988, publicists for *Good Morning, Vietnam* pitched a story on Williams, but they didn't want to give *People* access to the actor unless they were promised a cover. Gaines wasn't sure he wanted to make the agreement. Comedians traditionally didn't sell well on covers, and the once-hot actor was going through a lull in his career—films like *Popeye* and *The World According to Garp* were big box office disappointments. Then Williams's publicist said the actor would discuss the affair he was having with his nanny. Gaines was thrilled. He agreed and assigned writer Brad Darrach to do the piece. Darrach spent five days with Williams, then, late one evening during a break in a photo shoot and while the actor's P.R. agent was out of the room, the actor unburdened himself about his relationship with Marsha Garces, his son's nanny. Not long after the interview, Williams started getting nervous about what he had told the reporter. He insisted that he had cooperated only after being assured that the article would focus on his professional, not his personal, life. Jeffrey Katzenberg, the chairman of Disney, which was bringing out *Good Morning, Vietnam*, asked Jim Gaines to breakfast. Katzenberg warned Gaines not to publish anything that might upset Williams. He suggested that if *People* upset someone as popular in the Hollywood community as Williams was, other stars might retaliate. Gaines was furious at what he considered an attempt at coercion and refused to change the story.

The February 22 cover was pure tabloid: "Public triumph, private anguish. Robin Williams. *Good Morning, Vietnam* has made the comic genius into a movie star at last, but his life is a minefield. Having beaten alcohol and drugs, he's now entangled in a love affair with his son's nanny that has left his wife embittered—and Zachary, four, in the middle. It's the emotional challenge of his life. 'I'll do anything,' he says, 'to keep my son from harm.' "

Williams was outraged. "It feels like psychic rape," he said in an interview years later. "When you do these things, you get halfway through and you realize, my god, they're sticking it to me. It's like this feeling of violation. And what's weird is they're stabbing you with your own kitchen utensils."

After the appearance of the article, Hollywood, which had thought it could always depend on *People* for the sort of sympathetic treatment the magazine had given celebrities like Carol Burnett when the *Enquirer* threatened to expose her daughter's drug use, now began to consider the magazine just another tabloid. And treated it as such, for the boycott threatened by Katzenberg did take place. Top stars refused to speak to Gaines's staff. "You walk up to them looking for an item," complained one writer, "and they turn on you: 'How could you do that to Robin?'" Some celebrities might have been motivated less out of loyalty and more out of fear of the onetime celebrity-friendly magazine. Citing reasons they didn't want to cooperate with the magazine, publicists would say, "You might do a Robin Williams on us."

Richard Stolley, *People*'s founding editor, believed Gaines had made a fundamental mistake in antagonizing Williams and the Hollywood community. "The Robin Williams story was harsher than it needed to be," he says. "When he began yelping, people automatically rallied to his side. . . . In a fight between an icon and the press, there's no question who Hollywood will side with."

The press, so daunted by Williams's awesome power to punish publications that printed stories he didn't like, almost totally disregarded the news when shortly after the *People* flap a former cocktail waitress named Michelle Tish Carter filed a lawsuit alleging that the comedian had given her herpes. Williams countersued, saying that Carter had threatened to tell her story to the media unless he paid her. In July 1992, shortly before he was scheduled to testify, Williams and Carter reached an out of court settlement. Under the terms of the agreement, neither side was allowed to discuss the details of the settlement. "There was no way we were going to touch that story," says a reporter for a competing magazine. "The word was out: If you take a shot at Robin Williams, you're going to get hit yourself."

A year after the Robin Williams episode, after only two years at the helm of *People*, Gaines left the magazine to run *Life*. Sources at Time Inc. say that while profits were up 44 percent under Gaines, the company's management felt the magazine had become, in its pursuit of controversy, too much like a tabloid. The new editor, Lanny Jones, set out to reestablish the trust of the Hollywood community. But by then, stars didn't need *People* anymore. They had found a new celebrity-friendly magazine that gave them status and adulation that they had not dreamed possible. It was so upscale and glossy that it made *People* look like the *National Enquirer*.

13

tina brown

Tina Brown, wearing a cleavage-baring blood red dress with lips and nails painted to match, vamped for a photographer as a crowd of spectators gathered around the Condé Nast conference room, clutching their bottles of Evian and watching in awe. The editor of *Vanity Fair* tossed back her head and smiled mischievously on that spring day in 1989, her blond hair and pearl choker shimmering under the bright lights while Annie Liebowitz, *Vanity Fair*'s star photographer, took pictures for a profile scheduled to run on the cover of *Newsweek*. There once was a time, only a few years earlier, when a news magazine would have balked at such a cozy arrangement, but in the five years since Tina Brown had taken over *Vanity Fair*, she had rewritten the rules of journalism. While most mainstream magazines at least had pretenses of journalistic integrity and concern for the good of society, *Vanity Fair* unapologetically pandered to the wealthy and powerful who controlled the magazine's financial fate. Brown hired some of the world's best-known writers and most talented photographers to chronicle the lives of movie stars, socialites, moguls, and Euro-trash; the magazine celebrated fame, power, and whatever it took to get there. "I'm bored with these suppressed style snobs who say it's brave for an actress to play a bag lady," Brown said. "Ravish and polish are what I'm aiming for."

There were still those who sneered at *Vanity Fair* as an upscale *People*—or worse. As one magazine critic quipped, "Look, Muffy, a *National Enquirer* for us." Brown took gossip and celebrity journalism off the supermarket racks and put it on the coffee tables of the richest and most influential people in the country. In one issue, Patti Davis revealed her penchant for masturbation, Priscilla Presley discussed her thwarted romance with Julio Iglesias, and Mickey Rourke grimly recounted being "hit on" by transvestites when he worked as a bouncer in a crossdressers' club. Gene Pope invented the supermarket tabloid, Dick Stolley took it mainstream, Rupert Murdoch made it mass market, and Tina Brown took it upscale.

To get the cooperation of tabloid-shy celebrities, *Vanity Fair* made deals with subjects. Sometimes the deals were explicit, written agreements promising covers or photo and text approval; sometimes implicit, such as when Mick Jagger objected to a writer who was interviewing him because she kept asking questions about his past. Tina Brown assigned a different writer. *Vanity Fair* would go so far to make a celebrity happy that when Herb Ritts was shooting Warren Beatty for a cover, one of the photographer's assistants reportedly bared her breasts to get a smile out of the sulky actor. There was almost nothing *Vanity Fair* wouldn't do to get the cooperation of the rich and famous.

Vanity Fair's formula was such a hit with the public and advertisers that other publications were forced to follow or be left behind. Magazines had to put celebrities on their covers or die on the newsstands next to those that did. At Condé Nast, *GQ* took up the formula, then *Details*, then *Vogue* and the other women's magazines. Soon, news magazines like *Time* and *Newsweek* regularly had celebrity covers. New arrivals like *Premiere* and *Entertainment Weekly* joined the fray. "Movie magazines used to be a category," Gore Vidal lamented. "Now, everything is a movie magazine." Some publications, like *Esquire*, for years tried to resist doing exclusively celebrity covers, but circulation and advertising suffered. Only about twenty-five stars were big enough to guarantee newsstand sales. To get those celebrities, editors had to offer arrangements as attractive as *Vanity Fair*'s. Big stars would agree to a cover photo with the publication that made the most attractive offer. It was usually *Vanity Fair*. Journalists in *Newsweek*'s San Francisco bureau were outraged by the way the rules were changing, and they suggested that the magazine do a tough profile of this British invader who was corrupting the values of the industry and packaging tabloid stories as upscale news.

Brown wasn't surprised when she heard about *Newsweek*'s plans. Although she had won over the readers, the subjects, and the advertisers, many in the press were still quite hard on her. There were some favorable articles—*Adweek*, for example, named Brown hottest editor of the year in 1986—but Brown was continually ridiculed in elite media circles.* Brown knew she had to change that. "I had to win the opinion of my peers," she said. "I had to seduce the media."

When Brown sat down for an interview with *Newsweek* writer Tom Mathews, she turned on all of her considerable charm. She peppered her conversation with literary references, dismissing critics in a "silvery voice," said Mathews, that was "rippling with London elegance above Manhattan's barbaric yawp." Mathews rhapsodized over "the beauty who married the rakish Harold Evans," her "uptown élan and Front Page gusto," and the way her ankles were "sculpted into her drop-dead stiletto high heels."

Tina Brown had a beguiling way of leaning over and "confiding" tidbits to interviewers. Explaining how she rescued *Vanity Fair* from the dreary staff she had inherited, Brown did her best *Dynasty* persona: "We had quite a little blood around here," she laughed. "It was rather like *Scarface*." As she chatted, Brown leaned so far forward that, according to people who spoke with Mathews after the interview, her ample bosom escaped from her décolletage. Brown blushed as she adjusted her neckline and con-

---

* Some of the criticism may have been fueled by jealousy. Jane Amsterdam, editor of the then-hot *Manhattan inc.* considered Brown a rival. Amsterdam was married to Jon Larsen, the editor of the *Village Voice* and a good friend of Harold Evans and Brown, but according to one *Manhattan inc.* source, Amsterdam was regularly on the phone with Sally Quinn, making jokes about Brown and unkind references to her "udders."

tinued the interview. After Mathews left, Brown called a colleague and announced, "We have nothing to worry about."

When Mathews handed in his article, mayhem erupted at *Newsweek*. If anything, the *Vanity Fair* editor had worked her magic too well. There were screaming fights over whether the profile should run—much less as a cover story. "It was panting," said assistant managing editor Dominique Browning. "There was way too much heavy breathing. It was sexist. It was embarrassing." The alleged breast incident was a topic of much discussion around the office. "From the way Tom described it, she might have just been leaning way over," according to a colleague. "I can't absolutely say whether he saw any nipple, but he clearly saw more than he could handle. It obviously affected his thinking. The article gushed so much that it dripped."

After several heated meetings, the profile was taken off the cover. "It just didn't belong there," Browning said. "There was no substance to it." The article was passed directly to executive editor Steve Smith—rather than the standard route of going to an assistant managing editor first—prompting outcries of favoritism because *Vanity Fair* had excerpted a book by Smith's wife, Sally Bedell Smith. Even Steve Smith, however, was concerned about the tone of the profile. "Tom, one general observation on my third read," Smith wrote in a memo to Mathews, "I think we're being too friendly." One phrase that bothered him, for example, was Mathews's line: "To her presentations, Brown brought Jane Austen's ironic sensibility and Ayn Rand's will to power."

"Forgive me in advance, Mr. Princeton Man," Smith noted. "Is this Rand or Nietzsche? A tiny voice makes me think the latter." Rand and Austen were edited out of the piece and some skepticism was edited in, but even in its toned-down state, the *Newsweek* profile drooled. "Watching her is like watching a brightly polished red Porsche cruising down the highway at 55 miles an hour," the article concluded. "Given what she's got under the bonnet, if she really guns it, no one's going to catch her."

By the time the *Newsweek* article appeared, Tina Brown had won. She had seduced the media. It was a seduction that had begun long ago.

*　　*　　*

White paper bells fluttered in a hot August breeze and a Handel concerto blared out of the shrubbery at Grey Gardens where Ben Bradlee had tucked a tape player. The executive editor of the *Washington Post* and Sally Quinn, his wife and star writer, were preparing their East Hampton vacation house for a spur-of-the-moment wedding of another May-December media couple: Their good friend, fifty-three-year-old Harold Evans, was marrying *his* former star writer, twenty-seven-year-old Tina Brown.

It was Thursday, August 19, 1981, and Harold Evans was the most distinguished journalist in all of England, the editor of the august *Times* of London, as well as the *Sunday Times* of London. Tina Brown's detractors saw the romance as yet another one of her shrewd career moves—not that her professional life needed any boosts. In 1981, Brown was one of the hottest young journalists in London.

Tina Brown had not always planned to become a writer; she was a gifted mimic and at one point wanted to be an actress. Her father, George Brown, a producer of B-movies, encouraged his precocious daughter's endeavors. "Who shall we have to dinner to massage the Iranian/Swiss/Belgian money?" he would ask; afterward he would delight in angelic-looking little Tina's scathing impersonations of the guests. Tina was kicked out of boarding school three times—once for writing that a teacher's bosoms were "an unidentified flying object." After one expulsion, George Brown told the headmistress, "How depressing for you to know that you failed with this talented child." Despite her checkered school record, Tina entered Oxford when she was only sixteen years old.* She tried acting, but her father, who was once married to actress Maureen O'Hara, said that Tina found the endeavor "a rather depressing experience." Brown once worried that she was "fat and not amusing enough" and she was terribly shy. "I was the token crud at the parties who spent the

---

* Although this tidbit is repeatedly mentioned in profiles of Brown, an article in the *Sunday Times Magazine* of London quoted Brown's classmates who adamantly insisted that she was, in fact, eighteen when she went to Oxford. "I put the point to Tina Brown," wrote Georgina Howell, "who conceded, 'Well, I might have been just seventeen.' "

whole evening reading record covers," she once confessed, "but then I would go home and write this savage reportage about everybody else's ludicrousness." Brown turned her talent for ridiculing people's foibles into a journalism career. While at Oxford, her boyfriend Stephen Glover, who would go on to help found London's *Independent*, had an appointment to interview noted writer Auberon Waugh. Tina insisted on accompanying Glover, inserted herself into the conversation, and charmed Waugh, who invited her to a lunch at Private Eye. Brown wrote a wickedly funny account of the event, which was noticed by *Daily Mail* gossip columnist Nigel Dempster, who introduced Brown to the top editors of Fleet Street.

In serious relationships, Brown gravitated toward older, influential men, including Dudley Moore, Kenneth Tynan, and Auberon Waugh, though one of her suitors recalled that she seemed to have mixed feelings about sex: "She always kept her eyes tightly shut," he said. Brown's mother, a publicist turned gossip columnist, once joked that Tina's boyfriends were so much older that her father wondered whether he should call them "Sir."

"At parties," one friend said, "you would always find Tina sitting on the lap of the most important man in the room." In the 1970s, the most important man in the room was Harold Evans. The son of a railroad engineer from the northern working-class town of Yorkshire, Evans began his journalism career when he was sixteen, eventually taking over both the *Sunday Times* and the *Times* of London, the most revered paper in England, if not the world. Evans oversaw such triumphs as groundbreaking exposés of the Thalidomide drug scandal and the Kim Philby spy story. Brown became a writer for the *Sunday Times*, penning hilarious chronicles of adventures such as hiring a male escort, offering herself up as a centerfold to *Playboy*, and working as a go-go dancer in Hackensack, New Jersey. ("Put this on and move it," disco owner Big Ed told Brown as he handed her a G-string and complimented her backside. "No, really—we like our Show Go girls a little full.") She began dating rich or socially prominent cads and then writing about them under the pseudonym Rosie Boot. "She was so pretty, so funny, young and feminine,"* said

---

* Brown was third runner-up in the Miss Holiday Princess contest.

one of her editors, "that the men she got to talk never dreamed that she would remember what they said, let alone use it against them in print." One of Brown's victims called her description of him "the worst act of betrayal since the massacre at Glencoe."

She began lurking in the corridors around Harold Evans's office. "She stalked him," said a friend. She bombarded him with passionate letters—"a love correspondence really," said Evans. "Her letters were so marvelous I fell in love." The smitten Evans began a gradual transformation; one day staffers noticed that his glasses were replaced with contact lenses, he later appeared with his combed-back hair restyled into a modish, brushed-forward do, then he began arriving at work on a black BMW motorcycle. In 1978, he dumped his wife of twenty-five years and Tina Brown moved in. "It was very much a midlife crisis when Tina came along," said London *Times* features editor Anthony Holden. After co-workers complained that Brown was getting preferential treatment from her live-in lover editor, she left and took over *Tatler* magazine when she was twenty-five-years old. "I refused to be another Sally Quinn," she later explained.* One day, while visiting Quinn and Bradlee in America, Evans proposed. By lunchtime the next day, Brown had Evans at the altar.

Writer Marie Brenner, one of Brown's closest friends in America, arrived at Grey Gardens three minutes before the cere-

---

* The comparisons, however, are inevitable, including how Quinn also seduced her married boss with passionate letters. Brown made the comment after her infamous falling out with Quinn. *Vanity Fair* called Quinn's novel *Regrets Only* "cliterature" and "a one-pound beach cutting-board and sun-tan lotion absorber." Quinn disinvited Brown and Evans from Bradlee's sixty-fifth birthday party. "As a professional journalist who specializes in hatchet jobs in the *Washington Post*," Brown said, "I don't think she should complain." Replied Quinn, "Tina's desperate for success and nothing matters to her except her magazine." The two have supposedly reconciled, but Quinn maintained that she should have at least been warned about the seemingly unprovoked attack. According to a friend of Brown, it was not unprovoked and in fact was payback for a scathing review of *Vanity Fair* that ran in the *Washington Post* in the early days of the magazine—when Brown desperately needed good press. "It is one thing to make fun of soigné fatuities," Curt Suplee wrote. "It is quite another to wallow in them. And the sheer bulk of banality in much of this magazine suggests not ridicule of vanity, but the glad embracing of it."

mony. "I'm upset!" Brown declared. Brenner began to apologize for not arriving earlier when she realized that Brown's aggravation had nothing to do with the wedding. "I'm trying to do the photo spread for the October issue of *Tatler*," Brown said, "and I'm having trouble getting the right photographer."

Grabbing a bouquet of flowers plucked from Bradlee's garden and wearing a floral print dress she'd bought in a department store the day before, Tina headed to the makeshift altar. Her parents didn't have time to fly in for the wedding, so Brown was given away by *Times* feature editor Anthony Holden. Anna Blundy, the eleven-year-old daughter of one of Evans's foreign correspondents, was recruited minutes before the ceremony to be the sole bridesmaid. Bradlee was a rather nervous best man. The Honorable Judge Sheppard Frood—who was pulled off from the golf course that morning and proudly announced to the guests that he went round in seventy-nine—officiated over the five-minute ceremony wearing mirrored sunglasses.

Shortly after the vows were exchanged, Evans and Brown left for Manhattan, where Brown hopped on a flight to London to devote her attention to *Tatler*; Evans stayed behind and spent his wedding night at the Algonquin Hotel, chatting with an old buddy from the *Sunday Times*, discussing his glory days as a journalist.

Three years later, Tina Brown was no longer married to the most important journalist in England.

Life had, at that point, turned somewhat sour for Britain's hottest media couple. Rupert Murdoch had bought the *Times* of London, and Evans, after losing a power struggle with the new owner, was forced to resign. Evans and Brown had also become the target of ridicule in certain circles. *Private Eye* relentlessly lampooned Evans, calling him "Dame Harold Evans" or "small but perfectly formed." His wife was dubbed "titillating Tina" or "the lusty, busty Tina Brown."* Harry Evans sometimes referred

---

* Evans sued the magazine at least three times, and in 1983, Evans's lawyers demanded that the magazine stop writing about him and Brown for at least eighteen months: "We hereby give our solemn pledge that we will never, hereafter, in any circumstances, make any references whatsoever to these two clapped-out old has-beens," the magazine announced. "Frankly, who wants to hear about them ever again?"

to his wife as "Tina Evans," but the name didn't stick. By 1982, Brown's star was already beginning to eclipse Evans's. She nearly tripled the circulation of *Tatler* from 11,000 to 30,000, and the once-fusty magazine attracted so much attention that in 1982, American billionaire publisher Si Newhouse bought it. Except for a short, embarrassing stint as a television host on a show called *Film '82*, Tina Brown seemed incapable of failure.

When Newhouse resurrected *Vanity Fair* in 1983, Tina Brown became a consultant and contributed an article, "Kiss Kiss Kissinger" on hers and Harry's friend, Henry Kissinger. Evans had helped the former Secretary of State with his memoirs and Kissinger counseled and consoled Evans when he was battling Murdoch. Kissinger invited Tina to his exclusive sixtieth birthday party at the swank River House. "Nancy Kissinger glimmered like a moon through layers of black lace," Brown wrote under the pseudonymous byline "Ubiquitous." "Yet the more unreal the ambience, the more real Dr. Kissinger himself became, his precision-machine mind honed and ready to engage on any required level."

Whatever else might be said about "Kiss Kiss Kissinger," it was, at least, lively and gossipy, which made it an exception in the resuscitated *Vanity Fair*. The magazine was pretentious and ponderous—with its grim, black-and-white cover photos of writers like Philip Roth and Susan Sontag. It was a commercial and critical flop. The financial drain wasn't what upset Newhouse; he could afford to support the magazine with the family's profitable but unglamorous chain of newspapers. Newhouse wanted *Vanity Fair* for status; instead it was the laughingstock of the publishing world. "This is a disaster," he told one employee.

Tina Brown and Harry Evans were spending Christmas 1983 in Barbados when Si Newhouse called and offered Tina the editorship of *Vanity Fair*. Brown, who had just turned thirty years old, accepted on the spot. "Well, I'm going to New York," she told Evans. "What about you?"

Brown had complained that she was "sick to death" of England, but her notion of life in New York was based on fantasy. "I dreamed of huge white lofts in Manhattan," she noted, "sparsely populated with graffiti and trapezoid fifties furniture." Instead,

Brown at first lived in a characterless white brick building just off Second Avenue in an unchic area of Manhattan's Upper East Side. "I dreaded going home to the tacky apartment I had rented, with disgusting leopard-skin sofas," she once confessed. Harry got jobs teaching one course a semester at Duke University and being editorial director of *U.S. News & World Report*, which was owned by their friend, Mort Zuckerman. Harry often stayed with Ben Bradlee and Sally Quinn in Washington and saw Tina on weekends.

Tina Brown was repulsed by New York. "It's too money-fixated and hysterically competitive," she complained not long after arriving. "New York is obsessed with status and power and it's a very tough place. It accepts talent with open arms, but if you don't deliver the goods, you're utterly rejected."

Brown also discovered that the caustic wit that had served her so effectively in Britain didn't play as well in the United States. "In America," she complained, "I have to keep my irony in check." It wasn't easy. Hollywood glamour was reemerging with such a vengeance that it begged to be parodied. Wall Street had turned boorish traders into tycoons and the recently minted billionaires, with their borough accents and overdressed wives, were ripe for ridicule. "Here, it takes three years for a beer-can millionaire to become the equivalent of the Astors," Brown said. "It's something that would take four generations in England. That makes New Yorkers insecure. They do not want to be mocked for it."

She even looked down on American magazines and newspapers, which she called "the bland leading the bland." Americans watched so much television, Brown scoffed, that they weren't interested in reading and didn't know how to write. "It's inane what we have to read here," Brown told a British reporter. "I had to bring my own state-of-the-art sub editor, Miles Chapman, from England, who taught everyone in the office how to write a caption."

Brown's dislike for America was inflamed during her first year in New York by the continued dismal performance of *Vanity Fair*. The buzz on the magazine was so bad, she recalled, that people greeted her by saying, "I hear you're right down the toilet." In

July 1984, six months after she arrived, *Vanity Fair* carried only 14 pages of ads, down from 168 for the first issue—then a record for a magazine launch. Brown developed a Yuppie flulike condition—"some strange fantasy virus, like an emotional collapse," she said—but she continued to search for a formula for editorial success, quizzing people who worked for the most popular personality magazines—especially *People*. At the time, the magazine had a circulation of 3 million, a celebrity-friendly approach, and virtually unlimited access to Hollywood stars. "She invited me to tea on the pretext of interviewing me for a job at *Vanity Fair*," said a top *People* editor. "After a while it became obvious that she was more interested in *People* than she was in me. She was debriefing me about what works on the covers, what people are interested in reading, how we get stars to cooperate, what sells at the newsstands, real nuts-and-bolts stuff." The *People* staffer told her that American readers couldn't get enough of stories on British royalty, and that Princess Diana was the magazine's most popular subject. Brown was a bit of a Diana expert—in her repertoire of impersonations, the one of Diana was said to be the best. Brown started working on a *Vanity Fair* cover story on Princess Diana.

Brown lived in constant fear that she would be fired. Si Newhouse's dismissals were notoriously abrupt and ruthless; Annie Flanders, the founding editor of *Details*, had what she thought was a delightful, reassuring lunch with Newhouse, only to get fired within a month. Margaret Case, a *Vogue* editor who had been with the magazine for forty-five years, walked into her office one day in the early 1970s to find workers removing her desk. Soon afterward, her shattered but neatly dressed body was found on the ground under the window of her high-rise apartment. Newhouse dumped *Vanity Fair* founding editor Richard Locke after only three issues. His replacement, former *Vogue* features editor Leo Lerman, lasted nine months. When Newhouse bought the *New Yorker* in 1985, there was widespread talk that he planned to fold *Vanity Fair* into it. Brown repeatedly asked Si about the rumors of her demise, but he always denied them. Then, in May 1985, while Brown was in Hollywood trying to woo film industry heavyweights, she heard the rumors again.

Brown caught the redeye to New York and confronted her boss. This time, Newhouse told Brown that the rumors were true. "This hasn't worked," he told her. "I'm going to send you back to England." Newhouse told Brown that he was going to make her editor of British *Vogue*, the position previously held by her rival British import, Anna Wintour. The announcement would be made after Memorial Day.

"Please, just give us a few more issues," Brown begged Newhouse. She was on the verge of tears. She couldn't go back to London in disgrace. Brown promised Newhouse that she had a few blockbusters in the works, including the Diana profile. "I know we can turn this around." Eventually, Newhouse granted Brown a temporary stay of execution. Just in case, she devised an alternative plan. "I thought the magazine was going to fold," Brown later admitted. "I got pregnant so it would be something to do."

Brown had decided that the key to her magazine's—and her own—success was to ingratiate herself with the powerful, and she pursued this goal with what Evans once described as "a certain ratlike cunning." She befriended Newhouse's good friends David Geffen and Roy Cohn. She courted media lynchpins like Liz Smith and Barbara Walters. An early article she wrote herself was a paean to billionaire trophy wife Gayfryd Steinberg, the "fresh blood on Park Avenue," who Brown called a "heroine who seems to embody the new money, the new flash, and the new feminism." The editor made no apologies for the magazine's ingratiating tone. "For us, to be anti-rich would be dumb," Brown said. "One's betrayals here have to be rather more subtle."

The couple that to Brown epitomized American excess, glitz, and power was Nancy and Ronald Reagan. Privately, Brown had no particular affection for the Reagans.* When asked if Nancy Reagan was like royalty, Brown was amused. "Nancy Reagan could never be queen of England," Brown said. "She could not stand the food at Windsor Castle and would want to put central heating into Buckingham Palace."

---

* Not long after the Reagans were no longer in power, Brown assigned a hatchet job on them.

Although Newhouse publications had a history of being kind to the Reagans,* the White House was initially reluctant to cooperate because the Reagans were suspicious of New York's media. They also didn't see the value in spending much time with this fledgling magazine. Brown let the Reagans know that the profile would be written by their longtime friend and political ally, William F. Buckley, whom she knew because Buckley had helped Evans on Henry Kissinger's memoirs.† Brown even offered the Reagans "an early opportunity to approve the photo and the text." No interview was granted, but *Vanity Fair* was given "a few minutes" at the White House to take pictures of the first couple in a brief time slot Reagan had before he was scheduled to dine with the president of Argentina. Brown selected photographer Harry Benson, who had shot many of *People* magazine's more memorable photographs, and personally accompanied him to Washington for the shoot. At the White House, they were ushered into the map room, which—with its fusty charts and diagrams—would make an appropriately presidential backdrop. It was not, however, the glamour shot that Brown wanted.

As soon as the presidential handlers left, Benson pulled out a seamless white backdrop, set up his lights, and transformed the map room into a studio. When Nancy and Ronald Reagan appeared—he in a tux and she in a glittering black floor-length dress and a five-strand pearl choker—Benson popped in a Frank Sinatra tape and "Nancy with the Laughing Face" began to play. Reagan's handlers were clearly unhappy with the way Benson and Brown had manipulated the situation. The President himself was flummoxed; he didn't want to be photographed dancing, but the first lady knew a good photo op when she saw one, and she insisted. Before long, the Reagans were fox-trotting for Benson,

---

* In 1983, when the Reagan camp was worried that the President's age and health might become an issue in his reelection, political adviser Ed Rollins approached Si Newhouse's buddy Roy Cohn for help. "I can give you anything the Newhouse papers have," Cohn told Rollins. The resulting December 4 cover of Newhouse's *Parade* magazine, "How to Stay Fit" by Ronald Reagan, effectively quieted the concerns about Reagan's health.

† Buckley was so tight with the Reagans that he is said to have pulled strings to help Ron Reagan Jr. get into Yale.

while the Argentinean president was left to study the table settings.

The photo graced the June 1985 cover. Nancy Reagan nixed the original photos. She thought the retouching had gone too far. "She wanted some of her wrinkles back," said a *Vanity Fair* insider. Inside, Buckley defended Nancy's much-ridiculed Ronnie-gaze: "Affection, pride, uninhibited devotion, and just the redeemingly provocative touch of ginger (or I think I see it) of the kind that says, If you don't see what I see in him, you are blind."

Much of the rest of the issue was devoted to the ladys-who-lunch crowd that Brown had discovered was the key to entering New York's power elite. "I realized one day that New York is a matriarchal society and the way to crack it is to win over a crucial circle of power women," Brown said. "I noted names like Brooke Astor, Pat Buckley, Nan Kempner, Jane Herman, and Annette Reed, and I went to any event which had those names on the invitation." The June 1985 issue included an article "The Women You Want to Sit Next To"—a roundup of the powerful women Brown was wooing: Susan Gutfreund, Donna Karan, Pat Newcomb, Diane Sawyer. It was illustrated with a picture of Liz Smith, in a white tuxedo, tap dancing. *Nation* writer Alexander Cockburn called it "one of the most repulsive objects I have ever seen—all the more distasteful because it represents the cynical calculation of *Vanity Fair*'s young English editor Tina Brown, about what would appeal to the Mortimer's crowd, a 32-gallon bin of international white trash, whose approval she appears to crave." It was, Brown later said, the issue that saved her.

By the end of that year, Brown had clarified the formula for the magazine's success. *Vanity Fair* celebrated the rich, the famous, the powerful; it attacked the indicted, the fallen, the out-of-power. Those tactics were the very ones Brown had used to promote her own career—even before she came to the United States. "Perhaps because she was so keen to be famous, she was careful never to step out of line," said former *Private Eye* editor Richard Ingrams. "Her more wicked, mocking tone was reserved for the unimportant or those on their way down."

Indeed, when courting the powerful, she could sound unabashedly sycophantic, as she did in her infamous 1988 letter to CAA head Mike Ovitz, in which Brown tried to persuade the reclusive agent to sit for an interview. "Dear Mike," she wrote, "I was surprised to hear from a friend who works there that you are on the point of breaking your silence to the press in *Premiere*.* I felt sure this could not be true since it would be rather like Marlon Brando choosing 'Falcon Crest' as a vehicle for a comeback." Brown then went on to explain how well Ovitz would be treated by *Vanity Fair*. "As I see it, the world has a very limited and unsophisticated grasp of what an 'agent' does, particularly when that agent is you. Right now, the most hackneyed prevailing perception of you is a 'packager,' a term which has a connotation of crassness that has little to do with what you actually achieve on a daily basis. It seems to me that a better term for your role in the life of Hollywood would be a *catalyst*: activating creativity by a gifted sense of talent, material, timing and taste, plus, of course, extraordinary business acumen." Brown offered to assign a writer, Jesse Kornbluth, who was "knowledgeably well disposed toward CAA"—who was also actively involved in screenwriting at the time. Ovitz turned down the offer for a profile, but consulted with Brown regularly, suggesting profile subjects and, in an unspoken quid pro quo, arranging for his movie star clients to attend *Vanity Fair* parties.

In addition to wooing the key figures who controlled entrée into social and power circles, Brown shamelessly pandered to advertisers. *Vanity Fair*'s adoring articles on Ralph Lauren and Calvin Klein were most obvious: Of Calvin and Kelly Klein, Andre Leon Talley wrote that "you can almost hear the click of their exact fit." The cover story on Ralph Lauren, shot by his own photographer Bruce Weber, noted of the diminutive former Ralph Lipschitz: "Ralph Lauren, in fact, seems to be the archetypal outdoorsman: He could pass for a cowboy, pilot, wilderness outfitter or lumberjack." *Vanity Fair* also ran puff pieces on Giorgio Armani, Bill Blass, Donna Karan, Kenneth Cole, Valentino, and Karl Lagerfeld.

---

* Which, at the time, was owned by Brown and Evans's nemesis, Rupert Murdoch.

"Those were stories that deserved to be done," Brown declared, insisting that the Ralph Lauren story was "very hard for us to get." She brushed off criticisms as "sexist" saying that she would never be attacked for such things if she were a man. "The Calvin Klein thing was fluff," she said dismissively. "It was fun."

"It was so obvious, really, I don't think it compromised anyone," a supporter defended. "She really had to do things like that to keep the magazine alive."

It certainly worked. In 1985, *Vanity Fair* had 431 ad pages—up from 335 in 1984—but it still lost $7 million. By 1987, the magazine carried about 700 ad pages, but, according to Si Newhouse's calculations, it needed 1,000 pages to break even. In 1989, the year after the notorious Ralph Lauren cover story, it had 1,487 ad pages—one of the most amazing growth spurts in magazine history. After the Calvin Klein article, the designer took out an extraordinary 116-page advertising supplement. *Vanity Fair* became the undisputed industry leader and other magazines scrambled to compete; exposés of the rich and powerful were replaced with articles celebrating them.

The pages and masthead of *Vanity Fair* were filled with names of Brown's allies—or people she hoped to turn into allies. Brown hired Angela Janklow, the daughter of the well-connected literary agent Mort Janklow, as a Los Angeles correspondent, even though she had little journalism experience. Brown felt that such compromises were necessary for survival. "As you live here longer, you start to see the apparent freedom and the apparently limitless scope of it all is in fact something of an illusion because it's all so money-driven, so commercial," she complained. "There is that awful commercial fact that you can't make fun of Calvin Klein, Donald Trump, and Tiffany."

Brown had, in fact, once assigned a story on Trump Tower, alleging that the construction was so shoddy that the doorknobs kept falling off. Before it got into print, Trump called his friend Condé Nast president Steve Florio and the piece was killed. "When it comes to being really made fun of, I don't think Americans take kindly to it, largely because the whole Americana dream is about making it and getting respect for having done it," she told a British reporter. "They don't see why someone would come along and mock them. I mean 'I'm Donald Trump and I am *not* here to be laughed at.' But he should be laughed at, really.''*

And indeed, at dinner parties in England, Brown would regale friends with tales of those funny rich Americans. "There's this hilarious new tycoon who has just bought a cosmetics company, and at dinner the other night his wife started to get delusions of grandeur," Brown recounted. "She turned to the hostess and said, 'Ron's ready to eat now.' It broke me up!"†

Even Brown's boss wasn't safe from her stinging sarcasm. "It's why faceless millionaires buy publications," she once said. "So they can ring up Norman Mailer and ask him to dinner"—almost certainly a reference to Newhouse, who for years pursued the writer and considered signing Mailer as a contributor to be one of his great triumphs.

"Before I lived in America, I didn't believe women existed like you have on *Dynasty*, women with coifed hair and manicured nails who run steel-pipe companies," Brown said. "Then I met these women in New York." She became one herself: beautiful, powerful, ruthless, with an intimidating array of connections and no qualms about using them. Brown's and Evans's two children had between them nearly a dozen influential godparents, including Mort Zuckerman, literary agent Ed Victor, former *Daily News* publisher Jim Hoge, Marie Brenner, and then-hot Condé Nast editor Gabbe Dopelt. With such allies, few dared cross her. "I have a long shadow," she warned, "and it's going to get longer every month." Indeed, when her brother, movie producer Christopher Hambley Brown, pled guilty in 1988 to sexually assaulting three women on

---

* Soon after Brown arrived at the *New Yorker*, she assigned Mark Singer to write a scathingly funny dissection of Trump. Trump was furious. "I guess the only good news about your recent story on me is that people don't seem to be reading the *New Yorker*," he wrote in a letter to Brown. "Almost nobody mentioned it to me—unlike two recent covers of *People* magazine." Trump also sent a letter to his friend Steve Florio: "Steve, you will never make a profit with Tina Brown editing the *New Yorker*. She is *highly* overrated and the magazine is *very* boring. Best wishes, Donald." Florio was said to have taken the letter to heart.

† Brown was almost certainly referring to Ron Perlman, owner of Revlon, a big advertiser in *Vanity Fair*.

separate occasions on trains in London, no gossip columnist in America touched the story while Brown was at Condé Nast.

Brown's mornings began when she was picked up before dawn by her chauffeur from her Central Park South apartment. Her first stop was her hairdresser, who gave her a quick comb through, and soon she was in her office sitting behind a white desk shaped like a single quotation mark. Nearby was a paper shredder. Brown had the walls painted in a peach tone to remind her, she said, of the South of France. She would bring home shopping bags full of manuscripts every evening and she and Harry—who was hired by Newhouse to edit *Condé Nast's Traveler*—would read and edit them until the wee hours of the morning. The couple found a pretext to fly back to London—invariably on the Concorde—almost once a month. "You know, Tina invented a country that we called Trans-Atlantica," Evans once said. "It had all the virtues and none of the vices of England or America. Ideally, that's what we would like—to live in England and work in New York." Evans seemed unaware that he was precariously close to describing a character lampooned in Tom Wolfe's 1966 short story, "The Mid-Atlantic Man," which describes a London adman in New York who, lording his cultural superiority over the loud, childish Americans, while greedily feasting on the abundance of American wealth, thinks he has the best of both worlds, only to realize eventually he really has neither.

Although Brown professed to love America, with its openness and vigor, privately she was still scornful of it. She worried that her son, George Frederick, would grow up too American. "I would like him to have an English accent," she confided to a fellow Brit. "I hate whining American children." Once, when one of Brown's staff brought a baby into the office, Brown screamed. "Get that goddam child out of here!" Some thought Brown's reaction was peculiar for someone who, herself, had recently become a mother. "I adore being with George, but I don't believe in bringing him into the office life," Brown said. "Nor would I whip out a tit and feed him in the middle of the Four Seasons. It's not my style."

Although Brown could be warm, charming, and funny when necessary, it was often by design. When she worked the crowd at parties, she was accompanied by an assistant who wore an earpiece that was hooked up to an office; the assistant, relaying information from the office, would whisper in Brown's ear the names and bios of the people in the crowd with whom she should be friendly. People whose names weren't likely to be boldfaced in gossip columns sometimes complained that she could also be terribly chilly. "Oh, do get out of here," she reportedly once snapped at a member of her staff. "I want somebody with taste and class to talk to." "You've shaken hands with her," one editor said, "so you know what that limp, cold hand is like. And you certainly know about the eyes fixed pointedly over your shoulder in search of someone more to her taste, someone who will rescue her from the complete and utter tedium of you."

"She's not the kind to walk into the office saying, 'Good morning, good morning, good morning,' " said editor-at-large, Sarah Giles, one of several staffers Brown imported from England and who became involved in an ill-fated romance with Tina and Harry's friend, Mort Zuckerman. "For one thing, she's too focused. She's always planning the next month's issue. She's saying to herself, 'Right, I've got my sex scandal, I've got my murder mystery, I've got my celebrity profile. Now what else do I need to round it all out?' And then on the other hand, she doesn't say good morning to anyone because she doesn't know who they are."

By the early 1990s, Tina Brown had not only succeeded in "seducing" the American media, she had also redefined its yardstick of success, popularizing the notion that a magazine should be measured by the amount of "buzz" or media attention that it generated. Brown knew how deeply Newhouse cared about his public image. "Buzz means you're hot," she would say, clipping articles about *Vanity Fair*, sending them to Newhouse with little notes attached: "Are we hot or what?" Ad pages were flat at about 1,400, and the magazine was said to be breaking even or just barely turning a profit. Newhouse had reportedly sunk somewhere between $75 and $100 million into it. Although many other Newhouse publications earned much more money than *Vanity Fair*, Si Newhouse responded by publicly declaring Brown "the best editor in the world."

Yet Brown seemed discontented with her astonishing success. Like many ambitious people, once Brown had what she fought so hard to get, she no longer found it worth having. She began to express disdain for the stars whose access she had gone to such lengths to acquire. The culture of celebrity she had helped create in the eighties now seemed to bore and even disgust her. "I don't like Madonna particularly," she said of the woman who graced *Vanity Fair's* cover more than any other celebrity in Brown's tenure. "She was just something to sell magazines." Brown felt the same way about most of her other cover subjects, "I have no desire to meet Tom Cruise or Kevin Costner," she said, although *Vanity Fair* profiles of them were adulatory. Brown, who liked to say she seldom watched television or went to movies, put *Beverly Hills 90210* heartthrob Luke Perry on the cover of the magazine while telling friends that she had never seen the show that made him a star.

"Hollywood has no romance for me because I grew up practically in the lap of Margaret Rutherford,* and people like her," Brown said. "I saw nightmare egos all day long in the movie business, and I wanted no part of it."

Once, when planning a cover story on Sylvester Stallone, an editor suggested assigning the piece to acerbic critic James Wolcott, a writer whose work Brown admired. "What's the sense in wasting Wolcott on Stallone?" Brown said. "He's such a bore. . . . In some profound way, he's a joke to me. There's something deeply camp about Stallone romping on the beach with this bimbo [his girlfriend]." The profile was given to writer Kevin Sessums, a good friend of David Geffen's who had once worked in public relations. When someone protested that Sessums sometimes got a touch weak in the knees over his subjects, Brown replied, "It really doesn't matter what the story says." Then she added with a smirk: "Stallone is right up Kevin's street, actually."

Brown for the most part, only put proven Hollywood icons like Cruise and Madonna on the cover of *Vanity Fair*, but because there are only so many stars of the caliber Brown wanted, she began recycling cover subjects, adding to her anxiety that *Vanity*

---

* Miss Marple in the Agatha Christie films Tina's father produced.

Fair's formula was growing stale. Brown also grew increasingly concerned about how her fluffy, flashy magazine was going to age. She told associates that she was worried that *Vanity Fair* was too lightweight and "too gay" and needed to "go straight." "Americans have completely overdosed on celebrity," she said. "The pretentiousness of social life in the eighties will subside. Replacing it will be privileged men and women recharging the landscape."

Brown was so determined to tap into the serious zeitgeist she saw looming, that in 1990 she took Ellen Barkin off the cover and replaced the actress with Soviet leader Mikhail Gorbachev. Barkin was furious—she claimed that the only reason she had agreed to do the interview was that she was promised a cover—and she threatened to sue. By then, Brown knew she was too powerful for Barkin to fight with her. "It would be a bad career move," Brown said dismissively. Explaining her new, politically engaged priorities, she explained, "My passion is to put, for example, El Salvador on the cover and still have strong newsstand sales."

So, in 1992, when Si Newhouse offered Tina Brown the reins of the esteemed but financially troubled *New Yorker*, she grabbed them. "Seriousness will be sexy again," she declared. "Substance is back in style." She had taken gossip upscale; now she was convinced she would be able to take intellectualism mainstream. What she ended up doing, however, was extending the tabloid sensibility and culture of celebrity into the realm of literary journalism. While Brown ran some important and intelligent articles, those were often overshadowed by the "buzz" generated by fawning profiles of movie stars and Hollywood moguls as exemplified by the time Brown asked Roseanne to guest edit a special woman's issue. Longtime *New Yorker* writer George W. S. Trow quit after a sixteen-page photo spread of the O. J. Simpson case, including Kato Kaelin blow-drying his hair. "For you to kiss the ass of celebrity culture at this moment that way," Trow wrote in his resignation letter, "is like selling your soul to get close to the Hapsburgs—in 1913."* Brown had no choice but to go in for

---

* Brown gave Trow's letter a very public platform. At the *New Yorker*'s seventieth anniversary party, actor John Lithgow performed the part of Trow. Debra Winger, complete with a clipped British accent, read Brown's response: "I am distraught at your defection, but since you never actually write anything, I should say I am notionally distraught."

glitz, said her defenders. "The patient was moribund and the new doctor had take drastic measures to revive it—including regular colonics of power and celebrity," said writer John Seabrook. "Now that the patient seems to be getting healthier, hopefully the Barry Diller enemas can be cut back." That seemed unlikely. Brown, who truly did love good writing and incisive thinking, was falling victim to the celebrity culture that she was instrumental in creating. the *New Yorker* under Brown was reduced to holding regular "roundtables" for advertisers with celebrity lures, including a special lunch, attended by Elton John and Lauren Hutton, to celebrate the unveiling of a ten-page Gianni Versace advertising insert.

In March 1994, shortly before the Academy Awards, Brown held a party in Hollywood to celebrate the *New Yorker*'s first Hollywood issue. Three hundred guests mingled under a billowing white tent in the garden of the Bel Air Hotel. Five hundred white paper lanterns glowed on the assembled stars and potentates as they exchanged air kisses and industry gossip; they buzzed about how Emma Thompson had shown up without husband Kenneth Branagh; they fussed over Lassie, who was there to promote a new video and a new line of Lassie products; and they discussed what to wear to the upcoming Academy Awards. *The* topic of the evening, however, was the magnitude of the names that Tina Brown had attracted. At one table Anjelica Huston giggled with Shirley MacLaine; at another Whoopi Goldberg chatted with Oliver Stone; at another, Warren Beatty and Annette Bening cuddled for the cameras. At table number thirteen sat Michael Ovitz, Steven Spielberg and his wife Kate Capshaw, Ralph Fiennes, United Artists chief John Calley, Barbra Streisand—and Tina Brown. "This is as much Hollywood power as *anyone* can muster," producer Joel Silver marveled.

Brown made a short speech. "This issue is not about Hollywood glitz at all," she said. "It's about the creative process of film. It's about the life, rather than the lifestyle. It's about the work rather than the money. We're celebrating the work with this issue, not the money, not the lifestyle, not the planes, not the limos." The crowd applauded enthusiastically. Then Brown blasted what she called "the snide puff piece"—the article that pretends to praise its subject only to tear him down. A few of the writers there exchanged knowing glances; "snide puff piece" accurately described *Vanity Fair*'s specialty under Tina Brown. The editor then went on to chastise magazines for compromising their editorial integrity by making deals with publicists. The crowd was less enthusiastic. "When I heard that," said one writer, "I thought, 'Isn't this like Frankenstein complaining about the havoc his monster has caused?'"

Then Robin Williams spoke. The evening, he declared, was really a charity benefit to raise cash for the money-losing *New Yorker*. "Antiques," the actor said, "are a terrible thing to waste." Williams applauded Brown's Hollywoodization of the *New Yorker*. "You can't sell a magazine," he said, "with just literature and Connecticut haiku." The actor, who had been reluctant to give interviews since he was burned by *People* nearly a decade earlier, was the subject of a fawning piece in the *New Yorker*'s Hollywood issue; it was written by a friend of his wife. "I would like to thank Tina Brown for the puff," Williams said. "I still have a hard-on." The audience howled with laughter. "Or, as Jack would say," Williams said as he adopted a raspy Nicholson voice, "a *major* chubby."

Tina Brown threw back her head and her laughter echoed through the tent. She appeared to be quite amused, quite pleased to be there among the crowd that epitomized Hollywood glitz. But then again, Tina Brown was always a very talented mimic.

the good old gal and the tycoon

"This is a lousy time for gossip," Liz Smith complained. It was early 1990, and Liz Smith was America's queen of gossip, but she was feeling like an outsider in her own profession. "With all those supermarket tabloids paying for stories, you can't compete," she said. "Scandals like Gary Hart and Jim Bakker that used to belong to the columnists are on the front page of the *New York Times*. . . . It's died out. The column isn't that important because no one is shocked by anything." A handsome woman with a weary smile and a pageboy haircut that was getting increasingly blonder, Liz Smith was facing her sixty-seventh birthday. Her column wasn't just her job, it was her life. She would get up every morning at 9 A.M. in the cluttered, two-bedroom high-rise apartment she rented on East Thirty-eighth Street that doubled as her office; she would make coffee, read over the notes from the previous evening, skim ten newspapers, and she and her two long-time assistants, St. Clair Pugh and Dennis Ferrar, would field calls from press agents eager to get a mention in her column. "We need a lead!" she would always say. "We need a lead!" By 1 P.M. Liz Smith had filed her column; three times a week she would head over to the *Live at Five* offices to broadcast her regular segment there. Then, just about every evening, she'd go to some function—sometimes as many as three or four, but she was trying to cut down. She would greet and hug and kiss her "friends," people like Malcolm Forbes, Madonna, Barbara Walters, Gayfryd Steinberg, Elizabeth Taylor, David and Helen Gurley Brown, Mike Wallace, and Candice Bergen. Many of them, she knew, weren't really her friends. "Glamour, schlamor," she said. "It's all business." What she was really after was news to fill her column. Still, it wasn't an entirely bad life. "I am overpaid, overfed, overentertained, overstimulated," she said. "What's not to like about being Liz Smith?"

In early 1990, Liz Smith kept hearing upsetting stories about her friend Donald Trump: That he was cheating on his wife Ivana and their marriage was in trouble. Donald Trump was the most famous of the new celebrity tycoons—a billionaire who was adored by the masses. His name was plastered on his buildings and casinos; tourists gathered in front of his Trump Tower hoping to catch sight of him; his 1987 autobiography had been a bestseller. If Liz could get him to talk to her about his marriage problems, it would be a big scoop. Liz thought Donald was a scoundrel, but she liked him anyway. "He was very interesting and entertaining and funny," she said. "He was always sweeping me up in his arms and saying to everybody standing around, 'Isn't she the greatest?' Of course, he did that to just about everybody."

So, in January 1990, Liz Smith picked up the phone and gave Donald Trump a call. His assistant, Norma Foederer, cheerfully greeted Liz and put her right through. "Donald, there is a strong story going around and it just won't die," she told the tycoon. "Why don't you either decide that you're going to talk to me about it and let me print it in a way that won't be too inflammatory or sensational, or fix the situation so this story ends." She was concerned for Donald and Ivana, she says. "I thought he at least should know that things were going to explode if he didn't do something, one way or the other."

Donald was evasive. "When I told him the story, he said he would think about it," Liz said. "He didn't deny it." At that point, Liz had enough to write the story, but she didn't want to do it without Donald's approval. That wasn't her style. She waited to hear back from him, but he never called. During the next few weeks, she heard more tales, including one about a screaming fight between Ivana and the other woman in Aspen. The story was getting around and Liz was eager to lock it up. She figured that a letter to Trump might work better than another phone call so she sat down at her battered Texas Instruments typewriter and banged out a note to him. She warned him that if he didn't give her the story, "You're going to be in someplace a lot worse than the Liz Smith column."

Again, she waited for a response from him. Again, he didn't answer. So Liz did nothing. As important as the story was, there was something that was more important: access. Liz had been around the block long enough to know that if you turn on your sources, you lose them. You become a pariah—an enemy of the closely guarded circle of people that you had worked so hard to penetrate. You don't get invited to their parties and they don't call you with their stories. She had watched as Walter Winchell, once the most feared and influential columnist in the country, lost it all. "He'd come to El Morocco—this man who had been so powerful—and pass out mimeographed copies of his column as it was appearing out of New York," she says. "It was so pitiful. No New York paper picked him up because he was too much trouble. He'd made too many enemies." She'd seen what happened to her former boss Igor Cassini when he'd crossed the crowd he wrote about.

Liz had almost made the mistake of alienating her sources over a decade earlier. For five years, she had worked on a tell-all book about Jacqueline Onassis. Some of Jackie's defenders had warned Liz to drop the project, and eventually she had handed over the cartons of research to an ambitious reporter named Kitty Kelley. Thanks to Liz's material, Kelley's *Jackie Oh!* had become a huge best-seller, and the writer had gone on to skewer other powerful subjects. But she had become an enemy of the people Liz wrote about and they—and ultimately, Liz herself—had stopped speaking to Kelley. Going after the rich and powerful made you famous, but it also got you cut off.

"Access," Liz says, "is everything." Her good friend Barbara

Walters knew about access. "Barbara Walters's whole career wasn't made on her talent," Liz told reporter Jonathan van Meter. "It was made on her ability to get access. So access was worth millions of dollars to NBC and then to ABC and then to herself." Liz Smith, unlike so many of the upstart columnists who were trying to make a name for themselves, had a secret weapon: friendship. And it did help her get scoops. When Barbara Walters was getting a divorce, she gave the story to Liz. And when writer Nora Ephron split from Watergate reporter Carl Bernstein, she called up her friend Liz and gave her the story. Nora Ephron knew that it would be written in a way that was sympathetic to her.

When Liz heard that Elizabeth Taylor was getting married to construction worker Larry Fortensky, "I wrote her a letter and told her that after twenty-six years of friendship, I should be at that wedding," Smith says. She got the invite, and was the only journalist there.

Some people, especially those in the press, would attack and ridicule Liz, accusing her of being too close to her subjects, and it's true that she treated her friends well. Sometimes, she was so enamored of the glamorous people whom she wrote about that she was somewhat oblivious of their follies. When Liz Smith got invited to Saul Steinberg's jaw-droppingly extravagant fiftieth birthday party, she gushed in print over it. "I thought I was doing my job, and I got absolutely blown out of the water for ass-kissing the Steinbergs." In private, Smith is a little more circumspect about Gayfryd: "She's a very chic, severe, sort of frightened-looking person. She isn't terribly friendly. Looks like she could pass for a dominatrix."

Liz didn't believe that you have to write everything you know about people. She knew how it felt to have people hounding you about your private life—stuff that she felt was irrelevant. Staffers from a gay magazine were always threatening to reveal details about her sex life. "I think they're terrorists," she once told a reporter. "I think they must be very frightened and desperate people. They're so hateful and irrational. Talk about not living-and-let-living. I don't get it. I also think they're jealous of anybody that they think made it. I mean, what do they want me to be, the great lesbian of the Western world? Forget it! If I was Sandra Bernhard, maybe. But even then I'm not so sure."

"Jealousy," Liz says of her media critics. "I think a lot of it is just jealousy that they can't get invited to these parties. So they bitch and carry on that people who do get invited are all co-opted. But we're all co-opted by our friends to some extent. I don't know how you can avoid that."

Despite all her efforts to be nice, Liz still made some enemies. "I once had a terrible fight on the phone with Bette Midler, who called me up and said, 'I don't want to be in your fucking column.' " Mel Gibson and Burt Reynolds wouldn't speak to her. Sean Connery once got so angry with her that he told her, "I'd like to stick your column up your ass." Liz laughs: "I told him it was the best offer I had all week." Frank Sinatra was the cruelest. Liz knew better than to carry on a feud with the well-connected crooner; she and Sinatra later had lunch and she never mentioned his unkind comments. "It's like walking a tightrope," she explained. "If you disagree, in print, with anyone, they go nuts and try to kill you! Why do people get so inflamed abut being mentioned in a mere gossip column?"

Nearly a month had passed since Liz Smith first called Donald about his marriage. It was early February 1990, and she was working in her office, trying to make her 1 P.M. deadline when her assistant St. Clair Pugh told her that Ivana Trump was on the phone. "She knew," says Liz. "I heard she was a basket case over this whole thing. She wanted to have a private meeting." Donald was in Japan at the Mike Tyson fight so they could meet in the Trumps' Fifth Avenue apartment—the marble and mural-covered condo on the top three floors of the Trump Tower. Ivana answered the door herself, and Liz was shocked at the state she was in. She was nearly hysterical, tears streamed down her face and her nose and eyes were red and puffy. "She cried and wept and sobbed through the whole thing," says Liz. "She was in such a state of shock."

Ivana had accidentally discovered that Donald was seeing another woman. "I did find out first time on the telephone," Ivana recalled. "When I did pick up the phone in the living room and

Donald picked up the phone in the bedroom. In Aspen. And—
he spoke to a mutual friend of ours. And he was talking about
Mula and I really didn't understand. I never heard a name like
that in my life. And I came to Donald—I said who is Mula? And
he said, well, that's a girl who is going after me for the last two
years. And I said, Is that serious? And he said, Oh, she's just
going after me.''

Ivana, a one-time model and an alternate on the Czechoslova-
kian Olympic ski team, had immigrated to Canada in the early
1970s and married Trump in 1977 when he was just another
brash real estate developer. She worked with Donald on some of
his properties, especially the Plaza, and was the quintessential
1980s socialite: she loved to lunch at places like Le Cirque and
enjoyed wearing flashy jewels and designer clothes. "I don't ever
intend to look a day over twenty-eight," she once joked. "And
it's going to cost Donald a lot of money."

Liz Smith liked Ivana. "She's a nice woman," said Liz, though
she was, to put it kindly, "not a rocket scientist." For years, there
had been rumors linking Donald with high-profile women—the
reports were often denied by the women—including ice skater
Peggy Fleming, Mike Tyson's wife Robin Givens, socialite Georgette Mosbacher, and Dynasty star Catherine Oxenberg. Not long
before, Ivana had returned from a trip looking so dramatically
different that some friends didn't recognize her. She denied that
she'd gone under the knife, but the word among her crowd was
that she'd visited Michael Jackson's plastic surgeon, Steven Hoefflin, and had her face done to resemble Catherine Oxenberg's.

Ivana was distraught by the news that yet another woman was
going after her Donald. The next day in Aspen, Ivana confided in
a friend, who pointed out someone who knew this Marla. "I saw
[Marla's friend] in the line—in the food line [at a restaurant called
Bonnie's]—and I said, Will you give her the message that I love
my husband very much. And that was it. And I walk outside.
And I didn't know this Marla was standing behind the girl in line
because I never met her, I had no idea. And then Marla just
charged right behind me and she said—in front of my children—
'I love Donald. Do you?' And Donald was just looking up like
nothing happen or so . . . I said—I said—I really said—I said, 'Get

lost. I love my husband very much.' It was very unladylike, but it was as much as I really could—I—I—that was as much as I really—as harsh as maybe I could be.''

Donald was standing by, watching the whole thing, not saying a word. When the confrontation was over, he said to Ivana, "You're overreacting."

Word of the Aspen catfight spread quickly among members of the social set. Friends who had long known about the affair called Ivana to comfort her—and confirmed her worst fears, that Donald was seeing someone else. For two months, Ivana tried to live with the idea, but, she sobbed to Liz, she couldn't bear it. She had a lawyer, she wanted a divorce.

Now Liz had a dilemma: Ivana didn't want her to write the story. "She called to confide in me," said Liz. "She was afraid Donald was going to announce it. She said she knew Donald would ruin her, that he would take me away from her—he would take Barbara Walters and all her friends away from her. She asked if I knew of any good public relations people, because she was going to need one if the story came out. I left thinking it would be really dirty pool to betray her by printing the story.''

Liz had learned long ago, when she was a struggling writer trying to make a name for herself in New York, that the key to her success was helping her high-profile friends. Donald wasn't going to give her the story, but if she could talk Ivana into it, that might be nearly as good. "Within a day, I was talking to her lawyer and to the publicist, trying to convince them that it was in Ivana's best interest to release the story before Donald did," said Liz. "They agreed with me, and I guess they talked her into it." Sometimes, to maintain access, Liz knew, you had to take sides. Liz promised Ivana and her lawyer that she would treat Ivana well—and she lived up to her word.

On Friday February 9, 1990, Liz Smith had the manuscript hand-delivered, in secret, four blocks uptown from her office to the East Forty-second Street offices of the *Daily News*. She was biting her nails. It was two whole days before the *Daily News* was going to break the story in the Sunday paper. She included a note to Fran Wood, her editor: "I only got this by swearing in blood to do it their way and Ivana's lawyer doesn't want his name revealed yet. . . . After [Donald] gets off the plane Sunday night I'm afraid he's going to kill her—or me. But that's show biz. My chief hope is that we can keep someone on staff from leaking to the *Post* or *Newsday.* The lawyer (hers), however, says so far there are no calls or nibbles, so maybe nobody knows she has this lawyer yet. I will be available until the wee hours."

"LOVE ON THE ROCKS," the February 11, 1990, page one banner headline declared. "Mrs. Trump is reportedly devastated that Donald was betraying her" the article read. Ivana was so busy "rearing their three young children and being her husband's full-time business partner that she had absolutely no idea the marriage was in trouble . . . Intimates say Ivana had every chance to continue being Mrs. Trump by allowing her husband to live in an open marriage so he could see other women. But the bottom line is she won't give up her self-respect to do it."

It wasn't a big story—it was epic. The Trump Divorce erupted into a tabloid war like the city had rarely seen. For days, New Yorkers talked about little else. The couple that had it all— wealth, power, fame—was kaput. It signaled the real end of the eighties—the fall of the mighty, the comeuppance of arrogance and greed. It was, Liz later admitted, the biggest scoop of her career. It made Liz a celebrity and it put her in the center of the world that she had always covered. It was exactly the sort of story that she had once dreamed of writing.

Mary Elizabeth Smith was raised far from the glamour and power of New York. Born on February 2, 1923, in Fort Worth, Texas, to a cotton broker and his wife, Smith grew up in what she calls "the Booth Tarkington era, when America was innocent, when little boys fished with a bent pin and a dog could sleep in the middle of the street and not be run over." Like many Depression-era children, she was enthralled by the movies and religiously went to the nearby Tivoli Theatre. She wanted to become cowboy star Tom Mix, or, better yet, Fred Astaire. She became so fixated on the stars that she began to follow their real-life stories in the movie magazines and in Walter Winchell's column. Her father gave her a typewriter when she was eight and she made a fake newspaper—with columns and all. During World War II, she worked in an airplane factory while her first husband, an Army Air Corps pilot named Edward Beeman, fought in the Pacific. They divorced soon after he returned. "I really loved this guy a lot, but I sure wasn't meant to be anybody's wife," she says. "I had very high expectactions for myself. I wanted to be like Myrna Loy." She enrolled in the University of Texas, where she majored in journalism.

In 1949, the year after she graduated, she hopped a bus to New York with $50 in her pocket. She dreamed of becoming a serious writer for magazines like the *New Yorker* or *Time*, but was turned down everywhere. Actor Zachary Scott, about whom she had written a glowing profile while she was in college, pulled strings and got her a job at *Modern Screen*, the last of the old-time movie magazines. It was a valuable early lesson on favors. She held a number of jobs, including producer for Mike Wallace and ghostwriter for Igor Cassini. "New York was still very glamorous then—black-and-white floors, satin dresses, men in dinner jackets," she said. "I went to El Morocco every night for five years." Smith was briefly married a second time, to a travel agent named Freddie Lister, who mysteriously disappeared years after the divorce. After Igor Cassini was fired in a flap over his work for the Dominican Republic, Liz made an unsuccessful bid to take over the column. She wrote for several magazines, including *Cosmopolitan* and *Sports Illustrated*. She was also one of the anonymous contributors to a mean-spirited column called Robin Adams Sloan. Around this time, Liz started seeing a pyschiatrist, "a fabulous mother type" who helped her realize that one of the things that was keeping her back was envy. Liz had worked with a lot of famous people but "deep down, I was jealous, maybe, of their fame or their power or their money. And one morning, I asked myself, 'Do I like these people?' I did! They were very kind to me. I wanted them to succeed, because on top of everything else, their success would be my success. And at that moment, one career life ended and another began for me. When I sincerely started to want others to succeed, when I worked to help them do just that, my career took off. Real sucess followed." In 1976, Liz Smith got her own column in the *Daily News*, which was looking for a counterpart to its Aileen "Suzy" Mehl's society column. Liz Smith was a hit, and shortly after its debut it jumped from page twenty-two to page six, leapfrogging "Suzy"—who won't speak to her to this day.

In the 1980s, with the Wall Street boom and the emergence of nouvelle society, businessmen and moguls realized something that celebrities had long known—fame increases market value. They began angling to get mentions in the respectable gossip columns—especially Liz Smith's. By the time the Trump divorce erupted, Liz had redefined the art of access gossip journalism and had become the most prominent and most sought after in her field. When celebrities, authors, businessmen, or socialites knew that a detail of their private lives was about to become public because of some looming scandal, they would often turn to Liz for sympathetic treatment. It worked for Liz, it worked for them, and it worked for the *Daily News*. It never worked better for all three then it did with the Trump Divorce.

If there was one thing more humiliating for the staff of the *New York Post* than the looming prospect of bankruptcy, it was getting beat on a big story by the *Daily News*. "This shoulda been our story," *Post* editor Jerry Nachman was bellowing. "How did we get scooped by the Daily Snooze?" The *Post* staffers sat with their faces buried in Liz Smith's breathless report. The *Post* had the scrappiest, hardest working reporters in town—but they'd been under siege lately. The staff at the dingy, rat-infested offices overlooking the FDR Drive were being hit with layoffs and pay cuts. There was rampant speculation about who—if anybody— would buy the tabloid, which was hemorrhaging more than $10 million a year. The Trump story had been circulating for months. They couldn't use it. A while back, Page Six had run a blind item about Trump's other woman. Several weeks before Liz's story broke, word of the Aspen spat had reached executive editor Steve Cuozzo. He called "Suzy," who in 1985 had left the *News* and her nemesis Liz Smith for the *Post*. She knew the Trumps well. "It's absolutely true," Suzy said. "The girl's name is Marla Maples. She's a model from Georgia and they've been seeing each other for months."

Cuozzo was thrilled. "When are you going to write it?" he asked.

"I'm not going to touch it," "Suzy" said.

They all knew the story, says a *Post* reporter: "Trump was friends with Peter Kalikow [then the owner of the *New York Post*]. They had worked on deals together. There was even talk that Trump was going to buy the *Post* from Kalikow. There was no way we were going to piss off the boss's friend."

Donald Trump was flying home from the Mike Tyson fight in Japan when his assistant Norma Foederer called him in his private jet with the news. The story was page one of the *Daily News*. Trump, the master of media manipulation, had been scooped by his wife.

One of the first things Trump did when he got to his office was to call up his old friend Liz Smith. "I am leaving because I want to leave," he told Liz, desperately trying to respin the story to his advantage. "Ivana is a very wonderful woman and a very good woman and I like her. We might even get back together." Liz had given Donald a chance to break the story with her, and he didn't. "You gotta dance with the one who brought you," Liz said. She stuck with Ivana.

Ivana had snagged the best-read and most-liked columnist in town. Suzy would write some pro-Donald stories, but she had been around too long, and after Suzygate—a wildly publicized episode in 1988 in which it was revealed that many of the big names in one of Suzy's party columns had never actually attended the event—she was no longer a powerful enough ally. That left Donald with only one real option: Cindy Adams.

Readers looking for unbiased news and solid reporting didn't bother with Cindy Adams's column. Cindy Adams wasn't really a journalist—she was a character. If Liz Smith was the good old girl of gossip, Cindy Adams was the Dragon Lady of Dish. Liz Smith was small-town and star-struck while Cindy was a smart-mouthed, pushy New Yorker—and she cultivated the image. Her conversation and her column were heavy with attitude and peppered with words like *kiddo* and *chick*. Cindy always dressed to the nines: she wore big jewels and bigger eyelashes. She showed up for TV appearances with her own hair and makeup person in tow, and once there, she sometimes refused to go on with lesser guests. She once tried to get a hapless reporter fired for not recognizing her at a party. Cindy Adams and her husband, comedian Joey Adams, traveled around town in a white chauffeured Cadillac and ate free meals in restaurants that got plugged in Cindy's column.

By the mid 1970s, Cindy's career had not gone very far since she butted heads with Dorothy Kilgallen in the sixties. She had become friends with a number of politicians and Third World leaders from her touring days with Joey, and she sometimes wrote about her conversations with them for third-tier magazines and neighborhood newspapers. Then one day, she had to cancel a lunch that she and Joey were going to have with an editor from the *New York Post*, where Joey had a humor column. "I can't make it," she told the editor. "My close personal friend, the Shah of Iran, wants to see me." The toppled dictator was on his death bed, and journalists around the world were desperately trying to get a quote from him. The stunned editor asked if Cindy could possibly get an interview. "Of course," she said. The interview was short on facts but high on drama and it made international headlines. Cindy Adams was rewarded with her own column in the *New York Post*.

Cindy Adams's column quickly became the place where the world's maligned—the drug kingpins, tax cheats, sex harassers— could get sympathetic treatment. Old buddies like the Marcoses, the Sukarnos, and Adnan Khashoggi all cried on Cindy's shoulder and got a fiery defense in Cindy's column. Cindy would, in turn, get world exclusives from them. So, with Liz already taken, Donald Trump had nowhere else to turn. Cindy Adams became his ally.

The tabloid war was on—the battle lines were drawn. Ivana had as her defenders Liz Smith and the *Daily News*. And at Liz's recommendation, Ivana hired public relations guru John Scanlon, who also happened to represent the *Daily News*.

Donald Trump's side was being presented by Cindy Adams and the *New York Post*. Doing public relations for Donald Trump, not coincidentally, was Howard Rubenstein Associates, the company that also represented the *New York Post*.

A lot happened in the world that week. The Berlin Wall was toppled and Germany was reunited. Drexel Burnham Lambert, the wildly powerful junk bond company that spearheaded the 1980s financial boom, collapsed. And after twenty-seven years in prison, South African civil rights leader Nelson Mandela was freed. But for *eleven* straight days, the front pages of the tabs were devoted to the Trump Divorce.

Time and *Newsweek* did cover stories. Even the *New York Times* stooped to cover it. Some of the best coverage came from Carl Bernstein's old paper, the *Washington Post*. Bernstein, who was pulling an ill-fated stint at *Time*, was disgusted, calling it the "Three Mile Island of journalism: a meltdown waiting to happen." He seized the opportunity to attack Liz Smith and her "smarmy sort of New Journalism."*

"*Time* interviewed me for its story on gossip," says Smith. "The first questions its reporter asked me was whether I had a face-lift, dyed my hair and whether I was gay. I would never ask anybody any of those questions. And it had the audacity to make fun of me for being trivial."

Because she had a lock on one side of the story, Liz Smith wasn't just reporting the story, she was becoming part of it. She was getting embarrassed by this spectacle, but her editors and her WNBC-TV producer loved it. For three months she was allowed to write about hardly anything else. "I'm getting sick of myself," she confided to friends.

"If this isn't a tabloid story, there are no tabloids," said Matthew Storin, managing editor of the *Daily News*, who, in addition to Liz, had about a dozen reporters plus photographers on the story. Newspaper sales skyrocketed. Ratings for *Live at Five* jumped 50 percent.

---

* Liz suspected that Bernstein was still smarting over her coverage of his split from Nora Ephron. "He uses me in lectures as the great devil of American journalism," says Liz. "He came up to me at a party one night and threw himself in my arms and cried and said how much I'd hurt him. He blamed me for the divorce."

Smith's producer at WNBC was jumping up and down, calling her first thing in the morning: "What have you got?" he'd ask.

"Fuck you," Liz told him. "I'm asleep."

He'd call back in a few minutes. "I mean, he tormented me. We got some great stuff because he was so aggressive. It was the biggest story I ever saw happen that wasn't important—next to Elizabeth Taylor and Richard Burton."

Liz Smith was a star. She was on the cover of magazines. All because of access. But the serious journalist she had once wanted to be was slipping further and further away. "I hate myself," she said. And she was about to get in even deeper. On Valentine's Day, she and Ivana and about a dozen of Ivana's friends and family were scheduled to celebrate Ivana's forty-first birthday at La Grenouille, a ritzy Midtown restaurant.

Liz Smith, Barbara Walters, Carolyn Roehm, Shirley Lord, Ann Bass, Judy Taubman, Georgette Mosbacher, even Trump's mother, his sister, and their sister-in-law, Blaine Trump, were there for support. While an unruly mob gathered outside, the power women dined on lamb chops, asparagus en croute, and chocolate cake. Ivana, wearing a bright red designer jacket, cried throughout much of the lunch. She was showered with heart-shaped gifts and declarations of support; Adnan Khashoggi sent a cake. "Donald Trump's name was never mentioned," says Liz Smith "He was like a hovering presence."

Ivana had been escorted into the restaurant by two beefy guys who looked like they belonged with the Secret Service— with walkie-talkies, earphones, and all. When it came time to leave, "Ivana was scared to go outside," says Liz. So were most of the ladies who lunched. Reporters, photographers, cameramen—even her fans—were getting incredibly aggressive for a quote from the elusive Ivana, who would speak for the record only to Liz. "I'm not afraid of the press," Liz said. "Those were my pals out there, or my enemies—my peers, at least. I'm not afraid of them." Liz turned to Barbara Walters and said, "Come on, Barbara, you and I will go out there with Ivana."

So two of the best-known newswomen in the country became bodyguards, flanking the teary-eyed socialite. The crowd surged forward, and Barbara got pushed aside before they could make it through the door. Ivana was trembling. "I wanted to get out of there and get Ivana out," said Liz. "Barbara was shoved aside, so it was just the two of us." The crowd went crazy as the pair appeared.

"Get the money!" someone shouted.

"Get the Plaza! We're with you, Ivana!"

"Break his ass, blackmail him."

"Take Donald's money! Take his money, Ivana!"

"I said to Ivana 'Now smile. Be like Jackie Onassis,' " recalled Liz. "You don't want to go out there and let them see how sad you are. You look so beautiful. Just smile.' So we both went out with those idiot grins on our faces."

A huge photograph of the two women and their wide grins was plastered across the front page of the February 15 *Daily News*: "DOING OKAY" blared the headline. "Outside a crowd cheered Ivana. Inside posh La Grenouille, her pals, including our Liz Smith, moved her to tears with their support."

"I looked like her nurse taking her to a psychiatric ward," Liz says. "I was shocked. I didn't know the paper was going to be there."

Donald Trump had always enjoyed a cozy relationship with the press. Reporters were sometimes a bit awed when Trump himself returned their calls. He always asked about their health and their career and remembered the names of their spouses and children. He often told them they were "the greatest." He sometimes spoke to them off the record asking to be quoted as "a source close to Trump" and would tell them how fabulous business was and what an incredible deal he'd just made. And, presto, the next day there it was, word for word, in the papers. He would exaggerate his own personal wealth at say, $3 billion, and what do you know, the next day, according to the papers, he was worth $3 billion, and the banks would come knocking on his door to do business. He could make something come true by telling it to reporters.

Trump had expected his divorce to be big news, but not quite this big. "I've never seen anything like it," he declared. "Nelson Mandela's probably calling up 'Who is this guy? He blew me off the front page.' . . . It's been great for business. Business is hotter than ever." The *Post* headlines were making him out to be a superstud: Don Juan, they called him. Another declared that Donald gave Marla "The Best Sex I Ever Had." Ivana, according to the *Post*, was greedy. "Gimme the Plaza," one headline blared. They dug up a story on her first marriage and an old picture of her with brunette hair and ran the headline: "Ivana's Past as Dark as Her Natural Hair Color." But some of Donald's cronies didn't have his skill in dealing with the press. Trump's lawyer bragged to Cindy Adams: "I'm a killer. I can rip skin off a body. . . . I can cause pain. [I once made an opponent] collapse on the witness stand." He was playing it too hard.

Ivana's side seized the opportunity to play the victim. "Mrs. Trump emigrated to America from a repressive police state where violence was commonplace," said John Scanlon, Ivana's P.R. guy. "She did not expect that she and her children would ever be threatened again, particularly by her husband's lawyer."

The whole episode was beginning to turn into a public relations disaster for Trump. Liz Smith was a very effective advocate for Ivana. The press and the public, which had always seemed to adore him, began turning on him. According to a *Daily News* poll, 82 percent of the readers sided with Ivana. John Cardinal O'Connor consoled and counseled Ivana for forty-five minutes. Trump didn't want to be seen in public with Marla, so Garry Trudeau made fun of his "Bimbo Limbo." Trump began blasting the coverage as a "media circus." Cindy, who took to calling him "P. T. Barnum Trump," didn't always help his case. "Well, he just has too much juice or too many chromosomes, whatever it is God gave him," Cindy declared in Trump's defense. "He's got lots of aggression and he's just not going to lose. He has not made a great many friends on the way up but it's because that's the way he is. He's a killer and he knows it."

Trump demanded that Liz Smith be fired: "Liz Smith is being used, she was played like a fiddle." He accused Liz of making up quotes and writing "whatever comes into her head." He declared, "Liz Smith used to kiss my ass so much it was embarrassing." She had, he said, "disgraced the industry." There were rumors he might buy the *Daily News* and fire her.

Then he played his Trump card. Marla Maples, the Georgia Peach who hadn't spoken a word publicly, was going to be unveiled at the April 5 grand opening of the Taj Mahal—Trump's massive Atlantic City casino gamble. On March 1, Trump gave Cindy Adams the scoop. When Adams asked Donald whether he was unveiling Maples as a "devoted lover" or "savvy businessman" he replied, "Use your imagination."

Liz Smith was outraged. "It's just about the most tasteless thing I could imagine," she said. "It is the absolute nadir, after all his denials [that they were involved] and his saying he's worried about his children and his wife is a nice woman and blaming the press. It would just be the ultimate exploitation of this girl."

"So what if it's tacky?" Cindy shot back. "Calm yourself. We're talking about crap tables and slot machines, baby. We're talking about the quintessential hype. The Garden State Parkway will be a parking lot from New York to Atlantic City that day. This is a guy who is very savvy, and he will turn a negative stream of publicity into a positive one. He had her lying—laying—low for a purpose."

"That's like using her as a dishrag to wipe up some mess," said Liz. "I think he's finished in New York if he does something like this. I can't see really nice people wanting anything to do with someone who does something like that."

In mid-March, Marla got uninvited.

By late March, stories started appearing in Cindy Adams's column distancing Donald from Marla. Cindy assured her readers that Trump had no intention of marrying Marla. She began referring to Marla as "the future Miss Maples." The *Post* ran a story that Trump had dumped Marla, and that she "sobbed uncontrollably" during the "it's been real" phone conversation and "begged him not to leave her." Marla's spokesman Chuck Jones* angrily denied the reports and accused the media of sloppy and irresponsible reporting. If there was any mystery about who was behind the leaks, it was solved during a peculiar interview that Donald Trump gave *People* magazine reporter Sue Carswell.

---

* The shoe fetishist who would later admit to stealing and having "an intimate relationship" with Marla's pumps.

When Carswell called Trump's office to ask about the reported split with Maples, Trump wasn't sure he could trust her. He'd barely spoken with her and didn't have the relationship with her that he had with so many other reporters in town. Trump returned Carswell's call and said that his name was John Miller. "I'm sort of new here," Miller said. "I'm handling P.R. because Trump gets so much of it." He confirmed the sordid details of the split with Marla, and said it had never been that serious between them. "He's somebody who has a lot of options and frankly he gets called by everybody—everybody in the book in terms of women. . . . A lot of the people that you write about—and you do a great job by the way—but a lot of those people you write about, they call to see if they can go out with him," this "John Miller" told Carswell.

Donald Trump had a new woman in his life, he said, "Her name is Carla Bruni Fredesh. I don't know how to spell the last name. . . . She was having a very big thing with Eric Clapton and Eric Clapton introduced her to Mick Jagger and Mick Jagger started calling her and she ended up going with Mick Jagger and then she dropped Mick Jagger for Donald and that's where it is right now, and again, he's not making any commitments to Carla just so you understand." Madonna had called wanting to go out, too. Kim Basinger was also after Trump, said Miller. "She wanted to come up and discuss a real estate transaction. And you know, she wanted to go out with him. That was the reason she came up. Competitively, it's tough. It was for Marla and it will be for Carla." But, said Miller, Donald Trump wasn't in the marrying mode right now. "When he makes the decision, then that will be a very lucky woman."

Trump didn't know that Carswell had taped the twenty-minute conversation. When she played the tape for some other *People* reporters, they burst out laughing. "That's Donald Trump," one said. He had talked to Trump often enough to recognize his voice. Carswell didn't know whether to believe it. She played the tape for Ivana. That's him, Ivana confirmed. Marla Maples also recognized the voice, and was devastated. Trump was horrified. Trump the trickster, Trump the great media manipulator had been caught. The curtain had been thrown back to reveal the Great Wizard of Trump at the controls. The jig was up.

Over at *Forbes* magazine, the editors were eager to get an angle on the hot Trump story. A former cop named John Connolly was trying to pitch an article on casino operator Merv Griffin. Executive Editor Jim Michaels wasn't interested in Griffin. After years of running the magazine, Michaels was being eased out. He needed to make a big splash to keep his job. Years earlier, he had made headlines by running an exposé on the finances of William Zeckendorf, the high-flying real estate developer who was the Donald Trump of the 1960s. "I don't want Merv Griffin," Michaels told Connolly. "Get me Donald Trump. I want Donald Trump." Trump claimed that Malcolm Forbes was out to get him because he had kicked Forbes and some underage male friends out of the Plaza. The magazine hit the newsstands in May 1990, saying that the tycoon was worth considerably less than he claimed—Trump put his wealth at $5 billion; *Forbes* said $500 million would be a "generous" estimate. The spooked creditors came knocking, and that summer, Trump filed for bankruptcy.

Cindy Adams said the bad publicity over Trump's messy split directly led to his financial problems. "You cannot urinate on a long-term marriage and not have the white glare of spotlight publicity come down on you," she said. "And the bankers are a very conservative lot."

Says another Trump defender: "It was because he was so high flying that he became such a target."

Jim Michaels kept his job.

Ivana prospered. She got $25 million in the divorce settlement—what the pre-nup had called for—but, more important, she won over public favor. Ivana came out with her own line of clothing, a fragrance called Ivana, a newspaper advice column for the lovelorn, a line of jewelry that she hawked on television, and a novel about an immigrant socialite who bounced back after being cheated on by her tycoon husband. She denied that it was based on her life. She also denied that a wicked, smart-mouthed gossip columnist named Sabrina who sided with the husband was modeled after Cindy.

Liz Smith also prospered. On February 1, 1991, a year after the Trump story broke and while bankruptcy was looming over the *Daily News*, Liz Smith was snatched away by *Newsday*, at a salary that was reported to be as high as $1 million a year. The deal solidified her position as the highest paid print journalist in the country and, perhaps, the most powerful.

Donald Trump knew that. In June 1991, Liz Smith got a letter from her former foe, Donald Trump. "Liz, you crucified me for a whole year," Trump wrote. "But you're terrific."

the rise of tabloid television

"How can you do this to me, Jessica?" Steve Dunleavy shouted through the door. It was April 27, 1987, and Dunleavy, the senior correspondent for Rupert Murdoch's television program, *A Current Affair*, was standing outside the Massapequa, Long Island, apartment of Jessica Hahn, the curvaceous, big-haired former secretary who earlier that month had revealed that she had had an affair with the televangelist Reverend Jim Bakker. Dunleavy had been trying for weeks to get an interview with Hahn; he had offered her money, he said he would make her famous. He and Peter Brennan, one of the show's producers, had even stood under the window of her apartment serenading her at 4 A.M. But Hahn had so far resisted his importunities, and earlier that evening, while *Current Affair*'s host Maury Povich was watching the ABC *Evening News* at a bar with Dunleavy, he saw Ted Koppel appear in a teaser and announce, "Tonight, our guest will be Jessica Hahn, in her first interview since the scandal broke."

"I yelled out to Dunleavy, who had been promising he would get the first interview with Jessica," said Povich.

Dunleavy rushed off to the secretary's apartment. Through

the door, Hahn made apologies. The *Nightline* appearance, she explained, had been set up by the agent she had just been forced to hire. The agent thought Hahn needed to establish her credibility and that the best way to do this would be through one of the serious network news shows. Dunleavy was undeterred. As he stood out on the middle-class Long Island street contemplating his next move, the limousine that ABC had hired to drive Hahn to its New York studio arrived. And that was when Dunleavy, who is nothing if not resourceful, realized what he had to do. Identifying himself as a friend of Hahn's, he told the driver that the young woman had become sick and needed to go to the hospital. The limousine driver accepted this story, turned around and drove back to New York without his designated passenger. Dunleavy, meanwhile, summoned an ambulance and escorted Hahn out to the vehicle when it arrived. Meanwhile, at home in his New York apartment, Maury Povich turned on *Nightline*. "First, a schedule change," Koppel said when the show began. "Earlier this evening, Jessica Hahn, who was going to join us later in the program, went briefly to a hospital. She was seen by a doctor, treated, and is now back at home. I spoke to her a short time ago, and she'll be joining us another time."

But before that could happen, she gave her first exclusive, a few days later, to Steve Dunleavy.

Dunleavy, whom *Time* magazine once called "America's most renowned and reviled tabloid journalist," had been a central figure in the tabloidization of the American media since the mid-seventies. A native Australian who grew up in Sydney, Dunleavy was the head of a youth gang called the Blackhawks. When he was fourteen, Dunleavy quit school to work as a copyboy at the *Sydney Sun*. His father, a well-known news photographer, also worked at the *Sun*. "He taught me a few tricks in skullduggery," Dunleavy said. To escape charges of nepotism, Dunleavy went to work for the rival *Daily Mirror* at the age of fifteen. This put him into direct competition with his father, and according to one story, he slashed the tires of his father's car in order to beat him to a story. "I did not know at the time it was my father," he once said. "But after I did slash his tires, I snickered and he looked blankly at me and said, 'Son, wonderful. Dirty and wonderful.' "

In the sixties, Dunleavy worked for several Asian newspapers, including the *South China Morning Post*, and then in the seventies he caught the attention of Rupert Murdoch. The publisher—then in the initial stages of what came to be known as his "Australian invasion" of the American media market that would ultimately lead to a dominant presence in the newspaper, book, magazine, television, and movie industries—was launching the *Star*, his four-color tabloid, to compete with the *National Enquirer*. Impressed with Dunleavy's tenacity, his working-class sensibility, his energy, and his lack of scruples, Murdoch hired him as the *Star*'s chief reporter.

"If you wanted a miracle cancer cure, a flying saucer, a Hollywood scandal or a rip-off of an upcoming book in the guise of a 'review,' Dunleavy was your man," recalled Jim Brady, who was the paper's editor. "He wrote fast, he wrote, if necessary, all night. He knew policemen and shysters and charlatans and never took 'No Comment' for an answer." Dunleavy did more than just break news. "One of his great achievements was a 'hooray for America' column decorated with his picture and, I believe, several American flags," Brady continued. "The fact that Steve was an alien had nothing to do with it. He lashed out every week at the commies and pinkos and wimps and perverts he knew were scheming to take over."

Dunleavy was a slender, stooped man with a roguish Outback accent. He had an exaggerated pompadour haircut and chain-smoked Parliaments. In New York he became as notorious for his drinking and brawling—"going to the knuckles," as he called it—as for his right-wing politics and tabloid antics. He was never a graceful writer; in fact, when the journalist Pete Hamill learned that Dunleavy's foot had been run over by a car, he joked, "I hope it's his writing foot." Nonetheless, Dunleavy could concoct eye-catching headlines. He became a favorite of Murdoch—who had deeply involved himself in the *Star*, personally approving page layouts and rewriting stories—and when the Australian tycoon bought the *New York Post* from Dorothy Schiff in 1976—promoting "Aussie Takes Gotham" cover stories in both *Time* and *News-*

week—he appointed Dunleavy city editor. Dunleavy presided over the *Post*, where circulation had fallen below 500,000 and annual losses exceeded $50 million, during its fierce battle for New York tabloid supremacy with the *Daily News*. He was the man responsible for notorious Post headlines such as the legendary "HEADLESS BODY IN TOPLESS BAR" and for the fevered coverage of the 1977 blackout, "24 HOURS OF TERROR."

But the story that put Dunleavy on the map was the Son of Sam serial murder case. Since July 1976, when eighteen-year-old Donna Laurie was killed with a .44 pistol while sitting in a car outside her family home in the Bronx, the city had been stalked by a homicidal maniac named David Berkowitz. The police, however, did not know his identity and referred to him as the Son of Sam. "There's only one game in town and that's Son of Sam," Murdoch told his staff, which began pursuing the story relentlessly. In the summer of 1977, after two more people had been murdered, the *Daily News*'s star columnist Jimmy Breslin began addressing columns to the Son of Sam, who read the columns and wrote replies, which the *News* duly published. On July 31, when another woman was murdered, the *Post* ran the headline "NO ONE IS SAFE FROM SON OF SAM." Dunleavy, imitating Breslin, began to publish personal appeals to the killer to surrender to Dunleavy himself. These tactics, however egregious, doubled the *Post*'s circulation to 1 million. Some of its most controversial ploys occurred after Berkowitz was finally arrested. A *Post* photographer snuck into the jail and took a picture of the suspect as he slept in his cell. Another *Post* photographer, together with a *Daily News* photographer, was arrested for trespass after breaking into Berkowitz's Yonkers apartment. The *Post* published the photographs under the headline, "INSIDE THE KILLER'S LAIR." The *Post* also obtained letters, reportedly by paying for them, that Berkowitz had written to a former girlfriend and published them under the headline "HOW I BECAME A MASS KILLER BY DAVID BERKOWITZ," a headline that prompted criticism in the *New York Times* and the *New Yorker* and that Murdoch later apologized for, admitting that it was "inaccurate and wrong."

To many journalists, the entry of the once-liberal and literate

New York Post into the tabloid war came to epitomize the alarming debasement of their profession. Two years after the Son of Sam media frenzy, Osborn Elliot, the former editor of *Newsweek* who at the time was dean of the Columbia University School of Journalism, wrote an article in the *Columbia Journalism Review* viciously critical of Murdoch's values. "It is no longer enough to judge the paper solely by journalistic standards," Elliot wrote. "Here we enter a moral universe in which judgments are of a different order altogether, suggesting, as they do, that the matter ought not to be allowed to rest after the press critics have pronounced their anathemas. For the *New York Post* is no longer merely a journalistic problem. It is a social problem—a force for evil."

Murdoch, who had nothing but contempt for Elliot's "elitist journalism," made his position clear in a speech to the American Newspaper Publisher's Association during the height of the Son of Sam story. "A press that fails to interest the whole community is one that will ultimately become a house organ of the elite engaged in an increasingly private conversation with a dwindling club. . . . I cannot avoid the temptation of wondering whether there is any other industry in this country which seeks to presume so completely to give the customer what he does not want."

Dunleavy himself expressed identical sentiments in more colloquial terms. "Rupe doesn't dictate public tastes, you know," Dunleavy said. "He has a lot of bosses out there. Millions of them. The public tells him what they want to read and Rupe gives it to them."

In 1985, Murdoch, having already acquired, in addition to the *Post*, the *Chicago Sun-Times*, the *Boston Herald-American*, *New York* magazine, and the *Village Voice*, set out to purchase half interest in Twentieth-Century Fox for $250 million from Denver oil man Marvin Davis. The following year, Murdoch bought out Davis's interest for another $350 million, and at the same time negotiated a deal to purchase Metromedia—a collection of seven television stations in crucial markets such as WNYW in New York, WTTG in Washington, WFID in Chicago, and KTTV in Los

Angeles—from businessman John Kluge for $2 billion that allowed him to create the Fox Network.

Many media analysts felt Murdoch had vastly overpaid for the stations, but he believed he could increase their value far beyond what he had paid for them by merging them with Fox to create a fourth network. Fox would supply the product, entertainment, and the television stations would distribute it. "Entertainment you can take to be anything from a movie to a sporting event," Murdoch told his biographer Jerome Tuccilli. "The rest is a question of a distribution system. How do you distribute news, how do you distribute words? It's got to be a television screen, it's got to be a newspaper, it's got to be a magazine or a book. Is it cinema, a video cassette, is it the cable business or whatever?"

Murdoch announced in 1985 the founding of Fox, Inc., a division of his overall corporate body, News Corp., that would produce television shows as well as movies. This would enable Murdoch to cut his costs because, unlike the other networks, his would not have to bid for the television programs Hollywood produced—competition that, together with the loss of audience share caused by the expansion of cable television networks, was seriously eroding network profits. But since Murdoch's acquisitions had put him so deeply in debt, and since his fledgling network did not yet have the audience size that would enable him to air the sort of expensive prime-time comedies and dramas in which the other networks specialized, he needed shows that could both build a mass audience quickly and be produced on the cheap. The solution, he decided, was electronic versions of the print tabloids he had published so successfully.

In June 1986, Maury Povich was working as the host of *Panorama*, a daytime talk show blending celebrity interviews, cooking and travel spots, and breezy political discussion on WTTG in Washington, D.C. He also anchored the evening news. The station was one of those Murdoch had acquired the previous year in the Metromedia deal, and one night that June, after the ten o'clock news, the station's news director, Betty Endicott, told

Povich she'd just received a call summoning him to a meeting first thing the following morning with Murdoch.

Povich had never met his boss. What he had heard about him was at best mixed. When Harold Evans, the former editor of the *Times* of London, whom Murdoch had fired after taking over the paper, had been a guest on *Panorama*, he'd told Povich, off-camera, that Murdoch was a "killer." Wondering whether or not he was going to be fired, Povich caught an early shuttle flight up to New York. At the Fox offices, he was ushered into a conference room where Murdoch and a few aides awaited him.

"We intend to start a new show," Murdoch said after the preliminaries. "Here, in New York. If it works, we'll put it on the other Fox stations, and then across America. It is going to be unique. You will be the host."

Povich was astonished. After some discussion about the nature of the show, he told Murdoch he didn't understand what would distinguish it from other television news shows.

"You'll work it out," Murdoch said.

Murdoch introduced Povich to Peter Brennan, who had worked in Australian television, to Ian Rae, who'd been editor and publisher of the *Star*, and to J. B. Blunck, a graphic artist who worked at the *Village Voice*. The four of them, he said, would create the show. It would air in one month. "I was bowled over by the sheer audacity of it," Povich recalled. "Nobody mentioned focus groups or consultants or marketing research. These guys were so casual, as if nothing could be easier."

Ian Rae explained that the name of the show, *A Current Affair*, had been taken from the name of a similar show in Australia, "A kind of *Nightline* Down Under," in Povich's words. He was also told that he was not their first choice. They had hoped to hire Geraldo Rivera or Tom Snyder, but the two had demanded huge contracts. Povich, who was already on Murdoch's payroll, would be cheap. "They threw me in with all these crazy Australians," said Povich, though as host he would provide a comforting American tone. "I was the front man," he said. "I had certain advantages, because the people who knew me associated me with legitimate, respectable news."

Their first hire was Steve Dunleavy, whom Murdoch had

moved to Fox News when he was forced, after the Metromedia deal, to sell the *New York Post* because of FCC regulations designed to prevent media monopolies. Dunleavy suggested that for the first episode, they profile Jimmy Chin, who allegedly controlled organized crime in New York's Chinatown. Chin, a mysterious, elusive man, had never been interviewed on television but days before the show was to air, David Lee Miller, one of the show's new reporters, ambushed him on the streets of Chinatown. While Chin insisted he was just an ordinary citizen, the show's staff felt they had nonetheless scored an important exclusive. After it aired, however, the word was that Murdoch hated the segment so much that he wanted to fire Miller. "He wanted the guy in handcuffs and arrested by the end of the show," said Povich. "He wanted a brand-new kind of journalism. Activist . . . He expected our reporter to go out and arrest Jimmy Chin. A reporter he had in mind—his kind of reporter—would have clapped kindly old Uncle Jimmy in irons, in full view of his henchmen—which would have made an interesting part of the show if the henchmen didn't gun down Miller and the cameraman and the soundman first—then march him down to the Elizabeth Street police precinct, where he would present this known felon, this unrepentant villain, to the desk officer."

The program's trademark style became apparent shortly after its debut when Povich conducted a tearful, completely one-sided interview with Mary Joe Whitehead, the surrogate mother who'd decided to keep the child she was carrying for an infertile couple. Initially, the reaction of the establishment was surprisingly positive. " 'A Current Affair' is tabloid journalism," wrote John Corry in the *New York Times*. "Forget now the pejorative notions that cling to the phrase. 'A Current Affair' is tabloid journalism at its best. It is zippy and knowledgeable, and when it falls on its face at least it is in there trying."

In the early eighties, most television stations had to content themselves with reruns and game shows and local news when they were not showing network programs. But satellites and cable television had fueled the syndication business, enabling independent producers to sell regular shows or specials to stations whenever they wanted. Geraldo Rivera, abandoning his quest for establishment acceptance since leaving ABC, had produced and starred in "The Mystery of Al Capone's Vault," a critical flop—nothing was in the vault—that nonetheless became the highest rated syndicated show in television history. An astonishing 33.4 percent of the country's 87.4 million television sets tuned in. Geraldo had gone on to do a special on devil worship with ratings so high that, for the first time, *Roseanne* was knocked from the number one spot.

A Current Affair thrived in this tumultuous atmosphere. In addition to its run-of-the-mill stories on nude beaches and UFOs, on freeing dogs from Connecticut pounds and putting them in witness protection programs in Massachusetts, it consistently succeeded in making news. It aired a videotape of Robert Chambers, accused of murdering his date Jennifer Levin in Central Park, partying with four young woman on the eve of his trial, and at one point holding up a doll, twisting its head, and saying, "Oops, I think I killed it." When critics accused the show of bias because it paid $10,000 for the tape, Levin's family held a press conference defending the program. During the 1988 Democratic Convention, it bought and aired the videotape of Rob Lowe having sex with an underage woman, which resulted in a conviction of statutory rape for the actor.

Because it consistently made news, by 1988 the show, in addition to being shown on the six Fox stations, was being syndicated to more than 100 stations around the country to a total of 9 million homes. The *Atlanta Constitution* called it "the juggernaut of tabloid TV" and the networks, faced with declining audiences, found themselves imitating the tabloids in order to compete. ABC, for example, used what it called "dramatization"—nothing more than *A Current Affair*'s "reenactments"—to tell the story of the diplomat Felix Bloch, who was accused of spying for the Soviet Union. But the network, still bound by its traditional ethics, felt uncomfortable with the segment and Peter Jennings delivered an on-air apology for it.

A Current Affair's critics were of course legion. "The tabloid television shows have absolutely blurred the distinction . . . between news and titillation," Conrad Fink, a journalism professor at the University of Georgia, told the *Constitution*. "This creates a real problem. It confuses the public on who is a journalist and what is the role of journalism." The program's staff found such complaints tedious. "We wanted to do emotional stories and people stories," Peter Brennan, producer of Fox Television, said in 1989, "and not screw around with language or try to save the world or be Dan Rather."

But the critics were not limited to journalism professors. The moguls behind some of the programs were increasingly facing the wrath of friends and business partners who were being skewered by the shows. Barry Diller, who as head of Fox, Inc., was in charge of all programming and movies, was reportedly irritated by the show, if only because of its irreverent pieces on the private lives of the celebrities with whom he was trying to do movie deals. Diller was upset after *A Current Affair* ran a story on the rocky marriage of his good friend Sid Bass, who was in the process of dumping his wife Ann for Mercedes Kellogg. And, sources say director Steven Spielberg was incensed when *A Current Affair* ran a story, complete with background music from "Jaws," on his divorce from actress Amy Irving and his subsequent romance with actress Kate Capshaw. Spielberg reportedly called Diller and threatened never to work with him again.

And in 1990, a man named Stuart Goldman was arrested and led away in handcuffs for infiltrating *A Current Affair*. Posing as a producer, he had tracked down the tabloid's methodology; the word was that he was hired by a group of movie stars. He was celebrated by them; Oliver Stone reportedly optioned the movie rights to his story and Tom Cruise was interested in playing the lead.

But Murdoch, with decades of experience in dealing with powerful people his journalists had infuriated, refused to interfere. *A Current Affair's* real problems were brought about by its success. Just as the huge circulation of the *National Enquirer* in the early seventies produced a host of imitators, so too did the mass audience of *A Current Affair* spawn electronic competition. In 1988, Roger King, whose syndication company King World produced *Oprah* and *Wheel of Fortune*, lured away two producers from *A Current Affair*—Murdoch, wanting to keep costs down, had put hardly any of the staff under contract—to start *Inside*

Edition. The next year, Paramount started *Hard Copy.* "This is wild," Bill O'Reilly, host of *Inside Edition*, told the *Wall Street Journal* in 1989. "It's a shoot-out. It's the O.K. Corral."

The three programs were competing not just for staff but for stories. And the producers and reporters knew that, as in any tabloid war, victory goes to the most sensational. The first great battle in that war would take place in Palm Beach in 1991, when Patricia Bowman accused Willie Smith of raping her on a moonlit night on the lawn of the Kennedy family's oceanfront mansion— a news event in which for the first time the tabloid press not only competed with one another but drove the coverage for the entire media establishment. "We were the most watched newscast in the country," said Povich. "We relied on the great Shakespearean themes of revenge and violence and lust and betrayal. So the heads of the network news divisions realized that it's not just news about Washington and international news. And they began to chase the stories that dealt with these themes of lust and violence and revenge."

"One, two, William Kennedy Smith. William Kennedy Smith. William Kennedy Smith." Steve Dunleavy, standing on a ladder just outside the courthouse in West Palm Beach, in a surging crowd of reporters, photographers, camera crews, and spectators, was giving a sound check. "William Kennedy Smith," he repeated. "William Kennedy Smith."

The maroon Mercury station wagon owned by Jean Kennedy Smith, the sister of Ted Kennedy and the mother of William Kennedy Smith, turned down the street and came to a stop at the curb. The police restrained the crowd behind barricades. William Kennedy Smith, the pale, slightly pudgy medical student and accused rapist, climbed out of the car. Wearing slacks and a brown tweed sport coat, his face blankly amiable, he nodded at the crowd, then turned toward the contemporary brick building.

"Eight forty-six!" shouted Cynthia Fagen, Dunleavy's co-producer and one of ten *Current Affair* staffers assigned to cover the trial.

"Eight what?" asked Dunleavy.

"Eight forty-six."

"Okay."

"Go for it!" a crew member shouted.

Dunleavy looked into the camera and then, in his gravelly Australian drawl, a voice that managed to be at once snide and sanctimonious, he intoned, "William Kennedy Smith arrived at court today at eight-forty A.M., on the first day of his sensational rape trial. Outwardly he looks calm and confident, but now he faces some rough going as prosecution witnesses take the stand. I have spoken, *exclusively*, to one of those witnesses, who told me of the state of mind of the alleged victim and just how tough it's going to be for Mr. Smith!"

"Every famous trial has its chronicler," David Margolick, a reporter for the *New York Times*, would write a few days later, once the verdict was in. "The Scopes trial had H. L. Mencken, the Eichmann trial Hannah Arendt, and the just concluded rape trial of William Kennedy Smith had Steve Dunleavy." Indeed, Dunleavy, and *A Current Affair*, not only provided the definitive coverage of the trial, they influenced its outcome in a way that may have been unprecedented in legal history, and in doing so permanently redrew—and in the view of some, obliterated—the lines between the tabloid and the establishment press. "We wanted to own that story," said John Terenzio, the program's executive producer. They did.

What came to be known as "The William Kennedy Smith Rape Case"—even though Smith never used his middle name— was initially broken by freelance journalist Malcolm Balfour, a native South African and former *National Enquirer* reporter who worked out of a duplex apartment down the street from his old employer in the heart of Tabloid Valley. Although his office was cluttered with stacks of newspapers spilling from filing cabinets and the closet, and he could often be found in shorts and no socks at a battered metal desk, Balfour hardly fit the image of a struggling freelancer. He had ties to half a dozen British tabloids, as well as papers in Germany and Australia and the *New York Post*, and he could resell a single small item to any number of these publications, multiplying his earnings and turning him into, in effect, a one-man gossip syndicate. The living he made enabled him to drive a Mercedes, pilot his own airplane, put his two children through college, invest in real estate, and return to South Africa once a year.

Balfour, who had worked in Tabloid Valley since 1972 and who had been sued by Roxanne Pulitzer after reporting the details of her sex life in the *New York Post* under the famous headline "I SLEPT WITH A TRUMPET," had sources among the other journalists there, and among the criminal defense lawyers and law enforcement officers who could be found in the courts and police stations of South Florida. Within hours after Patricia Bowman had told investigators at the sheriff's office in West Palm Beach that William Smith had raped her, Balfour heard about the story from what he describes as a "police source" and filed it to the *Post*, which beat the competition by six hours with a story headlined "Kennedy Mansion Sex Probe."

The media began pouring into Palm Beach the next day. Among the 500 print and television reporters who descended on the scene was Steve Dunleavy, his two producers, and a camera crew from *A Current Affair*. They booked rooms in the Brazilian Court Hotel, which was favored by the tabloid press, and Dunleavy, an old nemesis of the Kennedys who had once written a book called *The Wild, Wild Kennedy Boys*, put Balfour on retainer, and the two began scouring Palm Beach, offering "finder's fees" for tips.

It was just as important to the mainstream press, and, as the case unwound, the distinction between the tabloid and the establishment did begin to collapse. In the most controversial incident, a British tabloid, the *London Mirror*, published Patricia Bowman's name and photograph, leading an American tabloid, the *Globe*, to do the same. This led *NBC Nightly News* anchor Tom Brokaw to use her name, on the grounds that it had already been made public, and that, in turn, decided the editors of the *New York Times* to do the same. Just as significant as an indicator of the collapsing distinction between tabloid and mainstream was that the article in which Bowman's name appeared, an extremely critical profile taking her to task for her "wild streak," was written by Fox Butterfield, a *Times* reporter in Boston who had no logical territorial connection to a Florida rape story but who did have strong connections to the Kennedy camp. Furthermore, the article contained, in true tabloid fashion, anonymous quotes, a description of the books on the shelf of Bowman's two-year-old daughter obtained by peering through her window, and material that some believe was supplied to Butterfield by Anthony Pellicano, a private investigator who was hired by celebrities and reportedly worked for the Kennedys.

The article caused a furor, both nationally and within the *Times*. Editorial writers at other papers castigated its editors. At a meeting attended by more than 300 reporters, people filled the *Times*'s auditorium and lined the aisles. Up front, *Times* editor Max Frankel, who had been in favor of publishing the victim's name even before NBC News broadcast it because he felt it unfair that Willie Smith's reputation should be damaged while she remained anonymous, received the brunt of the attacks. One female reporter said, "We don't understand why you've got *New York Times* reporters peeping in windows." Another complained the paper had "crucified" Bowman. A third described the article as "tabloid journalism." When nation section editor Soma Golden, who was standing with Frankel, said people who found fault with the article had "weird minds," many in the audience hissed, and one reporter responded, "The people with the weird minds are the ones who thought this was journalism."

Frankel defended his decision by pointing to NBC; one of the paper's columnists asked why the *Times* would rely on the judgment of others and wondered where the line would be drawn— at *Hard Copy* or MTV? "We'll know it when we see it," Frankel replied. By the end of the day, however, Frankel was retreating. A few days later, the editors published an "editor's note" regretting the article, but laying most of the blame for it on Butterfield. The editors of the *New York Times* appeared to have become completely disoriented. And indeed, Soma Golden told the *Washington Post* that the incident was "the most troubling time of my career." Dan Schwartz, editor of the *National Enquirer*, which had thoroughly reported the story without naming Bowman, said of the *New York Times*, "I think we took a more ethical stand than they did."

*　　*　　*

Willie Smith's uncle, Ted Kennedy, and his cousin Patrick, the Senator's son, had also been at the mansion the night the alleged rape took place but they could be expected to back up Willie's story. The other two crucial witnesses were Anne Mercer, a friend of the victim's who had gone with her to Au Bar, the nightclub where she met Willie Smith, and Michelle Cassone, a young off-duty waitress whom Patrick Kennedy had met at Au Bar that same night and had brought back to the family mansion. Among the journalists arriving in Palm Beach in the days after the report was filed, the competition to nail down the first exclusive from either of these witnesses, and from the victim herself, was intense.

At this time, not only were tabloid news organizations paying for interviews, they had vastly increased the amounts they could afford to pay by putting together consortiums—groups of news organizations from different parts of the world who would contribute to the payoff in exchange for exclusive rights to the interview in their geographical region. *Hard Copy*, having put together one such consortium with participating media from as far away as Australia, offered Bowman's attorney, David Roth, $500,000 for an exclusive with the victim and was prepared to go as high as $1 million.

Roth made it clear that his client would talk to no one for any amount until the trial was over. But the paying media had better luck with Bowman's two supporting witnesses. Less than a week into the story, the *Post* reportedly paid an undisclosed amount to Cassone for her account of the evening, including the claim that she had seen Ted Kennedy walking around the mansion late at night dressed only in a nightshirt—"pantless," as the *Post* called him—and published it under the headline "TEDDY'S SEXY ROMP!"

Soon, any journalist with the inclination had interviewed Cassone, who was also invited to New York, where she made the rounds of talk radio, such as Curtis and Lisa Sliwa's show, and appeared on *Geraldo* and *Sally Jessy Raphael*. Then, once her usefulness as a witness had been corrupted by overexposure and payoffs, she herself became a victim.

In late May, in exchange for £9,400, a former boyfriend of Michelle Cassone gave Balfour photos of her, naked, performing oral sex on him. Balfour passed them on to Dunleavy, who invited Cassone to New York to make a studio appearance on the show. After lunch at the 21 Club, they arrived at the *Current Affair* set. With the cameras rolling, Dunleavy asked Cassone about the rumors that she was going to pose nude for *Penthouse*. Cassone replied that she could never take her clothes off for a photographer. "It would kill my mother," she told Dunleavy. At that point, Dunleavy pulled out the photographs of Cassone having sex that Balfour had purchased. Cassone, mortified and incensed, grabbed at the pictures and began hitting the man who had just taken her to lunch at 21. She kneed him in the groin and bit his hand—all while the cameras rolled. When the footage was aired that night, the show earned the highest ratings it would receive all year. Dunleavy treated the entire incident as a joke. "As a man you can't run away," he said of Cassone's attack. "As a gentleman you can't respond. So you just had to take it. And when she pulled up the knee, then suddenly I was in the Lutan Boys Choir, you know, singing my high C."

It was *A Current Affair* that also got the first exclusive from Anne Mercer, the woman Patricia Bowman had called to come rescue her from the Kennedy mansion. The fee she finally received, $25,000, was far less than the $150,000 she had originally been offered because by the time she agreed to talk to the show, the police had released the transcripts of her statements, which significantly reduced the news value of what she would say on air.

By the time the trial started the following fall—"Gentlemen," an article in the *Palm Beach Post* declared as it began, "to the sewers!"—*A Current Affair* and its staff had gone from covering the story to playing a crucial role in its outcome. It had produced some forty segments on the case, and a number of them were indeed pivotal, newsmaking "Exclusives!" In addition to the pieces on Mercer and Cassone, it had interviewed Tony Liott, the bartender whose testimony undermined Patricia Bowman's credibility, and Ewell Tournquists, a waiter who'd provided an account of Senator Kennedy's alleged drunkenness. During jury selection, Willie Smith's attorney Roy Black mentioned the program and Dunleavy as often as once an hour while quizzing potential jurors about which segments they had seen. Overexposure to the show was grounds for disqualification.

Then on the opening day of the trial, prosecutor Moira Lasch, having decided not to call Michelle Cassone at all because she had been so tainted by her involvement with *A Current Affair*, called Anne Mercer as her first witness. Under cross-examination by Roy Black, Mercer, the thirty-year-old daughter of a wealthy real-estate developer with reported ties to organized crime, admitted that *A Current Affair* had paid her $25,000 for her first interview, which she had spent on a vacation to Mexico with her boyfriend, and another $15,000 for a second interview that very evening. The admission discredited her testimony. Dunleavy, together with Mercer's attorney, Raoul Felder, escorted her from the courthouse. Later, Felder turned on Mercer, appearing on *A Current Affair* and saying she "once was a poor little rich girl who was used to getting her way with everything. She still had this air that she was rich, famous, and arrogant. There was this attitude, 'Who are you to question me?' It was that attitude that killed her on the stand."

In the end, the trial damaged almost everyone it touched. Patricia Bowman was forever scarred. The Kennedy family's reputation had received yet another serious blow. The editorial judgment of the *New York Times* had been denounced throughout the country. Cable television, however, had profited handsomely. The day the trial opened, CNN's audience increased 57 percent. The following day it rose 71 percent. And on the day Patricia Bowman testified, it climbed 142 percent. But the biggest winners were the tabloid news shows. During the sweep-month ratings in November as the trial was getting under way, *Hard Copy* had a 6 Nielsen rating, up from the 4.6 of the previous year, and *Inside Edition* had a 6.8 rating, up from a 5.6. But the leader was *A Current Affair*, with an 8.8 rating, up from an 8.2 a year earlier.

Shortly after the verdict, in acknowledgment of the show's moment of triumph, the *New York Times*, whom Dunleavy regularly excoriated as stuffy and stiff and boring, ran its affectionate profile of the reporter, calling him "the undisputed maharajah of tabloid television" and "the ringmaster" of "a media circus." It was an ironic tribute coming from a paper that had so publicly bungled its coverage of the story. But it was significant nonetheless. The media establishment seemed to be admitting that, in 1991, it had ceded the field—or at least the role of defining the news—to the tabloid press that one of its reigning members had once haughtily denounced as a "force of evil."

16

---

the gatekeepers

Tom Cruise, the world's biggest movie star, was coming to New York the first weekend in December 1996, and entertainment reporters from around the country flew in to interview him. TriStar was releasing Cruise's *Jerry Maguire* and the elusive star was attending the glittering premiere onboard the luxury liner *Galaxy*, as well as the world premiere of *Portrait of a Lady*, starring his wife Nicole Kidman. "The couple that premieres together stays together," declared Liz Smith.

In recent months, however, rumors were swirling that the couple's marriage was troubled. There were reports of ugly arguments and talk that the couple was spending more and more time apart. When Kidman showed up at the black tie post-premiere party for her movie, she looked lovely in a shimmering green gown. She carefully fielded questions about her marriage. "Tom and I are heterosexuals," the actress said in an even voice. "We have a great marriage. We have two wonderful children. It's all just vicious, hurtful lies dreamed up to sell magazines and newspapers." Tom Cruise didn't have to deal with the prying reporters. He ditched the party and left his wife to fend for herself.

At the Regency Hotel that Saturday, journalists had been invited to interview the stars of *Jerry Maguire*. When they realized that Cruise was going to be a no-show, a halfhearted revolt erupted. "Show Me the Money!" the reporters chanted.

"I know it's frustrating for you guys," said director Cameron Crowe, himself a former journalist who had profiled Cruise for *Interview* magazine. Crowe explained that Cruise was just too busy with Stanley Kubrick's *Eyes Wide Shut* to meet with them. "Kubrick only let him loose for forty-eight hours," Crowe said. "I'm grateful that he's packing everything into that time." In that time, Cruise gave interviews to the *Today Show*, *Larry King Live*, and avowed Cruise fan Rosie O'Donnell. He also gave a press conference to the Hollywood Foreign Press Association.

It wasn't just that Tom was rushed for time, the reporters knew. The actor hated the American press. Journalists who showed up at the Regency with hopes of interviewing Cruise were left quoting the nice things his co-stars said about him. Some of the reporters felt used—they grumbled about the absurdity of gathering flattering comments about a celebrity who refused to speak to them. "Why don't you guys lighten up on Tom?" said Bonnie Hunt, the actress who played the sister of Cruise's love interest in *Jerry Maguire*. "He's a bit press-shy but he's a truly nice person. It's not easy being a superstar."

And no one was a bigger star than Tom Cruise. There's a Hollywood axiom that on the way up, stars hire publicists to get them press, once they've arrived, they hire publicists to protect them from the press. Now, Tom Cruise was doing the seemingly impossible. He was getting good press without having to deal with reporters.

The journalists knew who had created this situation. It was Cruise's publicist, Pat Kingsley. Among many reporters, Kingsley was the most feared, most loathed woman in Hollywood. In recent years, she had virtually denied print access to most of her bigger clients. Newspaper and magazine reporters, she complained, were always digging for information on stars. Facts, reporting, and real information were enemies of the Hollywood image machine. If Kingsley had her way, she once admitted, profiles of her clients would include almost no information about them. "I don't like interesting stories," Kingsley said. "Boring is good. Good reporting and good writing don't help my client. New information is usually controversial. I don't need that. People don't read. The text doesn't matter." All she really cared about was getting her clients' pictures on the covers of magazines. "Why do you always get to decide who's on your cover?" she asked an editor in 1990. By 1997, Pat Kingsley sometimes got to decide.

It had all begun five years earlier, during the publicity campaign for *Far and Away*. The movie was imminently forgettable, but the junket had a major turning point in the world of entertainment journalism. It was then that Pat Kingsley first made journalists sign contracts, imposing terms on their interviews with Cruise. At the time, there was outrage over the then-unheard-of restrictions. With each of Cruise's movies, however, the conditions had gotten increasingly prohibitive. By the time of the *Jerry Maguire* screening, the *Far and Away* junket seemed like the good old days.

Pat Kingsley arrived at the Four Seasons Hotel on the morning of May 9, 1992, and braced herself for a harrowing experience: protecting Tom Cruise from the media. Nearly one hundred reporters from around the country meandered around that Saturday, eager to interview Cruise. Kingsley eyed them suspiciously, interrogating people with a cutting Southern twang that softened into a soothing drawl when it was directed at her high-strung movie star clients. Kingsley was a tall, formidable woman whose blond hair fell in a blunt bob around her strong jaw; she had unflinching eyes and a determined gait that followed wherever her chin led. Pat Kingsley was the first and most powerful of the new breed of publicist: the gatekeeper. She did not subscribe to the theory that any publicity is good publicity; she spent more time squashing stories than she did peddling the celebrities she represented. "The people get used to you awfully fast," Kingsley would warn her clients. "You never want them to get too much of you."

Unfortunately, there were times when even stars as big as Tom Cruise had to deal with the media, and this weekend was one of those times. Cruise and Nicole Kidman were starring in

Far and Away, a $62 million historic, romantic, comic epic directed by Ron Howard and distributed by Universal. The studio had an especially tough job with *Far and Away*. The movie was a clunker, and Universal knew it. It was one of Cruise's few misfires, and only his star power—and a skillful manipulation of the press—could save it from being a box office bomb. Cruise was getting paid $12.5 million to appear in the movie, and under the terms of his contract, he was required to do a "reasonable amount" of publicity. Cruise's contract also forced Universal to hire Kingsley and her firm, PMK, to promote *Far and Away*.

The arrangement rankled Universal, which already had its own promotion staff. Studio press agents complained that personal publicists like Kingsley were more interested in pacifying their temperamental stars than they were in promoting films. The criticism didn't bother Kingsley. "That kind of rap has been around," she said dismissively. Studio publicists had too many films to promote to give each one sufficient attention, Kingsley said. What's more, "studio publicists don't have the confidence" of stars like Tom Cruise, Kingsley said. "That's why a publicist like myself is there—to act as a liaison and work on cooperation."

There was nothing cooperative, some Universal executives grumbled, about Kingsley's work on *Far and Away*. The studio was sponsoring a junket to promote the movie: at Universal's expense, journalists from around the country were flown into Los Angeles and put up at the Four Seasons for the weekend. The print reporters were divided into groups of about ten and led into rooms where they would be granted short group "interviews" with the stars and principals of *Far and Away*. The drill with television journalists was similar: each would be escorted into a room for four-minute interviews that would be taped by the studio's production team, so that the individual TV stations didn't even have to send a camera crew to the junket.

Junkets were one of the studios' favorite ways of promoting a film. For a weekend that cost about $100,000 to $200,000, they received literally millions of dollars worth of publicity. Studios would pay for the reporters to be flown—often first class—to top hotels in New York or Los Angeles or even overseas, where they were fed fine food and wine, given bags full of freebies, reimbursed for expenses like taxis, and sometimes even given $100 or so pocket money. Reporters were told what they could and couldn't ask the stars: don't quiz Bruce Willis about his family; Sean Young was a forbidden topic when interviewing James Woods; don't interrogate Arnold Schwarzenegger about reports that his father was a Nazi; and don't ask Tom Cruise *anything* personal. The resulting articles were almost invariably puff pieces. Journalists who wrote or broadcast anything negative would be blackballed on the junket circuit, losing precious access to top movie stars, as well as the cushy, all-expense-paid weekends that had become a cherished perk for some Hollywood reporters. Reporters who covered junkets—regulars are sometimes called "junketeers"—were bought and paid for, and they knew it. "There should be an editorial note at the top of the articles, like health warnings on cigarettes," said one writer. "Danger: this is a puff piece that has been totally negotiated with the subject's publicist and is worthless." Nevertheless, most newspapers and TV stations loved junkets. While some insisted on reimbursing studios when they sent reporters on junkets, the interviews were a godsend for smaller newspapers and local TV stations that normally wouldn't have the budget or the clout to get face time with a star like Tom Cruise.

Celebrities, for the most part, hated junkets. Some called them "gang bangs." They were better than the multicity promotional tours that studios used to force celebrities to make, but junkets were grueling, two- or three-day performances for celebrities who had to appear enthusiastic, friendly, and spontaneous as ten or twenty gangs of reporters peppered them with inane questions like "How does it feel being so famous?" "What toothpaste do you use?" and "Is your mother proud of you?" Some stars, like Arnold Schwarzenegger, were so professional and cooperative during junkets that studio publicists held them in awe. The action hero has been known to give more than sixty interviews in one day—and make each seem like his first. "Arnold deserves the ironman endurance award in junkets," according to one publicist, who said the actor surprised and flattered reporters by remembering their names and details from conversations he had had with them years earlier. "The only way you can tell that Arnold is getting tired is when his accent starts to get a little stronger," said one reporter, or when his hostility toward journalists began to show through, like the time one asked him for an autograph—an unwritten taboo at junkets—for his mother. "Sure," Schwarzenegger said genially. "We wouldn't want you to disappoint your mother." Then he added with a loud laugh, "I'm sure you've already disappointed her enough."

Some stars were notoriously terrible at junkets. Once, when asked what she thought of the assembly-line interviews, Carrie Fisher threw herself on the ground and started pounding the floor. Meryl Streep practically refused to do them; she was just no good at censoring herself. At the *Postcards from the Edge* junket, Streep blurted out that she was upset that Madonna would edge her out from *Evita*, declaring "I can sing better than she can!" Once, when promoting *Navy Seals*, Charlie Sheen showed up slurring his words and looking like a gangster with a yellow fedora and a pin-striped suit. When a reporter asked Sheen to describe his character, the actor got belligerent. "You saw the movie," Sheen snapped, "so why should I describe the character?" Then he started "buying" drinks for reporters—even though it was an open bar. None of the junketeers reported on Sheen's peculiar behavior.

Perhaps no major star is as bad on junkets as Julia Roberts. When promoting *Hook*, the actress was asked how she had prepared for the role of Tinkerbell. "I don't know," Roberts said, then with some irritation added, "she's just sort of this thing that happens. Who wants to know how Tinkerbell comes about?"

Asked if recent press reports about her erratic behavior had upset her, Roberts replied: "I just wish the public at large would concern themselves with their own lives, with their own personal business and affairs and then probably divorce rates would be lower, there wouldn't be so many fractured families and troubled people and things would be a lot easier for everybody."

After a long, awkward silence a reporter finally said, "You're not happy being here, are you?"

"I've learned the hard way to be more frugal with words around people like you," Roberts shot back. When a reporter phoned in a story that some people were disappointed with *Hook* and Roberts, she was asked to leave the junket early.

*　　*　　*

Kingsley had a problem with junkets. They were grueling work for her stars. They also created the sort of media blitz that made her clients seem more accessible than she liked. Reporters who went on junkets would stockpile quotes or footage and trot them out whenever that star was in the news. Even worse, as far as Kingsley was concerned, junketeers would sometimes repackage the interviews and sell them to other publications—including the dreaded supermarket tabloids. The studios didn't care, but Kingsley certainly did. She did not want it to look like her hard-to-get celebrities were chatting it up with enemies like the *National Enquirer*. What's more, appearing to give interviews to tabloids cheapened the value of the star's words and put Kingsley in a weaker position when she negotiated exclusive interviews with upscale magazines. Kingsley was determined to tighten up the market for the precious Cruise interviews, so she teamed up with Kidman's publicist, Nancy Seltzer, and demanded that reporters who wanted to interview Cruise or Kidman at the *Far and Away* junket had to sign a "consent agreement." The contract stipulated, among other things, that quotes from Cruise and Kidman could be used "only during or in connection with the initial theatrical release" of *Far and Away*. All hell broke loose.

"Outrageous!" said an editor of the *Dallas Morning News*.

"Blackmail!" charged one broadcast reporter.

"Manipulation!"

"A threat to freedom of the press!"

"This is the final insult," said New York *Newsday* movie critic Jack Matthews. "Publicity has taken over. It's really offensive. This is entertainment extortion."

"Since when is it a bad thing to make tough demands on behalf of your client?" Kingsley said. "The person who has the goods has a much stronger position. Why not exercise that position? In which business do you not do that?"

"Marlin Fitzwater wouldn't have Sam Donaldson sign this," HBO's assignment editor Glen Meehan complained. "I had to sign it and I didn't like it because it put me in a situation that makes us non-news."

"I don't see what all the fuss is about," Kingsley said. "If they don't like it, they don't have to participate." Kingsley had some very sound reasons for wanting the journalists to sign the agreements. For one thing, freelance reporters would sometimes sell articles in countries where Kingsley had negotiated exclusive interviews. "It makes us look like we've reneged on an agreement," she said. Kingsley knew she'd lose a few journalists, but not many. Despite their noisy protests, Kingsley knew that the media needed Tom Cruise; they wanted a piece of his star power. It translated into TV ratings and newsstand sales that they needed to survive. And indeed, as she anticipated, the Four Seasons was packed that Saturday.

The junketeers were shepherded into rooms where reproduction Queen Anne chairs were arranged in semicircles around a coffee table and an overstuffed couch. Publicists escorted in the interview subjects, and the reporters politely sat through question-and-answer sessions with Nicole Kidman, Ron Howard, and producer Brian Grazer. When Cruise walked into a room, however, the excitement was palpable. Cruise flashed his movie star smile and appeared genuinely happy to be there. He wore pointy-toed buckskin boots with heels at least an inch high, black jeans, and a white tee-shirt under an embroidered black shirt. He looked quite relaxed and fit, though a few journalists thought he looked a tad shorter than the five feet nine inches listed on his official biography.* "He reached over and gave you a handshake with such a firm grip," recalled one reporter. "He looked you right in the eye. He connected. He had real personal power." One journalist made the terrible faux pas of asking for Cruise's autograph. Several of her colleagues gasped—many of them were starstruck, but they weren't supposed to be so *obvious* about it. There was an embarrassed silence for a moment, then Cruise grinned and gave the reporter his autograph.

Some reporters who had interviewed Cruise before recognized the charm that he could turn on and off like a light switch. "His smile was a little too quick," according to one writer. "And

---

* The word was that Cruise stood on a "cheater box" to make him as tall as Kidman. He also allegedly used one to stand above his *Top Gun* co-star Kelly McGillis. He also had to use one in *Interview with the Vampire* so that the six-foot-tall Brad Pitt wouldn't tower over him.

his laugh was a little too loud." His grammar wasn't great either: "alls I'm saying" seemed to be a favorite phrase. Still, they lapped it up—including comments like, "Comedically, dramatically, physically, this movie opens up new avenues for me." In a typical revelation, Cruise confided: "The story was enchanting. My character had a lot of dimensions I had never before explored." He discussed the joys of being married to Kidman. "It's just gotten better," he gushed. "You just get to share everything. It's really incredible."

It all seemed so heartfelt, so spontaneous, so genuine. But when some reporters compared notes afterward, they realized that Cruise said nearly the same thing to each of the groups. Regarding the Irish brogue he learned for the film, for example, Cruise told one group: "This isn't your old Lucky Charms accent." To another, he said: "We didn't just do the old Lucky Charms sort of accent." To another he spoke of his "all-out Irish accent. Not the Lucky Charms type of stuff." As with most junkets, the star's answers were most likely scripted in advance.

That didn't matter. The reporters weren't there to expose the publicity ruse they were perpetrating. To the contrary. The junket-produced stories were usually worded to make it sound as though the writer had sat down for an exclusive interview with the star. "When a confident, smiling Cruise arrives at the Four Seasons hotel for a recent interview, he considers what drew him to *Far and Away* . . ." read one article. "Cruise passes on coffee for a bottle of Canadian Glacier spring water, then, settling into an overstuffed couch, he says *Far and Away* demanded he master horseback riding and bare-knuckled boxing . . ." read another. The headlines were fawning: "Tom and Nicole: Far and Away a Dynamic Duo on Screen" declared one headline. "Romantic Leads On Screen and Off," went another. There were a few unpleasant incidents at the junket—a reporter who had refused to sign the consent agreement was forcibly escorted out of a Cruise interview—but overall, it was a resounding success.

Far and Away needed all the good press it could get. When the film premiered in Cannes, it was met with outright ridicule. The audience hooted and howled with contempt. Viewers threw things at the screen. Though *Far and Away* fell short of Cruise's biggest hits—*Top Gun* earned $171.6 million, and *Rainman* grossed $173 million domestically—if the studio's accounting is to be believed, the movie actually made money. It cost about $62 million to make and, according to one estimate, grossed about $100 million worldwide. *Far and Away* was a critical flop, but Cruise's star power—and the glowing articles from the junketeering reporters—saved what might have otherwise been a box office bomb. Pat Kingsley had created a relationship between the stars and press that had not existed since the studios spoon-fed stories to Louella Parsons and Hedda Hopper: she had turned the mainstream media into a public relations machine for the stars.

Back in her cluttered office in a nondescript building near West Hollywood, Pat Kingsley put in long hours, negotiating with journalists who were willing to cut deals, screaming at those who weren't, and comforting distraught stars who thought reporters didn't keep their end of the agreement. Kingsley's desk was a former blackjack table, covered with green felt and surrounded by newspaper and magazine clippings, videocassettes, unopened mail, and still-wrapped gifts from grateful stars and hopeful journalists. On her desk was a group photo of Sally Field, Jane Fonda, Jessica Lange, Goldie Hawn, and Barbra Streisand, autographed by each of them.

Considering her power and her influence, Pat Kingsley was not particularly well-paid by Hollywood standards. The $3,000 to $7,000 monthly retainer most clients paid was a pittance compared to what producers and agents made. PMK, which Kingsley owned with Lois Smith and Leslee Dart in New York, had a staff of 45—about half of them in Los Angeles. It had 135 clients in 1992 and an annual billing of about $4 million.

Kingsley did not lead the life of a Hollywood mogul. She lived alone in Pacific Palisades—she had a grown daughter from a twelve-year marriage that ended in divorce in 1978—and avoided the party circuit except when working. She disliked crowds. "I get panicky when I'm in a big department store," she confessed. "I have to go into one of the changing stalls, put my head between my knees, and concentrate on breathing deeply."

Kingsley hadn't always wanted to be a publicist. When she

was growing up, she didn't want to be anything in particular. "I figured I was just going to get a job until I got married and had a child," she said. "I had no ambition." She was born in Gastonia, North Carolina, in 1932 and her family moved from one Southern town to another, following her father's work as a civilian quartermaster in the army. She enrolled in Winthrop College in South Carolina but wasn't a particularly motivated or scholarly student, and dropped out after two years. "I never read Shakespeare or the classics," she once admitted, "and when I'm with people who have read them, I have always felt the lack." After dropping out of college, Kingsley held a variety of odd jobs, once vaccinating cows in Reno, Nevada, before a friend got her a stint in the publicity department of the Fountainebleau Hotel in Miami Beach. That led to a publicity job at NBC in New York and with syndicator Ziv TV. In 1959, she moved to Hollywood where she worked as a secretary at Rogers and Cowan, the most powerful of the independent publicity firms that emerged after the fall of the studio system. Rogers and Cowan's clients included Marilyn Monroe, Frank Sinatra, Natalie Wood, and Doris Day. Kingsley's various duties included going to a Dodgers game with Day and helping Monroe's cat give birth.

When Kingsley started in the business, publicity was a poor cousin of the movie industry. Publicists sat around concocting stories about the stars they represented—some true, some not—and the best ones were rewarded with space in the gossip columns and fanzines. Groveling publicists pleaded with powerful columnists like Walter Winchell for mentions of their clients—as epitomized in the 1957 film *The Sweet Smell of Success*. The philosophy was simple: celebrities needed the press. "Dog food and movie stars are much alike," Warren Cowan's partner Henry Rogers once decreed, "because they are both products in need of exposure."

Cowan made Kingsley a "planter"—someone who gave gossip columnists tidbits about clients. "Hedda and Louella were still there, and getting the lead in one of their columns was vitally important, but when there would be some news item or gossipy item, I would almost never think to call up a columnist," Kingsley recalled. "I never really went in for the side of the business most people think of when they think of publicity—the gimmicky stuff, the stunts. . . . Calling columnists about where stars had lunch and all that. I was never any good at it. Besides, it doesn't have anything to do with anybody's career.''

In 1971, Kingsley and two partners formed Pickwick Public Relations, which merged with a competitor in 1980 to become PMK.* The agency formed ties with Creative Artists Agency in Los Angeles and ICM in New York, and together, the agents and publicists filled the function that studios once had: controlling access to the stars. "I hesitate to say that Pat does my public relations,'' Sally Field said. "It's way beyond that. I send her material, the scripts I'm thinking about doing or developing. And I'm not the only one who does. Jim Brooks, Goldie Hawn—a whole bunch of people ask her about scripts, about writers, about almost everything. . . . With Pat, a sort of safeness came over me I'd never felt before.''

In the early years of Kingsley's career, celebrities were very much at the mercy of the few publications that covered television and Hollywood. Then the mainstream press discovered what the stars could do for their ratings and circulation, and the balance of power began to shift. By the 1980s, there were more TV shows and publications that needed big movie stars than there were big stars. It was, quite simply, a seller's market, and Kingsley began to set the terms. She would withhold her clients, seeing who would offer best deal: the most favorable coverage, the most flattering photographs. At first, Kingsley would only allow her bigger stars to give interviews if they were promised a cover; soon the stars began insisting that the publicist be present for the interview; then they demanded veto power over the writer.† Then they asked for photo approval, quote approval, and sometimes, even veto power over text and headlines. Stars loved the gatekeeper style of publicity; they were not only getting better placement for less work—they were being publicized like movie stars, rather than dog food.

---

* Pat Newcomb, the press agent who had always remained so mum about Marilyn Monroe's last day, was a partner for a while, but she left to form her own company.

† Tom Cruise once rejected fourteen writers before agreeing to sit for a *Rolling Stone* profile.

Pat Kingsley's gatekeeper style of public relations caught on and other publicists adopted—and even exaggerated—Kingsley's methods. New York–based Peggy Siegal was so renowned for her hardball tactics that *Los Angeles* magazine called her "Doyenne of the Dragons." Her tirades are legendary. Ex-*Vogue* features editor Randall Koral butted heads with Siegal when he ran a piece on Mel Gibson's *Air America*, which called the movie an "ill-informed, half-baked and unfunny comic caper." Siegal, who was representing the film, called Koral. "Siegal told me I was wet behind the ears and ready to learn a thing or two; I was just a kid who wouldn't last long," said Koral. "It was very, very threatening." When *Dick Tracy* was released, Siegal blackballed *Vogue* from interviewing her client Warren Beatty. It was a pattern Koral would see repeated many times in his career.

Publicist Nancy Seltzer has a similar reputation. Journalist Ivor Davis, whose column was syndicated to about fifty newspapers, was invited to a press junket for *My Life*, starring Michael Keaton and Nicole Kidman. Seltzer had clashed with Davis in the past, and when she found out that he was scheduled to attend the junket, she announced that Kidman would boycott the event unless Davis was barred from attending. "I didn't even want to write about Kidman," Davis complained. "I wanted to do Keaton, but she succeeded in getting me disinvited. The studio said it was out of their hands. So Michael Keaton lost press in fifty papers for an interesting film about a man dying of cancer that desperately needed help at the box office."

Despite the competition, PMK remained the most powerful agency because it had the most impressive roster of clients. In addition to Cruise, PMK represented Demi Moore, Arnold Schwarzenegger, Jodie Foster, Sharon Stone, Richard Gere, Al Pacino, Goldie Hawn, Candice Bergen, Roseanne Arnold, and Courtney Love. If a reporter wrote anything critical about any PMK client, he would risk losing access to the other stars—effectively destroying his career as a celebrity writer.

Once a celebrity went under PMK's protective umbrella, the press's treatment of him or her changed dramatically. When Courtney Love was merely a Seattle grunge rocker, *Vanity Fair* did a scathing profile of her that resulted in her temporarily losing custody of her daughter.* After Love decided she wanted to be a movie star, she hired PMK, and *Vanity Fair* did a cover story on Love, depicting her as an angel. PMK further cleaned up Love's image by mailing out glamour shots of the former grunge queen along with a thinly veiled threat. "We got calls telling us to discard any old photos of Courtney, like the ones where her makeup was smeared all over her face and you could see her underwear," according to one reporter. "We were told that we would be 'monitored' and anyone who used old photos instead of the ones of her looking like a Hollywood goddess would risk losing her cooperation and other PMK clients too." Such threats usually worked. Hollywood journalists couldn't afford to antagonize PMK. In 1993, *Vanity Fair* had agreed to put PMK client Andie MacDowell on the cover, but when a last-minute interview with Bill Clinton came through, the magazine's editors were so worried about upsetting PMK that they published two versions of the magazine: one with Clinton and one with Andie MacDowell.†

Kingsley's power was such that at times, she could almost manufacture a star out of whole cloth. In 1997, she teamed up with director Joel Schumacher to perform such sleight of hand on the virtually unknown Matthew McConaughey, a twenty-six-year-old Texas law school student whose biggest role had been in *The Return of the Texas Chainsaw Massacre*. Schumacher cast him as an idealistic lawyer in *A Time to Kill* and Kingsley got the publicity machine rolling, and before long, McConaughey was profiled by *48 Hours*, Liz Smith praised him in her syndicated column, and he was the first virtually unknown actor to have the cover of *Vanity Fair* to himself. Articles in *Newsweek*, the *New York Times*, and *Us* magazine followed. Even before *A Time to Kill* was released, McConaughey was turning down multimillion-dollar of-

---

* The article alleged that Love used heroin while she was pregnant, a charge the singer vehemently denied. In that article, however, *Vanity Fair* did clean up Love's image somewhat. Fearing backlash from readers, Tina Brown had a cigarette airbrushed out of a barely dressed and very pregnant Love's hand.

† *Vanity Fair* was then being edited by Graydon Carter, who in his early years was less sure of his power than Tina Brown. A *Vanity Fair* spokeswoman, however, denied that scenario, saying hat PMK had nothing to do with the decision and that the magazine just wanted "the best of both worlds."

fers, including the role opposite Julia Roberts in *My Best Friend's Wedding*. Schumacher jokingly called McConaughey "my Frankenstein," but some in Hollywood say the creation was equally Pat Kingsley's. "This guy's salary is being built on buzz alone," noted one observer. "It's what's wrong with Hollywood." Kingsley dismissed talk that she "made" McConaughey. "He was made a star because of his startling debut in *A Time to Kill*," she said. "He delivered the goods."

By the time of the *Far and Away* junket, Pat Kingsley was succeeding in reversing the power relationship between the press and the publicists that existed since the days of *Sweet Smell of Success*. It was now the journalists who did the groveling. "Publicists control every word, every picture, every caption and if anybody says they don't, they don't know what time it is," said Koral. "They have enormous power. If you want their stars, you've got to play by their rules." With journalists feeling increasingly strongarmed by publicists, the relationship became incredibly antagonistic. Horror stories abounded about Kingsley. "I used to be a war correspondent, but entertainment journalism is much nastier," said one reporter. "Hollywood has made me very, very tough. War might be hell, but the people you have to deal with are nicer."

Even Pat Kingsley, however, had her failures. Julia Roberts was one of them. The actress was notoriously prickly. Once, when she moved into a very upscale apartment complex while her house was being renovated, she reportedly had notices sent to the other well-to-do tenants that if they ran into her in the hallways, they were not to speak with her or even look at her. She was also very demanding about her publicity. When a *People* magazine photographer snapped photos of Roberts onstage with Lyle Lovett the day after the two got married, she had police confiscate the film. *People* sued and a judge sided with the magazine, so Roberts's publicist gave *People* flattering, authorized wedding photos instead. But later, when Roberts was trying to get some good press as a UNICEF goodwill ambassador in Haiti, she recognized the *People* photographer and became so belligerent that UNICEF officials had to apologize to the members of the media for her outburst.

In 1991, the actress was being represented by publicist Susan Geller when she learned that *Vanity Fair* had wanted to do a cover story on her, but Geller turned down the magazine. Tina Brown had reneged on an agreement, according to Geller, to put her client Ellen Barkin on the cover. Geller insisted that she simply didn't want to deal with a magazine whose editor didn't keep her word, but the buzz was that Geller was also punishing Tina Brown. Julia Roberts was furious; she thought she was being used and so she dropped Geller and signed up with PMK. It was a big coup for Kingsley, but shortly after the deal was done, Roberts's life became tabloid fodder. The actress canceled a lavish Hollywood wedding to Keifer Sutherland less than a week before it was scheduled to happen. Within days, she was spotted nuzzling with Jason Patric. There were reports of erratic behavior on the set of Steven Spielberg's *Hook*. There were rumors of drug abuse. The actress became the butt of jokes. Jay Leno said he was taking the toaster he had bought for Julia and Keifer and giving it to Marla and Donald.

"Why can't you make it stop?" Roberts sobbed on the phone to Kingsley. The publicist called some of the reporters who had written unkind things about Roberts. She insulted and threatened them, but she had no leverage with the tabloids because they would never be given access to Roberts anyway. So Kingsley sought out friendly reporters—like her good friend Liz Smith—to deny a story about friction between Roberts and Steven Spielberg on the set of *Hook*. "The only way it was finally stopped was that Steven Spielberg got on the phone with Liz Smith," said Kingsley. That finally quieted everyone down, but the damage was done. "It was one thing after another, and it was all about her personal life," Kingsley said. "It seemed like any time I would talk to her, I was the bearer of bad news, I was the messenger." By the end of the year, Roberts dumped Kingsley. "I don't blame her," said Kingsley. "I was sorry to lose her, but I don't fault her for what she did."

Shortly after Kingsley lost Roberts, she got an even bigger star. Tom Cruise had been represented by publicist Andrea Jaffe since 1981, but when Fox hired Jaffe to do publicity in 1992, she had to drop all her clients. Cruise was by then perhaps the most image-conscious, controlling star in Hollywood. He bought up the rights to photos of himself and made people who worked with him sign confidentiality agreements. The crews on the sets of movies were often given long lists of do's and don'ts—mostly don'ts: don't talk to him unless he speaks first, don't ask for his autograph. Cruise surrounded himself with a small circle of close friends, family, and co-workers.* Andrea Jaffe knew how important control and privacy were to the powerful, somewhat prickly star; when she moved to Fox, she recommended Cruise consider Kingsley.

Kingsley became fiercely protective of Cruise. The brighter Cruise's star became, the more control he wanted over his career. When Columbia released *A Few Good Men* in 1992, Cruise forced the studio to bring Kingsley on board, and again she insisted that the journalists who interviewed Cruise sign a consent agreement. Under the conditions of the agreement, the interviews from the *Few Good Men* junket could be "printed and/or broadcast only once during or in connection with the initial domestic theatrical release" of the movie. "The one-time airing defies all knowledge of what it takes to promote a movie," complained one person close to the film. "Columbia wants the interviews to air as much as possible and promote the movie. That's the point of having a junket."

But the second restriction was even more shocking: PMK demanded approval of wording of the on-air "teasers" that television stations used to announce any Cruise interviews. "Teasers are fine, but sometimes they're very misleading," Kingsley said. "We have no problem if they announce that they have an exclusive interview with Tom Cruise, but if it gets into a lengthy description of what the interview is about, we want approval." An embarrassed Columbia told irate reporters that other stars from *A Few Good Men*—including Kevin Bacon and Kevin Pollack, as well as direc-

---

* Cruise knew and trusted Jaffe because her brother, Stanley Jaffe, was his producer in Cruise's 1981 breakthrough film, *Taps*.

tor Rob Reiner—would be happy to chat with journalists who didn't sign the consent forms. "That would be like doing a story on U2 and not getting Bono," grumbled one broadcaster, who reluctantly signed the agreement. "We're signing it because our station was already expecting the interview. It's Tom Cruise and it's a big movie."

Pat Kingsley could have her choice of covers, and with the release of *A Few Good Men*, a men's magazine like GQ seemed a good place for a cover story on Cruise. Writer Stephanie Mansfield interviewed the actor at the Bel Air Hotel in Los Angeles; Pat Kingsley was sitting in the next room.

"The interview lasted probably the requisite hour and a half," Mansfield recalled. "He seemed very congenial if somewhat—I would say—aloof. He's not a real easy person to get to know—certainly in that situation." But, according to Mansfield, she felt she and Cruise had "bonded in a mutually self-serving way" that journalists and their subjects often do.

Shortly after the interview, Mansfield mentioned to a friend that she was profiling Cruise. "My friend said 'This is such a coincidence. You should call my cousin who grew up with him,' " said Mansfield. "So I called this young girl who went to Glen Ridge High School in New Jersey with Tom Mapother . . . As it turned out, she was very positive about Tom. She thought he was a really nice guy."

When Cruise telephoned Mansfield for a scheduled follow-up interview, she casually mentioned the conversation with Cruise's old classmate. "He went ballistic," Mansfield recalled. "He started yelling into the phone: How dare I talk to someone he went to school with. What is this, a profile or a biography? He accused me of conducting a 'covert operation.' He was so *irrational*. He didn't make any sense. I tried to explain that the former friend didn't say anything negative, but it didn't matter. He was obviously very upset that I had done any reporting, that I hadn't just taken the interview with him and printed it verbatim."

Cruise slammed down the phone, and Mansfield just sat there, somewhat stunned. In a few minutes, the phone rang again. It was Pat Kingsley. "She basically threatened me," said Mansfield.

"I've been in the business too long to threaten someone," said Kingsley. "What I did say is that it would be a long time before I would subject a client to be interviewed by her."

But Mansfield has a different recollection. "She said, and this is a direct quote, 'Tom is going to be around for a long time and I'm sure that you want to be around in your business for a long time.' I said, 'Pat, I don't know what you're driving at.' She made it very clear that if I used any of this interview from this young girl, I would be blacklisted from her clients."

Mansfield decided to use the material anyway, and when the piece was published, it was one of the most revealing portraits ever written about Cruise. Kingsley decreed that Mansfield would never interview another one of her clients. "Am I stupid?" she said of such blackballing tactics. "If they burn me once, won't they burn me twice? I will absolutely not work with them again. I'll tell a magazine, 'Listen, this writer has a bad history with my clients so give us another writer.' The same with a photographer. If a client doesn't wish a particular photographer to shoot him, why should we allow it?"

"I guess I'm perceived in the industry as a junkyard dog by making a phone call and doing some reporting," Mansfield said. "If you want to stay in the business of interviewing celebrities, you better write the sort of piece that is fawning and adoring and has no facts."

After the junket for *A Few Good Men*, a few editors grumbled that it was high time to take action against publicists like Kingsley. The cause was taken up by Lanny Jones, the top editor at *People*. Pat Kingsley had been battling with *People* for some time, ever since she claimed that the magazine reneged on a promise to give Mary Tyler Moore photo approval in the early eighties. The feud intensified when, according to Kingsley, the magazine used some pictures of Goldie Hawn without her permission. "The photographs made her look heavy," Kingsley says. The accompanying article—a "write around" done without the cooperation of the subject—further infuriated Kingsley, who accused the magazine of "subterfuge" and "misrepresentation" by using quotes that had appeared elsewhere. Kingsley started withholding her clients from

People. That July, Jones invited a group of top journalists from *Vanity Fair, Newsweek, Time, E!, Premiere,* and *TV Guide* to a meeting at the Regency Club in Westwood, California. Jones urged them to establish a written set of rules that every publication and television show—except "the bottom feeders like the tabloids"—would follow when dealing with press agents. "He's just mad because *People* has lost the monopoly it used to have on celebrity interviews," according to another journalist, who said that *People* still hadn't recovered from the backlash to its 1988 Robin Williams interview. "*People* used to be able to call the shots. Now it's finding it hard to find any big stars who'll sit down for an interview." The problem wasn't just the fallout from the Robin Williams debacle. *People* had to compete for interviews with mainstream magazines like *Time* and *Newsweek,* upscale newcomers like *Premiere* and *Vanity Fair,* and men's and women's magazines like *Mademoiselle* and *Esquire* that almost never used to put celebrities on their covers. *People* magazine was still hugely successful, but by the time of the junket for *A Few Good Men,* celebrities were no longer coming to it. In its early years, virtually all of *People*'s covers were done with the celebrities' cooperation, ten years later that number was closer to 75 percent, by the mid-1990s, it was down to about 20 percent. "One problem we at *People* face in a seller's market is that, while we can stand on principle and say, 'No, we won't allow you photo approval,' or whatever, someone like a Pat Kingsley can always go to another magazine who will," Jones complained.

"Jones said that if we bond together and agree to stop making deals with publicists," one attendee recalled, "they will lose their grip over us."

Kingsley wasn't worried. "The media is incapable of sticking to any code," she said. "All you have to do to break one of those alliances is offer someone an exclusive interview."

The alliance crumbled.

After the Mansfield fiasco and the failed *People* rebellion, Kingsley decided to deny most of the print media access to her bigger stars. "The articles are just too tough, have too much of an edge," she said. "It's easier to do television. The public sees what you have to say, rather than some writer's interpretation of what you said. . . . Besides, people don't read anymore."

At junkets for Cruise's next film, *The Firm*, TV reporters were given interviews but print reporters were greeted with a note from Cruise, explaining that he had to leave town. "I look forward to the opportunity to speak with you again in the future." That opportunity did not come. Even Kingsley's ally Liz Smith was told that Cruise didn't want to speak with her. The actor was, it seems, upset by an extraordinarily gentle barb that less sensitive types would have taken as a compliment. Smith had written that Cruise and Jeanne Tripplehorn's characters in *The Firm* "are wildly good-looking, have fabulous bodies and a fantastic sex life [so] don't be surprised if the real-life Mrs. Cruise, Nicole Kidman, appears on the set with Tom's lunch once in a while."*

"Tom was hurt by your item," Kingsley told Smith, "he may not want to do an interview with you." The gossip columnist was flabbergasted. "Here is a guy I've praised to the skies—his looks, his talent, his obvious adoration of Nicole Kidman. I even loved *"Far and Away"*!† . . . I suppose I should be used to this irrational supersensitivity. But it's always a surprise. And always a disappointment."

Pat Kingsley and other celebrity protectors argued that Tom Cruise's personal life—his religion, his romances—were nobody's business. "Where is it written that stars are public figures? That the press has a right to know?" Kingsley said. "If they were elected officials, I could see it. . . . But where is it written that the star's life is news?" Cruise's life was news, some journalists countered, because he used his tremendous clout behind the scenes to advance his agenda. There was the issue of his religion, which, on the face of it, would certainly seem to be Cruise's

---

* Kingsley recalled the dispute being over something another actress had said, though she couldn't recall the specifics.

† Smith called the film "a winner—a lush, romantic, vigorous, sexy and spectacular piece of movie making. And Cruise is spectacular as well. He is appealing, photogenic, and charismatic as ever. Yes, yes, he IS a good actor, but Cruise can't escape his looks and charm. . . . Relax you guys at Universal; 'Far and Away' looks like a blockbuster from my vantage point."

private business. It was, however, a factor in the film industry; Cruise reportedly put pressure on studios he was working with to use ClearSound—a sound system developed by the Church of Scientology. While some, including non-Scientologists, swear by ClearSound, others are less taken with the system. Cruise tried to get producer Don Simpson to use ClearSound in *Days of Thunder*, but Simpson refused. When the producer, after having spent $25,000 on Scientology classes at Cruise's urging, called the church "a con," Cruise reportedly retaliated by having Simpson eased out of directing a *Top Gun* sequel. Cruise did succeed in persuading director Ron Howard to use the system in *Far and Away*—although it cost $120,000, when most sound systems cost about $5,000. Cruise, who also got Reiner to use ClearSound in *A Few Good Men*, was angered by reports that ClearSound was a "squeak-suppressing system" designed to lower the actor's sometimes high-pitched voice. "Bullshit!" he said. "Alls it is, is a recording system, designed to capture the voice—not to enhance or change it."

Given PMK's demonstrated willingness to retaliate, few journalists dug into the story of Cruise's involvement in Scientology, a subject he went to great lengths to keep out of the press. "He didn't want people to know he belonged to the church, and they had promised him anonymity," said *Star* gossip columnist Janet Charlton, who broke the story of Cruise's membership. "It created a big stir. They went insane and they tried to track down my source." Someone claiming to be from the phone company tried to get her phone records, she said. A man who said he was the *Star*'s lawyer tried to get Charlton to tell him the name of her source. Charlton said she later found out he was working for the church. "Reporting on Scientology can by very intimidating," Charlton said. "But I deeply believe it's an important, newsworthy story. Tom Cruise is a very powerful guy."

In Germany, an anti-Scientology movement was led by Chancellor Helmut Kohl, who said that the religion bore a resemblance to organized crime and posed a threat to democracy. When some Germans organized a boycott of *Mission Impossible*, thirty-four non-Scientologist celebrities—including Dustin Hoffman, Oliver Stone, and Goldie Hawn—signed a letter to Chancellor Kohl, comparing Germany's persecution of Scientologists to the oppression of the Jews during the Holocaust. "In the 1930s, it was the Jews," said the ad. "Today it is the Scientologists." The letter, which ran as an ad in the *International Herald Tribune*, turned out to have been placed by Bert Fields, the Los Angeles lawyer who represented Cruise as well as fellow Scientologist John Travolta. When asked if he had attached his name to the letter for moral or more pragmatic reasons, one signer replied, "Do we all want to be in business with Tom Cruise and John Travolta, and would we sign a letter just to make them happy, make them like us? What do you think?"

Pat Kingsley was having to deal with questions not just about Cruise's religion, but also his sexual orientation. In 1987, when Cruise was twenty-four, he had married Mimi Rogers, who was seven years his senior. The ceremony was so secretive that even Andrea Jaffe, who was his publicist at the time, didn't know about it. Stories soon began to circulate that the couple was having trouble conceiving a child. Cruise denied any problems. In late 1989, he told a number of publications how happy he and his wife were. "I just really enjoy our marriage," he said to Jann Wenner's *Us* in December 1989. "I couldn't imagine being without her." One month later, Cruise announced that they were splitting and refused to discuss it. When *Playboy* asked Rogers if she had dumped Cruise, she bristled. "Is that the story—that I was bored with that child and threw him over, chewed him up and spit him out?" Rogers said. "Well, here's the real story. Tom was seriously thinking of becoming a monk. At least for that period of time, it looked as though marriage wouldn't fit into his overall spiritual need. And he thought he had to be celibate to maintain the purity of his instrument. My instrument needed tuning. Therefore, it became obvious that we had to split."

Almost immediately, Rogers withdrew the comment. According to some reports, Cruise's lawyers had warned Rogers that she could lose her multimillion-dollar divorce settlement if she didn't keep quiet about the marriage, but Rogers insisted she got no pressure from Cruise. She went on the *Tonight Show* and told Johnny Carson that she had made the comments as a spoof of the way tabloids make up outrageous stories. "I came up with the most implausible thing I could think of," she said. "Like a guy thinking of becoming a monk would be doing *Days of Thunder!*"*

Speculation about the actor's sex life didn't die down after his marriage to Nicole Kidman. Cruise's new wife was put in the awkward position of defending her husband's sexuality to the media. "I don't know what [Mimi Rogers] meant, but I can assure you my husband's no monk!" Kidman once said. "He's a very sexual guy." Kidman was even asked, point blank, if her husband was gay. "Gay? Really?" she said. "Well, ummm, he's not gay in my knowledge. You'll have to ask him."

Kidman, who had grown up in Australia, was once described as "breathtakingly determined . . . She has pursued her career with the relentlessness of a heat-seeking missile." Her first big film, the 1989 Australian suspense thriller *Dead Calm*, got some attention in the United States, but produced no offers of roles, so Kidman took charge of the situation. She got hold of a pur-loined copy of a script for *Ghost*, in which she recognized a poten-tial blockbuster, and videotaped a private production of the film, with herself in the role that would go to Demi Moore. She sent the unorthodox audition video—unsolicited—to director Joel Rubin. "I don't know how she got the script," a stunned Rubin said. "But the video was an elaborate production—fully cast, blocked and acted with little sets and lights and everything. I've never seen anything like it."

Rubin was impressed, but not impressed enough to give Kid-man the role. She got her break playing a brain surgeon in Tom Cruise's *Days of Thunder*; after the movie appeared, she converted to Scientology, married Cruise, and the couple adopted two chil-dren in Florida, where a controversial Republican gubernatorial candidate, Anthony Martin, called for an investigation into the adoptions, calling them egregious examples of "baby selling." Some critics questioned whether Kidman's marriage to Cruise was a career move for both of them. Entertainment reporters debated

---

* In fact, Tom Cruise as a man of the cloth isn't as bizarre as Rogers tried to make it sound. When he was a teenager, Tom spent a year studying for the priesthood in a Franciscan seminary in Cincinnati.

about whether or not the media had an obligation to investigate the possibility. On the one side, there were those who agreed with Pat Kingsley that stars' private lives are nobody's business; others countered that celebrities were among the richest, most influential people in the country and that the press should not put itself in the position—as it did in the days of Hedda and Louella—of perpetrating public relations myths. The rumors about the Cruise-Kidman marriage were so rampant, this argument went, that even if they weren't true, the media had an obligation to address them. Accordingly, in a profile of Kidman, *McCall's* ran an anonymous quote, attributed to "a prominent movie critic" who said he had "heard rumors" that Cruise and Kidman had married "to squelch the gay stuff" and that "Nicole was told that if she married Tom, CAA would make her a movie star." The article also quoted a number of people who dismissed the speculation and said that Cruise and Kidman had an ideal marriage. Printing the rumor, however, spread it beyond the media and entertainment circles that traffic in such things and put them in mainstream America. "I spoke with Pat the day that story appeared," said a writer. "She was devastated and crazed. When something like that happens, her fury knows no bounds."

Cruise and Kidman were prepared to sue, but lawsuits—as everyone in Hollywood knew from the Carol Burnett episode—were too lengthy and too messy. Kingsley wanted a retraction and she wouldn't wait until the next issue of *McCall's* came out; it was delivered through Pat Kingsley's office the day the offending magazine hit newsstands: "*McCall's* knows of no evidence indicating that Mr. Cruise is sterile or homosexual, or that Ms. Kidman is anything other than a highly competent actress, or that they married for any reason other than mutual love and respect, or that any of the other reported rumors is true."

Liz Smith also weighed in on the controversy. Ever since she'd been lured to *Newsday* and her column started appearing in the parent company's *Los Angeles Times*, Smith was more eager than ever to make a big splash in Hollywood. The gossip columnist was a frequent house guest of director Joel Schumacher, who had set aside "the Liz Smith" room for her. "All this continuing controversy over Tom's private life reminds me of a well-known director who was asked what he thought about the much-gossiped-about Cruise-Nicole Kidman marriage," Smith wrote. "He said, 'You know, it's none of my business. It's none of your business. And frankly, I don't care.' Great answer." The unnamed source in the item was Joel Schumacher; he also happened to be Kidman's director in *Batman Forever* and Cruise's director in *The Firm*.

Vanity Fair writer Jennet Conant also rushed to Cruise and Kidman's defense. Conant, who was married to *60 Minutes* reporter Steve Kroft, told *USA Today* and the *New York Post*'s Page Six that the *McCall's* story was inaccurate and unfair. "What reporters were doing to Tom and Nicole was a rabid invasion of their privacy," Conant said. Tom and Nicole were "deeply in love" Conant insisted; she knew, she said, because they were friends. "I profiled Nicole twice, and she liked what I wrote," said Conant. When the writer profiled Kidman for *Redbook*, she didn't address the rumors. "It's nobody's business," Conant maintained. *McCall's* was just jealous, Conant told Page Six, because it didn't have access like *Redbook*. After Conant's comments appeared, Kingsley called the writer to thank her. The next year, when Kingsley was negotiating with *Vanity Fair* for the first ever joint interview with Nicole Kidman and Tom Cruise, Kingsley asked for—and got—Jennet Conant. The reporter had no apologies for the fawning tone of the story. "This is not an investigation of criminals," she said. "It's fun stories about nice people who I happen to like a lot." Later, when *Vanity Fair* profiled Tom Cruise's good friend George Clooney,* also a PMK client, Conant got that assignment too. The Stephanie Mansfields of entertainment journalism were being edged out by writers who were more cooperative with the Pat Kingsleys of the world. "Pat and I deal with each other on a very professional level," said Conant. "There's never been any restrictions, she's never asked me to sign anything . . . They know they can trust me. They know I never hit below the belt."

Indeed, by the late 1990s, negative articles about Cruise, like the one in *McCall's* or fact-filled ones like Stephanie Mansfield's,

---

* Clooney once dated Kelly Preston, who was married to John Travolta and was Cruise's co-star in *Jerry Maguire*.

were a rarity. Kingsley had succeeded in intimidating the entertainment press so thoroughly that it was willing to publish increasingly implausible celebrations of the actor's good deeds.

In 1996, around the time *Mission Impossible* was being released, Tom Cruise, who both directed and starred in the movie, was being depicted in the media as a real-life action hero for a series of heroic rescues: he had saved the life of a boy being crushed by his throng of fans and paparazzi, he had come to the aid of a woman who had been hit by a car. In August, Cruise made headlines for saving the lives of a French family whose yacht exploded off the Isle of Capri. Articles and TV segments around the world applauded the actor's bravery: "No Mission Impossible" declared one newspaper. "Tom Terrific," proclaimed *People* magazine. The only problem was—it never happened. While there *was* an accident, neither Cruise nor anyone on his yacht participated in the rescue in any way, according to a spokesman for the coast guard in Capri, which rescued the family and brought it to safety on the yacht on which the star was sailing. Cruise, according to the coast guard spokesman, never lifted a finger in the actual rescue. The star did, however, visit the victims in the hospital. When questioned about the story, Kingsley at first praised Cruise's heroics and courage. "If I'm ever in danger," she said, "I hope Tom Cruise is around!" When pressed for a specific description of Cruise's heroism, however, she got vague. And when presented with the coast guard's official version of events, Kingsley backed off.

"The press made up the story!" she declared angrily. "They got it wrong!" And then she added triumphantly: "They always do."

p.r. muscle

Private Investigator Anthony Pellicano was on the *Dangerous* tour in Bangkok with Michael Jackson when he got the call: police had raided Neverland, the singer's 2,700-acre ranch; they had a search warrant; they brought in a locksmith; they seized videotapes and photographs. This is trouble, Pellicano knew, but then again, trouble was Pellicano's business.

It was Sunday, August 22, 1993, still before dawn in California, but Pellicano telephoned criminal lawyer Howard Weitzman in Los Angeles anyway. "Wake up," Pellicano told Weitzman. They had a lot of work to do.

Hard Copy correspondent Diane Dimond spent most of Monday, August 23, at her cubicle in the Mae West Building of Paramount Studios, tracking down the names in Heidi Fleiss's little black book. Shortly before 4 P.M., Dimond's boss, Executive Producer Linda Bell Blue, tapped her on the shoulder. "In about seven minutes, Channel 4 is going to run a story about Michael Jackson," Blue said. "I don't really know what it is, but come to my office. Let's watch it."

"The L.A.P.D just a few moments ago confirmed for us that entertainer Michael Jackson is the subject of a criminal investigation," reported KNBC-TV's Colan Nolan. This should be interesting, Dimond thought as she and Blue leaned forward, eager to find out why the police were investigating the world's biggest pop star. They didn't find out from KNBC-TV. "It was an odd story," said Dimond. "They said police were looking for something, but they didn't say what or why."

Bell turned to Dimond: "You're on the Michael Jackson story."

Dimond elbowed her way through the crowd of other reporters, photographers, and camera crews that crowded into Howard Weitzman's Century City office the following day for a press conference the lawyer had called in reaction to the mysterious investigation of Michael Jackson. Bert Fields, the smooth-talking, powerhouse attorney whose clients included Dustin Hoffman, John Travolta, Warren Beatty, David Geffen, and Tom Cruise, was also on the case, but the front man was the more combative Weitzman. "I'm going to make a statement in a moment," Weitzman told the crowd. "If you guys will act like humans, which is real difficult for you all . . ."

Weitzman then introduced Jackson's "security consultant," Anthony Pellicano. A slight, well-groomed man with receding wavy hair and hound-dog eyes stepped up to the mike. There is no truth, Pellicano told the crowd, to the child molestation charges against Michael Jackson. A collective gasp came from the journalists. This was the first time anyone officially disclosed why police were investigating Jackson. Then Pellicano threw a curve ball: What the case was really about, the security consultant said, was blackmail. "A demand for twenty million dollars was presented and it was flatly refused," Pellicano told the stunned reporters. "We had no intention to do anything with it. We wanted to see how far they went." When Jackson's people refused to pay, the accusers went to the authorities, Pellicano said. "I am actively engaged in investigating that extortion attempt."

Dimond's jaw dropped. She was stunned—not just by the charges of child molestation, and not just by the blackmail allegations—but because she believed she recognized Pellicano's voice.

After Dimond reported on the apparent ties between the Hollywood Madam and Columbia Pictures, an anonymous man with a Chicago accent began calling her, trying to persuade her that certain people were trying to frame Columbia executives.

"That's him!" Dimond whispered to her producer. "That's the guy who's been trying to spin my Heidi Fleiss story." Dimond wondered why the same person would be involved in the two biggest scandals in Hollywood. "This guy must be one slick operator," she thought. She didn't yet know the half of it.

By 1993, the culture of celebrity was so pervasive that movie stars and recording artists were among the richest, most powerful people in the country—and no one was bigger than Michael Jackson. Jackson wasn't just a pop star; he was a multibillion-dollar conglomerate. He had signed a contract with Sony worth $1 billion, the biggest entertainment deal in history. He had an endorsement deal with Pepsi and was credited with the soft drink's two-point increase in market share; each point was worth $470 million, so Jackson was a very valuable commodity to Pepsi.*

The power of celebrities, however, extended way beyond their financial clout. They were modern society's most sacred icons. Celebrities had a cultural significance and an emotional impact on Americans that they didn't find in religious or political leaders. In the early 1990s, no performer personified the celebrity-as-demigod syndrome more than Michael Jackson. It was an image Jackson worked hard to cultivate. Although his actual philanthropic work was limited mostly to singing songs about the underprivileged and hugging children in hospitals, Jackson was seen as one of the world's great humanitarians. Presidents wanted to be photographed with him; he was honored by Carter, Reagan, Bush, and Clinton. Los Angeles Mayor Tom Bradley declared a Michael Jackson Day.

The entire scandal industry, however, was built on bashing such icons. By the time the Michael Jackson story broke, the scandal industry was very big business. In addition to the super-

---

* Jackson privately said he didn't like Pepsi. "I don't drink that crap," he once confided.

market tabloids, there were twelve news magazines on television in 1993—up from three five years earlier—each one trying to come up with revelations more shocking than the other. The scandal business, according to one estimate, was a $28.3-billion-dollar industry.

With so much at stake, both sides became *very* aggressive. As tabloid reporters increasingly resorted to tactics like paying sources and going undercover to get the goods on celebrities, an equally combative industry evolved that specialized in suppressing scandal. When a salacious bit of information threatened to wreck a star's career, when police reports and criminal charges were involved, traditional public relations—even gatekeepers like Pat Kingsley—were useless. At times like those, celebrities turned to a breed of aggressive private detectives usually billed as "security consultants."

The best-known of these operators worked in and around Hollywood. Pellicano's key competitor was probably Gavin de Becker, who for years was on the William Morris payroll and whose clients included Michael J. Fox, Cher, and Bill Cosby. Fox hired de Becker when he married actress Tracy Pollan in 1988. At first, Fox thought de Becker was going overboard on the job. When the actor showed up at the quiet Vermont inn where he was to be married, he was startled to see what he later described as "half a dozen Arnold Schwarzenegger look-alikes in business suits and mirrored shades in Adirondack chairs scanning the woods with binoculars and searchlights." To execute Operation Fox, de Becker had prepared a thirty-six page manual, referring to Michael Fox as Coyote 1 and Tracy Pollan as Coyote 2. "The *National Enquirer* and its ilk have the whole industry more or less wired," the young and attractive de Becker warned a startled Fox. "You've got two-bit publicists, chauffeurs, and secretaries all over Hollywood selling information to the junk press. Whenever you go to a restaurant frequented by celebrities, you can assume that the guy who parks your car is working with a paparazzo. He's got a slip of paper in his pocket with the name of a photographer on it." Fox came to the conclusion that de Becker wasn't overreacting after the detective sent Fox's publicist, Nanci Ryder, undercover answering phones at the *National Enquirer*'s makeshift headquarters at a nearby hotel. Not only did Ryder discover the *Enquirer*'s plans—including an idea to rent a llama suit to cross a meadow—but she also got her hands on a copy of the *Enquirer*'s confidential source list, including some people on Fox's payroll.

"When you arrive at the scene of a story and a bunch of guys are talking into their cufflinks, you know de Becker is on the job," said a tabloid reporter.

Pellicano couldn't stand de Becker. He referred to his biggest competitor as a "fucking wimp." Pellicano was of the tough-talking Philip Marlowe gumshoe school of private detectives. Also known as "The Private Investigator to the Stars," "The Publicist of Last Resort," or "The Celebrities' Thug," Pellicano was born in 1944 in the working-class Chicago suburb of Cicero. "I'm a kid from the streets," he admitted. "I could have been a criminal just as easily." A high school drop-out raised by a single mother, he earned a GED in the army signal corps and went to work at the Spiegel catalogue company "skip tracing" customers who didn't pay their bills. From there, Pellicano joined a private detective agency he found in the back of the Yellow Pages. In 1969, he set up his own shop, solving several highly publicized missing persons cases, working for the government, and becoming a minor celebrity around Chicago. He loved publicity, drove a huge Lincoln Continental, hung samurai swords in his office, and sealed his letters with monogrammed wax. In 1974, however, Pellicano declared bankruptcy and in the filing revealed that he had borrowed $30,000 from Paul "The Waiter" de Lucia, the son of a reputed mobster. "Paul de Lucia is my daughter's godfather," Pellicano protested. "He's just like any other guy in the neighborhood." Nevertheless, the scandal forced Pellicano to resign his prestigious position on the Illinois Law Enforcement Commission. His business and his reputation were in shambles, and he needed a high-profile case to restore his reputation. It came in the form of Elizabeth Taylor.

In 1977, the body of the actress's third husband, Mike Todd, was stolen from its grave in a Chicago area cemetery. After police searched and found nothing, Pellicano showed up at the cemetery with the camera crew from a local news station, went to a spot seventy-five yards south of the excavated grave, reached under some scattered branches and leaves, and produced a plastic bag containing Todd's remains. Pellicano insisted that "underworld sources" had told him the body's whereabouts, but rivals snickered that the private detective had staged the entire escapade for publicity. If so, it worked. The recovery of Todd's body made headlines, and a grateful Elizabeth Taylor introduced Pellicano to her Hollywood friends. Los Angeles criminal attorney Howard Weitzman hired Pellicano to work with him, and the pair successfully defended auto executive John DeLorean in a cocaine-trafficking case—even though the FBI caught DeLorean on videotape selling cocaine to an undercover agent.* In 1983, Pellicano left Chicago and opened an office on Sunset Boulevard in Los Angeles. There, sources say, he was coached by the notorious Fred Otash, the private investigator for *Confidential.* In Hollywood, Pellicano quickly became what he calls "the ultimate problem solver."

Pellicano didn't tackle the problem, he went after the accuser. He has, foes say, boasted of his underworld contacts and threatened people with violence. He insists he didn't, however, carry a gun. "That's a physical solution to a mental problem," says Pellicano, a proud member of Mensa, the organization whose members all have genius-level I.Q.s. Pellicano used "Sherlock Holmes–type stuff," he explained, by digging up the dirt on the people who were maligning his clients. And there always was dirt. When a woman sold a story to a British tabloid that she had an eleven-year affair with Kevin Costner, the actor called Pellicano, who fed damaging facts about her to the tabloids. "She was trying to extort Kevin Costner," said Pellicano. "We exposed her for what she was." In cases of blackmail, Pellicano said, he starts by "appealing to their sense of values," he said. "If they don't have any, then I have to counter black 'em."

Before O. J. Simpson was accused of murdering his wife Nicole and Ron Goldman, the ex-football star hired Pellicano to silence a secretary who accused him of abusive behavior. The accusations went away after Pellicano found potentially embarrassing information on the secretary. When James Woods was

---

* There were later charges, denied by Pellicano, that he had intimidated potential government witnesses.

going through a messy breakup with Sean Young—a split so acrimonious it was said to have involved mutilated dolls, threatening letters, and bizarre tales of Woods's penis stuck to his thigh with Krazy Glue—Woods hired Pellicano. The private detective also worked on the William Kennedy Smith rape trial. He is said to be the one who dug up information about accuser Patricia Bowman's personal life that appeared in the *New York Times* and the supermarket tabloid *The Globe*.

One of Pellicano's mandates was to track down *Spy* magazine's aggressive but pseudonymous Hollywood reporter Celia Brady. "It's a secret society," Pellicano said. "If somebody wants to investigate a member of the group, they have to be willing to take the heat themselves."

Don Simpson had used Pellicano's services before. When a former receptionist sued Simpson for $5 million, claiming the producer of *Top Gun* and *Days of Thunder* made her schedule hookers for him and that he used cocaine and watched pornographic videos in front of her, Pellicano produced evidence that the accuser herself had used drugs, rented porn movies, and had stolen letters from Simpson's wastebasket. "He goes in like a junkyard dog to find dirt," said the receptionist's lawyer. One witness who testified against the receptionist got a $4,500 "loan" from Pellicano, which, the detective said, didn't have to be paid back. "Anthony is one of those people who is, shall we say, a lion at the gate," Simpson gleefully said after the case was dismissed. "He is not a man to be on the wrong side of."

So when a doctor named Stephen Ammerman, who was said to be treating Don Simpson for drug addiction, died of a drug overdose at Simpson's Bel Aire estate, the producer immediately called Pellicano. Later, Ammerman's family filed a wrongful death suit, alleging that the doctor hadn't willingly taken the drugs that killed him and that Pellicano and others destroyed evidence before police arrived on the scene. The charges against Pellicano were dismissed after Simpson himself died the following year of a drug overdose.

Not everyone was always impressed with Pellicano's tactics. After Heidi Fleiss was arrested, Pellicano publicly denied that Columbia executive Michael Nathanson was one of her clients. The problem was, until the denial, Nathanson hadn't been publicly linked to Fleiss. The denial prompted *Variety* to give Pellicano the PR Boner Award.

Then there was the Roseanne case. The comedienne paid Pellicano $25,000 to locate a daughter she'd given up for adoption seventeen years earlier. The story appeared in the *National Enquirer*, and Roseanne claimed that Pellicano—whom she called "a low-life scumbag"—split the fee with reporters from the tabloid who then tracked down her daughter and ran the story. Pellicano denied giving the story to the *National Enquirer*; he blamed the leak on Roseanne's husband Tom Arnold, who did, in fact, sell stories about Roseanne to the *Enquirer* to support his drug habit.*

The truth is that Pellicano did work for the *National Enquirer* from time to time. When *Los Angeles* magazine was preparing an exposé of the tabloid, reporter Rod Lurie said the detective threatened him and tried to get the piece killed. "There was consistent cultlike phone intimidation from Pellicano," said Lurie. "He would call my friends and family and editors I worked for at other magazines, saying I was through in this town." According to Lurie, Pellicano paid the reporter's research assistant to steal his notes. *Enquirer* sources, meanwhile, insist that Lurie's biggest source on the story was actually working for tabloid foe Gavin de Becker.

"I can't do everything by the book," Pellicano once admitted. "I bend the law to death in gaining information." Pellicano would sometimes remind people that he carries an aluminum baseball bat in the trunk of his black Nexus. "Guys who fuck with me get to meet my buddy over there," he once told a reporter, gesturing toward the bat. Pellicano also tells people that he is an expert with a knife—"I can shred your face" he has said—and that he has a blackbelt in karate. "If I use martial arts, I might really maim somebody," he said. "I have, and I don't want to. I only use intimidation and fear when I absolutely have to."

Anthony Pellicano had worked for Michael Jackson for four years. His services didn't come cheap. The investigator's usual fee

---

* Pellicano and Roseanne have "resolved their differences," according to a spokeswoman.

was $500 an hour; Jackson paid Pellicano a retainer of $100,000 a month. The singer, according to Pellicano, was the victim of twenty-five to thirty extortion attempts every year. He also had family problems. When Jackson's sister La Toya wrote a tell-all book that included allegations that Michael had been molested as a child, Pellicano launched a campaign to discredit La Toya and her husband, Jack Gordon. He succeeded. Before the book came out, newspaper articles appeared saying that Gordon was a convicted panderer who had owned massage parlors and had changed his name twice. Despite Pellicano's efforts, the book was a bestseller. The detective, however, insists that Jackson was pleased with his work. "We finished that job," Pellicano said. "Michael is happy."

During the child molestation allegations, Pellicano completely took over the function of public relations. Jackson's usual publicist, Lee Solters, referred all calls—more then seven hundred in the first week—to Pellicano. "I had to lay out the chessboard and say, what does the public think?" Pellicano said of the situation. "How will this affect Michael and all of the other deals that are in the works for him? And the sponsors involved?"

Even before the child abuse scandal broke, Jackson and his handlers were masters at manipulating the press. Actual interviews were minimal and were limited to journalists who were bona fide friends or allies. Although articles frequently appeared about Jackson's bizarre behavior, most of them were amusing tales of Jackson's wacky eccentricities or stories of his love for stars like Elizabeth Taylor and Diana Ross. Almost all the stories were planted by the singer or at his direct orders. When Jackson and Madonna had a "date" at the Los Angeles restaurant Ivy, paparazzi were waiting by the time they arrived. They had been tipped off by both Jackson's people and Madonna's. A similar scene occurred when he had a "date" with Brooke Shields—whose other highly publicized romances included George Michael, John Travolta, and Dodi Fayed.* Some believed that Jackson's friendship

---

* After Jackson told Oprah Winfrey and her 90 million viewers that he and Shields were in love, the grateful Jackson gave Shields a $100,000 ring and a $200,000 necklace.

with Elizabeth Taylor was also largely for public consumption. They fed off each other's fame: she gave him old Hollywood credibility, he gave her cutting-edge hipness. "They rarely saw each other privately," according to writer Chris Anderson, who said the friendship was both a public relations ploy and a financial arrangement because Jackson was a big investor in Taylor's various merchandising efforts.

"Jackson would leak stories to us all the time," says the *National Enquirer*'s Mike Walker. "Then he'd do this whole 'the tabloids lie' routine." Jackson regularly planted items that he was feuding with rival singer Prince; one of his favorite tabloid stories reported that Prince was using ESP to drive Jackson's beloved chimp Bubbles crazy. "This is the final straw," the story quoted Jackson as saying. "What kind of sicko would mess with a monkey?" Jackson personally orchestrated the publication of stories that he wanted to buy the Elephant Man's bones and that he slept in an hyperbaric oxygen chamber because he wanted to live to be 150. Jackson wanted the hyperbaric chamber story to run on the cover of the *National Enquirer*—the one condition was that the writer use the word "bizarre" at least three times. "He really liked the word *bizarre*," according to Charles Montgomery, the reporter who did the piece. When Jackson was told that the Polaroid that showed him sleeping in the chamber wasn't good enough quality to run as a cover, he posed for a second photograph. "I did more articles on Jackson than I did on anyone else," said Montgomery. "Before I ran anything, I would always check with people close to Michael to see how accurate it was. I almost always had full cooperation from his camp."*

Jackson was shocked that the mainstream press, including *Time*, *Newsweek*, the AP, and UPI, picked up the oxygen chamber story. "It's like I can tell the press anything about me and they'll buy it," Jackson said. "We can actually control the press. I think this is an important breakthrough for us."

---

* Among those who confirmed the hyperbaric chamber story for the *Enquirer* was Michael Jackson's plastic surgeon, Dr. Steven Hoefflin, whose other patients are said to include Liz Taylor, Ivana Trump, Tony Curtis, Don Johnson, Joan Rivers, Nancy Sinatra, and Sylvester Stallone (who denies he's a patient). Dr. Hoefflin would later be involved in a scandal when some staffers accused him of sexual harassment. He was cleared of the charges.

By the time Jackson did his highly rated interview with Oprah Winfrey in February 1993, his handlers told him he had gone too far with the "bizarre" front; he had to distance himself from the "Wacko Jacko" stories.

"I have been in this house looking for that oxygen chamber," Oprah said to Jackson. "I cannot find the oxygen chamber anywhere in the house."

"That story is so crazy," Jackson dolefully said. "I mean, it's one of those tabloid things. It was completely made up. It's a complete lie."

For the first few days after the Pellicano press conference, the Michael Jackson story was reported largely as the private detective had spun it: an extortion attempt gone awry. "Michael Jackson Tells Fans He Did No Wrong: Complaint Linked to Extortion," read one typical headline. "Don't Believe the Dirt!" advised another. "This Is a Guy Who Doesn't Even Swear!"

While *Hard Copy* correspondent Dimond was working the phones on the story, she got a call from someone who started reading from a police report on the Jackson investigation. It was filled with phrases like "masturbation" and "oral copulation." "I've got to meet with you now," Dimond said. That evening, at a small Italian restaurant in Santa Monica, the informant showed Dimond a confidential report from the Los Angeles Department of Children's Services. "I saw an extremely graphic, detailed narrative from this child," said Dimond, "right down to the sexual acts." Dimond knew a big story when she saw one. "[The informant] was upset by the way the whole story was being reported as a botched extortion," said Dimond. "He said, 'You've got to promise me this story won't get buried.' " He needn't have worried. "It was either going to be a superstar being falsely accused or it was going to be a superstar perhaps guilty of one of the most heinous crimes we know," said Dimond. "Either way, I couldn't lose." The report was stolen property so Dimond's producer forbade her to take it or pay money for it; she spent three hours transcribing the twenty-five-page report in longhand.

*   *   *

"Tonight, on *HARD COPY!*" a teaser blared the next day. "Diane Dimond reveals the exclusive details behind the Michael Jackson child abuse allegations!"

The story became the biggest sexual scandal in decades. Competition for scoops was furious—and was often fueled by money. Within hours of Dimond's broadcast, a news agency called Splash was selling copies of the Child Services report for $750 each. ABC, CBS, and NBC all got copies. The *National Enquirer* assigned a team of twenty reporters who canvassed Los Angeles, knocking on 500 doors in the neighborhood where the accuser lived. Even *Nightline* and *60 Minutes* sent letters to participants, begging them to appear. "First let me say that I am sure this week has been overwhelming to you," Ted Koppel wrote to the accuser's father. "You have had a first-hand crash course in dealing with the media. I'm sure it has not been easy. . . . Anthony Pellicano and the Jackson people have been trying to tip the balance of the media coverage in their favor by making allegations that you were the perpetrator of an extortion attempt. . . . Therefore, I am offering you and/or your attorney the opportunity to be my sole guest on 'Nightline' tomorrow evening." The father turned down the offer, but Koppel devoted an entire segment of *Nightline* to the scandal on the evening of the State of the Union address.

Jackson's long-running antagonism toward the press actually worked in his favor during the child abuse scandal. His advisers cast the story as a media vendetta against the singer. One of Pellicano's strategies was to hire dozens of Michael Jackson look-alikes to show up in various locations around the world. "Michael Jackson spotted in London!" a news report would declare. His handlers would then prove that Jackson wasn't near London, adding, "This is yet another example of the media's sloppy, irresponsible coverage of Michael Jackson. How can you believe anything they say?"

Pellicano also produced young boys who insisted that their intimate friendships with the singer were entirely chaste, although some thought that strategy backfired when one of the kids volunteered information that he shared a bed with Jackson. "It's a very big bed," Pellicano explained.

The detective had more success persuading people not to talk to the media and discrediting those who did. Reporters who tracked down potential sources were constantly told, "Mr. Pellicano has told us not to say anything." Four former security guards who filed suit against Jackson, alleging that they were fired because they "knew too much," sold their story to *Hard Copy* for $100,000. They accused Pellicano of threatening them. When two ex-employees, Mark and Faye Quindoy, sold their story, Pellicano immediately called their credibility into question, pointing out that they were involved in a back-pay dispute. He also called them "cockroaches" and "failed extortionists."

Jackson's supporters, including his own family, were hardly more honorable. "Every single person I've contacted on Jackson's side or in his family has wanted money," said Dimond. "People would say, 'Michael's a lovely well-balanced young man and if you give me $5,000 I'll go on the record with that.' " The singer's father, Joseph Jackson, wanted $150,000 to appear on talk shows to defend his son. He negotiated with *Hard Copy*, but talks fell apart because the show wanted Michael's mother to appear too, and Joe couldn't deliver her.* When PBS did an exposé on how checkbook journalism fueled the Jackson controversy, Jackson's parents said they'd be willing to speak out against it—for $100,000.

Pellicano's most successful tactic, however, was taping the accuser's father apparently negotiating the terms of a screen deal or settlement. The detective had been dealing with the father for four months and had been recording the calls. He gave reporters twenty-five-minute tapes of the conversations, and although the evidence from the recordings was far from conclusive, the fact that anyone would have financial discussions with someone who supposedly molested his son was enough to turn the tide in Jackson's favor. After Pellicano released the recording, a poll showed that only 12 percent of those questioned believed the allegations against Jackson; most believed that he was the victim of extortion.

---

* In late 1993, Katherine and Michael's brother Jermaine appeared on CNN and *Hard Copy* to speak in Michael's defense, but Joseph refused to appear. He was still holding out for payment.

*　　*　　*

It wasn't from his biological family that Jackson would find his most effective supporters. It was from his Hollywood family, particularly Elizabeth Taylor. Chen Sam, Taylor's spokeswoman, had urged the star to disassociate herself from the messy controversy. On August 29, Sam got a call from the *New York Post's* Richard Johnson, checking out a story that Taylor was on her way to Singapore to publicly support Jackson. Sam convinced the columnist that the story wasn't true. Later that day, Johnson called back. He'd heard the story again. He had details. Chen angrily denied the story, threatening to sue Johnson if he printed anything. Soon after she hung up the phone, Sam got a call from Liz Taylor. The star was on the plane heading to Singapore.

"You can't do this!" Sam screamed at Taylor. Sam slammed down the phone. "Goddamn her!" Sam said. "She thinks she's going to get another bauble from Cartier!"

"What do you mean?" an assistant asked.

Sam explained that once, to thank Taylor for her public support, Michael Jackson gave the star a $250,000 canary diamond necklace. "Now every time he's in trouble, she rushes to his side hoping for another little gift." Whatever Taylor's motives, the former screen goddess's trip to Singapore turned into a minor media event in itself. Taylor and two members of her entourage took three of the seats in the first class cabin; the other twelve were all filled with tabloid reporters. Chen Sam's office suspected Jackson's people had tipped off the reporters.

"Michael is one of my best friends in the whole world, and I can't think of anything worse that a human being could go through than what he's going through now," Taylor told one reporter during the flight. "He's a very sensitive, very vulnerable, very shy person. I believe totally that Michael will be vindicated." Asked about the motive for the allegations, Taylor said, "Well, I think all of that is becoming quite clear—extortion."

Sam watched furiously as the woman whose image she had spent much of her adult life shaping appeared on *A Current Affair*, defending Jackson. "She looked like Elvis on a bad day," said a member of Sam's staff. "She was wearing an unflattering Hawaiian shirt and Chen was furious because her hair and makeup hadn't been done. The lighting was terrible."

"How could she do this to me?" wailed Sam.

But with Elizabeth Taylor's support, others were more willing to defend Jackson. Sharon Stone spoke in his defense. Donald Trump stood up for the singer, at one point putting Jackson up in his Plaza Hotel. "If anyone wants to mess with Michael," said Trump, "they have to come through me first." Liz Smith weighed in, urging Pepsi not to drop his sponsorship on the basis of unsubstantiated charges.* Smith attacked Diane Dimond and *Hard Copy* for so aggressively exploiting the scandal. When Dimond reported a Jackson biographer's unsubstantiated and apparently untrue claims that a video existed of the star having sex with a minor, Smith wrote, "Diane Dimond glowed as she hasn't in months, squeezing out every scintilla of innuendo from what appears to be a totally baseless rumor." Jackson filed a $100 million lawsuit against *Hard Copy* and Dimond.

The reaction to Dimond's coverage was, she said, "swift and threatening and violent." Her phones were tapped, she believed, her car was followed, her past investigated, her friends and family called and harassed. Some of it came from irate Michael Jackson fans—a gang of them once physically attacked her. More often, she said, it was from Pellicano and his team.

"For months, the Michael Jackson story consumed every waking moment of my life. At every turn, Anthony Pellicano kept popping up," said Dimond. "I started hearing from friends that Anthony Pellicano had called, asking questions like where does she live? Where did she come from? Does she have any kids?" Other reporters would pass along veiled threats, she said, from Pellicano—which he denied making. "He'd say, 'Tell Diane Dimond I'm watching her.' or 'Tell her I hope her health is good.' " Dimond became convinced that her phone was tapped. "Paramount was pretty convinced too," she said. "They got a security expert to come to my house. . . . They found evidence of some weird tampering." Dimond also believed that her phones at *Hard*

* Pepsi and other corporate sponsors were understandably noncommittal.

Copy were tapped. She decided to do her own detective work and devised a plot with her husband.

One morning at 9 A.M., Dimond's husband called her at her office: "How's that special on Anthony Pellicano coming?" he asked.

"Oh, it's great," Dimond replied. "We've got all sorts of things on him. We're going to expose everything, including the whole story about Elizabeth Taylor's husband's grave."

At 9:28 A.M., Dimond got a call. "What kind of story are you doing on Anthony Pellicano?" someone from Paramount's legal department wanted to know. Dimond said she wasn't doing any story on the detective. "I just got a call from Weitzman's office," the caller told Dimond. "They were quite sure you are doing a story on Pellicano."

"After that," said Dimond. "I never used my desk phone."

By late 1993, some of Pellicano's tactics started to backfire. For one thing, the tabloid media had realized that if celebrities like Jackson could hire private investigators to dig up the dirt, so could they. Private investigator Don Crutchfield, another of Pellicano's Los Angeles area competitors, was uncovering unsettling information about Jackson's relationships with children and was appearing on *Hard Copy* with it.

Some people close to Jackson were persuading the singer that his lawyers and Pellicano were making mistakes and talking to the press too much. "If it were in my camp, I would get rid of everyone," said the singer's brother Jermaine Jackson. "His representatives are just plain stupid." By then, Jackson was said to have been spending $100,000 a week on his legal defense. Faced with these expenses and with four months of uninterrupted tabloid hysteria, Jackson switched tactics, parting company with Pellicano in December 1993. "I swear on my children [he has nine of them] this decision was not Michael Jackson's," said the detective. "If I wanted to, I could be working on this case today." Pellicano also continued to maintain that Jackson was innocent. Weitzman stayed on the case but Bert Fields also quit and was replaced by Johnnie Cochran, the flamboyant attorney who would later defend O. J. Simpson. The following month, the case was settled for a reported $27 million.

Pellicano claimed he was dead set against paying any money. "There was no way that Bert Fields and I would have settled that case," Pellicano said. "No chance, no way." And indeed the settlement, which was publicly viewed as a tacit admission of guilt, effectively crippled Jackson's career.

Part of the problem was that he could no longer afford his high-priced help. "Michael Jackson is teetering on the edge of financial ruin," according to John Connolly, the reporter who exposed Donald Trump's dire financial straits in 1990. "The pay-offs, the lawyers, the protectors cost him a fortune."

Jackson quietly tried to sell tainted Neverland, but no one was willing to pay $26 million for the spot where the alleged child molestation had taken place. The lucrative product endorsements were gone. The audiences no longer filled up stadiums. In 1997, paychecks issued to employees of Jackson's company, MJJ, bounced. No more $100,000 a month retainer fees. No more $250,000 canary diamond necklaces.

Jackson's Hollywood defenders began disappearing from the picture. Eventually, even Elizabeth Taylor reportedly started avoiding Jackson's phone calls. Liz Smith also stopped defending him, and one day repeated a comment attributed to the singer's ex-manager, Sandy Gallin, suggesting that Jackson was, indeed, a pedophile.* "Why is Liz always picking on me?" Jackson complained. "Liz is always nice to Lisa Marie, and Lisa Marie is much weirder than I am!"

"Michael's problems with the media are mostly of his own making," Smith responded. "Too much spin control and not enough common sense."

One by one, Jackson lost the circle of high-powered, high-priced Hollywood heavyweights who had for years protected him from public scrutiny. They were replaced by figures from New

---

* "Does Michael Jackson like boys?" Gallin allegedly said to *E!* columnist Bruce Bibby. "Does a bear shit in the woods?" Gallin denied he ever said any such thing, but Bibby stood by the story. "The remark came out of the woods," Bibby said. "I certainly didn't ask him."

Age religions or the Third World. A number of cult watchers claim that his marriage to devout Scientologist Lisa Marie Presley was arranged by the controversial religion. Jackson, who proposed to Elvis's daughter over the telephone, was such a tarnished star that some wondered why the Scientologists wanted him among its members, but Presley effectively used Jackson to do public relations for the church.* Deepak Chopra, according to one source, took up Michael Jackson's cause and orchestrated an extraordinary *Life* magazine cover story, photographed by Harry Benson, that showed Jackson playing with his son, Prince. In 1997, a Saudi prince named Waleed bin Talal—who is also a big investor in EuroDisney, Donald Trump's properties, Steven Seagal films, and Planet Hollywood—took over much of Jackson's financial empire.

Michael Jackson hasn't entirely disappeared, however. Stories regularly appear in the tabloids about Jackson's sexual prowess and about the "love triangle" between him, Lisa Marie, and his second wife, Debbie Rowe. "Jacko's Wacko Plan to Have 2 Wives" read the *National Enquirer*. "Michael Jackson has hatched a bizarre plan to have two wives—and his pregnant wife Debbie couldn't be happier." He also sold pictures of his newborn son to the tabloid *OK!*, reportedly for $1.3 million.†

Although no formal charges were ever brought against Michael Jackson, the scandal effectively ruined his career. Anthony Pellicano loudly and repeatedly said that he was opposed to settling, and the perception in some Hollywood circles was that if the singer had stuck with the private detective and Fields, he would have never gone down in flames. The collapse of Michael Jackson's career showed Pellicano and the rest of Hollywood that in the face of scandal, the best strategy was to fight back—and fight dirty if necessary. Ever since the Michael Jackson scandal, Pellicano has never been busier.

---

* When MTV was working on an exposé on alternative religions, for example, Lisa Marie called the president of the music network and told them that if they were tough on Scientology, they would lose access to Jackson's music.

† Jackson has said that he was giving the proceeds to charity, but at least one of his charities reportedly has been under investigation for not giving any money to the needy.

When Cheryl Shuman, Hollywood's "optician to the stars," went on a tabloid TV show and claimed that she had evidence that Steven Seagal beat his wife, Seagal hired Anthony Pellicano. Shuman claimed she was harassed and followed and once was beaten so badly that she ended up in the emergency room of a hospital, though she could never prove who was behind the attacks. When *Time* magazine writer Richard Zoglin looked into her allegations in early 1995, he got a seven-page threatening letter from Seagal's attorney, including dirt that had been dug up by Pellicano. "It included everything down to Shuman's exact prescription for Prozac," said Zoglin. They had effectively undermined Shuman's credibility as a source. *Time* dropped the story. "I don't blame them," said Zoglin. "On the one hand, it's a story that deserved to be told, on the other hand, it just wasn't worth the hassle."

Reporter John Connolly also experienced Pellicano's hardball P.R. when he wrote an article on Seagal. Connolly claimed that he had evidence that Seagal was linked to the mob, had lied about his CIA experience, and had paid to have someone killed. Seagal turned Pellicano loose on Connolly. The reporter, a former cop, didn't back down, but the experience was harrowing. "Most journalism schools don't teach reporters how to respond to a Louisville Slugger," said Connolly. "His tactics have a real chilling effect."

Pellicano's star continued to rise. He was hired as a technical consultant in the films *Ransom* and *The Firm*. He butted heads again with Diane Dimond when *Hard Copy* reported on the Jerry Springer scandals and the controversial talk show host hired Pellicano. "I really think I am the best in the world," Pellicano said shortly before the Jackson scandal. "I would say that in the next ten years, I'm going to make millions of dollars."

The lesson for the media was equally bottom-line oriented: If they'd ever doubted it before, the Michael Jackson episode showed that scandal sells. That was hardly a new insight—the media feeding frenzy during the Trump divorce was still fresh in everyone's minds—but that was a soap opera; the Jackson story was a tragedy. The public said they were disgusted by it, but the ratings indicated otherwise. Thanks to Dimond's series of scoops,

Hard Copy's ratings were up 24 percent during the Michael Jackson coverage. Ratings were also up at *A Current Affair*—which at one point hired a professional actor to play the part of the young accuser as he gave his deposition describing Jackson's alleged molestation. By the early 1990s, even the networks were poised to embrace tabloid journalism. ABC News executives told *World News Tonight* anchor Peter Jennings and his producer Paul Friedman to do more "R&P" stories—rape and pillage stories. Network news looked to the tabloid news magazines for direction. When ABC's *PrimeTime Live* broadcast Diane Sawyer's interview with Jackson and Lisa Marie Presley, the struggling show got a huge ratings boost—60 million Americans watched, more than twice as many viewers as watched anything else on television that week.* If the celebrities and the media learned anything from the Michael Jackson episode, it was to up the stakes on both sides. Yet nothing, people thought, would ever compare with the Michael Jackson saga. A story could not possibly be more sordid, more disturbing—or more of a ratings bonanza—than a worldwide superstar brought down because of his alleged fondness for young boys.

That was before the O. J. Simpson story.

---

* The interview was especially embarrassing given the set of Jackson's demands that ABC agreed to, including letting the singer see the taped portions of the interview before broadcast and altering them when Jackson thought that the lighting was unflattering, keeping the air conditioning on high so that his pancake makeup wouldn't melt, showing his entire four minute, forty-five second video from HIStory, and agreeing to air ten promotional spots from HIStory. ABC didn't concede to one of Jackson's requests, however, which was to have Princess Diana introduce him.

a struggle for respectability

On June 14, 1994, when two people on the fringe of celebrity were discovered hacked to death in Brentwood, California, it seemed like another run-of-the-mill Hollywood murder. At the *National Enquirer*'s headquarters in Lantana, Steve Coz, the executive editor and second in command after Iain Calder, got the tip that Monday morning, before any of the news bulletins flashed it. "O.J.'s ex-wife and someone else are dead," Coz told senior editor David Perel. "You run it."

"Okay," said Perel.

The story was a natural one for the *Enquirer*. Its readers, two-thirds of whom are women, loved stories about abused wives, about the dark side of fame, about how rich people who seem to have it all actually lead lives that are desperately unhappy. Initially, it had an advantage over other publications in covering the murders of Nicole Brown Simpson and Ron Goldman. The crime of the century, Steve Coz later boasted, occurred "in the middle of our source network." Reporters from the tabloid appeared at the murder scene shortly after the coroners did—and before any other reporters. The *Enquirer* editors also knew the history of O.J.'s violence against

Nicole; when the former football star was convicted of beating his wife in 1989, most publications virtually ignored it, but the *National Enquirer* played up the incident in a full-page story: "O.J. Simpson Charged with Wife-Beating—The Shocking Details!"

But what no one—not Coz nor Perel nor editor-in-chief Iain Calder nor anyone else at the *National Enquirer*—realized the day the news of the murders broke was that the O.J. Simpson murder story would not only take over their lives, entirely dwarfing the Michael Jackson story, and for that matter any other event the tabloid had covered, but that it would also change the very nature of the American media. As a result of the O.J. Simpson story, tabloid values, tabloid techniques, and tabloid standards would become the values, techniques, and standards accepted by the mainstream media. The tabloid version of reality would prevail, but with the ultimate irony that the tabloids themselves would suffer for it, for when the mainstream press went tabloid, the tabloids began to look irrelevant.

As the story unwound, the appetite of readers for continuing coverage surprised, and then astounded, the *Enquirer*'s editors. "Elvis dying was absolutely immense," Iain Calder said. "Chappaquiddick was absolutely immense. Princess Grace dying was absolutely immense. But nothing has come close to the tremendous staying power of this." The *Enquirer*'s sales, which had fallen about 15 percent since 1990, increased 10 percent in the wake of the murders. Editors at the other tabloids, the *Globe*, the *Star* and the *Examiner*, saw similar results. "With times being bad in papering, O.J. has taken care of us," said reporter Ken Harrell of the *Globe*, where sales were also up 10 percent. "After this is over, we're going to send him a letter of thanks."

Readers punished editors for straying from the story. In August, three months after the murders, when the *Enquirer* acquired pictures of Michael Jackson and Lisa Marie Presley's wedding, Calder thought he had an irresistible tabloid scoop, but when he put it on the cover of the August 23, newsstand sales actually dropped. His readers were interested in nothing but O.J. "Who would have thought that wouldn't be the number one story for the *Enquirer*?" said Calder. "Never in my wildest dreams could you have told me . . . that O. J. Simpson would be bigger than that."

Once they realized the scope of the story, Iain Calder and Steve Coz and David Perel spared no expense; they assigned twenty *Enquirer* reporters to knock on doors and whip out their checkbooks if a good source was reluctant to talk for free. The *National Enquirer* ended up spending more than $150,000 on tips that resulted in one scoop after another, including $12,500 to the dealer who sold O.J. his hunting knife and $18,000 to Nicole's housekeeper, who said that O.J. would abuse his wife and then send her flowers. The *Enquirer*'s practices earned its reporters and editors the familiar criticism about ethical compromises. But something unprecedented also took place; the establishment media began grudgingly to concede that the tabloid was beating them on the story. "Many of us in the established media have discovered just how good the *Enquirer* can be," said Ted Koppel. "They've been strong and in there on this story," said Bill Boyarsky who covered the trial for the *Los Angeles Times*. "They've had a lot of stuff first." The *Columbia Journalism Review*, which had published Oz Elliot's essay denouncing tabloids as a "force of evil" twenty years earlier, actually called Steve Coz and David Perel "the Woodward and Bernstein of tabloid journalism." And the *New York Times* ran a lengthy article praising the tabloid for its "aggressiveness and accuracy." Iain Calder was stunned by the *Times*'s benediction. "It took my breath away," he said. Others at the tabloid were more wary. "It was one of the worst things that ever happened to us," groused one reporter who had worked at the tabloid since the Elvis story. "It was like the kiss of death for us."

Indeed, even as it was accruing these accolades, the *Enquirer* had begun to encounter a problem that had to do with the reality that the O.J. Simpson story riveted not just tabloid readers but the entire nation. Ninety-five million people had watched the Bronco chase on television. Economist Bernard Lentz of Ursinus College in Collegetown, Pennsylvania, estimated that workers were so distracted by watching and talking about the trial that businesses lost more than $25 billion. The elite were just as fascinated; Congressional hearings and the daily State Department briefings were scheduled around the important developments in the O.J. case. Foreigners were also obsessed. When Benazir Bhutto, the Prime Minister of Pakistan, visited Los Angeles and was asked who she would like as dinner guests, she requested Marcia Clark and Robert Shapiro. And President Clinton said that when Russian President Boris Yeltsin visited the United States in 1994, his first comment to Clinton was "Do you think O.J. did it?"

The media both responded to and generated this interest. More than a thousand journalists from around the world descended on Los Angeles to cover the trial. A huge $1 million media encampment of tents and transmitters served by caterers and garbage collectors, was erected around the courthouse. An *Advertising Age* survey found that in 1994, more magazine covers were devoted to the O.J. Simpson case than any other subject.*

And in the quest for exclusives, previously fastidious print outlets sunk to and sometimes below the standards of the tabloids. When the *New Yorker*, now edited by Tina Brown of *Vanity Fair* fame, teased a controversial O.J. story on its cover, newsstand sales went up by 50 percent. The magazine—which had published an influential essay during the 1977 Son of Sam hysteria castigating the tabloids for unethically involving themselves in the unfolding story—also published photographs of a shirtless Kato Kaelin and of Paula Barbieri posing seductively while clad only in a shirt. And its correspondent Jeffrey Toobin—who said at the time, "Some of us in so-called respectable journalism get a lascivious charge out of saying how good the *Enquirer* is, but it's unreliable crap, and it's important to remember that"—reported in its pages the defense theory that the murders were a Colombian drug hit and a Los Angeles police detective had planted the bloody glove on Simpson's property. "That story was a blatant plant by the defense, and printing it was the height of irresponsibility," said the *Enquirer*'s David Perel.

The *Enquirer*'s editors grew alarmed about the number of publications crowding in on their turf. "Fifteen years ago we would have been out there alone, or with two or three other

---

* In *Advertising Age*'s cover story survey of more than thirty of the nation's leading magazines, Oprah Winfrey came in second; Jacqueline Onassis, who died that year, ranked third; Tonya Harding and Nancy Kerrigan were fourth; Julia Roberts fifth; President Clinton, sixth; Michael Jackson and Lisa Marie Presley were seventh; Tom Cruise and Roseanne tied for eighth, and Princess Diana came in tenth.

reporters," groused Calder. "Now we're elbowing the *New York Times* and the *Washington Post* out of the way. *ABC News* is camping out on the lawn and running after people with cameras." Indeed, the O.J. Simpson story had an even greater impact on television than on print. *Inside Edition* and *American Journal*, produced by King World, shored up their Los Angeles bureau of twenty by more than fifty additional staffers. The eleven network magazine shows were all in bitter competition, and they pursued the story as well. NBC's *Dateline* featured O.J.'s two children from his first marriage. CBS's *Eye to Eye with Connie Chung* interviewed Simpson's mother; *20/20* and *PrimeTime Live* had interviews of various members of Nicole's and Ron Brown's families; and Barbara Walters interviewed O.J.'s personal assistant. The news departments of CBS and NBC each spent about $30,000 a week just on the trial. ABC, which scaled back coverage, spent a mere $20,000 a week. ABC, CBS, and NBC evening news ran 1,392 stories on the Simpson case in 1995—almost twice the number of stories as the second-place subject—which was Bosnia, with 762 stories. In an *ABC News* poll, 84 percent of those questioned said they weren't interested in hearing about O.J. But when the network cut away from coverage of Simpson's preliminary hearing in July 1994, ratings instantly dropped.

As Dan Rather explained at the time: "In every newsroom in the country—and that includes ours—there's somebody, usually several somebodies who say, 'You know, Dan, you can love the Balkans story all you want . . . you can say it's of great, lasting historical significance . . . and you can argue all you want that it ought to lead the broadcasts, and I'm gonna tell you, in a tight ratings fight, O.J. spikes it up there and you better keep that in mind. The average local news director is a guy with his back to the wall, his shirttail on fire, the bill collector at the door and a guy with a straight razor right at his throat. If his ratings don't get up, he may be out of a job in three months, six months, nine months. So when somebody says O.J. gets the ratings, even if his better sense or his conscience tells him to go with something else as the lead, he's gonna go long and strong with Simpson."

Once the trial began, however, cable television owned the O.J. Simpson story. CNN's ratings went up an astonishing 600 percent.

It jacked up the cost of a commercial accordingly: from $3,000 for a typical thirty-second spot to $24,000. Ed Turner, executive vice president of CNN, put fifty staffers on the story and declared that the network would cover every minute of the trial. "We have paid our dues with plenty of Nigerias and Somalias and Bosnias over the years," he said. "But you can't get fifteen people to sit down and watch that if you put a gun to their heads."

The effect of the scandal on viewership patterns was profound—and permanent. "Whenever there's a big migration from one medium to another," noted media analyst Ed Atorio of Dillion Reed, "there's never a 100 percent migration back." More and more, the nation was turning to cable, which in turn was devoting itself more and more to scandal. Geraldo Rivera gave over his CNBC show *Rivera Live* almost exclusively to the Simpson trial and in so doing became the first cable show to beat CNN's Larry King in the ratings. "From that time on," noted *Vanity Fair*, "all cable networks focused obsessively on scandals."

As the mainstream media leaped over what was a quintessential tabloid story, something ironic happened: circulation fell dramatically at the tabloids. People didn't need to buy the *National Enquirer* to find out what was going on in the O.J. case: it was all over the evening news and the *New York Times*. The tabloids not only lost whatever gains they had made in the early months of the scandal, circulation fell below what they had been in the pre-O.J. days. By the fall of 1995, when the trial began, the O.J. story had turned into a disaster for the tabloids. Circulation at the *Enquirer* fell to an average 2.7 million a week from 3.15 million in 1994. Its parent company went from operating in the black to losing money: in the three months ended in June 1995, it had a net loss of $880,000, versus a $7 million profit in the same quarter a year earlier. Revenue in that period dropped from $80.3 million to $73.5 million.

Tabloid TV was going through a similar crisis. Gavel to gavel coverage of the O.J. Simpson trial was on CNN, so viewers no longer had to tune in to *A Current Affair* or *Hard Copy* for tabloid stories. *A Current Affair* decided it would try to go in the direction of *60 Minutes*, and in 1995 the show's producers fired the man who personified tabloid TV, Steve Dunleavy. "As soon as it was decided that the show was going to go another direction," Dunleavy said, "it was fairly clear that whatever skills I do or do not have would not necessarily be there for the show."

To boost circulation, the *Globe*, the *Enquirer*'s chief competition, resorted to the time-tested tabloid strategy of taking sides. And the side it chose to take was Simpson's. The *Globe*, founded in 1954 by Joe Azaria, an Iraqi who immigrated to Canada before World War II, was the *bête noir* of supermarket tabloids, an outcast among outcasts. With a circulation of about 1 million in 1994, much smaller than that of the *Enquirer*, it had customarily made its mark by running stories that no other tabloid would touch. The *Globe* had first published the name and pictures of Patricia Bowman, the woman who claimed she was raped by William Kennedy Smith; it had published bizarre stories about satanic orgies that were held during fund-raisers for California Governor Jerry Brown. It had run an article claiming that Bill Clinton had fathered a child with a black prostitute—a story that was later disproved when the *Star* paid the alleged child to take a blood test.*

---

* There was one tabloid that was even more aggressive than the *Globe: News Extra*, which was formed by Paul Azaria, the younger brother of the original founder of the *Globe. News Extra* kept getting sued for increasingly daring stories: Rod Stewart sued over a story alleging that he had cheated on his wife, and Sylvester Stallone sued over an article claiming he had a penile implant after his use of steroids had rendered him impotent. Finally, the tabloid was done in when it ran an article: "New Oprah Shocker! Fiancé Stedman Had Gay Sex with Cousin" in the March 24, 1992. Oprah and Stedman sued for $300 million. A private investigator hired by Winfrey discovered that *News Extra* had never even interviewed Carlton Jones, Stedman Graham's gay cousin who had been quoted extensively in the *News Extra* article. His comments had apparently been stolen from the files of the *Globe*, which had pursued the story, but had decided that the story was too flimsy and that Carlton Jones wasn't credible as a source. "The investigator also discovered that the other tabloid plied Jones with liquor and agreed to pay him money in exchange for his statements to the other tabloid," according to the suit. "Additionally, the other tabloid engaged in tactics such as: asking suggestive and leading questions of interview subjects in an effort to have them provide information which would be embarrassing to Stedman Graham; failing to take minimal steps to corroborate statements made by sources; and failing to determine the veracity and credibility of sources." Soon after the suit was filed, *News Extra* fired its entire staff, disconnected its phones, and stopped publishing. No one from the defendant's side—not even a lawyer—showed up at the trial, and Oprah won the case by default.

The *Globe*'s Los Angeles bureau was located on Wilshire Boulevard and Bundy Drive, a mere two blocks away from where Nicole Simpson and Ron Goldman had been killed, and it had surpassed the *Enquirer* in its tabloidy approach to the O.J. story. Budgeting $20,000 to $40,000 each week to cover the story, it hired a lip reader to decipher what O.J. whispered to his lawyers, it paid a genealogist to trace O.J.'s family history, and it used a lie detector test to determine whether Simpson was telling the truth in the audio edition of his book. It paid $30,000 for a seven-year-old photo of Simpson brandishing knives and wearing combat fatigues.

And then it declared O.J.'s innocence. "World Exclusive: OJ was Framed" the tabloid declared. "America writes to OJ: You're Innocent" said another headline. "Shocking New proof O.J. Didn't Do It!" Then, in the ultimate tabloid tactic, the *Globe* offered a $1 million reward for anyone who could provide conclusive evidence that Simpson was framed. It was marketing genius and a journalistic travesty. Circulation shot up about fifty percent to 1.4 million, and the tabloid beat *People* magazine—which that week put Axl Rose on the cover—for the first time ever. Nearly 200,000 readers wrote or called the *Globe* to give the tabloid information about the "real killer." Phil Bunton, the *Globe*'s editorial director, admitted that the tabloid's position on the story was pandering to its readers. "It's amazing how many people out there don't think O.J. really did it, or don't want to believe O.J. did it," he said.

Over at the *Enquirer*, the editors and reporters reacted in horror. The *Globe* was giving supermarket tabloids a bad name. "I don't think they've done any real reporting," sniffed the *Enquirer*'s David Perel. "I've yet to read anything with credibility in that publication." When the *Boston Herald* wanted to do an article on the *Globe* and the *National Enquirer*'s coverage of the case, Iain Calder refused to be interviewed unless he could be assured that photographs of his publication wouldn't appear alongside those of the *Globe*. "I don't want us to appear next to a magazine that runs headlines about alien babies from outer space," he said. After all, he had the tabloid's reputation to think about.

By the peak of the O.J. story, Iain Calder was growing weary.

The *National Enquirer* had been sold in 1988, after its owner, Gene Pope, died of a heart attack at the age of sixty-one. ("National Enquirer Owner Goes to Meet with Elvis," ran the headline in the *New York Post*.) The new owner, Peter Callahan, proudly described himself as cheap and pronounced that there were plenty of excesses that could be eliminated from the *National Enquirer*'s budget. The first thing to go was Pope's beloved "World's Tallest Christmas Tree."*

Iain Calder had stayed on under the new ownership with a stunning salary of $600,000, but by 1995, the work was no longer fun. He was fifty-six years old, and was still working sixteen- and eighteen-hour days. He had started having dizzy spells. To relax, he and his wife of forty-one years, Jane, took a visit to his hometown in Scotland. There, thousands of miles away from O.J. and Jackson and Tom Cruise and Donald Trump, the dizzy spells stopped. When Calder got back to the United States in November 1995—in the midst of the biggest tabloid story of the century—he declared that he would retire. "It's an epic moment in tabloid history," said Dan Schwartz, an *Enquirer* alum who was working at the competing *Globe* at the time.

To replace Calder, Callahan chose Steve Coz, the thirty-eight-year-old who had been heading up the O.J. coverage. Coz was, in many ways, the polar opposite of Calder. He was the product of an exclusive New England prep school—and he looked it. He had a square, aristocratic chin and wore tortoiseshell glasses and Ralph Lauren Polo shirts. He had been hired by the *Enquirer* in 1982, shortly after graduating from Harvard cum laude with an English major. His mother was always embarrassed that he worked for the tabloid—"He's smarter than that," she would insist—but Coz was impressed by the aggressiveness and intelligence of the reporters, and, he argued, the mainstream media was every bit as tabloidy as the *Enquirer*. "The other night, I'm watching

---

* Several in the Palm Beach area tried to continue the tradition of the world's tallest Christmas tree, including an entrepreneur who bought Pope's decorations and erected a 158-foot polyester and steel tree—which was cheaper than importing a real one from the West Coast—and charging $6 to see the display. The operation was a bust, the owner was forced into bankruptcy, and the tradition was discontinued.

television and there's Mike Wallace, hosting a show called '20th Century' and it's all about the cover-up of UFOs," Coz said. "So here I have a *60 Minutes* correspondent telling me about visitors from outer space! The next morning, I'm listening to an ad on the radio and it's saying 'Tonight! On the Discovery Channel! The Curse of the Cocaine Mummies!' And then I open our local newspaper and there's a story on page two, underneath all the celebrity news, that says, "Lobster Boy Dies. . . . It's so close to our stuff," Coz said, "I can't believe it."

Because the rest of the media had embraced tabloid topics, those subjects were now considered mainstream. And what that meant, in Coz's view, was that the *Enquirer* had become in effect a mainstream publication. But for every seven people who looked at it in the supermarket, only one bought it. "People are still embarrassed," Coz said. "So we're trying to change the common perception of the *Enquirer*." In the wake of the Simpson trial, he hoped to reposition the magazine, to establish it as a legitimate, even celebrity–friendly publication. He had celebrities sing the praises of "the new *Enquirer*" in the pages of the tabloid. "I love the new *Enquirer*," celebrities such as Montel Williams would declare. "It is the tabloid of integrity!"

The strategy appealed to the corporate owners of the *Enquirer*, who figured they could make up in advertising revenue what they had lost in newsstand sales. Being a "good" tabloid had another advantage as well. Focus groups repeatedly showed that one reason that people weren't buying tabloids was because readers found them hostile toward the celebrities they revered. If Coz could establish the *Enquirer* as celebrity-friendly, he figured, he could reverse the circulation losses. He set out to accomplish this on January 16, 1997, a year after the Simpson trial ended, when Bill Cosby's son, Ennis, was shot and killed on a Los Angeles freeway.

Bill Cosby, who in several surveys was ranked the most-loved man in America, had long had a complicated relationship with the tabloids. The *Enquirer*'s detractors claimed that the tabloid had "blackmailed" Cosby. In 1989, a woman had called the *Enquirer*'s Los Angeles offices, claiming Cosby had an illegitimate daughter and she had the photos to prove it. The tabloid had

approached Cosby and promised not to go with the story, according to several people familiar with the arrangement, if Cosby
could cooperate with it on other stories. Cosby, according to the
sources, agreed, but resented the tabloid's intimidation and intrusiveness. When his son was murdered, he blasted the tabloid practice of paying sources, and challenged the tabloids to use the
money instead to offer a reward for information about his son's
killer. At that time, the *Globe* revealed that they, too, had been
pursuing the story of Cosby's alleged illegitimate daughter. After
Ennis's murder, according to *Globe* editor Tony Frost, people at
the *Globe* became suspicious and revealed that they had been
negotiating with Autumn Jackson to pay her $25,000 for the story
that she was Cosby's illegitimate daughter.

Coz, seizing the opportunity to polish the *Enquirer*'s reputation, quickly responded by putting up a $100,000 offer for infor-
mation leading to the arrest of Ennis Cosby's murderer. Much to
Coz's horror, the *Globe* followed suit, offering a $200,000 reward.
The Cosbys were mortified at having the *Globe* and *Enquirer* as
their allies. They hired security expert and tabloid foe Gavin de
Becker to help them with their dilemma and they demanded that
the tabloids rescind their offers. Despite the increased respect
for the *Enquirer* among certain figures in the mainstream news,
celebrities continued to loathe it. "My husband and I do not want
their money to be associated with our son," Camille Cosby said.
"These publications have lied about me and my family and have
enriched their coffers at our expense."

Both refused to withdraw their offers. "The reward stands
until we talk to Bill Cosby and find out what's at issue here,"
Steve Coz said at the time. "We feel we have handled the Cosby
family with respect throughout our coverage," responded *Globe*
editor Tony Frost. "We were offered the photographs of Ennis
Cosby in a pool of blood at the murder scene. A terrible, terrible
tragedy. We turned them down. It was totally inappropriate to
publish those photographs."

A week after the *Enquirer* offered its reward, a thirty-four-
year-old named Chris So called in to say he knew who killed
Ennis Cosby. A friend of his, Mikail Markhasev, So later testified,
said, "I shot a nigger. It's all over the news." So's testimony led

to the conviction of Markhasev. When in July 1998, Mikail Markhasev was convicted of murdering Ennis Cosby in a botched robbery attempt, police said the *Enquirer*'s tip was crucial. "We will take help wherever we can get it," said Los Angeles Police Department Commander David Kalish. "We appreciated the *National Enquirer*'s help. Their reward money was very, very important to us in solving this case."

"It was our finest hour," beamed Coz. "We hope this has ended any anger Camille may have towards us."

The "new *Enquirer*" also found itself in the somewhat ironic role of ombudsman of the tabloid press, castigating its rivals for their journalistic lapses. It particularly found itself at loggerheads with the *Globe*, which it repeatedly accused of using sleazy tabloid tactics. When Steve Coz saw the May 20, 1997, issue of the *Globe*, "FRANK CAUGHT CHEATING ON KATHIE LEE WITH BLOND!" his first reaction was professional envy. "Wow," Coz said to himself, "that's a great tabloid story!" Then, when the Giffords denied the allegation—"We live in what I call a 'cash for trash' society," Kathie Lee declared in a speech at Marymount College, "where anyone can say anything about you, anything unkind about you, then they're rewarded for it financially"—the *Globe* released the videotape of Gifford cavorting with Suzen Johnson. Coz seized the opportunity to moralize. "It's a major crossing of the line," said Coz. "We chase celebrities, we chase cheating celebrities. We try to find out what's going on in Hollywood. We uncover and report the news. We don't create the news. What happened here is that the *Globe* commissioned an act of prostitution to entrap Frank Gifford to sell a story which bordered on pornography. . . . When you do what the *Globe* has done, you violate the whole journalistic process. . . . It's not a question of the tabloid press, it's a question of the press."*

While the *Globe*'s editors ridiculed such language as shameless

---

* In a rather ironic twist, Suzen Johnson later sold her story to the *National Enquirer*. On January 12, 1999, she told the tabloid "I was paid $250,000 to help set up Frank Gifford. I had sex with Frank, and I'd like to tell Kathie Lee: 'I'm sorry it ever happened.' " She then declared that the *Globe* had tricked her into setting up Gifford. The *Globe* fired back by publishing copies of the contracts she had signed.

posturing—"Sour grapes," said *Globe* editor Tony Frost—it seemed to be working. That year, circulation climbed 4 percent—from 2.6 million to 2.7 million. The increase was small, but it was significant—the first time readership had gone up since the early days of the O.J. scandal.

Coz celebrated the entré of the *Enquirer* into the mainstream media by hanging four framed magazine covers on the wall of his office. There was a *Time* cover of a bug-eyed alien, a *Newsweek* cover with lesbian couple Melissa Etheridge and Julie Cypher declaring "We're having a baby," *People* magazine's exposé of "Men Behaving Badly" (Eddie Murphy, Joe and Michael Kennedy, Donald Trump, and Frank Gifford), and the *Enquirer*'s scoop detailing the confession given by Ennis Cosby's murderer. Over the four covers Coz hung a sign with the words: "Which one is the tabloid?"

The *Enquirer*, Coz was convinced, was on the road to respectability. And so was he. He was writing op-ed pieces for the *New York Times* and appearing on Sunday morning talk shows along with other media pundits. *Time* called Coz one of the twenty-five most influential people in the country, and the *Enquirer* took out full-page ads in the *New York Times* touting the honor. Reporters were calling the *Enquirer* for story leads, and citing the tabloid in their articles. Upscale advertisers were even beginning to approach it. Then something happened that would darken the reputation of the *National Enquirer* and the tabloid press for years to come.

19

the tabloid princess

Tabloid reporter James Whitaker bobbed in a boat called the *Fancy* 150 yards off the coast of Saint Tropez, watching the woman he had helped become the most famous person in the world. Whitaker, a reporter for the *Daily Mirror*, had known Princess Diana for nearly twenty years—since she was an anonymous apple-cheeked teenager with dreams of marrying a prince. Whitaker, a dapper dresser with a round, ruddy face and a chipmunk smile, became Diana's biggest champion; she secretly gave him scoops about herself and he reciprocated with relentlessly adoring coverage. Diana had long since dropped Whitaker as her favorite confidante—he had been "traded up," he knew, for the more upscale Richard Kay at the *Daily Mail*—but he was still quite friendly with Diana, and there were those who believed that Whitaker, more than any other person, had launched the remarkable worldwide fame of Princess Diana.

Whitaker watched with a certain amount of proprietary affection that cloudless Monday in July 1997 as the Princess, dressed in a bold gold jungle print bathing suit and dark sunglasses with gold trim, cavorted on the beach in front of the fleet of journalists and paparazzi offshore. "She was absolutely parading herself," Whitaker said.

The Princess's vacation had been on the front page of every tabloid in London that weekend; "Di and Sleaze Row Tycoon!" the *News of the World* announced. "Di's Freebie!" blasted the *Sunday Mirror*. Diana couldn't have been surprised that her little holiday was big news: the Princess and her two sons, the heirs to the throne of England, were vacationing with the man who helped topple the conservative government by revealing that he had bribed top Tory officials.

After about half an hour of being photographed, Diana got into a speed boat and headed out to the *Fancy*. Clinging to the side of the boat, she giggled and joked with Whitaker, but she also complained about the press. "How long are you going to be here?" Diana asked. The attention was embarrassing, she protested, and her son William "gets really freaked out" by all the photographers. "My sons are always urging me to live abroad and to be less in the public eye," she said. "Maybe that is what I should do, given the fact that you won't leave me alone. I understand I have a role to play, but I have to be protective of my boys." She didn't speak French, Diana said, so Whitaker and the British journalists were going to have to pass her message on to the French press. "I am going to make an announcement in two weeks that is going to put an end to all this," she told them, "and boy will you be surprised."

Some of the media horde were already surprised by Diana's behavior. Until that point, she seemed quite happy to be photographed. "She would flash a complicit smile toward the photographers whenever she appeared or left," one of them said. She had "delighted" the photographers noted *Hello!* "Aware of the lenses but, for once, totally unfazed by them." The Princess was so cooperative that at one point, the paparazzi chipped in and bought her one hundred red roses to thank her. Whitaker and others who had covered the Princess for years were less confounded by her behavior; they knew there were times when Diana cooperated with the press, and times when she didn't. During her Saint Tropez vacation, Diana apparently wanted to be in the papers, and some of the British journalists thought they knew why:

although she was no longer married to Charles, Diana was still quite jealous of his longtime mistress, Camilla Parker Bowles, whom she blamed for wrecking the marriage. "If there was a good shot of Camilla in the paper looking good and sexy, then you can guarantee that the Princess would be out the next day looking even sexier," said royal photographer Glenn Harvey, "sort of saying, you know, 'I'm number one.' " The week that Diana spent with the Al Fayeds, Charles was throwing a lavish fiftieth birthday party for Camilla at his Gloucestershire estate. Camilla had gone through a number of makeovers to redeem herself in the eyes of the British people, and she was finally getting a boost in the public opinion polls. London was buzzing with the rumor that Charles was finally going to ask Camilla to marry him— which Diana bitterly opposed. The thought of her rival, gussied up and grinning on the arm of Charles on the front of London's tabloids, infuriated Diana. The Princess knew that her vacation with Mohammed Al Fayed was guaranteed front-page news.

"She drove Camilla to the back of the papers," marveled Whitaker. Princess Diana had, once again, won the public relations battle.

Princess Diana—contrary to her brother's famous "blood on their hands" speech—was never "baffled" by the tabloids. She lived by them. "I read everything that's written about me," she once told Lady Colin Campbell. Every morning, she pored over the papers, studying each article about her, every photograph taken of her, and all the press devoted to her enemies and rivals. "If the stories were positive, she was ecstatic," according to a member of her household staff, "but if they were negative she would tailspin and bemoan the cruelties of the world. Then she'd hit the telephone and make sure that the journalists she had in her pocket put her side of whatever story she felt needed to be respun in the following day's papers."

Those reporters "in her pocket" felt that Diana was justified; the Princess was engaged in a public relations war, with both sides leaking to their allies in the media. Diana was much better at it than Charles and his side were. "She may have been tricky, contrary and manipulative at times," Whitaker said, "and why not after what she had been put through in life?"

Whitaker had good reason to be defensive about the Princess. He had, some might say, discovered her. Actually, it was she who discovered him. One day in 1978—when the only royal story of interest was who Prince Charles would marry and Whitaker was one of about seven royal reporters following the story—Diana Spencer walked up to Whitaker outside Buckingham Palace and introduced herself. "I know you," Diana said playfully. "You're the wicked Mr. Whitaker, aren't you? I'm Diana." Whitaker, who wrote for the *Star* back then, spotted Diana again several months later, fishing on the River Dee with Prince Charles. When Diana saw the royal press pack, she scampered off and hid behind a tree. She delighted the reporters, however, by spying on *them*, using a makeup mirror as a periscope. "What a cunning lady," Whitaker thought. "This one is going to give us a lot of trouble if she is indeed the new girl in the life of Prince Charles."

Whitaker and others covering Prince Charles became enchanted with Diana. "She was delightful," said Whitaker. "She was immensely flirtatious. . . . And she did definitely seduce the media that were with her." Diana became friendly with the reporters, greeting each of them by name. She was, according to Whitaker and others who covered her then, never shy. " 'Shy Di' " was always a silly tabloid cliché that made headline writing easy," said Whitaker. "She was a girl with a lot of guts."

Some were a tad more cynical than Whitaker about Diana's "friendship." "I always thought that she had a very well-developed native cunning," said photographer Harry Arnold. "She knew how to manipulate men quite early on in terms of looking at them in a certain way and making them feel special and using a little phrase now and again. And she did it with all of us."

"I had to court them. Make them like me. Make them my friends," Diana later said. "I may have been only nineteen, but I wasn't stupid." Behind his back, Diana called Whitaker the Fat Red Tomato.

She joked with *Sun* photographer Arthur Edwards about giving him a knighthood if she ever became queen. Edwards never took her attention personally. "The reason is most likely that thirteen million readers will see her at her gorgeous best," he said. "Funnily enough, it is always the papers with the highest circulation to whom Diana is the most cooperative."

One day, Whitaker, worried about the effects of the media glare on the young woman, wrote Diana a note:

> *This is to say that we, all of us in Fleet Street, love you very much. If ever we do anything that upsets you—which, of course, will happen—we are very sorry . . . Keep your chin up and keep going.*

Two days later, Diana approached the crowd of photographers and reporters waiting outside her apartment. "Please leave me alone for a second," she said. "I want to speak to Mr. Whitaker in private." Diana asked for his advice in dealing with the press and he counseled her. She began calling Whitaker daily, planting certain stories, killing others.

Whitaker used the *Star* shamelessly to lobby for the Princess. When word circulated that Diana's past might not be as pristine as the tabloids had made it out to be, Whitaker ran an interview with Diana's uncle, declaring—inaccurately, it appears—that she was a virgin. When the *Mirror* ran a sensational article claiming Diana had spent the night on a train with Charles, Whitaker ran a story refuting it. "I just didn't want this romance to go wrong," Whitaker said. "I wanted her to marry him because I thought it would be good for everyone."

One day Whitaker advised Diana to be less forthcoming with reporters. "Look, Diana, if you go on talking to the press as much as you have done lately you can only damage any chance you might have of marrying Charles," he told her. Other would-be Princesses had been dropped by the Prince for talking too much. "It is not liked by the Royal Family and I urge you to stop. There will be times when I will ask you a question to which I need an answer desperately. I am telling you now, don't answer me. I know I am cutting my own throat, but I believe that marrying Prince Charles is very much more important than me writing another exclusive." After that, all of Diana's conversations with reporters were off the record. "She was a brilliant operator," said Whitaker.

Whitaker wrote a four-part series on Diana for the *Star*, urging Charles to marry her. "I took a decision, and I think some of my colleagues did, that she was a pretty suitable person to become the Princess of Wales." The *Star*'s circulation shot up and the other tabloids followed. Diana became a superstar.

"To DI For!" headlines declared.

"Charles: Don't DIther!" one headline demanded.

"She's 19 and a perfect English Rose," declared the *Sun*.

"DIvine," announced the *Mirror*.

"There was to be no turning back for the Prince from now on," Whitaker noted. "The great British public would have lynched him if their beloved Diana had been hurt in any way. She had grown more popular than he by now."

Indeed, the Royal Family saw Diana's popularity as its possible salvation. The press and public were so uninterested in uncharismatic Windsors that the Royal Family—which has little real function other than one of public relations—was in danger of becoming obsolete. Prince Charles never much liked the media—he called reporters "gutter rats" and "bloody animals"—but he knew the Royal Family needed the good press that Diana would bring. "You know, the time we all have to worry is when you don't write about me or want to take photographs," he once said to a royal reporter. "Then there would be no great point in us being around." The duty-bound Prince agreed to marry the smitten teenager that the people loved—even if he didn't. The marriage was little more than a worldwide publicity stunt, but the romance of it temporarily silenced even the most cynical journalists. "Let's talk about the size of Di's feet," Tom Brokaw said to a colleague during a commercial break of the broadcast of the royal wedding. "I mean, she's got gunboats down there." But even Brokaw seemed moved by the wedding kiss on the balcony of Buckingham Palace, although it, too, was fake.

"Give her a kiss," Prince Andrew urged Charles.

"I'm not getting into that caper," Charles snapped.

"Oh, go on, give her a kiss."

Charles turned to his mother. "May I?"

The queen consented and the fairy tale was complete. For a while, everyone—the press, the public, the palace—was happy to believe in the fairy tale. Diana, however, grew increasingly unhappy about the disparity between the public facade and her private unhappiness. "The fairy tale was killing me," she said, so she decided, "I'm going to kill the fairy tale."

Diana, like many celebrities, lived through her public image. While she did resent the constant intrusion of her privacy, she also depended on the press attention. "She got her emotional sustenance from the newspapers," said biographer Andrew Morton. "She really defined herself in their terms. If they were nice to her she felt good."

Diana, photogenic and charismatic, understood the media and understood the power of images. She courted the media brilliantly. When the couple went on outings, royal handlers were reduced to pleading with photographers surrounding Diana to take a few shots of Charles. At a speech in Australia, Diana once upstaged her husband by merely crossing her legs. The photographers, eager to get a shot of a royal thigh, all rushed to the side of the stage where Diana was sitting, nearly toppling the platform where Charles was speaking. Charles started getting jealous of Diana's good press. He accused Diana of being an exhibitionist, acting out her own celebrity fantasies when she danced onstage for his birthday.

Diana often spoke of "my public" and her "special relationship with the people." She was terrified of losing that public love. Before Prince Andrew got engaged, Diana worried that his bride would steal her spotlight. "I'm the flavor of the month," she once said to photographer Edwards, "but if Andrew marries a black girl or a Catholic, they'll be the story." When Andrew married Sarah Ferguson, and the press briefly adored the vivacious redhead, Diana was jealous. "I suppose you're going to drop me like a hot potato?" she fretted. "I suppose you'll be fussing over Sarah now."

Meanwhile, Diana brilliantly planted favorable stories about herself, squelched negative ones, and cast herself as a victim of a cold, uncaring husband and an oppressive monarchy. When Diana refused to let Charles attend her thirtieth birthday party—her lover James Hewitt was a guest—he released the face-saving story that he had pressing business matters to attend to; she told reporters, off the record, that it was yet another example that his work was more important to him than she was. The tabs ran with her spin on the story. Buckingham Palace's ploy to get good press through a loveless marriage had backfired.

"They kept saying I was manipulative," she told *New Yorker* editor Tina Brown. "What's the alternative? To just sit there and have them make your image for you?"

In addition to Whitaker, the Princess courted and regularly confided in Clive Goodman of the *News of the World*, Charles Rae of the *Sun*, and Robert Jobson of the *Express*. By the mid-1990s, Diana's favorite confidante, however, was Richard Kay of the *Daily Mail*. Diana spoke with Kay almost every day. The journalist reported her agenda so faithfully that he was known among colleagues as Diana's minister of propaganda. When the Princess was photographed sunbathing topless in Spain, Kay wrote stories blasting the media, quoting "a friend" of the princess saying that "it was as if the Princess had been raped." The friend, of course, was Diana. Later, when the *News of the World* got a story that harassing phone calls to art dealer Oliver Hoare were traced back to Diana's private phone lines, Kay tried to persuade the paper that Diana didn't make the calls. A few hours later, the Princess was spotted in Kay's car; the two had a three-hour strategy meeting. Diana ended up giving Kay an on-the-record interview. "Somewhere someone is trying to make out that I am mad," Diana said. "Do you realize that whoever is trying to destroy me is inevitably damaging the institution of monarchy as well?"

Usually, however, Diana's press manipulation was conducted entirely behind the scenes. Once, when a paper was preparing an article on a private speech Diana gave on eating disorders, an editor there called Kensington Palace for comment. To his surprise, Diana got on the phone and spoke for forty minutes. "She told me exactly what she had been saying, what she hoped to achieve and what her own suffering had been in incredible detail," he said. "The understanding was that I would not quote her directly, but to do it as a reported speech." The editor was shocked, therefore, when the next day the Princess issued a statement, deploring the article as an invasion of her privacy. "I rang her immediately," recalled the editor, "and congratulated her on a brilliant operation."

When Diana leaked her version of events to Andrew Morton for *Diana: Her True Story*, the Palace was almost successful in dismissing the book as "tabloid rubbish." Diana confirmed the book by embracing one of Morton's on-the-record sources; she also contacted photographers beforehand to make sure they were on the scene to record it all for the newspapers. The day the pictures were published, Diana appeared at a public event and broke down into sobs. "She said in the morning that she was going to burst into tears," according to Morton, "just as a way of getting criticism off her."

Diana had conquered the tabloids and was on her way to coopting the broadsheets. She began a campaign of meeting with top editors in London. She would chat with them about Buckingham Palace's war against her and would describe how editors could help her.

"She was very entertaining company," said one editor. "Her conversations were laced with confessions and revelations. It was pretty riveting stuff, but it was all on the understanding that you wouldn't pass them on. After that we would be briefed regularly about what she was thinking and where she was going . . . off the record of course."

Rupert Murdoch was one of the editors Diana courted. After Murdoch's *Times of London* serialized the Morton book, Diana thought he was squarely on her side. She invited Murdoch to lunch at Kensington Palace, but the publisher, according to several people who work with him, was not entirely charmed. "He kept his distance," said one of his staff. "He didn't want her phoning him twice a day trying to influence his editors through him." She learned just how much Murdoch was not on her side when his *Sun* published the "Squidgy" tapes of her in a conversation with James Gilbey.*

---

* In fact, Murdoch had the Squidgy tapes for eighteen months before publishing them. He was afraid of public backlash—afraid that he would be accused of trying to destroy the monarch. Finally, they were leaked to the *National Enquirer*, then picked up by the *Sun*. Many suspect the leak was orchestrated by Murdoch's camp, which Murdoch vehemently denies.

Diana also courted Peter Stothard, the editor for the *Times of London*. They met for lunch on May 18, 1994, and the pattern was much the same as it was with most of the editors she wooed: personal revelations interwoven with tales of the plot against her by allies of Prince Charles. That day, the papers carried a story saying Diana spent £3,000 a week on grooming and personal care. As she sipped her bottled water, Diana explained to Stothard that the story was a leak from those inside Buckingham Palace who were trying to destroy her; she told Stothard that he and the *Times* could help save her. "She felt that her only recourse was to fight like with like, and on this day, she had a plan," according to Stothard. "To my horror, she began to set out a complicated story about how she had helped a tramp who had fallen into the Regent's Park canal and was going to see him in the hospital that very afternoon." The next day, without Stothard's help, the story about her heroism and kindness in rescuing the "tramp" was in all the papers.

Diana was training Prince William in media manipulation; she brought her eldest son along with her to at least two of these meetings with journalists. "I just wanted to talk to you about a few things—get to know you," Diana explained. "I think it would be useful for William to meet an editor."

"It is an undisputed fact that the Princess connived with the media and exploited it for her own interest, just as much as we exploited hers for ours," observed Sir David English, editor-in-chief of Associated Newspapers. English, like many editors, used to give Diana advice on how to deal with the media, but he grew exasperated when he realized that she was much more clever at it than he was. "You're the finest P.R. operator, man or woman, I have ever met," English told her.

Princess Diana was so shrewd in shaping her public image that by early summer 1997, she was probably the most famous, most loved woman in the world. Her public persona bordered on sainthood, but her private life was a mess. She had packed on fifteen pounds after being dumped by Hasnat Khan, a Pakistani heart surgeon whose deeply religious Muslim parents didn't approve of their romance. There were reports that she was calling him constantly.

Diana was caught in the trap experienced by every celebrity who invites the media into their lives and then gets angry about the intrusion. She desperately wanted to be in a romance, but she had become a prisoner of the fame she worked so hard to cultivate. "I'm never going to meet anyone, because who would go out with me?" Diana complained to her friend Cindy Crawford. "I have my picture in the paper every single day. Who would want to take that on?"

Dodi Fayed wanted to find that woman, he told friends, who could get him on the cover of *People* magazine. For years, the Egyptian playboy had desperately been trying to become famous, but his father's immense wealth and his own meager accomplishments weren't doing the trick. He had produced several movies—including Academy Award winner *Chariots of Fire, Hook, The World According to Garp, Brenda Star, Reporter,* and *The Scarlet Letter*—but his actual involvement in the films was only minimal, and certainly didn't warrant much media coverage. Dodi would visit places like Elaine's, a Manhattan restaurant favored by journalists, trying to get someone to do a story on him. He courted gossip columnists, like Mike Walker at the *National Enquirer* and Hollywood writer Jack Martin. "He was always bugging me to write something about him," said Walker. "He was constantly sending me gifts, inviting me out, and trying to give me items about himself." According to his former girlfriend Carole Mallory, he had a Hollywood columnist on his payroll.

Dodi Fayed hired PMK, Hollywood's most powerful public relations firm, to raise his profile. PMK would sometimes offer publications interviews with some of its bigger stars if they would do articles about the firm's unknowns, but even with this sort of publicity muscle behind him, Dodi wasn't getting much ink. The most press he got was for dating famous women. Dodi had been linked to Brooke Shields, Cathy Lee Crosby, Joanne Whalley, Julia Roberts, Britt Ekland, Mimi Rogers, Daryl Hannah, Stephanie Powers, Tina Sinatra, former *Charlies' Angel* Tanya Roberts, Valerie Perrine, Prince Andrew's ex-girlfriend Koo Stark, Winona Ryder, and O.J.'s ex, Tawny Kitaen.* Dodi was drawn to women in the news.

---

* Some of these women, including Winona Ryder and Julia Roberts, have denied that any relationship ever existed.

Dodi Fayed worked for his father, Mohammed Al Fayed, but people who knew him say he was actually much closer to his uncle, arms dealer Adnan Khashoggi, the brother of his late mother. Once, according to the *London Times*, Al Fayed discovered that his son had developed a taste for cocaine and after that, had Dodi regularly tested. "As far as I know, he always tested clean," according to a business associate, who says Dodi never got the respect of his father, who would sometimes introduce him as "my useless son."

Despite a monthly allowance of $100,000, Dodi was always in debt. He was once sued for $1 million for allegedly selling film rights he didn't own. He was served eviction papers after failing to pay rent on a $3 million Beverly Hills mansion. A New York nightclub claimed he had an unpaid $20,000 tab. Usually, his father's money would make the problem go away, but not always. One man who sued Dodi for back rent was told he could collect the $135,000 he was owed if he would claim that the bill had been run up by an imposter. The outraged man refused. "Even for $135,000 I'm not going to say that he's a stand-up guy," he fumed. "That imposter trick is at least five years old," said one reporter who knew Dodi well. At least one debt, however, was publicly blamed on an imposter.

In Dodi's courtship of Diana—as with many things in his life—his father did much of the behind-the-scenes work. Mohammed Al Fayed, a bonafide Anglophile, had been pursuing Princess Diana and her family for years. He had befriended Diana's father, Earl Spencer, and made him a special guest at the Ritz. He had appointed Diana's stepmother, Raine Spencer, to the board of Harrods. Although Mohammed Al Fayed barely knew Diana's father when she became Princess, by the time the Earl died in 1992, Al Fayed claimed that the two had become so close that they were "like brothers." He also said that shortly before he died, Diana's father had asked him to "keep an eye" on his children. Al Fayed would send expensive gifts to Diana's sons, with a note inscribed "with love from Uncle Mohammed." He had been trying to get Diana to take a vacation with his family for years, inviting her to come to his villas in Gstaad or Saint Tropez or to his castle in Scotland, but she always declined.

On June 3, Mohammed Al Fayed sat next to Princess Diana at a benefit dinner at the Churchill Intercontinental Hotel. Over a dinner of roasted lamb and lentils, Mohammed invited Diana to vacation with him in Saint Tropez. To Al Fayed's surprise, she accepted. Mohammed had his helicopter pick up Diana and her boys and he sent for his son, who was living with model Kelly Fisher in Los Angeles.

Mohammed Al Fayed told Dodi that if he could land Diana, he could have the mansion in Paris that had been owned by the Duke and Duchess of Windsor. Mohammed footed the bill for the romance, including paying for the ring Dodi bought for Diana. He also encouraged—or at the very least, didn't discourage—the publicity about the romance. Brian Vine, an editor at the *Daily Mail*, telephoned the tycoon to ask if his reporters and photographers were annoying the vacationers. Al Fayed assured Vine that the Princess was not bothered by the attention. A week after Diana's initial vacation in Saint Tropez, Mohammed gave Dodi carte blanche to use his helicopters, yachts, and villas to woo the Princess. On one of those cruises they had The Kiss.

Some believe The Kiss in the Mediterranean was just as staged as the kiss between Charles and Diana on the balcony of Buckingham Palace sixteen years earlier. "A woman who's been followed by the press as much as she has," observed *Newsweek* Paris Bureau Chief Christopher Dickey, "does not embrace her Egyptian lover in public on a boat where she knows there are going to be people floating around offshore taking pictures unless she means to make a statement."

The Kiss pictures weren't even taken by a paparazzi—they were shot by fashion photographer Mario Brenna, who had frequently worked with Diana's old friend Gianni Versace. Brenna, like the photographers at Saint Tropez, was shocked by how exhibitionistic Diana seemed. "They kissed for ten seconds and after that her head went back," Brenna said. Diana pulled down the straps on her bathing suit and Dodi slowly rubbed suntan oil on her shoulders. "She looked so happy. It was almost like she was putting on a show for the camera."

Some believed Diana wasn't the only one who wanted to make a statement. Dodi's former publicist, Jim Sliman, suspected that Dodi had tipped off the press to give their whereabouts to make sure his picture would be plastered all over the world. "I don't know if he loved her," said columnist Jack Martin, who knew Dodi for nearly twenty years. "Actually, 'like' is better. Dodi went out with loads of famous women he didn't like."

"She's not reacting in the way she has in the past by getting upset at reports of the romance," said her confidant Richard Kay. "Dodi has obviously said, 'Look, I don't care about the publicity, so she can relax.' " Kay compared Diana and Dodi Fayed to Jackie and Aristotle Onassis.

The pictures sparked a bidding war among the tabloids. In the United States they were published by the *Globe*—which paid $200,000 for them. Within a few weeks, all the tabloids had The Kiss photos, along with breathless details about the romance. The stories, for the most part, depicted Dodi as an incredible lover and the man of Diana's dreams.

"It's the best sex I've ever had," Diana supposedly told a friend. "Being with Charles was never like this—I never knew it could be this good. I can't get enough!"

"For the first time, Di has seen fireworks!" read one tabloid.

"He's taken her to places she's never been before," one "friend" was quoted as saying, "and I don't mean the Italian Riviera!"

"Dodi knows all the right buttons to press" another "friend" said, "and he presses them all night long!" read one tabloid.

"A Guy for Di" the cover of *People* magazine blasted.

"It's destiny," Al Fayed was quoted as saying.

"We welcome Diana into the family," Dodi's uncle, Adnan Khashoggi, gleefully announced.

The stories about Dodi's sexual prowess elicited scorn from some of his former girlfriends. "We never had sex with the lights on. There was virtually no foreplay," said Texas model Denise Lewis said. "And I can't recall one session that lasted longer than twenty minutes." Another former girlfriend, Traci Lind, claimed that Dodi was abusive and volatile, that he hit her, tried to choke her, and had threatened her with a gun. The romance also came as a real shock to Kelly Fisher, who claimed she had slept with Dodi just hours before his tryst with Diana. Dodi had, ironically, bought an engagement ring for Fisher that was almost identical to the one Charles gave Diana when they were betrothed. Fisher hit Dodi with a $2 million lawsuit.

Nevertheless, the unlikely love birds were the talk of Great Britain—and much of the rest of the world. It was Diana's first public romance since her divorce from Charles. Dodi Fayed, according to the gossip circuit, was going to set Diana up in Hollywood. He was going to make her a movie star. There was talk that he would finance *Bodyguard II* with Kevin Costner. A script was written with Diana playing the beautiful but lonely princess. There were nude scenes. Diana had several conversations with Kevin Costner about the movie, he said. "Diana had a crush on Kevin Costner," says a source. "It was a harmless infatuation like she was always getting over celebrities. . . . She talked endlessly about the time she danced with John Travolta."*

Stories circulated that Diana was planning to marry Dodi; that he was buying Julie Andrews's former mansion for $7.3 million so they would have a Hollywood home together; that she was ten weeks pregnant with his child. The stories were so pervasive that several of Diana's friends called her to caution her against doing anything too hasty. Diana assured them that no wedding was in the works. She also was not ten weeks pregnant with Dodi's child—despite rumors and even a fake medical test that was later leaked to the media.†—"Don't worry," she assured one friend, "I'm having a wonderful time, but the last thing I need is a new marriage. I need it like a bad rash on my face." She told another pal: "I haven't taken such a long time to get out of one poor marriage to get into another."

By late August, some say that Diana was starting to have a

---

* Diana also had a bit of a crush on President Clinton. "I think he's dishy," she told gossip columnist Taki Theoracoupolos. "And tall, too." Diana was also said to be smitten with John Kennedy Jr. There were also reports—which Diana denied—that she had a crush on Tom Hanks and pestered him with phone calls.

† Stories circulated that Diana was ten weeks pregnant with Dodi's child when she had only known him for eight weeks. What's more, a friend who was close enough to Diana to be familiar with her bodily rhythms said it would have been "biologically impossible" for her to have been pregnant as reported.

few doubts about her new suitor. It wasn't just on account of Dodi's caddish behavior; reports circulated that Dodi liked to secretly videotape himself having sex with his girlfriends and there were rumors that he planned to tape Diana. The Princess told friends she resented the way the Fayeds were so obviously trying to buy her affection with expensive trips and gifts. "I don't want to be bought," she complained to her friend Rosa Monckton, and giggled about the Fayeds' vulgar furnishings and ostentatious taste, such as the private jet decorated with pharaoh heads and plush pink upholstery.

Diana was, however, still eager for the romance to get into the papers. At 6:30 on the evening of August 30, Diana briefed reporter Richard Kay on her plans. Maybe she would marry Dodi, she told Kay, and maybe not. She might, she said, withdraw from public life altogether—as long as she could still remain an international humanitarian.

That night, the paparazzi followed Dodi and Diana to the Ritz in Paris. Dodi wanted to drive to his father's Paris villa. He had another expensive gift he wanted to give Diana.* The Princess, according to some reports, didn't want to go. It was late and she was tired. She didn't feel like being photographed or having to outrun the paparazzi. Diana suggested they get a room at his father's hotel. They argued. Dodi was overheard assuring Diana it would be all right. Dodi Fayed was smitten; he had found the woman who got him on the cover of *People* magazine.

It was the sort of international tragedy that news people live for. Networks all over the world canceled all regular programming and covered Diana's death around the clock. It wasn't just the biggest story of the day, it was the only story. Andrew Morton called it "one of the most awful tragedies of the late twentieth century—if not the greatest." The public was deeply grief-stricken by the death of a woman they had never met but felt they knew. Through the constant coverage of Diana's soap opera–like life,

---

* Mohammed Al Fayed later revealed that the gift was an ornate silver platter inscribed with a love poem; when a former girlfriend heard that, she was outraged, telling friends that it sounded suspiciously like a platter she bought him when they were dating.

the Princess had become part of the public consciousness. Diana was, perhaps, history's most profound example of the artificial intimacy that results from celebrity. "She was a friend," sobbed one mourner. "She was a big part of my life. I can't imagine going on without her."

Diana's funeral was the most watched event in the history of television: an estimated 2.5 billion tuned in. It was broadcast live on every continent except Antarctica. In the United States, competition among the media got fierce. A battle broke out between ABC and NBC over the rights to the BBC feed. Then, CNN president Rick Kaplan, a friend of President Clinton, called the White House the day before Diana's funeral to get help in getting BBC footage of the funeral—eliciting outrage from ABC.

Although it was a tabloid story, no news outlet was above covering it. Diana's death was a moment of the complete melding of elite news and tabloid news. Perhaps that's why CBS blew it. The so-called Tiffany Network, which had also botched the story of Elvis's death, initially didn't want to commit resources to the death of Princess Diana. Reports of the car crash reached CBS headquarters around 8:20. CBS staff called Lane Venardos, the vice president for hard news and special events, who was making decisions that Labor Day weekend. Venardos, a twenty-seven-year veteran of the network, was not a big fan of celebrity news. He urged his staff to hold back on the story. This didn't seem like such a big deal, he said; early reports indicated that while Dodi Fayed and the driver were killed, the Princess had apparently survived. Venardos told his staff to wait until all the facts were in, so, while the other networks were marshaling their forces, CBS waited. Even after CBS got official news of Diana's death, it didn't act. Venardos was trying to reach CBS News President Andrew Heyward at his Westchester country club, but, Heyward later explained, he was in a "black hole" where his beeper couldn't be activated. Some in the newsroom say he admitted that he had turned off the beeper. The CBS staff didn't reach Heyward until after midnight. The other networks and most cable stations had long since switched over to full coverage of Diana's death; CBS's bewildered and outraged affiliates were being fed footage of pro wrestling. At 1:15 A.M., CBS finally decided to give affiliate stations a feed from Britain's Sky TV.

It was a debacle that went beyond embarrassing; press critics blasted the network for "the stench of incompetence" and "stunning ineptitude." Heyward later sent angry affiliates a letter of apology and assurances that nothing like that would ever happen again. Venardos was demoted, and Heyward turned to Don Hewitt to help CBS News save face.

"It's irresistible," Hewitt said. "A high-speed crash kills the mother of the future King of England. She was beautiful, glamorous, running around with an Egyptian playboy whose father owns Harrod's. You couldn't make this up!" Hewitt, the consummate showman, put together a special segment of *60 Minutes* devoted entirely to Diana. A great story, Hewitt once said, needs a bad guy—and in this case, the tabloid press was the bad guy. The program took the media to task for pursuing stories about Diana's private life—never mentioning Diana's role in leaking those stories. Mike Wallace interviewed Katharine Graham, who cautioned viewers about the difference between paparazzi and the "legitimate" press. Dan Rather, choking back tears, said the princess was "a victim of the uncontrolled cult of fame and celebrity gone mad." Then *60 Minutes* added its own celebrity touch: Elizabeth Taylor, the world's second biggest tabloid fixture after Princess Diana, was interviewed by Eleanor Mondale. "I know what it's like to be chased by paparazzi, and it's one of the most frightening, claustrophobic-making feelings in the world," Taylor said. She didn't mention that she was a longtime friend of Dodi's uncle, Adnan Khashoggi, brother-in-law of Mohammed Al Fayed. It didn't matter how drugged or drunk the chauffeur was, Taylor said, Diana was killed by the tabloids. "They're responsible," a tearful Taylor declared. "The world's Princess was killed by the greed of the paparazzi."

The Diana special edition of *60 Minutes* was applauded by critics. "It did more in that sixty minutes to help the reputation of CBS News," wrote one reviewer, "than did the previous twenty hours." Hewitt's showmanship had once again redeemed CBS.

For days, television, magazines, and newspapers relentlessly covered Diana's death—often lamenting the media's relentless coverage of celebrities. Even tabloid editors joined in on the tabloid bashing. Steve Coz, the Harvard-educated editor of the *National Enquirer*, went on TV to blast media excesses. Coz, continuing his bid to reposition the *Enquirer* as celebrity friendly, said that he had been offered exclusive U.S. rights to the pictures of blood-soaked photographs of Diana. He had turned them down, he boasted, and he piously urged other tabloids to do the same. When it was pointed out that the *National Enquirer* that week had paparazzi shots of Dodi and Diana with the headline "Di Goes Sex Mad!" Coz, mumbled something about "unfortunate timing."

Reporters and editors tried to come forward to say that they had good relationships with Diana. *New Yorker* editor Tina Brown, who while at *Vanity Fair* wrote one of the snidest stories in print about the Princess, devoted much of that issue of the *New Yorker* to Diana. She also wrote about the off-the-record lunch she had with the Princess and *Vogue* editor Anna Wintour. It turns out that Diana had begun cultivating the United States media in much the same way that she had been courting the British press: the Princess had befriended Barbara Walters, Katharine Graham, and Oprah Winfrey, among others. "I never thought I would say this publicly," Walters said on ABC. "I never have until tonight, but I considered her a friend. She was warm, huggable, and I grieve." Graham wrote an essay for *Newsweek* entitled "A Friend's Last Goodbye."

Magazines and newspapers that reported on celebrities were scrambling for the high road. *People* magazine, which at the time of Diana's death had put her on the cover more than any other person—a record forty-three times*—ran an editor's letter about how much Diana liked *People* magazine, including the articles about herself. "Unlike much of the tabloid press, we do not pay

---

* Liz Taylor was a distant second with fourteen covers.

story subjects or sources," *People* editor Wallace wrote.* "We work hard to avoid buying pictures taken by so called stalkarazzi photographers who menace their subjects, trespass or operate under false pretenses." *People* abruptly canceled plans to excerpt Kitty Kelley's *The Royals*, for which it had reportedly paid $25,000. Among the book's revelations were that Diana wasn't a virgin when she married Charles and that she had bad breath and an insatiable sexual appetite. "I happen to think it's a legitimate piece of journalism and history, and that we should not back away from it," said her publisher, Warner Books head Larry Kirshbaum. "I think *People* is gutless. I find it shocking that so many journalists have gotten squeamish about telling the truth." At the New York *Daily News*, the book editor broke down in tears and begged her boss not to excerpt *The Royals*. "People will hate us," the editor sobbed. She won the argument.

Diana's death unleased a torrent of celebrity hatred toward the press. One of the first stars to blast the press was, unsurprisingly, Tom Cruise. "What's this world coming to?" Cruise complained to CNN a few hours after the crash. "It is so disgusting. . . . We need laws concerning what is harassment when these people put price tags on people's heads."

Cruise was quickly joined by his close friend, George Clooney, who had also been leading a campaign against the media. Like Tom Cruise and Dodi Fayed, Clooney was represented by PMK. On the news of Diana's death, Clooney held a press conference to blast the paparazzi, and mocked Coz's promise not to buy the crash photos. "Pictures of a dying Princess trapped in her car—I'm impressed," Clooney said. "What ethics!"

Arnold Schwarzenegger, who was run off the road by paparazzi while driving with his wife, joined the chorus: "Many of us in public life have had the chilling experience of being chased and hunted down like animals simply for a photograph."

---

* *People* has paid sources on several occasions. The magazine paid Donna Rice's friend Lynn Armandt. In 1991, it paid Elizabeth Taylor $175,000 for photos of her wedding. *Star* and *People* reportedly joined forces to spend $400,000 for pictures of Lisa Marie Presley's first child. According to a *New York Post* reporter, he was turned down for an interview with a woman who survived two weeks at sea because she had sold the story exclusively to *People* for $10,000.

Michael Jackson, who had repeatedly leaked stories about himself to publications like the *National Enquirer,* joined in on the press bashing. "I'm not Jacko! I'm Jackson!" he fumed to Barbara Walters for a *20/20* segment. "Wacko Jacko! . . . Where did that come from? Some English tabloid! I have a heart and I have feelings."

Carol Burnett—who waged one of the longest and most expensive battles against the tabloids—rejoiced when she saw that some supermarkets in Los Angeles had removed the tabloids from the racks and customers who wanted to buy them had to ask.

Fran Drescher angrily called on the American public to boycott the tabloids. *The Nanny* star had apparently forgotten that in her autobiography, she made fun of Diana when the Princess "started to get bitchy, and I thought to myself, 'Nobody likes a bitchy princess, Princess.' "

Almost anyone who had come under media scrutiny joined in on the tirade against the press. O. J. Simpson compared his plight to Diana's. "I, like Princess Diana, have been hounded by the press," he said. "It has gone too far." JonBenet Ramsey's mother, Patsy, called *Larry King Live* to urge a boycott of the tabloids. "We are normal, everyday Americans and [the tabloids] have ruined our lives," Ramsey complained. "I would ask in the memory of my daughter for everyone worldwide to boycott these publications."

The world's biggest publicity hounds were blasting the media. Donald Trump refused to give the *Daily News* the name of his date one evening. "He wants to keep his private life private," said a spokesman. "He said it is not fair to expose this girl to the mean world of the paparazzi." Trump also said that one of the few regrets in his life was that he never dated Diana.

Ivana Trump, not to be upstaged by her husband, said that she learned of Diana's death while appearing on the Home Shopping Network in Canada. She was so overcome with grief, she had to leave the air. "I wept for a true friend," she said. "When her marriage to Charles was near its end, Diana turned to me for advice. . . . Both of us also knew the bitterness of betrayal by the one we trusted the most. Sometimes we'd laugh about the bad choices our husbands had made. Other times, we'd just exchange knowing glances."

"People have the same fixation with her that they do with me," Madonna told the *London Times*. They had met and talked once for ten minutes. Madonna told the Princess that she was "about the only person who seemed to get more attention than me." Demi Moore called Madonna to compare notes. Madonna called George Clooney and discussed organizing a tabloid boycott.

Any suggestion that Diana courted the press was met with disgust and outrage. "They say she wanted it," said *Mad About You* star Paul Reiser. "That's how they talk about rape victims!"

Even after the photographers were exonerated, they were not forgiven. It was the nature of their work that disgusted people; they were like parasites or vultures, as Sylvester Stallone said, like "birds that sit on tombstones." After it was revealed that the driver had almost four times the legal limit of alcohol in his system, the anger still focused on the photographers. "One could almost hear the audible, smug sighs of relief at the news that the driver from the Ritz was legally drunk," wrote Liz Smith, "not that this group of tabloid assassins was prepared to accept any criticism even if the driver had been cold sober." No celebrity crusades were organized against drunk driving. "I think that as far as the issue of this guy who was driving the car being drunk is a kind of bizarre joke on everyone," said Alec Baldwin, who had recently been found not guilty after punching out a photographer who tried to take pictures of his newborn child. "I certainly hope that this guy's intoxication doesn't wind up letting these [paparazzi] off the hook."

After Dodi's death, Mohammad Al Fayed kept PMK on retainer, and some reporters who tried to write stories not favorable to the Al Fayeds were told they risked losing access to the impressive roster of celebrities represented by PMK—including Tom Cruise and George Clooney. "We were working on a story about the real Dodi Fayed," said a producer. "We got a threatening call from PMK and decided that the tradeoff wasn't worth it. We dropped the story."

*   *   *

A "Cult of Diana" quickly emerged. "Bigger than Jackie!" the London papers declared. "Bigger than JFK." "Bigger than Grace Kelly." Diana's burial site, predicted one headline, "will become the new Graceland." Diana's brother Lord Spencer cashed in on the cult by charging people to visit the "New Graceland." Charles Spencer—who had been at war with the tabloids since they revealed his marital infidelities, but who had also worked as a royal commentator for *Today* and had sold pictures of his newborn son to a British tabloid—asked that tabloid editors be banned from the funeral. Although some editors had already accepted invitations, they agreed not to attend.

One tabloid reporter who could not bear to stay away, however, was James Whitaker. Shortly after the crash, Whitaker told a television reporter that sometimes the Princess would "use" photographers to advance her causes. The public was so outraged by Whitaker's comments that his editors forced him to apologize. "I regret now that I said anything that caused offense to anybody listening to what I thought was a balanced appraisal of Diana and her complicated life with photographers," a repentant Whitaker wrote. Whitaker was as grief stricken as most Brits. He was haunted by a conversation he had had with Diana not long before her death. "Would you come to my funeral if I were to die?" the Princess asked. Shocked, Whitaker assured Diana that she would outlast him. To the reporter's horror, Diana persisted with the morbid conversation.

"Why would you want to come to my funeral?" she asked.

"For two reasons," he said. "Professionally, to report and record your death. And, second, because you are an astonishing lady who often confuses me but always intrigues. It is an event I could not miss." At Diana's funeral, distraught mourners carried hand-painted signs blasting the press. "You murdering bastards," a middle-aged woman wept at she spat on a photographer. "You killed her, you pigs. You murdered her." Two people who knew Whitaker, however, told him that they enjoyed a tribute he wrote to Diana. When the third person told him that she knew he had loved the Princess, Whitaker burst into tears.

Although no one could bring back Diana—the press and the public seemed to agree on one thing: Diana's tragic fate should not be passed on to the sons she loved and protected so desperately. The consensus was clear: leave the boys alone. The public was shocked and outraged; therefore, when the day after the funeral, a photograph appeared in almost every national paper in England showing the young princes and Charles in a car heading to the funeral. Newspaper switchboards lit up across London as horrified readers protested the media's continuing tasteless intrusiveness. Some of the editors were too embarrassed to tell the grieving callers that the photo op had been arranged by Buckingham Palace.

EPILOGUE

The members of the media were so mortified at being implicated in the death of Princess Diana that it seemed possible that finally gossip columnists and scandal rags—as well as the mainstream press that had come to follow their lead—would be shamed, or legislated, into behaving themselves. Six months after Diana died, California Senator Dianne Feinstein and Utah Senator Orrin Hatch introduced the Personal Privacy Protection Act. The law would make it a crime to persistently follow or chase a person in order to film or record them for commercial purposes. It also allowed celebrities to bring suit against photographers who use high-powered lenses, microphones, and other devices to invade people's privacy. "If Senator Feinstein is able to steer this bill through the Senate, we owe her a great debt of gratitude," said Pat Kingsley.

"The bill *will* be passed," said Feinstein, "we owe it to the memory of Princess Diana." Michael J. Fox and Paul Reiser testified on behalf of the bill. Tom Cruise, Tom Hanks, Goldie Hawn, Julia Roberts, Billy Crystal, Brooke Shields, Sharon Stone, Ed Asner, Mel Gibson, Michelle Pfeiffer, Antonio Banderas, Melanie Griffith, and Whoopi Goldberg also threw their weight behind the bill. While the celebrity support was not surprising, the mainstream media, for the most part, also supported the bill. In late 1998, state legislation containing many of the provisions of the federal bill sponsored by Feinstein and Hatch was signed into law by California Governor Pete Wilson.

In the year since Diana's death, it seemed as if the industry had come full circle since the *Confidential* scandal forty years earlier. Just as had happened in 1957, politicians and celebrities, with the support of the public and the establishment press, were working together to curb the power of the paparazzi and the tabloid publications that employed them.

And, indeed, they seemed to be succeeding, for the tabloid press at large, both print and broadcast, was suffering. The *National Enquirer*, with its circulation continuing to fall, was sold again in 1999 to a group that included former Treasury secretary Robert Altman, and in a wild effort to demonstrate its increasingly deferential attitude to celebrities invited Roseanne, who had once sued the publication, to guest-edit an issue. The same group also bought the *Enquirer*'s nemesis, *The Globe*.

People had so alienated top-tier stars that it was publishing mostly tabloid-style write-arounds and cover stories on ordinary people in extraordinary situations. To fill the void, Time Warner had started up *In Style*, a celebrity magazine that did no reporting. Utterly fawning, it took the place that *People* had occupied when that magazine was celebrity friendly, and it was a stunning success.

The situation was, if anything, even more grim in the broadcast field. Faced with increasing competition from the proliferation of new network news magazine shows like *48 Hours* and *Dateline NBC*, and from softer-edged syndicated programs like *Access Hollywood*, both *Hard Copy* and *A Current Affair* tried to reposition themselves in the mid-nineties as serious news shows. Neither succeeded. Ratings continued to fall. Fox, in desperation, fired Steve Dunleavy, the "ringmaster of the media circus," from *A Current Affair* in 1996. When that didn't work, Fox canceled the show altogether in 1997. *Hard Copy* managed to hang on for another two years but in the fall of 1999 it, too, was taken off the air.

At the same time, many of the figures instrumental in the "tabloidization" of the media had fallen by the wayside. Rona Barrett left the gossip business altogether and spent the 1990s selling real estate in Los Angeles, quite successfully by most accounts. Doris Lilly was less fortunate. She died in 1991, destitute and forgotten, screaming from her hospital bed, "Call the newspapers! Call Richard Johnson [of Page Six]! Call Cindy Adams!" Others were trying to create post-tabloid incarnations for themselves. Geraldo Rivera, who had joined NBC with a serious news show on CNBC, declared his hopes to establish himself as the "anchorman for the new millennium." His co-host was former *Hard Copy* reporter Diane Dimond. Cindy Adams and Liz Smith ended up at the same tabloid, the *New York Post*, and although the rivalry between them was still keen, they no longer fought the great tabloid wars that they had when they were at competing papers. Gossip foes, such as Anthony Pellicano, were back in business. Although the White House has denied it, the private detective reportedly was working for the Clinton administration, and is said to have been a major source for unflattering stories on Monica Lewinsky. Tina Brown left the *New Yorker* and launched *Talk* magazine. But the articles—like a cover story in which Liz Taylor and Michael Jackson gushed over each other—seemed like a tired formula.

Richard Stolley, who had paved the way for celebrity journalism to enter the mainstream, had long retired from being an editor, and was spending much of his time lecturing crowds about the evils of gossip. "I think gossip can be the enemy of civilization," he told a group of journalists in 1998. "I think the dissemination of cruel, mean-spirited information which is fundamentally disturbing to a human being, to his family, to his friends is a blow to civilized society."

There will always be a complicated dance among the public, the media, and the rich and famous and powerful. Celebrities, whether politicians or movie stars, crave certain types of controlled publicity but detest uninvited airings of their foibles and excesses. The media, which profit by selling celebrity, require both access to the celebrated and the freedom to publish unflattering details of their private lives if that serves either a journalistic or commercial purpose. The public, for its part, is indisputably titillated by celebrity gossip but also disapproves of the media for the invasion of privacy required to provide them with the gossip it finds so fascinating.

The tensions within this triangular relationship can never be overcome more than temporarily. Any attempt at voluntary restraint by the media will always be undone by some shameless outsider, from *Confidential*'s Robert Harrison to the *Enquirer*'s Gene Pope to Internet maverick Matt Drudge, who believes that society at large, and his own bank account, is best served by placing no limits on what the public has a right to know. Whenever the "legitimate" media swears off gossip, another medium comes along to fill the void.

And by 1999, that medium was clearly the Internet. That year Matt Drudge, who had once preached that journalists should not earn too much money, was making more then $4,000 a day (or more than $1 million a year) from his column, according to a well-placed source. In addition to launching his own Fox TV talk show, he ditched his beat-up Geo Metro and bought a Porsche. He angrily left his talk show in late 1999, after Fox officials refused to let him show a photo of a fetus on air. He had, he declared, been "spoiled" by the freedom of the Internet. "The Internet," Drudge insisted in his talk to the Washington Press Club, "is going to save the news business."

It may not save the news business, but it had certainly rescued Druge from a life of obscurity. It had also given new life—for better or worse—to gossip. By killing certain stories and editing or cutting others, the power of the establishment media to control what information reached the public had been virtually extinguished by the Internet. And that, rather than the fear of yet another lurid scandal, may have been what made the mainstream journalists at the Press Club shudder when Drudge, in conclusion, declared, "Let the future begin."

SOURCES

A note on sources: In the course of reporting this book, I conducted hundreds of interviews, recorded transcripts from scores of television shows, and read hundreds of books and thousands of newspaper and magazine articles. As it would be too daunting a task to name all the sources consulted, I have listed the most important books, articles, and television shows in the bibliography. Some sources were especially essential to the reporting; I have listed those in the chapter notes.

1   "Citizen Reporter"

Matthew Drudge's address before the National Press Club, 2 June 1998. Also author's interview with Doug Harbrecht, 23 April 1999.

For an account of the penny press, see Andie Tucher, *Froth and Scum: Truth, Beauty, Goodness, and the Ax Murder in America's First Mass Medium.* Also see Frederick Allen, "Up from Humbug," *Columbia Journalism Review.*

For a fascinating history of the gossip and society in America during the nineteenth and early twentieth centuries, see Nicholas Lemann, "Confidence Games." See also Mitchell Stephens, *A History of News.*

For the definitive account of Winchell's power and influence, see Neal Gabler, *Winchell: Gossip, Power and the Culture of Celebrity.* For further discussions of Winchell, see also Lehman and Herman Klurfeld, *Winchell: His Life and Times.*

I interviewed a number of people who know or knew Matthew Drudge, including Dan Mathews and David Cohen. Other sources consulted for this chapter include Howard Kurtz, "It's Ten Past Monica, America. Do You Know Where Matt Drudge Is?"; Janet Wiscombe, "What Hath the Web Wrought?"; Michael Finley, "Drudging up Change on the Internet"; Robert B. Gunnison, "Drudge Dredges Up the Dirt." The notion that Drudge hacked into computers is based on reports from several sources as well as William Powers, "Punctured Franchise."

2   The War Against *Confidential*

The description of the courtroom setting and trial was taken from a variety of contemporary news accounts as reported in the *New York Post,* the New York *Daily News,* the *New York Times,* the New York *Mirror, Time,* and *Newsweek.* In addition, the author interviewed scandal magazine expert Alan Betrock and publisher Lyle Stuart.

Among the profiles of Harrison consulted were Tom Wolfe's "Public Lives: *Confidential* Magazine. Reflections in Tranquility by the Former Owner, Robert Harrison, Who Managed to Get away with It"; Mike Wallace's "The Man Behind *Confidential*"; a 1957 series on Harrison in the New York *Mirror.* Neal Gabler also discusses the relationship between Harrison and Winchell.

For more on Fred Otash, see his book *Investigation Hollywood!* See also Bill Davidson, "The Dick"; Howard J. Rutledge, "Gossipy Private Peeks at Celebrities' Lives Start Magazine Bonanza. *Confidential*'s Racy Exposés Crack Newsstand Records."

3   Mike Wallace—Shaking the Building

The material in this chapter is based on an interview with Mike Wallace as well as interviews with a number of people who work for him, many of whom asked not to be identified. See also Wallace's autobiography, *Close Encounters*; the excellent Edward Klein, "Hidden Mike"; *Vanity Fair* and a collection of his early interviews, published in *Mike Wallace Asks.* In addition, these published sources were consulted: "Mike Wallace: In the Spotlight"; Marvin Barrett, "Turnabout on Mike Wallace, *Newsweek*"; the series on Mike Wallace in the *New York Post,* 13–18 February 1957; William A. Coleman, "Mike Wallace's Sunday Punch," *Parade.* For Oliver Treyz's visit to ABC, see Leonard Goldenson, *Beating the Odds.*

4   The Birth of a Tabloid

Details of the *Enquirer*'s early years are based on a number of interviews with Generoso Pope Jr.'s son, Paul Pope, with John Miller's son, John Miller

Jr., and with Igor Cassini. Also, an unpublished interview with Lois and Paul Pope by Noel Botham and Brian Hitch, provided to the author by Paul Pope.

Details of the Costello dinner are taken from a variety of newspaper accounts at the time of the hit, as well as Leonard Katz's excellent *Uncle Frank: The Biography of Frank Costello*. Also see George Wolf with Joseph Di-Mona, *Frank Costello: Prime Minister of the Underworld*, and Kenneth Jackson, *The Encyclopedia of New York City*.

For a biography of Generoso Pope Sr., see Philip Cannistraro's *Italian Americans: New Perspectives in Italian Immigration and Ethnicity*, and Pope's obit, "Generoso Pope, 59, Publisher, Is Dead," *New York Times*, 29 April 1950.

Details on the relationship between Roy Cohn and Pope are based on a number of interviews, but particularly one with his friend and biographer, Sidney Zion. See also Zion's book, *The Autobiography of Roy Cohn*, as well as Nicholas Von Hoffman, *Citizen Cohn: The Life and Times of Roy Cohn* and Roy Cohn, *A Fool for a Client*.

For a rousing account of the early years at the *National Enquirer*, see George Bernard, *Inside the National Enquirer: Confessions of an Undercover Reporter*. See also Reginald Potterton, "I Cut Out Her Heart & Stomped on It!," *Playboy*.

Other important printed sources for this chapter include William R. Amlong, "Pope: The High Priest of Lowbrow," *Tropic*; "Goodbye to Gore," *Time*; and Sid Kirchheimer's "Enquiring Minds Want to Know the Man Behind the *National Enquirer*," *Fort Lauderdale News & Sun-Sentinel*. See also Kent A. MacDougall's "Going Straight: The National Enquirer Finds Gore Doesn't Pay but Reassurance Does," *Wall Street Journal*.

5   "They've Got Everything on You . . ."

Information in this chapter came from interviews with Benjamin Bradlee, Igor Cassini, Lawrence J. Quirk, and Sidney Zion. I also consulted the Dorothy Kilgallen collection at the New York Public Library.

Among the most startling accounts of Ben Bradlee's relationship with the Kennedys is in his own words in *Conversations with Kennedy* and in *A Good Life: Newspapering and Other Adventures*.

J. Edgar Hoover being a source for Winchell is documented in several places, but see especially Anthony Summers, *Official and Confidential: The Secret Life of J. Edgar Hoover*; Zion, *The Autobiography of Roy Cohn*, and Herman Klurfeld, *Winchell: His Life and Times*.

For further details of Kennedy's manipulation of the press, see Klurfeld; Thomas C. Reeves, *A Question of Character: A Life of John F. Kennedy*; Wesley O. Hagood, *Presidential Sex*; Earl Wilson, *Show Business Laid Bare*; Sidney Skolsky, *Don't Get Me Wrong—I Love Hollywood*; Lee Israel, *Kilgallen*; and Lawrence J. Quirk's *The Kennedys in Hollywood*.

For more information about the Cassini episode, see Peter Maas, "Boswell of the Jet Set," *Saturday Evening Post*; Cassini's "Personal Lives: When the Sweet Life Turns Sour; A Farewell to Scandal," *Esquire*; and "Igor Cassini Indicted as Failing to Register as Trujillo Agent," *New York Times*, 9 February 1963.

For biographical information on Fred Otash, see Anthony Cook, "The Man Who Bugged Marilyn Monroe," *GQ*; Bill Davidson's "The Dick," *Los Angeles* magazine; Otash's *Investigation Hollywood!* and his obituary by Myrna Oliver, "Fred Otash, Colorful Hollywood Private Eye and Author," *Los Angeles Times*. The account of Otash's bugging of the Kennedys was taken from a variety of sources, including Robert Welkos and Ted Rohrlich, "Marilyn Monroe Mystery Persists," *L.A. Times*. A similar account is in Anthony Summers, *Goddess: The Secret Lives of Marilyn Monroe*. See also James Spada, *Peter Lawford: The Man Who Kept the Secrets*.

6   The Divas

I conducted interviews with a number of people who dealt with the subjects, including Dan Shaw, Patricia Bosworth, Eleanor Lambert, John Springer, and Mimi Strong. Published sources consulted include Paul O'Neil, "The Little Queen that Hollywood Deserved," *Life*; George Eell, *Hedda and Louella*; and Richard Lemon and Mary Ann Norbom's "The Warrior Queens of Gossip," *People*. Several of Sheila Graham's books, particularly *Hollywood Revisited*; Lawrence Laurent, "Telling Tales: Still Rewarding," *Newsday*; Nikki Finke, "Miss Rona Ready for Another Run at TV," *Los Angeles Times*; Tom Shales, "Some Enchanted Rona: The Woman Who Made TV Safe for Hollywood Gab," *Washington Post*; John Hallowell, "Miss Rona Barrett Gossips," *New York Times*; and Joanne Wasserman, "Miss Rona's Snit Over Barbara Plums," *New York Post*. The dishiest source of information on Rona Barrett is probably her autobiography, *Miss Rona*.

7   Tabloid Glory Days

This chapter is based mostly on interviews with current and former *National Enquirer* employees who wish to remain anonymous. In addition, some printed sources were used. Among those that were particularly helpful are an account of working at the *Enquirer* by P. J. Corkery, "Exclusive! Inside the *National Enquirer*," *Rolling Stone*; Jim Hogshire, *Grossed-Out Surgeon Vomits Inside Patient! An Insider's Look at Supermarket Tabloids*; and an account by then-*Enquirer* writer George Bernard, *Inside the National Enquirer: Confessions of an Undercover Reporter*.

Other sources consulted include David Lamb, "Into the Realm of Tabloids," *Los Angeles Times*; Beth Ann Krier, "When the *National Enquirer* Pounces, Sales Jump—And So Do Its Critics," *L.A. Times*; Matt Spetalnick, "Tabloids Create Strange, Wacky World on Florida's East Coast," *Reuters*; John A. Byrne, "Slugging It Out in the Supermarkets," *Forbes*; Isadore Barmash, "Enquirer Promoting New Image," *New York Times*; Rudy Maxa, "This Reporter Rifles Garbage," *Washington Post*; Elizabeth Peer and William Schmidt, "Up From Smut," *Newsweek*; and James Lardner, "Can 17,000,000 Readers Be Wrong? Life on a Journalist's Funny Farm," *Washington Post*.

8   *60 Minutes*

In addition to an interview with Mike Wallace, this chapter is based on interviews with dozens of current and former employees of *60 Minutes*, all of whom wished to remain anonymous. A number of published sources were consulted as well, including Mark Hertsgaard's excellent "The 60 Minute Man," *Rolling Stone*, 30 May 1991, and a follow-up by Carol Lloyd, "A Feel for a Good Story," *Salon*. See also Edward Klein, "Hidden Mike," *Vanity Fair*; Richard Zoglin, "What Makes '60 Minutes' Tick," *New York Times*; John O'Connor, "Still the Best of TV's 'News Magazines,' " *N.Y. Times*; Peter Bart, "Seer of '60 Minutes,' " *Variety*; Donovan Moore, "60 Minutes . . . tick, tick, tick, tick, tick, tick . . ." *Rolling Stones*; Les Brown, "How '60 Minutes' Stumbled into Prime Time," *N.Y. Times*. A number of books were consulted for information on Mike Wallace and the history of *60 Minutes*, particularly Wallace's *Close Encounters* and Don Hewitt's *Minute by Minute*. See also Robert Metz, *CBS: Reflections in a Bloodshot Eye*; Barbara Matusow's *The Evening Stars: The Making of the Network News Anchor*.

9   Gossip Goes Mainstream

This chapter is based largely on interviews with current and former *People* staffers, particularly founding editor Richard Stolley.

Articles consulted include Michael Gross, "Up with People," *GQ*; Jennifer Bojorquez, "Idol Minds," *Sacramento Bee*; Kimberly Goad, "Richard Stolley: His *People* Skills Set the Tone for Two Decades," *Dallas Morning News*; John McGuire, "*People* at 20," *St. Louis Post-Dispatch*; Janet Cawley's "People Who Need People Marks 20th Year," *Chicago Tribune*.

Among the books consulted, Judy Kessler, *Inside People*, was immensely informative and useful, as was Curtis Prendergast with Geoffrey Colvin, *The World of Time Inc.: The Intimate History of a Changing Enterprise, Vol. 3: 1960–1980*.

10   The Death of a King

This chapter is based on contemporary articles and interviews with reporters and editors who covered Elvis's death and funeral, including Tom Kuncl and Peter Herbst. A number of books were particularly useful, including Neal and Janice Gregory, *When Elvis Died*; Lee Cotten's *All Shook Up: Elvis, Day-by-Day, 1954–1997*; Patricia Jobe Pierce, *The Ultimate Elvis: Elvis Presley Day by Day*.

11   The Networks Go Tabloid

This chapter is based on interviews with current and former employees of ABC, including Barbara Walters and past interviews with Av Westin, Geraldo Rivera, and others who wished to remain anonymous. Among the published sources: Desmond Smith, "The Wide World of Roone Arledge," *New York Times Magazine*; Richard Zoglin, "ABC Ya, Roone," *Time*; Marc Gunther, *The House That Roone Built*; Elizabeth Gleick, "Geraldo Rivera: Fresh from a Triumph in the O.J. Wars, the Rogue Reporter Still Hungers for Respect," *People*; Geraldo Rivera, *Exposing Myself*; William Plummer, "The Monroe Report: News Staffers at ABC-TV Cry 'Cover-up' When Their Bosses Kill a 20/20 Magazine Segment on Marilyn Monroe," *Time*; Kim Mills, "Author Charges Politics in Cancellation of '20/20' Segment on Monroe," Associated Press; Jay Sharbutt, "ABC Boss Defends Monroe Decision," *Los Angeles Times*; Paul Rosenfield, "How Does It Feel to Be Barbara Walters," *L.A. Times Calendar*; Jeff Greenfield, "The Showdown at ABC News," *N.Y. Times Magazine*.

12   Celebrities Fight Back

Carol Burnett's trial was covered by a number of newspapers and magazines at the time; especially useful were Myrna Oliver's articles in the *Los Angeles Times*. See also Clark Taylor, "Carol Burnett: 'I'd No Idea I Was This Strong,' " *L.A. Times*; and Jay Mathews's "Burnett Wins Enquirer Suit," *Washington Post*. For a lively account of Michael J. Fox's wedding, see his own article: "Michael J. Fox's Nuptials in Hell!" *Esquire*.

See also P. J. Corkery; Judy Kessler, *Inside People*; Linden Gross, "So Rich, So Famous, So Pestered," *Cosmopolitan*; William Sherman, "Rockin' with the Rock Impressarios,"*Cosmopolitan*; Jon Underwood, "Axl Rose Won't Sign a Contract That Makes Him Sing in a Town Starting with the Letter *M* Because He Thinks *M* Has a Curse on It," *Daily Mail*; Richard Harrington, "Whatever the Promoter Will Bear," *Washington Post*; Fred W. Wright, "Special Requests," *Tampa Tribune*; and Patrick Goldstein, "Hollywood's Real True Lies," *L.A. Times*.

13   Tina Brown

This chapter is based largely on my reporting on Tina Brown and *Vanity Fair* over the last decade, including brief conversations with Brown in the course of that reporting. In addition, a number of former staffers spoke on the condition of anonymity. Numerous printed sources were consulted, including Alan Franks, "Party Animus," *The Times Saturday Review*; Bill Higgins, "Connecticut Haiku Goes Hollywood," *Los Angeles Times*; Georgina Howell, "All Is Vanity; Nothing is Fair," *London Sunday Times Magazine*; Bill Thomas, "Mighty Tina," *L.A. Times*; Neil Mackwood, "The Girl from Little Marlow Bites the Big Apple," *Daily Mail*; Greg Easley, "Ms. Brown, Mr. Mailer Wants to Know If You Picked Up His Dry Cleaning," *Spy*; Geordie Greig, "Hollywood Babble On," *Times of London*; Alexander Cockburn, "Nausea: Critique of Vanity Fair," *The Nation*; Geoffrey Stokes, "The Trouble with Tina," *Spy*.

14   The Good Old Gal and the Tycoon

This chapter is based on my reporting on Trump over the last decade, including
numerous interviews with Donald and Ivana Trump and the various players in the Trump divorce. In addition, a number of printed sources were
particularly useful, especially, Jonathan Van Meter, "The Sour Smell of
Success," *7 Days*. Other sources include daily coverage of the Trump saga
in the newspapers, particularly Howard Kurtz's articles in the *Washington
Post*; Walter Anderson, "Liz Smith: The Lady Behind the Gossip," *Cosmo-
politan*; Cliff Jahr, "Loose Lips: Gossip Columnist Liz Smith Gives the
Lowdown on Celebrities," *Ladies Home Journal*; David Sheff, "The Play-
boy Interview: Liz Smith," *Playboy*; Lorne Manly, "Off the Record," *New
York Observer*; Divina Infusino, "Liz Smith Serves Gossip in Big Scoops,"
San Diego Tribune; Richard Bernstein, "Gossip's Hot, and Hers Is the
Name to Drop," *New York Times*; Clifford Pugh, "Texas Boots and Texas
Roots: Columnist Still Talks with a Thick Drawl," *Houston Chronicle*; and
Merrie Morris, "The World's Most Famous Gossip Columnist Is Wearing
Jeans," *Washington Times*.

15   The Rise of Tabloid Television

Interviews included Maury Povich and other sources at Fox and the *New York
Post*. Printed sources include the transcript of CNBC, 14 September 1994,
"Steve Dunleavy of 'A Current Affair' Discusses His Job and That of
Tabloid Reporters"; Maury Povich, *Current Affairs: A Life on the Edge*;
Mike Thomas, "It's Scandalous! Malcolm Balfour, King of the Trash Tabs,
Tells the Titillating Truth!", *Orlando Sentinel Tribune*; David Margolick,
"A Peek Under the Tent of the Palm Beach Media Circus," *New York
Times*; David Shaw, "Obsessed with Flash and Trash," *Los Angeles Times*;
James Brady, "Now Stand By, America: Here Comes Steve Dunleavy,"
Crain's New York Business.

16   The Gatekeepers

This chapter is based largely on my reporting and experiences with publicists,
as well as an interview with Pat Kingsley. Several journalists who attended
the various junkets spoke on the condition of anonymity. Other interview-
ees include Stephanie Mansfield, John Springer, Lee Grant, and Jennet
Conant. A number of valuable articles were consulted, particularly Christopher Robbins, "The Woman Behind Tom: Pat Kingsley," *Times of London*; John Seabrook, "Kingsley's Ransom," *The New Yorker*; Ivor Davis
and Sally Ogle Davis, "Flacks Fatales," *Los Angeles* magazine; Jeffrey
Goodell, "The Fame Machine," *Mirabella*; Paula Span, "Invasion of the
Movieflackers," *Washington Post*; Peter Howell, "Cruise Control by Play-
ing Cat and Mouse with the Media," *Toronto Star*; Richard Roeper, "A
Star is Bored," *Spy*; Melanie Warner and Marty O'Loughlin, "Cover or
Nothing," *Inside Media*; Tom Maurstad, "Hero Worship," *Dallas Morning
News*; Divina Infusio, "It's a Reporter's Feast (or Famine)," *San Diego*

Tribune; Rick Marin, "They're Hot!", *Des Moines Register*; Anita M. Busch, "Media Up in Arms Over Studio Publicity Contracts," *Hollywood Reporter*; Sharon Waxman, "The Hollywood Junket," *Washington Post*; Bernard Weinraub, "Hollywood and Tough Journalism Don't Mix," *New York Times*; Nigel Andrews, "Sunset on the Boulevard of Inflated Egos," *Financial Times*; Claudia Eller, "A Star Is Born—Before He's Even Been Seen," *Los Angeles Times*; and Michael Cieply, "Hollywood's High-Powered Image Machine," *L.A. Times.*

17   P.R. Muscle

This chapter was based on my own reporting on the Michael Jackson story as well as interviews with a number of people who have dealt with Jackson or Anthony Pellicano, including Diane Dimond, John Connolly, and Maureen Orth. Hundreds of articles were consulted for this section. Among the most useful were Orth, "The Jackson Jive" and "Nightmare in Neverland," *Vanity Fair*; and Connolly's "The Pellicano Brief," *Los Angeles* magazine. See also Ian Katz, "Hollywood's Star Gumshoe," *Washington Post*; Larry Katz, "King of P.R.: Jacko's Not Wacko, He's Just Crazy Like a Fox," *Boston Herald*; Peter Wilkinson, "The Big Sleazy," *GQ*; Steve Oney, "Anthony Pellicano: The Private Eye Who Dogged the DeLorean and Belushi Cases Talks About the Tools of his Trade: Guts, Guns and Gizmos," *Playboy*; David Ferrell and Chuck Philips, "Gloves Come Off in Damage Control by Jackson Camp," *Los Angeles Times*; Gordon Smith, "Jackson's Investigator a Vanishing Breed," *San Diego Union-Tribune*; Shawn Hubler and James Bates, "Streetwise Gumshoe to the Stars," *L.A. Times*; and Claudia Eller, "Company Town: A Partnership on the Rocks?," *L.A. Times.*

18   A Struggle for Respectability

Saturation coverage of O. J. Simpson makes it difficult to narrow down the hundreds of articles consulted for this chapter, but some of the most important include David Shaw, "The Simpson Legacy: Is the Media Overfeeding a Starving Public?," *Los Angeles Times*; David Margolick, "The Enquirer: Required Reading in Simpson Case," *New York Times*; John Lyttle, "Exposed! America's Biggest Scandal Sheet," *The Independent*; M. L. Stein, "Supermarket Tabloids Set O.J. Case Pace," *Editor and Publisher*; Gordon Edes, "Simpson Crowned New King of Tabloids," *Fort Lauderdale Sun-Sentinel*; Mark Washburn, "Checkout-Line Tabloid Approaches Respectability on O.J. Case," *Charleston Gazette*; David Lieberman, "Rivals Have Descended on Tabloids," *USA Today*; Bill Boyarsky, "Tabloids Affecting Trial Coverage—And the Trial Itself," *L.A. Times*; Felicia Levine, "O.J. Saga Juices Enquirer Sales," *South Florida Business Journal*; Elizabeth Gleick, "Leader of the Pack," *Time*; David Beard, "Tabloids Inquiring: Will There Be Life After the O.J. Trial?," *Fort Lauderdale Sun-Sentinel*; Jane Sutton, "Simpson Outsells Babies from Mars!," Reuters; and Katy Butler, "The Accidental Feminist," *L.A. Times Magazine.*

See also Diane Cyr, "Acquiring Minds," *Inside Media*; Andra Sachs, "Mud and the Mainstream," *Columbia Journalism Review*; David Lamb, "Into the Realm of Tabloids," *L.A. Times*; Si Liberman, "Supermarket Tab King Steps Down," *Editor and Publisher*; Jon Nordheimer, "Mild-Mannered Buyers Tame Wild Tabloids!," *N.Y. Times*; Marguerite M. Plunkett, *"Enquirer* Editor Calder Steps Down," *Palm Beach Post*; M. G. Lord, "The *Enquirer* in Bed with the *Star!*," *Newsday*; Howard Kurtz, "Checkbook Journalism: The Globe & Cosby's Alleged Extortionist," *Washington Post*; and Lyle Slack, "Alien Brainchild Lands in Supermarket, Libels Oprah, Dies," *Saturday Night*.

19   The Tabloid Princess

Princess Diana's death resulted in massive media coverage, but PBS's unedited, sometimes unbroadcast interviews from the superb "The Princess and the Press" were especially useful. Also, Peter Stothard, "A Perrier with the Princess," *Times of London*; Richard Attenborough's "A Shy Start Soon Gave Way to a Wicked Sense of Humour," *Times of London*.

Also, *Larry King Live* shows "Guests Discuss How Tabloid Photographers Effect Stars' Lives" and "The Impact of Tabloids in America."

BIBLIOGRAPHY

Selected Articles

Adalain, Josef. "Mike Wallace's Pot-Smoking Past." *New York Post*, 1 November 1996.

Alexander, Max. "Not-so-Private Eye Who May or May Not Be Your Friend." *Daily Variety*, 6 September 1993.

Allen, Frederick. "Up from Humbug." *Columbia Journalism Review*, March 1995; April 1995.

Alter, Jonathan. "America Goes Tabloid." *Newsweek*, 25 December 1994/2 January 1995.

———. "The Art of the Deals." *Newsweek*, 9 January 1989.

Amlong, William R. "Pope: The High Priest of Lowbrow." *Tropic*, 14 January 1973.

Anders, Marjorie. "Liz Smith: Small-Town Girl Swims with the Big Fish." Associated Press, 20 August 1987.

Anderson, David. "2 Pope Brothers Indicted by U.S." *New York Times*, 20 July 1960.

Anderson, Walter. "Liz Smith: The Lady Behind the Gossip." *Cosmopolitan*, March 1989.

Andrews, Nigel. "Sunset on the Boulevard of Inflated Egos." *Financial Times*, 3 September 1994.

Armstrong, Lois. "Carol Burnett Welcomes Her Daughter Carrie Back from the Grim World of Drugs." *People*, 1 October 1979.

Arnold, Roseanne. "What Am I Anyway, a Zoo?" *New York Times*, 30 September 1990.

Attenborough, Richard. "A Shy Start Soon Gave Way to a Wicked Sense of Humour." *Times of London*, 6 September 1997.

Auletta, Ken. "Don't Mess with Roy Cohn." *Esquire*, 5 December 1978.

Baer, Atra. "Atra Baer Turns the Tables, Puts Mike on Hot Seat." *New York Journal American*, 23 February 1957.

Bain, George. "Sensational Sales for the Tabs." *Maclean's*, 22 December 1986.

Balfour, Malcolm. "Camille Cosby Rips Tabs' 'Abuse.'" *New York Post*, 2 February 1997.

Barmash, Isadore. "Enquirer Promoting New Image." *New York Times*, 31 August 1987.

Barnhart, Aaron. "Drudgery Indeed: Wannabe Winchell Would Do Well to Stick to Web Work." *Kansas City Star*, 15 August 1998.

Barrett, Marvin. "Turnabout on Mike Wallace." *Newsweek*, 16 September 1957.

Barrymore, Drew. "The Secret Drew Barrymore." *People*, 1 January 1989.

Barsky, Neil. "Shaky Empire: Trump's Bankers Join to Seek Restructuring of Developer's Assets." *Wall Street Journal*, 4 June 1990.

Bart, Peter. "Seer of '60 Minutes.'" *Variety*, 21 December 1993.

Barthel, Joan. "Rona Barrett: TV Snoop." *Life*, 21 March 1969.

Beard, David. "Tabloids Inquiring: Will There Be Life After the O.J. Trial?" *Fort Lauderdale Sun-Sentinel*, 11 April 1995.

Bennett, Vanora. "Editors at 5 Tabloids Agree to Stay Away from Funeral." *Los Angeles Times*, 6 September 1997.

Bernstein, Richard. "Gossip's Hot, and Hers Is the Name to Drop." *New York Times*, 3 April 1991.

Berthelsen, Christian. "Tabloid Offers Reward and Gets Small Thanks." *New York Times*, 6 July 1998.

Bird, Robert S. "2 Pope Brothers Named by U.S. in $375,000 Plot." *New York Herald Tribune*, 20 July 1960.

Bojorquez, Jennifer. "Idol Minds." *Sacramento Bee*, 1 March 1994.

Borders, William. "Stylish 26-Year-Old Takes Over Tatler." *New York Times*, 30 November 1979.

Boulard, Garry. "Giving People What They Want to Read." *Editor and Publisher*, 4 May 1991.

Bourne, Brendan. "Cosby Slay Informer Collects 100G." *New York Post*, 10 July 1998.

Boyarsky, Bill. "Tabloids Affecting Trial Coverage—And the Trial Itself." *Los Angeles Times*, 17 January 1995.

Boyd, James L. "Only the Birds and the Bees Saw . . . What Dorothy Dandridge Did in the Woods!" *Confidential*, May 1957.

Bradford, Krista. "The Big Sleaze." *Rolling Stone*, 18 February 1993.

Brady, James. "Now Stand By, America: Here Comes Steve Dunleavy." *Crain's New York Business*, 31 July 1988.

Brennan, Judy. "A Publicity Giant Spins for Itself." *Los Angeles Times Magazine*, 14 June 1994.

Brick, Mike. "Cindy Is a Model Number." *New York Star*, 9 January 1949.

Briskin, Hy. "How Mike Todd Made a Chump of a Movie Mogul!" *Confidential*, 3 March 1957.

Brock, Pope. "Steve Dunleavy: Quick with a Buck and a Fist, A Current Affair's Nervy Aussie Never Met a Story Too Lurid to Love." *People*, 7 June 1993.

Broeske, Pat H. "After Death, 'It Was War'; Even Elvis's Coffin Made It to the Front Page." *Los Angeles Times*, 16 August 1977.

Brower, Brock. "The Brothers Cassini." *Esquire*, February 1963.

Brown, Les. "CBS Tipster Decision on Highest Level, Salant Says." *New York Times*, 10 December 1975.

———. "Haldeman Said to Get $25,000 for CBS Interview by Wallace." *New York Times*, 6 March 1975.

———. "How '60 Minutes' Stumbled into Prime Time." *New York Times*, 23 November 1975.

———. "Networks Reviewing Policies on Paying for Exclusive Interviews." *New York Times*, 2 April 1975.

Brown, Mick. "English Flair at Vanity Fair." *Sunday Times of London*, 1 April 1984.

Brown, Tina. "Editor's Letter: Transatlantica." *Vanity Fair*, October 1985.

———. "Hi, Society." *Sunday Times of London*, 18 September 1983.

———. (under the pseudonym "Ubiquitous") "Kiss Kiss Kissinger." *Vanity Fair*, August 1983.

———. "The Mouse that Roared." *Vanity Fair*, October 1985.

———. "A Woman in Earnest." *The New Yorker*, 15 September 1997.

Busch, Anita M. "Cruise's Junket Orders Draw Fire from Journalists." *Hollywood Reporter*, 11 November 1992.

———. "Media up in Arms over Studio Publicity Contracts." *Hollywood Reporter*, 29 May 1992.

Butler, Katy. "The Accidental Feminist." *Los Angeles Times Magazine*. 10 December 1995.

Byrne, John A. "Slugging It Out in the Supermarkets." *Forbes*, 14 March 1983.

Campbell, Richard. "Don Hewitt's Durable Hour." *Columbia Journalism Review*, September/October 1993.

Carlson, Gus. "Enquirer Exposed! Documents Reveal Tabloid's Untold Story." *Miami Herald*, 9 June 1991.

Carmody, Diedre. "Life to Cease Publishing Dec. 29." *New York Times*, 9 December 1972.

Carmody, John. "Buying Time from Haldeman." *Washington Post*, 7 March 1975.

Carmody, John. "Turbulence at ABC News Results in Executive's Suspension." *The Record* (Bergen, N.J.), 3 March 1987.

Carroll, Jerry. "Psst! Did you hear. . . ." *San Francisco Chronicle*, 25 April 1990.

Carswell, Sue. "Trump Says Goodbye Marla, Hello Carla." *People*, 8 July 1991.

Carter, Bill. "Now It Can Be Told: Tabloid TV Is Booming." *New York Times*, 23 December 1991.

Cash, William. "Drudging Through the Muck." *The Sunday Star Times (Auckland)*, 15 February 1998.

Cassidy, John. "The Lady and the Trump." *Times of London*, 18 February 1990.

Cassini, Igor. "How the Kennedy Marriage Has Fared." *Good Housekeeping*, September 1962.

———. "Personal Lives: When the Sweet Life Turns Sour; A Farewell to Scandal." *Esquire*, April 1964.

Castro, Peter. "Goodbye, Friend." *People*, 3 February 1997.

Cawley, Janet. "People Who Need People Marks 20th Year." *Chicago Tribune*, 3 March 1994.

Chittenden, Maurice. "Fayed the Fateful Outsider Sits with Establishment." *Sunday Times of London*, 7 September 1997.

Cieply, Michael. "Hollywood's High-Powered Image Machine." *Los Angeles Times*, 10 July 1988.

Ciolli, Rita. "After O.J., What?" *Newsday*, 20 July 1994.

Clines, Francis X. "Gossip Guru Stars in 2 Roles at Courthouse." *New York Times*, 12 March 1998.

Cockburn, Alexander. "Nausea: Critique of Vanity Fair." *The Nation*, 7 September 1985.

Colacello, Bob. "Anything Went." *Vanity Fair*, March 1996.

Coleman, William A. "Mike Wallace's Sunday Punch." *Parade*, 2 December 1957.

Collins, Jay. "The Skeleton in Mike Wallace's Hidden Closet." *Hush-Hush*, January 1958.

Collins, Scott, and Sallie Hofmeister. "Simpson Case a Big-Ticket Boon for Tabloid Media." *Los Angeles Times*, 13 October 1995.

Conant, Jennet. "The Professional." *Vanity Fair*, June 1996.

Connolly, John. "The Pellicano Brief." *Los Angeles Magazine*, February 1994.

Cook, Anthony. "The Man Who Bugged Marilyn Monroe." *GQ*, October 1990.

Corkery, P. J. "Exclusive! Inside the *National Enquirer*." *Rolling Stone*, 11 June 1981.

Cosby, Camille O. "Don't Believe the Tabs." *USA Today*, 6 February 1997.

Cox, Dan. "Movie Junkets Woo the Freebie Press." *Variety*, 27 June/3 July 1994.

Crosson, John. "Young Pope Causes Stir." *New York Herald Tribune*, 15 October 1950.

Cyr, Diane. "Acquiring Minds." *Inside Media*, 20 November 1991.

Darrach, Brad. "A Comic's Crisis of the Heart." *People*, 22 February 1988.

Davidson, Bill. "The Dick." *Los Angeles Magazine*, May 1991.

Davies, Hugh. "Kennedys Savaged by the TV Pit Bull." *Daily Telegraph*, 3 November 1991.

Davis, Ivor, and Sally Ogle Davis. "Flacks Fatales." *Los Angeles Magazine*, August 1991.

Dean, John. "Haldeman Is No More Innocent Than I Am." *The New York Times*, 6 April 1975.

Denton, Archer. "Why Kennedy and Winchel Phfft! Behind WW's War with the White House." *Confidential*, January 1963.

DiGiacomo, Frank. "Bam! Pow! Suck! Liz and Joel, Dynamic Duo." *New York Observer*, 23 June 1997.

Donahue, Diedre. "Brown Turns the Pages on to Pizazz." *USA Today*, 19 February 1988.

Dougherty, Philip H. "Advertising: Life Magazine's Post-Mortem." *New York Times*, 11 December 1972.

Duffy, David, John South, and Michael Glynn. "Bill Cosby: My Tragedy." *National Enquirer*, 4 February 1997.

Dunphy, Catherine. "Coming to America." *Toronto Star*, 22 May 1992.

Dutka, Elaine. "The Law of Attraction." *Los Angeles Times*, 29 July 1996.

Easley, Greg. "Ms. Brown, Mr. Mailer Wants to Know If You Picked Up His Dry Cleaning." *Spy*, September/October 1995.

Edes, Gordon. "Simpson Crowned New King of Tabloids." *Fort Lauderdale Sun-Sentinel*, 4 October 1994.

Eller, Claudia. "Company Town: A Partnership on the Rocks?" *Los Angeles Times*, 29 August 1995.

———. "A Star Is Born—Before He's Even Been Seen." *Los Angeles Times*, 11 June 1997.

Fannin, Rebecca. "Tina's in Vogue at Vanity Fair." *Marketing & Media Decisions*, May 1984.

Farrell, Mary H. J. "The Trumps Head for Divorce Court." *People*, 26 February 1990.

Federici, William, and Henry Lee. "Charlene Cassini Dies; Find Empty Pill Bottle." *Daily News*, 10 April 1963.

Ferrell, David, and Chuck Philips. "Gloves Come Off in Damage Control by Jackson Camp." *Los Angeles Times*, 3 September 1993.

Ferretti, Fred. " '60 Minutes' Seeks to Fill Reasoner's Chair." *New York Times*, 12 November 1970.

Finke, Nikki. "Miss Rona Ready for Another Run at TV." *Los Angeles Times*, 26 January 1989.

Finley, Michael. "Drudging up Change on the Internet." *The Times Union* (Albany, N.Y.), 10 February 1998.

Fiore, Faye. "Senators, Actors Focus on Bill to Curb Paparazzi." *Los Angeles Times*, 16 February 1998.

Firestone, David. "Murdoch's Post Made Headlines." *Newsday*, 7 February 1988.

Fisher, Jim. "Supermarket Shocker! Tabloid Checks Facts." *Lewiston (Idaho) Morning Tribune*, 21 October 1990.

Fleming, Charles. "In Hollywood, Female Publicists Rule Roost." *Daily Variety*, 7 August 1992.

Flippo, Chet. "Funeral in Memphis." *Rolling Stone*, 22 September 1977.

Fong-Torres, Ben. "Broken Heart for Sale: Elvis' Bodyguards Talk About What Happened." *Rolling Stone*, 22 September 1977.

Fox, Michael J. "Michael J. Fox's Nuptials in Hell!" *Esquire*, June 1989.

Franck, Linda Bird. "Gossipmania." *Newsweek*, 24 May 1976.

Franks, Alan. " 'I Hope That Now She Is Free.' " *Times of London*, 3 September 1997.

———. "Party Animus." *London Times Saturday Review*, 9 February 1991.

Galbraith, Jane. "If She Keeps Talk of the Town, Will Readers Know What Town It Is?" *Los Angeles Times Calendar*, 5 July 1992.

Gerard, Lou. "You'll Have to Guess How She Shapes Up." *National Enquirer*, 5 July 1959.

Gewen, Barry. "The News at Any Cost: How Journalists Compromise Their Ethics to Shape the News." Book Reviews, American Labor Conference on International Affairs, *The New Leader*, 27 January 1986.

Glaberson, William. "Times Is Criticized for Using Simpson Account from Tabloid." *New York Times*, 23 December 1994.

Gleick, Elizabeth. "Geraldo Rivera: Fresh from a Triumph in the O.J. Wars, the Rogue Reporter Still Hungers for Respect." *People*, 17 March 1997.

———. "Leader of the Pack." *Time*, 9 January 1995.

Goad, Kimberly. "Richard Stolley: His *People* Skills Set the Tone for Two Decades." *Dallas Morning News*, 20 March 1994.

Goldman, John J. "Life Magazine to Fold Dec. 29 Due to Heavy Financial Drain." *Los Angeles Times*, 9 December 1972.

Goldstein, Patrick. "Hollywood's Real True Lies." *Los Angeles Times*, 31 July 1994.

Goodell, Jeffrey. "The Fame Machine." *Mirabella*, April 1992.

Goodwin, Christopher. "Is He a Man or Is He a Mouse?" *Sunday Times of London*, 10 May 1998.

Graf, Hobart. "Why Rock Hudson's Giving Hollywood the Willies." *Uncensored*, December 1955.

Granville, Kair. "A Tangle for Inquiring Minds." *Los Angeles Times*, 29 September 1990.

Green, Tom. "Tina Brown, the Toast of the Town." *USA Today*, 3 March 1999.

Greenfield, Jeff. "The Showdown at ABC News." *New York Times Magazine*, 13 February 1977.

Greig, Geordie. "Hollywood Babble On." *Times of London*, 20 March 1994.

Gross, Linden. "So Rich, So Famous, So Pestered." *Cosmopolitan*, November 1993.

Gross, Michael. "Inside Gossip: The Scoop on Suzy, Liz, 'Rat' Revson, and the Big Feud." *New York*, 9 May 1988.

———. "Up With People." GQ, March 1997.

Grossman, Lawrence K. "Spot News: The Press and the Dress." *Columbia Journalism Review*, November/December 1998.

Grutzner, Charles. "State Body Finds Wide Dishonesty in City Salt Deals." *New York Times*, 18 August 1960.

Guart, Al, and Cathy Burke. "Con Man Eyed as Mastermind of Cosby Plot." *New York Post*, 31 January 1997.

Gunnison, Robert B. "Drudge Dredges Up the Dirt." *San Francisco Chronicle*, 24 January 1998.

Hallowell, John. "Miss Rona Barrett Gossips." *New York Times*, 22 September 1968.

Harrington, Richard. "Whatever the Promoter Will Bear." *Washington Post*, 31 August 1980.

Henry, David. "Tough Slogging." *Forbes*, 8 September 1986.

Henry, William A. (III) "Pssst . . . Did You Hear About?" *Time*, 5 March 1990.

Hentoff, Nat. "Pawning the Constitution to Repay a 'Damaged' Star." *Los Angeles Times*, 5 April 1981.

Herbers, John. "Former Aide Interviews Nixon." *New York Times*, 9 April 1984.

Hertsgaard, Mark. "The 60 Minute Man." *Rolling Stone*, 30 May 1991.

Hester, Clyde. "How His Marriage Saved Rock Hudson from Double-Scandal." *TV Scandals*, December 1957.

Hewitt, Bill, with Lyndon Stambler, John Hanna, and Leah Eskin. "Trouble Shooter." *People*, 20 September 1993.

Higgins, Bill. "Connecticut Haiku Goes Hollywood." *Los Angeles Times*, 16 March 1984.

Hiscock, John. "Stars' Stand Stuns Scandal Sheets: Hollywood Turns the Tables on Tabloid Gossips." *Sunday Telegraph*, 15 December 1991.

Holden, Benjamin A. "O.J. Case Spawns Its Own 'Economy.' " *Wall Street Journal*, 9 April 1995.

Honigsbaum, Mark. "The Princess and the Press." *The Spectator*, 27 September 1997.

Horine, Don. "Tabs up for Grabs." *Palm Beach Post*, 25 July 1995.

Howell, Georgina. "All Is Vanity; Nothing Is Fair." *London Sunday Times Magazine*, 26 October 1986.

Howell, Peter. "Cruise Control by Playing Cat and Mouse with the Media." *Toronto Star*, 13 December 1996.

Hubler, Shawn, and James Bates. "Streetwise Gumshoe to the Stars." *Los Angeles Times*, 11 September 1993.

Infusino, Divina. "It's a Reporter's Feast (or Famine)." *San Diego Tribune*, 8 July 1990.

———. "Liz Smith Serves Gossip in Big Scoops." *San Diego Tribune*, 13 March 1986.

Ingrams, Richard. "Only Connect." *Spy*, May 1992.

Jahr, Cliff. "Loose Lips: Gossip Columnist Liz Smith Gives the Lowdown on Celebrities." *Ladies Home Journal*, January 1989.

James, Clive. "Requiem." *The New Yorker*, 15 September 1997.

Jermone, Jim. "The Cher & Gregg 'Soap Opera' Finds a New Time Slot: The Family Hour." *People*, 27 September 1976.

———. "Cher Takes a Pay Cut (from $60,000 a Day to $4,000 a Week) and the Boldest Step of Her Career." *People*, 2 January 1992.

———. "Now That Cher Has Helped Show Him the Way, Gregg Allman Takes to the Road Again." *People*, 8 September 1975.

Johnstone, Lammy. "A Look at Mike Wallace—Circa '78." *New York Tribune*, 3 February 1978.

Jones, Robert A. "Planet Tabloid." *Los Angeles Times*, 22 January 1997.

Katz, Ian. "Hollywood's Star Gumshoe." *Washington Post*, 2 September 1993.

Katz, Larry. "King of P.R.: Jacko's Not Wacko, He's Just Crazy Like a Fox." *Boston Herald*, 2 July 1995.

Keillor, Garrison. "An Institution Gone to the Dogs." *Los Angeles Times*, 4 April 1995.

Kennedy, Caroline. "Graceland: A Family Mourns." *Rolling Stone*, 22 September 1977.

Kennedy, John. "Showdown: Shocking Truth Behind JFK Jr's Secret Summit with Tabloid Honcho Iain Calder!" *George*, August 1996.

Kidwell, David. "Tabloids in Bidding Battle for Exclusive O.J. Stories." Knight-Ridder, 15 July 1994.

Kilday, Gregg. "Haldeman on TV: The $25,000 Question." *Los Angeles Times*, 20 March 1975.

Kirchheimer, Sid. "Enquiring Minds Want to Know the Man Behind the National Enquirer." *Fort Lauderdale News & Sun-Sentinel*, 25 February 1987.

Klein, Edward. "Hidden Mike." *Vanity Fair*, November 1991.

———. "The Unstoppable Peggy Siegal." *Vanity Fair*, January 1996.

———. "Winning Diane." *New York*, 13 March 1989.

Kleinfield, N. R. "Magazines Battling for Checkout Racks." *New York Times*, 4 April 1979.

Knight, Michael. "Mood Muted at Life as Last Issue Goes to Press." *New York Times*, 20 December 1972.

Koch, Neal. "The Hollywood Treatment." *Columbia Journalism Review*, January 1991.

Kolbert, Elizabeth. "How Tina Brown Moves Magazines." *New York Times Magazine*, 5 December 1993.

Kowet, Don. "Media and the Moral of the Tale." *Washington Times*, 12 December 1991.

Kracht, Alvin R. "Can There Be Life After Death?" *New York Times*, 24 December 1972.

Krier, Beth Ann. "When the National Enquirer Pounces, Sales Jump—And So Do Its Critics." *Los Angeles Times*, 11 June 1987.

Kunen, James S. "Pop! Goes the Donald." *People*, 9 July 1990.

Kurtz, Howard. "After the Diana Debacle, the News Hasn't Gotten Any Better for Andy Heyward." *Washington Post*, 15 October 1997.

———. "Checkbook Journalism: The Globe & Cosby's Alleged Extortionist." *Washington Post*, 1 January 1997.

———. "Fast & Flawed." *Brill's Content*, July/August 1998.

———. "Gifford Tumbles into Tabloid Trap." *Washington Post*, 17 May 1997.

———. "It's 10 Past Monica, America. Do You Know Where Matt Drudge Is?" *Washington Post*, 28 March 1999.

———. "Ivana Won't Deal With Hubby's 'Killer' Lawyer." *Washington Post*, 10 February 1990.

———. "This Year's Fall Classic May be O. J. Simpson Trial." *Washington Post*, 7 September 1994.

———. "The Trump Divorce: Day 2." *Washington Post*, 13 February 1990.

Lacher, Irene. "Trump Watchers Already Are Choosing Sides in the Billion-Dollar Divorce." *Los Angeles Times*, 15 February 1990.

Lahr, John. "Dealing with Roseanne." *The New Yorker*, 17 July 1995.

Lamb, David. "Into the Realm of Tabloids." *Los Angeles Times*, 13 February 1992.

Lardner, James. "After Ten Years, the Hard Edge of '60 Minutes' Is, If Anything, Harder." *Washington Post*, 18 September 1977.

———. "Can 17,000,000 Readers Be Wrong? Life on a Journalist's Funny Farm." *Washington Post*, 2 April 1978.

Lauerman, Connie. "Sheila Graham's 50 years 'In the Gossip.' " *Chicago Tribune*, 9 April 1985.

Laurent, Lawrence. " 'Miss Rona' Barrett Survives the Knocks." *Los Angeles Times*, 30 September 1972.

———. "Telling Tales: Still Rewarding." *Los Angeles Times*, 5 September 1972.

LeClair, J. E. "The Real Reason for Marilyn Monroe's Divorce." *Confidential*, September, 1955.

Lemann, Nicholas. "Confidence Games." *The New Republic*, 5 November 1990.

Lemon, Richard, and Mary Ann Norbom. "The Warrior Queens of Gossip." *People*, 13 May 1985.

Levine, Felicia. "O.J. Saga Juices Enquirer Sales." *South Florida Business Journal*, 4 November 1994.

Levitt, Shelley. "Lovett First Sight." *People*, 13 July 1993.

Liberman, Si. "Supermarket Tab King Steps Down." *Editor and Publisher*, 13 July 1996.

Lieberman, David. "Rivals Have Descended on Tabloids." *USA Today*, 9 August 1994.

———. "Trial Rewrites Media's Rules on Coverage." *USA Today*, 4 October 1995.

Linderman, Lawrence. "Liz Smith: The Golden Girl of Gossip." *Cosmopolitan*, May 1995.

Lindsey, Robert. "Reopening of Inquiry into Marilyn Monroe's Death Raises Imbroglio in Los Angeles." *New York Times*, 29 October 1985.

Lloyd, Carol. "A Feel for a Good Story." *Salon*, 17 March 1998.

Lord, M. G. "The Enquirer in Bed with the Star!" *Newsday*, 8 April 1990.

Lowrie, Katharine. "Topsy-Turvy World of Fan Mags." *Los Angeles Times (Calendar)*, 30 March 1980.

Lubrano, Gina. "Newspapers That Dance to Hollywood Tune Need Refresher Course in Ethics." *San Diego Union-Tribune*, 18 May 1992.

Lurie, Rod. "I Was on the Enquirer's 'Hit List.' " *Los Angeles Magazine*, October 1990.

———. "No More Mr. Nice Guy." *Los Angeles Magazine*, October 1993.

———. "Now They're Playing Dirty: Hey, If You Thought the Enquirer Was Sleazy Before, Look What It's Up to Now." *Los Angeles Magazine*, February 1992.

Lyttle, John. "Exposed! America's Biggest Scandal Sheet." *The Independent*, 21 July 1996.

Maas, Peter. "Boswell of the Jet Set." *Saturday Evening Post*, 19 January 1963.

MacAlan, Carlton. "Why TV's Mike Wallace Always Asks That." *Uncensored*, March 1958.

MacDougall, Kent. A. "Going Straight: The National Enquirer Finds Gore Doesn't Pay but Reassurance Does." *Wall Street Journal*, 9 April 1971.

Mackwood, Neil. "The Girl from Little Marlow Bites the Big Apple." *Daily Mail*, 9 July 1993.

MacLeod, Hope, and Charles Gruenberg. "A Festive Evening with Frank Costello, and Then. . . ." *New York Post*, 3 May 1957.

Manly, Lorne. "Off the Record." *New York Observer*, 2 December 1996.

Mansfield, Stephanie. "Tom Cruise From the Neck Up." *GQ*, December 1992.

Margolick, David. "Deputy Tells of Emotions of Simpson." *New York Times*, 15 December 1994.

———. "The Enquirer: Required Reading in Simpson Case." *New York Times*, 24 October 1994.

———. "A Peek Under the Tent of the West Palm Beach Media Circus." *New York Times*, 15 December 1991.

Marin, Rick. "They're Hot!" *Des Moines Register*, 22 August 1993.

Martin, Greg. "Errol Flynn and His Two-Way Mirror!" *Confidential*, 3 March 1955.

Martz, Larry. "The War of the Trumps." *Newsweek*, 26 February 1990.

Marx, Andy, and Adam Sandler. "Flacks Aflutter Over Star PR War." *Daily Variety*, 5 January 1994.

Massa, Joe. "Hoffa 'Bodyguard' in Orleans Trying to 'Sell His Story.'" New Orleans, *Times-Picayune*, 10 December 1975.

———. "Tip from T-P Turns FBI onto Con." *New Orleans Times-Picayune*, 11 December 1975.

Mathews, Jack. "Topless Days, Tuxedo Nights." *Newsday*, 19 May 1992.

Mathews, Jay. "Burnett Wins Enquirer Suit." *Washington Post*, 27 March 1981.

Mathews, Tom. "High Gloss News." *Newsweek*, 1 May 1989.

Maurstad, Tom. "Hero Worship." *Dallas Morning News*, 20 June 1993.

Maxa, Rudy. "This Reporter Rifles Garbage." *Washington Post*, 4 February 1979.

McCall, Cheryl. "Barbara Meets Willie." *People*, 21 June 1982.

McCarthy, Harry. "Mae West's Open-Door Policy!" *Confidential*, November 1955.

McCormick, Erin. "Secrets of a Tattler." *San Francisco Examiner*, 3 November 1992.

McDaniel, Jobeth. "Roseanne Sings a New Tune." *Ladies Home Journal*, January 1991.

McDonald, R. E. "It Was the Hottest Show in Town When Maureen O'Hara Cuddled in Row 35." *Confidential*, March 1957.

McGrory, Daniel. "Althorp 'Will Be New Graceland.'" *Times of London*, 10 September 1997.

McGuire, John. "People at 20." *St. Louis Post-Dispatch*, 12 January 1994.

McKerron. "A Brown Study." *Sunday Times Magazine*, 22 January 1984.

Mehegan, David. "Harry Evans Has Turned His Fleet Street Savvy into Best-Selling Books." *Boston Globe*, 1 February 1995.

Mehren, Elizabeth. "Road to the Fair: For Tina Brown, a Decade of Detours." *Los Angeles Times*, 30 January 1985.

Meskil, Paul. "Columbus Parade Loses Its Fortune." *New York Daily News*, 4 October 1972.

Mills, Kim. "Author Charges Politics in Cancellation of '20/20' Segment on Monroe." Associated Press, 4 October 1985.

Mitchell, Emily. "Two for the Money." *People*, 26 February 1990.

Moore, Donovan. "60 Minutes . . . tick, tick, tick, tick, tick, tick. . . ." *Rolling Stone*, 12 January 1978.

Moore, Martha T. "Simpson Case Will Leave Its Mark on Airwaves." *USA Today*, 31 January 1997.

Morris, Merrie. "The World's Most Famous Gossip Columnist Is Wearing Jeans." *Washington Times*, 25 October 1993.

Natale, Richard. "How Hollywood Protects Its Stars." *San Francisco Examiner*, 31 January 1993.

Negri, Miguel. "No Wonder John Wayne Was the Topic of the Tropics!" *Confidential*, November 1956.

Newman, Bob. "Will Mike Wallace Give Himself the Hot Seat?" *On the QT*, November 1957.

Newton, Jim, and Sonia Nazario. "Investigator, Lawyer Quit Jackson's Defense Team." *Los Angeles Times*, 22 December 1993.

Nordheimer, Jon. "Mild-Mannered Buyers Tame Wild Tabloids!" *New York Times*, 4 February 1988.

O'Connor, James and Jean Adams. "Frisky Cops Put Costello in Clink." *New York Mirror*, 10 May 1957.

O'Connor, John. "Sometimes, Crow Can Be Tasty." *New York Times*, 18 February 1973.

———. "Still the Best of TV's 'News Magazines.' " *New York Times*, 27 January 1974.

———. "Wallace Interviews Haldeman on CBS." *New York Times*, 24 March 1975.

O'Connor, Meg. "Crime Panel Member Quits After Loan Is Bared." *Chicago Tribune*, 4 May 1976.

O'Donnell, Frank. "Confessions of a New Producer." *Regardies*, February 1992.

Oliver, Myrna. "Burnett Tells of Anger over Gossip Item." *Los Angeles Times*, 18 March 1981.

———. "Burnett Win May Spark More Libel Suits." *Los Angeles Times*, 21 March 1981.

———. "Carson's Bitter TV Blast Affects Burnett Libel Trial." *Los Angeles Times*, 19 March 1981.

———. "Fred Otash: Colorful Hollywood Private Eye and Author." *Los Angeles Times*, 8 October 1992.

———. "Reporter Testifies at Burnett Libel Trial." *Los Angeles Times*, 14 March 1981.

———. "Smiling Burnett in Court to Do Battle with Tabloid." *Los Angeles Times*, 12 March 1981.

O'Neil, Paul. "The Little Queen That Hollywood Deserved." *Life*, 4 June 1965.

Oney, Steve. "Anthony Pellicano: The Private Eye Who Dogged the Delorean and Belushi Cases Talks About the Tools of His Trade: Guts, Guns and Gizmos." *Playboy*, February 1986.

Orth, Maureen. "The Jackson Jive." *Vanity Fair*, September 1995.

———. "Nightmare in Neverland." *Vanity Fair*, January 1994.

Parker, Jerry. "Zinging Her Way to Fame." *Newsday*, 23 July 1974.

Peer, Elizabeth, and William Schmidt. "Up from Smut." *Newsweek*, 21 April 1975.

Peterson, Iver. "The National Enquirer Cuts Back on Sensationalism, But Is Still Haunted by Its Past." *New York Times*, 8 September 1997.

Plaskin, Glenn. "Ivana's Heartache." *Ladies Home Journal*, May 1990.

Plummer, William. "The Monroe Report: News Staffers at ABC-TV Cry 'Cover-up' When Their Bosses Kill a 20/20 Magazine Segment on Marilyn Monroe." *Time*, 21 October 1985.

Plunkett, Marguerite M. " 'Enquirer' Editor Calder Steps Down." *Palm Beach Post*, 11 November 1995.

Potterton, Reginald. "I Cut Out Her Heart and Stomped on It!" *Playboy*, April 1969.

Powers, William. "Punctured Franchise." *National Journal*, 27 March 1999.

Pristin, Terry. "Roseanne, Husband Drop Enquirer Suit." *Los Angeles Times*, 25 January 1992.

Pugh, Clifford. "Texas Boots and Texas Roots: Columnist Still Talks with a Thick Drawl." *Houston Chronicle*, 5 December 1995.

Randolph, Eleanor. "The Powers That Be." *Los Angeles Times*, 30 December 1996.

Rappleeye, Charles. "A Reporter's Fall from Grace." *Columbia Jounalism Review*, July/August 1993.

Remnick, David. "Harold Evans, at the Ready: The Fleet Street Editor Comes to U.S. News." *Washington Post*, 21 November 1984.

Resner, Jeffrey. "A Walk on the Sleazy Side with the New Breed of Tabloid Reporters." *Rolling Stone*, 30 June 1988.

Reston, James. "CBS and Haldeman." *The New York Times*, 7 March 1975.

Richman, Alan. "Black Belt, White Lies." GQ, March 1991.

Ringel, Eleanor. "Studios, Stars Have Some Writers Eating Out of Their Hands." *Atlanta Journal and Constitution*, 7 June 1992.

Rivera, Geraldo. "What Ever Happened to Geraldo Rivera?" *Esquire*, April 1986.

Robbins, Christopher. "The Woman Behind Tom: Pat Kingsley." *Times of London*, 26 March 1994.

Roberts, Johnnie L. "Time for a Tuneup: Why ABC News Is in the Throes of a Midlife Crisis." *Newsweek*, 24 June 1996.

Roberts, Johnnie L., and Cynthia Crossen. "Suzy May Be Queen of Gossip Mongers, but She's Threatened James Revson, Parvenu Rival, Is Getting Much Publicity Attacking Her Methods." *Wall Street Journal*, 31 March 1988.

Roberts, Roxzanne. "The Princess and the Press." *Washington Post*, 4 September 1997.

Roeper, Richard. "A Star Is Bored." *Spy*, April 1992.

Romano, Lois. "Vanity's British Import." *Washington Post*, 12 January 1984.

Rosenberg, Howard. "Camera in Court: The Burnett Case." *Los Angeles Times*, 23 March 1981.

———. "Gossip Surrounds Ms. Rona's Move." *Los Angeles Times*, 4 August 1980.

———. "TV Marriage on the Rocks for Rona, Tom." *Los Angeles Times*, 14 November 1980.

Rosenfield, Paul. "How Does It Feel to Be Barbara Walters?" *Los Angeles Times Calendar*, 20 November 1988.

——. "Tina Brown: The Magic of High Style." *Los Angeles Times Magazine*, 21 December 1986.

——. "Where Did All the Gossip Go?" *Los Angeles Time Calendar*, 14 December 1986.

Rushmore, Howard. "Rory Calhoun: But for the Grace of God—Still a Convict!" *Confidential*, May 1955.

Rutledge, Howard J. "Gossipy Private Peeks at Celebrities' Lives Start Magazine Bonanza: Confidential's Racy Exposés Crack Newsstand Records." *Wall Street Journal*, 5 July 1955.

Sachs, Andrea. "Autumn of His Life?" *Time*, 21 July 1997.

——. "Mud and the Mainstream." *Columbia Journalism Review*, May/June 1995.

Safire, William. "Who Needs People?" *The New York Times*, 28 February 1974.

Sanchez, Rene. "One Woman's Pleasure Is the President's Pain." *The Washington Post*, 17 February 1998.

Sanger, Elizabeth. "Keeping Tabs: How Weeklies Run with O.J." *Newsday*, 26 February 1995.

Schickel, Richard. "It Was the Strongest Rumor Yet." *New York Times*, 10 December 1972.

Seabrook, John. "Kingsley's Ransom." *The New Yorker*, 21 March 1994.

Seely, Nancy, and Marcy Elias. Series on Mike Wallace. *New York Post*, 13–18 February 1957.

Sessums, Kevin. "Cruise Speed." *Vanity Fair*, October 1994.

Shales, Tom. "CBS News Is Out $10,000 with No Clue to Hoffa Body." *Washington Post*, 10 December 1975.

——. "Geraldo Rivera, Like He Is." *Washington Post*, 16 April 1987.

——. "Some Enchanted Rona: The Woman Who Made TV Safe for Hollywood Gab." *Washington Post*, 3 December 1981.

Sharbutt, Jay. "ABC Boss Defends Monroe Decision." *Los Angeles Times*, 8 October 1985.

——. "Reaction to Westin's Suspension." *Los Angeles Times*, 28 February 1987.

Sharkey, Betsy. "Publicists Battle for the Perfect Magazine Cover and Content." *MediaWeek*, 6 November 1995.

Shaw, David. "Obsessed with Flash and Trash." *Los Angeles Times*, 16 February 1994.

——. "The Simpson Legacy: Is the Media Overfeeding a Starving Public?" *Los Angeles Times*, 9 October 1995.

Sheff, David. "The Playboy Interview: Liz Smith." *Playboy*, February 1992.

Shenon, Philip. "CBS Is Said to Have Paid 2 Fugitives for Interview." *New York Times*, 22 September 1983.

Sherman, William. "Rockin' with the Rock Impressarios." *Cosmopolitan*, February 1995.

Shortell, Brad. "Does Desi Really Love Lucy?" *Confidential*, 1 January 1955.

——. "Open Letter to General Mills: Here's Why Frank Sinatra Is the Tarzan of the Boudoir!" *Confidential*, May 1956.

Sipchen, Bob. "An Attack on Flacks and Hacks." *Los Angeles Times*, 15 August 1991.

Skelton, Nancy. "Bank Catches Interviewer Mike Wallace Off Guard." *Los Angeles Times*, 10 January 1982.

Slack, Lyle. "Alien Brainchild Lands in Supermarket, Libels Oprah, Dies." *Saturday Night*, November 1992.

Small, Michael, and Todd Gold. "Message from Michael." *People*, 12 October 1987.

Smiglis, Martha. "In Florida: The Rogues of Tabloid Valley." *Time*, 15 August 1988.

Smith, Desmond. "The Wide World of Roone Arledge." *New York Times Magazine*, 24 February 1980.

Smith, Gordon. "Jackson's Investigator a Vanishing Breed." *San Diego Union-Tribune*, 10 September 1993.

Smith, Liz. "Julia & 'Hook' Forever!" *Newsday*, 17 July 1991.

———. "90 Minutes." *Vogue*, August 1986.

Smith, Sally Bedell. "ABC Monroe-Report Cancellation Is Argued." *New York Times*, 5 October 1985.

Span, Paula. "Invasion of the Movieflackers." *Washington Post*, 27 June 1989.

Spetalnick, Matt. "Tabloids Create Strange, Wacky World on Florida's East Coast." Reuters, 30 October 1986.

Stein, Jeannine. "Di, Liz, Tonya, the Bobbitts . . . For 20 Years, People Has Covered All Types." *Los Angeles Times*, 28 February 1994.

Stein, M. L. "Supermarket Tabloids Set O.J. Case Pace." *Editor and Publisher*, 4 February 1995.

Stein, Ruth. "Sheila Graham: Fame as a Mistress." *San Francisco Chronicle*, 4 April 1985.

Stern, Richard L., and John Connolly. "How Much Is Donald Worth?" *Forbes*, 14 May 1990.

Stokes, Geoffrey. "Queen Tina." *Spy*, May 1992.

———. "The Trouble with Tina." *The Guardian*, 23 May 1992.

Stothard, Peter. "A Perrier with the Princess." *Times of London*, 2 September 1997.

Strauss, Robert. "Geraldo Dumps Trash, Moves to Higher Ground." *St. Louis-Post Dispatch*, 4 September 1996.

Streete, Horton. "Why Liberace's Theme Song Should be 'Mad About the Boy.' " *Confidential*, 7 July 1957.

Strickland, Leif B. "Inside the Byte-Way, with Insider Gossip (and In-Cyber Gaffes), Matt Drudge Becomes an Icon of Internet Political Reporting." *The San Diego Union-Tribune*, 11 June 1998.

Suplee, Curt. "Vanity Fair's Trivial Pursuit." *Washington Post*, 4 April 1984.

Sutton, Jane. "Simpson Outsells Babies from Mars!" Reuters, 19 July 1994.

Szulc, Ted. "Igor Cassini Indicted as Failing to Register as Trujillo Agent." *New York Times*, 9 February 1963.

Taki. "The Princess." *London Sunday Times*, 7 September 1997.

Taylor, Clarke. "Carol Burnett: 'I'd No Idea I Was This Strong.' " *Los Angeles Times*, 1 June 1981.

Taylor, John. "Trump: The Soap." *New York*, 5 March 1990.

Thomas, Bill. "Mighty Tina." *Los Angeles Times*, 3 November 1991.

Thomas, Mike. "It's Scandalous: Malcolm Balfour, King of Trash Tabs, Tells the Titillating Truth!" *Orlando Sentinel Tribune*, 19 May 1991.

Turner, Richard. "With Roseanne Barr in News, Tabloids Don't Need Aliens." *Wall Street Journal*, 16 February 1990.

Ulmer, James. "Cruise Playing Businessman at Cannes Film Festival." *Hollywood Reporter*, 18 May 1992.

Underwood, Jon. "Axl Rose Won't Sign a Contract That Makes Him Sing in a Town Starting with the Letter M Because He Thinks M Has a Curse On It." *Daily Mail*, 23 October 1992.

Ungless, Janet. "Mocking the Gods Is Her Cup of Tea." *Newsday*, 10 September 1986.

Utne, Eric. "Tina's New Yorker." *Columbia Journalism Review*, March 1993.

Van Meter, Jonathan. "The Sour Smell of Success." *7 Days*, 14 March 1990.

Waldron, Martin. "Hoffa Tipster Gone; CBS Is Out $10,000." *New York Times*, 9 December 1975.

Walker, Jerry. "Editor Wants to End Deals with Publicists." *Jack O'Dwyer's Newsletter*, 25 August 1993.

Wallace, Mike. "The Man Behind Confidential." *New York Post*, 3, 4, 5, September 1957.

———. "Wallace Defends Haldeman Interview." (Letter to the Editor) *New York Times*, 13 April 1975.

Walston, Charles. "Tabloid TV Has Changed the Rules." *Atlanta Constitution*, 17 November 1991.

Wark, Penny. "My Life with the Princess by Her Man at the Palace." (Interview of Patrick Jephson) *London Sunday Times*, 7 September 1997.

Warner, Melanie, and Marty O'Loughlin. "Cover or Nothing." *Inside Media*, 16 February 1994.

Washburn, Mark. "Checkout-Line Tabloid Approaches Respectability on O.J. Case." *Charleston Gazette*, 25 January 1995.

Wasserman, Joanne. "Miss Rona's Snit over Barbara Plums." *New York Post*, 17 April 1980.

Waters, Harry F. "The People Perplex." *Newsweek*, 6 June 1977.

———. "The Sting." *Newsweek*, 22 December 1975.

Waxman, Sharon. "The Hollywood Junket." *Washington Post*, 30 December 1996.

Weinraub, Bernard. "Hollywood and Tough Journalism Don't Mix." *New York Times*, 3 June 1992.

———. "Michael Jackson's Lawyer and Investigator Quit Jobs." *New York Times*, 22 December 1993.

Welkos, Robert, and Ted Rohrlich. "Marilyn Monroe Mystery Persists." *Los Angeles Times*, 29 September 1985.

Werts, Diane. "Forget the Tabloids, Tattoos and Taunts: Roseanne and Tom Arnold Want to Be Taken Seriously." *Newsday*, 9 February 1992.

White, Jim. "Hi, I'm Dave. Lovely to See You." *The Independent*, 17 February 1994.

Whitworth, Damian. "Dawn of the Paparazzi." *Times of London*, 10 September 1997.

Wilkins, Barbara. " 'Even the Promiscuous Feel Pain,' Says Warren Beatty, Coming Clean in 'Shampoo.' " *People*, 14 April 1975.

Wilkinson, Peter. "The Big Sleazy." GQ, January 1992.

Willens, Michele. "Aiming the Spotlight." *USA Today*, 21 June 1991.

Wilson, Theo. "Burnett Beats Enquirer for $1.6 M." *New York Daily News*, 27 March 1981.

Wiscombe, Janet. "What Hath the Web Wrought?" *Los Angeles Times Magazine*, 16 August 1998.

Wolfe, Tom. "The Mid-Atlantic Man." New York section of *World Journal Tribune*, 27 November 1966.

———. "Public Lives: Confidential Magazine; Reflections in Tranquility by the Former Owner, Robert Harrison, Who Managed to Get Away with It." *Esquire*, April 1964.

Wright, Fred W. "Special Requests." *Tampa Tribune*, 22 January 1995.

Wulf, Steve. "Sportscasters Behaving Badly?" *Time*, 2 June 1997.

Younger, Irving. "Memoir of a Prosecutor." *Commentary*, October 1976.

Zito, Tom, and Larry Rohter. "The Lives of Elvis Presley." *Washington Post*, 18 August 1977.

Zoglin, Richard. "ABC Ya, Roone." *Time*, 17 March 1997.

———. "The Press and Steven Seagal." *Buzz*, August 1996.

———. "What Makes '60 Minutes' Tick." *New York Times*, 11 September 1977.

Zuber, Amy. "Time Inc.'s People Person." *Folio*, 15 December 1994.

No Byline

"Barbara Walters: Star of the Morning." *Newsweek*, 6 May 1974.

"Cindy Says." *Editor and Publisher*, 9 March 1960.

"Cronkite Views '60 Minutes.' " *New York Times*, 26 November 1983.

"Dame Herald Evans Memorial Issue: A Nation Mourns." *Private Eye*, 26 March 1982.

"Drudge Tells Journalism Students He's Not Bound by Rules of Journalism." Associated Press, 26 February 1999.

"Elvis." *People*, 29 August 1997.

"Enquirer Belted: Burnett's $1.6 Million Punch." *Time*, 6 April 1981.

"From Worse to Bad." *Newsweek*, 8 September 1969.

"Generoso Pope Buys New York Enquirer." *New York Times*, 4 April 1952.

"Generoso Pope, 59, Publisher, Is Dead." *New York Times*, 29 April 1950.

"Goodbye to Gore." *Time*, 21 February 1972.

"Hollywood Goes to War: The Stars Are Coming Out to Sue the *National Enquirer*." *Time*, 21 January 1980.

"House Unit Decries Tour by Joey Adams." *New York Times*, 10 July 1962.

"It's Star Wars on the Tabs." *People*, 15 October 1990.

"The Man from T.R.A.S.H." *Newsweek*, 21 July 1975.

"Mr. and Mrs. Harold Evans: A Solemn Pledge." *Private Eye*, 20 May 1993.

"Murphy Dismisses Pope Jr. as Honorary Police Deputy." *New York Times*, 26 October 1950.

"Oprah Winfrey and Beau Win Defamation Suit Against Tabloid by Default." *Jet*, 18 May 1992.

"Oprah Winfrey and Stedman Graham File $300 Million Suit Against Toronto-Based Tabloid." *Jet*, 13 April 1992.

"The *People* People." *Newsweek*, 4 March 1974.

"*People's* Premiere." *Time*, 4 March 1974.

"People Who Hate People." *Esquire*, August 1976.

"Phew, What a Tattler!" *Private Eye*, 27 February 1981.

"Tabloid Wars Rage!" *Newsday*, 15 October 1989.

"Tattling on a Tattler." Associated Press, 1 November 1990.

"Trashy Journalism." *Time*, 21 July 1975.

"TV: CBS News Magazine Opens." *New York Times*, 25 September 1968.

"Yorkshire Terrier is 'Top Dog.' " *Private Eye*, 26 February 1982.

"Young Man Loses His Badge." *New York Herald Tribune*, 17 October 1950.

Books

Adams, Cindy. *My Friend the Dictator*. Indianapolis: Bobbs-Merrill, 1967.

———. *Sukarno: An Autobiography*. Indianapolis: Bobbs-Merrill, 1965.

Adams, Joey. *Cindy and I: The Real Life Adventures of Mr. and Mrs. Joey Adams*. New York: Crown Publishers, 1957.

———. *From Gags to Riches*. New York: Frederick Fell, 1946.

———. *On the Road for Uncle Sam*. Bernard Geis Associates, 1963.

Andersen, Christopher. *Michael Jackson Unauthorized*. New York: Simon & Schuster, 1994.

Anderson, Jack, with James Boyd. *Confessions of a Muckraker*. New York: Random House, 1979.

Anson, Robert Sam. *Exile: The Unquiet Oblivion of Richard M. Nixon*. New York: Simon & Schuster, 1984.

Aronson, Steven M. L. *Hype*. New York: William Morrow, 1983.

Auletta, Ken. *Three Blind Mice: How the TV Networks Lost Their Way*. New York: Random House, 1991.

Barr, Geraldine, with Ted Schwarz. *My Sister Roseanne: The True Story of Roseanne Barr Arnold*. New York: Birch Lane Press, 1994.

Barrett, Rona. *Miss Rona: An Autobiography*. Los Angeles: Nash Publishing, 1974.

Barrett, Wayne. *Trump: The Deals and the Downfall*. New York: HarperCollins, 1992.

Bates, Stephen. *If No News, Send Rumors*. New York: St. Martin's Press, 1985.

Bernard, George. *Inside the National Enquirer: Confessions of an Undercover Reporter*. Port Washington, N.Y.: Ashley Books, 1977.

Betrock, Alan. *Sleazy Business: A Pictorial History of Exploitation Tabloids 1959–1974*. Brooklyn, N.Y.: Shakes Books, 1996.

Bird, S. Elizabeth. *For Enquiring Minds: A Cultural Study of Supermarket Tabloids*. Knoxville: University of Tennessee Press, 1992.

Boorstin, Daniel J. *The Image*. New York: Atheneum, 1962.

Boyer, Peter J. *Who Killed CBS?* New York: Random House, 1988.

Bradlee, Benjamin C. *Conversations with Kennedy*. New York: W. W. Norton, 1975.

Bradlee, Ben. *A Good Life: Newspapering and Other Adventures*. New York: Simon & Schuster, 1995.

Cannistraro, Philip. *Italian Americans: New Perspectives in Italian Immigration and Ethnicity*. Edited by Lydio F. Tomasi. New York: Center for Migration Studies, 1985.

Cassini, Igor, with Jeanne Molli. *I'd Do It All Over Again*. New York: G. P. Putnam's Sons, 1977.

Cassini, Oleg. *In My Own Fashion*. New York: Simon & Schuster, 1987.

Cheshire, Maxine, with John Greenya. *Maxine Cheshire, Reporter*. Boston: Houghton Mifflin, 1978.

Clarke, Gerald. *Capote: A Biography*. New York: Simon & Schuster, 1988.

Cohn, Roy. *A Fool for a Client*. New York: Hawthorne Books, 1971.

Collier, Peter, and David Horowitz. *The Kennedys: An American Drama*. New York: Summit Books, 1984.

Corkery, Paul. *Carson: The Unauthorized Biography*. Ketchum, Idaho: Randt & Company, 1987.

Cotten, Lee. *All Shook Up: Elvis, Day-By-Day, 1954–1997*. Ann Arbor: Pierian Press, 1985.

Cramer, Richard Ben. *What It Takes: The Way to the White House*. New York: Random House, 1992.

Crutchfield, Don. *Confessions of a Hollywood P.I.* New York: Dunhill Publishing, 1997.

Cuozzo, Steven. *It's Alive: How America's Oldest Newspaper Cheated Death and Why It Matters*. New York: Times Books, 1996.

Davies, Nicholas. *Diana: A Princess and Her Troubled Marriage*. New York: Birch Lane Press, 1992.

Diamond, Edwin. *Behind the Times: Inside the New New York Times*. New York: Villard Books, 1994.

Downs, Hugh. *On Camera*. New York: G. P. Putnam's Sons, 1986.

Eells, George. *Hedda and Louella*. New York: G. P. Putnam's Sons, 1972.

Fairey, Wendy W. *One of the Family*. New York: W. W. Norton, 1988.

Felsenthal, Carol. *Power, Privilege, and the Post*. New York: G. P. Putnam's Sons, 1993.

Fisher, Eddie. *Eddie: My Life, My Loves*. New York: Harper & Row, 1981.

Gabler, Neal. *Winchell: Gossip, Power and the Culture of Celebrity*. New York: Alfred A. Knopf, 1994.

Gates, Gary Paul. *Air Time: The Inside Story of CBS News*. New York: Harper & Row, 1978.

Goldberg, Robert, and Gerald Jay Goldberg. *Anchors: Brokaw, Jennings, Rather and the Evening News*. New York: Birch Lane Press, 1990.

Goldenson, Leonard H., with Marvin J. Wolf. *Beating the Odds*. New York: Charles Scribner's Sons, 1991.

Goulden, Joseph C. *Fit to Print: A. M. Rosenthal and His Times.* Secaucus, N.J.: Lyle Stuart, 1988.

Govoni, Albert. *Cary Grant: An Unauthorized Biography.* Chicago: Henry Regnery Company, 1971.

Graham, Katharine. *Personal History.* New York: Alfred A. Knopf, 1997.

Graham, Sheila. *Confessions of a Hollywood Columnist.* New York: William Morrow, 1969.

———. *Hollywood Revisited.* New York: St. Martin's Press, 1984.

———. *A State of Heat.* New York: Grosset & Dunlap, 1972.

Granger, Stewart. *Sparks Fly Upward.* New York: G. P. Putnam's Sons, 1981.

Gregory, Neal, and Janice. *When Elvis Died.* Washington, D.C.: Communications Press, 1980.

Gunther, Marc. *The House That Roone Built.* New York: Little, Brown, 1994.

Haden-Guest, Anthony. *The Last Party: Studio 54, Disco, and the Culture of the Night.* New York: William Morrow, 1997.

Hagood, Wesley O. *Presidential Sex.* New York: Birch Lane Press, 1995.

Hamblin, Dora Jane. *That Was the Life.* New York: W. W. Norton, 1977.

Hewitt, Don. *Minute by Minute.* New York: Random House, 1985.

Hogshire, Jim. *Grossed-Out Surgeon Vomits Inside Patient! An Insider's Look at Supermaket Tabloids.* Venice, Calif.: Feral House, 1997.

Hopper, Hedda. *The Whole Truth and Nothing But.* Garden City, N.Y.: Doubleday & Company, 1962.

Hurt III, Harry. *Lost Tycoon: The Many Lives of Donald J. Trump.* New York, W. W. Norton, 1993.

Israel, Lee. *Kilgallen.* New York: Delacorte Press, 1979.

Jackson, Kenneth T., ed. *The Encyclopedia of New York City.* New Haven: Yale University Press, 1995.

Katz, Leonard. *Uncle Frank: The Biography of Frank Costello.* New York: Drake Publishers, 1973.

Kelley, Kitty. *Elizabeth Taylor: The Last Star.* New York: Simon & Schuster, 1981.

———. *His Way: The Unauthorized Biography of Frank Sinatra.* New York: Bantam, 1986.

———. *Jackie Oh!* Secaucus, N.J.: Lyle Stuart, 1978.

Kessler, Judy. *Inside People.* New York: Villard Books, 1994.

———. *Inside Today.* New York: Villard Books, 1992.

Kessler, Ronald. *Inside Congress.* New York: Pocket Books, 1997.

Kiernan, Thomas. *Citizen Murdoch.* New York: Dodd, Mead & Co., 1986.

King, Larry, with Peter Occhiogrosso. *Tell Me More.* New York: G. P. Putnam's Sons, 1990.

Klurfeld, Herman. *Behind the Lines: The World of Drew Pearson.* Englewood Cliffs, N.J.: Prentice-Hall, 1968.

———. *Winchell: His Life and Times.* New York: Praeger Publishers, 1976.

Lawford, Lady May, and Buddy Galon. *Bitch! The Autobiography of Lady Lawford.* Brookline Village, Mass.: Branden Publishing, 1986. (Originally published in England in 1972.)

Lawford, Patricia Seaton, with Ted Schwarz. *The Peter Lawford Story*. New York: Caroll & Graf, 1988.

Leamer, Laurence. *Playing for Keeps: In Washington*. New York: Dial Press, 1977.

Leapman, Michael. *Arrogant Aussie*. Secaucus, N.J.: 1984.

Lerner, Max. *Ted and the Kennedy Legend*. New York: St. Martin's Press, 1980.

Machlin, Milt. *The Gossip Wars*. New York: Tower, 1981.

Maier, Thomas. *Newhouse: All the Glitter, Power, and Glory of America's Richest Media Empire and the Secretive Man Behind It*. New York: St. Martin's Press, 1994.

Manchester, William. *Controversy and Other Essays in Journalism*. Boston: Little Brown, 1976.

Matusow, Barbara. *The Evening Stars: The Making of the Network News Anchor*. Boston: Houghton Mifflin, 1983.

Metz, Robert. *CBS: Reflections in a Bloodshot Eye*. Chicago: Playboy Press, 1975.

Morton, Andrew. *Diana: Her True Story—In Her Own Words*. New York: Simon & Schuster, 1997.

Navasky, Victor S. *Naming Names*. New York: Viking Press, 1980.

Oppenheimer, Jerry. *Barbara Walters: An Unauthorized Biography*. New York: St. Martin's Press, 1990.

———. *The Other Mrs. Kennedy; Ethel Skakel Kennedy: An American Drama of Power, Privilege and Politics*. New York: St. Martin's Press, 1994.

Otash, Fred. *Investigation Hollywood!* Chicago: Henry Regnery, 1976.

Parker, John. *Warren Beatty: The Last Great Lover of Hollywood*. New York: Caroll & Graf, 1994.

Pedrosa, Carmen Navarro. *Imelda Marcos*. New York: St. Martin's Press, 1987.

Pierce, Patricia Jobe. *The Ultimate Elvis: Elvis Presley Day by Day*. New York: Simon & Schuster, 1994.

Pilat, Oliver. *Drew Pearson: An Unauthorized Biography*. New York: Harper's Magazine Press, 1973.

Povich, Maury, with Ken Gross. *Current Affairs: A Life on the Edge*. New York: G. P. Putnam's Sons, 1991.

Prendergast, Curtis, with Geoffrey Colvin. *The World of Time Inc.: The Intimate History of a Changing Enterprise*. Vol. 3: 1960–1980. New York: Atheneum, 1986.

Preston, Charles, and Edward A. Hamilton, eds. *Mike Wallace Asks*. New York: Simon & Schuster, 1958.

Quinn, Sally. *We're Going to Make You a Star*. New York: Simon & Schuster, 1975.

Quirk, Lawrence J. *The Kennedys in Hollywood*. Dallas, Tex.: Taylor Publishing, 1996.

Reeves, Thomas C. *A Question of Character: A Life of John F. Kennedy*. New York: The Free Press, 1991.

Rivera, Geraldo. *Exposing Myself*. New York: Bantam, 1991.

Rogers, Henry C. *Walking the Tightrope*. New York: William Morrow, 1980.

Rose, Frank. *The Agency: William Morris and the Hidden History of Show Business*. New York: HarperCollins, 1995.

Salinger, Pierre. *P.S.: A Memoir*. New York: St. Martin's Press, 1995.

Salisbury, Harrison E. *Without Fear or Favor: The New York Times and Its Times*. New York: Times Books, 1980.

Sancton, Thomas, and Scott MacLeod. *Death of a Princess: The Investigation*. New York: St. Martin's Press, 1998.

Shawcross, William. *Murdoch*. New York: Simon & Schuster, 1993.

Skolsky, Sidney. *Don't Get Me Wrong—I Love Hollywood*. New York: G. P. Putnam's Sons, 1975.

Smith, Ronald L. *Johnny Carson: An Unauthorized Biography*. New York: St. Martin's Press, 1987.

Smolla, Rodney A. *Suing the Press: Libel, the Media and Power*. New York: Oxford University Press, 1986.

Spacks, Patricia Ann Meyer. *Gossip*. New York: Alfred A. Knopf, 1985.

Spada, James. *Peter Lawford: The Man Who Kept the Secrets*. New York: Bantam, 1991.

Spoto, Donald. *A Passion for Life: The Biography of Elizabeth Taylor*. New York: HarperCollins, 1995.

Stephens, Mitchell. *A History of News: From the Drum to the Satellite*. New York: Viking, 1988.

Stolley, Richard. *People Celebrates People: The Best of 1974–1996*. New York: People Books, 1996.

Summers, Anthony. *Goddess: The Secret Lives of Marilyn Monroe*. New York: MacMillan, 1985.

———. *Official and Confidential: The Secret Life of J. Edgar Hoover*. New York: G. P. Putnam's Sons, 1993.

Swanberg, W. A. *Luce and His Empire*. New York: Charles Scribner's Sons, 1972.

Taraborelli, J. Randy. *Laughing Till It Hurts: The Complete Life and Career of Carol Burnett*. New York: William Morrow, 1988.

———. *Michael Jackson: The Magic and the Madness*. New York: Birch Lane Press, 1991.

Taylor, Elizabeth. *Elizabeth Takes Off: On Weight Gain, Weight Loss, Self-Image and Self-Esteem*. New York: G. P. Putnam's Sons. 1987.

Thompson II, Charles C., and James P. Cole. *The Death of Elvis: What Really Happened*. New York: Delacorte Press, 1991.

Thornton, Penny. *With Love, from Diana*. New York: Pocket Books, 1995.

Toobin, Jeffrey. *The Run of His Life*. New York: Random House, 1996.

Tucher, Andie. *Froth and Scum: Truth, Beauty, Goodness, and the Ax Murder in America's First Mass Medium*. Chapel Hill: University of North Carolina Press, 1994.

Von Hoffman, Nicholas. *Capitalist Fools*. New York: Doubleday, 1992.

———. *Citizen Cohn: The Life and Times of Roy Cohn*. New York: Doubleday, 1988.

Wallace, Mike, and Gary Paul Gates. *Close Encounters*. New York: William Morrow, 1984.

Warhol, Andy. *The Andy Warhol Diaries*. Edited by Pat Hackett. New York: Warner Books, 1989.

Whitaker, James. *Diana vs. Charles: Royal Blood Feud*. New York: Signet, 1993.

———. *Settling Down*. London: Quartet Books, 1981.

Wicker, Tom. *On Press*. New York: Viking, 1978.

Wilson, Earl. *Show Business Laid Bare*. New York: G. P. Putnam's Sons, 1974.

———. *The Show Business Nobody Knows*. Chicago: Cowles Book Company, 1971.

Winans, Christopher. *Malcolm Forbes: The Man Who Had Everything*. New York: St. Martin's Press, 1990.

Witcover, Jules. *The Year the Dream Died: Revisiting 1968 in America*. New York: Warner Books, 1997.

Wolf, George, with Joseph DiMona. *Frank Costello: Prime Minister of the Underworld*. New York: William Morrow, 1974.

Zion, Sidney. *The Autobiography of Roy Cohn*. Secaucus, N.J.: Lyle Stuart, 1988.

Selected TV Shows

"Barbara Walters Interviews Ivana Trump." *20/20*, ABC, 9 May 1991.

"Controversy over Tabloid Journalism." *Charlie Rose*, PBS, 14 February 1994.

"Dick Stolley Discusses 20 Years of People Magazine and Current Anniversary Issue." *Tom Snyder*, CNBC, 1 March 1994.

"Digital Dirt: Fact, Fiction and Cyberspace." *Nightline*, ABC, 8 January 1998.

"Equal Time: Latest Development in the Alleged Affair Between President Clinton and Monica Lewinsky." CNBC, 10 February 1998.

"The Gossip Culture." *Charlie Rose*, PBS, 13 June 1991.

"Guests Discuss How Tabloid Photographers Affect Stars' Lives." *Larry King Live*, CNN, 2 September 1997.

"How Do Tabloids Get Their Stories?" CNN, 6 August 1995.

"The Impact of Tabloids in America." *Larry King Live*, CNN, 19 June 1997.

"Larry King Live Welcomes Cosby Family's Consultant Gavin De Becker." *Larry King Live*, CNN, 14 March 1997.

"Latest Developments in the Alleged Affair Between President Clinton and Monica Lewinsky." *Equal Time*, CNBC, 10 February 1998.

"The National Enquirer." *60 Minutes*, 30 September 1990.

"The Princess and the Press." *Frontline*, PBS, November 1997.

"Princess Diana." *60 Minutes*, CBS, 31 August 1997.

"Showbiz Today." CNN, September 15, 1998.

"Steve Dunleavy of 'A Current Affair' Discusses His Job and That of Tabloid Reporters." CNBC, 14 September 1994.

"Tabloid Truth: The Michael Jackson Story." PBS, 15 February 1994.

INDEX